EDEXCEL

BUSINESS

YEAR **1**

Including AS

IAN MARCOUSÉ
Andrew Hammond
Nigel Watson

HODDER
EDUCATION
AN HACHETTE UK COMPANY

Orders: please contact Bookpoint Ltd, 130 Milton Park, Abingdon, Oxon OX14 4SB. Telephone: (44) 01235 827720. Fax: (44) 01235 400454. Lines are open from 9 a.m. to 5 p.m., Monday to Saturday, with a 24-hour message answering service. You can also order through our website: www.hoddereducation.co.uk

If you have any comments to make about this, or any of our other titles, please send them to educationenquiries@hodder.co.uk

British Library Cataloguing in Publication Data

A catalogue record for this title is available from the British Library

ISBN: 978 1 471 84776 9

This edition published 2015.

Impression number   10 9 8 7 6 5 4 3 2 1

Year   2015, 2016, 2017, 2018

Hachette UK's policy is to use papers that are natural, renewable and recyclable products and made from wood grown in sustainable forests. The logging and manufacturing processes are expected to conform to the environmental regulations of the country of origin.

Cover photo © peshkova/Fotolia

Illustrations by Aptara

Typeset in 11/13 pt Bembo Std by Aptara, Inc.

Printed in Italy for Hodder Education, an Hachette UK Company.

A catalogue record for this title is available from the British Library.

ISBN 9781471847769

Contents

How to use this book

What distinguishes Business from most A level subjects is the importance of context. Not much business theory is 'true' in an abstract way; it becomes true only when intelligently placed into a business situation. So not only does the book have many 'Real business' cases within the chapters, it also makes constant reference to actual, up-to-date examples of the main subject matter. In this way, the reader learns the richness of the subject – and finds it easier to remember the key issues.

This book has been designed to be useful in several ways. For students:

1. To be read: either before the teacher tackles a topic or after, as a reinforcement of the theory. Be sure to ask your teacher what she or he would prefer. When you've finished the chapter, have a go at the Revision questions, which are designed to help you absorb the material you've just been reading.

2. As a reference resource. This book has an excellent index at the back, to help you track down a small section on 'overdrafts' or 'cash cows'. So it can be helpful in class – or for homework – as a reference book.

3. As a revision resource. The book has several features in every chapter that help with revision. When revising, start by reading the 'Five whys and a how' feature. This asks questions relating to the text – and then answers them. If you feel confident with the questions and the answers, move on to the 'Evaluation'. If this also makes sense, you can move on to another chapter/topic. If, however, you still feel in the dark, you'd better read/re-read the chapter.

Having gone through that process, it's time to test yourself against the specification. This can be seen online or downloaded from http://qualifications.pearson.com/en/qualifications/edexcel-a-levels/business-2015.html. When you have the specification in front of you, go through Themes 1 and 2, making sure to think about the headings (on the left) as well as the detailed subject content (on the right).

Finally, during revision, tackle ALL of the numerical questions in Chapter 48 (the answers are at the end of Chapter 49).

For teachers:

1. I want a text book I can trust so that I can change things up a bit. 'This week, you're teaching yourself Quality management. Read Chapter 44 with care, taking notes as you go – and answer Revision questions 1–5. Next Tuesday I'll test you on what you know.' This book is a reading book more than a reference book, with lots of examples of application to the real world. I try to set a reading homework early on, then occasionally further reading for homework. Overall, though, I'm hoping that students will start to take their own initiative with the reading.

2. All the short questions, case studies and 'extended writing' questions at the end of the chapters have answers and mark schemes in the *Edexcel Business A level Year 1 Answer Guide*. This is available as a photocopiable pack or as part of the Dynamic Learning digital package. If you feel the need for extra exam papers, my *Exam Pack for Edexcel Business AS/First Year* is published by A–Z Business Training Ltd (see www.a-zbusinesstraining.com).

I hope this new book is as enjoyable to use as it was to write.

Acknowledgements

When I started writing text books, research meant going to libraries and tracking down businesspeople for interview. These days, Google is hugely helpful, as are the *Financial Times*, *The Grocer* and the many business websites I subscribe to. Happily, face-to-face conversations remain vital. Salvatore Falcone at Panetteria Italiana and Matteo Pantani at Scoop are my constant sources of slices of real business life.

I also want to acknowledge some colleagues who have helped along the way. This excellent Edexcel specification owes a great deal to Isla Billett and Colin Leith. And the qualities of the book are partly due to my co-authors Nigel and Andrew, and partly thanks to the hard work of Beth Cleall and Graeme Hall at Hodder.

And then there are the students and student teachers who chipped in along the way. My writing career started with a student saying, 'You should write a book of these (case studies)', so thank you Leda Barrett. More recently Yan Wu, Sujagan Sivananthan, Lauren Cox, Neetu Rathore and Yasmin Safar have been hugely helpful in keeping me inspired by teaching in general – and particularly by Business as a challenging, ever-fascinating subject.

Writing a textbook is time-consuming and energy-sapping. So the most important acknowledgement is to my family, especially my wife Maureen, and to my grandchildren, who sometimes have to dig me out of my office so that we can do more important things such as playing trains or digging up the flower patch.

Finally, the subject itself. It's a cliché to say that business is ever-changing. Thankfully, it's true. So writing a book in 2015 is wonderfully different from ten years ago.

I hope you enjoy that difference.

Ian Marcousé, April 2015

The Publishers would like to thank the following for permission to reproduce copyright material.

Every effort has been made to trace all copyright holders, but if any have been inadvertently overlooked, the Publishers will be pleased to make the necessary arrangements at the first opportunity.

Pages 1 & 185: © peshkova/Fotolia; p. 2: © Libby Welch/Alamy; p. 7 **left** © Newscast-online Limited/Alamy, **right** © Roger Cope/Alamy; p. 16: © Paul Sakuma/AP/Press Association Images; p. 20: © Doris Heinrichs/Fotolia; p. 40: © FremantleMedia Ltd/REX; p. 45: © Richard Naude/Alamy; p. 49: **top**: © Oli Scarff/Getty Images, **bottom**: © Mediablitzimages/Alamy; p. 56: © The Asahi Shimbun via Getty Images; p. 66: © Eranga Jayawardena/AP/Press Association Images; p. 67: © Noam Galai/Getty Images; p. 71: © Bernardo De Niz/Bloomberg via Getty Images; p. 76 © Sunil Saxena/Hindustan Times via Getty Images; p. 95: © Richard Levine/Demotix/Press Association Images; p. 104: © Monkey Business/Fotolia; p. 140: © fotum/ Fotolia; p. 152: © Share Radio; p. 153: © Nancy's Nails; p. 159: © Randy Duchaine/Alamy; p. 197: © Chivote; p. 213: © Patrick Hemdé/Fotolia p. 253: © The Asahi Shimbun via Getty Images; p. 261: © Stadium Bank/Alamy; p. 264: © Photofusion/REX; p. 267: © epa european pressphoto agency b.v./Alamy; p. 291: © fotolincs/Alamy; p. 302: © Noah Berger/Bloomberg via Getty Images

Theme 1

Marketing and people

1 Introduction to marketing

Definition

Marketing can be defined as the department tasked with targeting the right product at the right target market using the right combination of price, promotion and place.

Linked to: The market, Ch 2; Market positioning, Ch 4; Product and service design, Ch 10; Branding and promotion, Ch 11; Marketing strategy, Ch 15.

1.1 Introduction to marketing

Peter Drucker, a famous business academic, says that, 'The aim of marketing is to know and understand the customer so well, the product or service fits him and sells itself.' In other words marketing is about gaining an understanding of what product or service is needed to match customer requirements. This might be through great market research, or through the kind of brilliant insight shown by the founders of Google, Facebook or Apple.

'Think like a customer.'

Paul Gillin, author, *The New Influencers*

To turn this understanding into a profitable business requires the ability to communicate the customer benefits clearly and consistently. L'Oréal has been transformed from an also-ran into the world's biggest cosmetics business on the back of the brilliant claim of quality and superiority: 'Because I'm worth it'. Tesco went from number two in the grocery business to unrivalled number one with 'Every Little Helps'. The problems Tesco has suffered since is a reminder that marketing isn't simple. If circumstances change, the marketing may have to change – which, in the case of Tesco, may mean all four aspects of its marketing: product, price, promotion and place.

1.2 Marketing objectives

A **marketing objective** is a marketing target or goal that an organisation hopes to achieve, such as to boost market share from 9 to 12 per cent within two years. Marketing objectives steer the direction of the business. Operating a business without knowing your objectives, is like driving a car without knowing where you want to go. Some businesses achieve a degree of success despite the fact that they choose not to set marketing objectives, stumbling across a successful business model by accident. But why should anyone rely on chance? If firms set marketing objectives, the probability of success increases because decision making will be more focused.

To be effective, marketing objectives should be quantifiable and measurable. Targets should also be set within a time frame. An example of a marketing objective that Nestlé might set is: 'To achieve a 9 per cent increase in the sales of KitKat by the end of next year.'

Real business

Marketing objectives in the non-profit sector

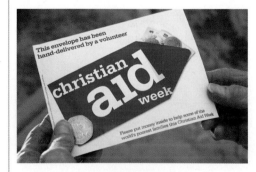

Figure 1.1 Christian Aid Week logo

Charities such as Oxfam and Christian Aid need marketing to keep their brands alive and donations coming in. Typical marketing objectives that a charity may set could include the following.

- *Raise brand awareness.* Brand awareness is the percentage of the market that knows of your brand; that is, they can recognise it from a list of brand names, or they can quote it unaided. Raising brand awareness could be a very important marketing objective for a smaller charity that is at yet unknown. If a greater percentage of the general public is aware of a charity's existence and its activities, donations may increase, enabling the charity to expand its work.
- *Brand loyalty.* Brand loyalty exists when consumers return to your brand rather than swapping and switching between brands. A charity could set a marketing objective to improve brand loyalty. If existing donors can be persuaded to set up a direct debit to the charity, the charity's cash flow will improve.
- *Corporate image.* A scandal-hit charity could set a marketing objective of trying to improve its reputation, in order to protect its income stream from donors.

1.3 Marketing strategy

Marketing strategy is the medium- to long-term plan for how to achieve your marketing objectives. The process of thinking it through requires rather more, though, than simply writing down a plan. In his book *Even More Offensive Marketing*, Hugh Davidson says that effective marketing strategy requires POISE (see Table 1.1).

P	Profitable	A proper balance between the firm's need for profit and the customer's need for value
O	Offensive	Getting on the attack, leading the market, taking risks and forcing competitors to be followers
I	Integrated	The marketing approach must flow through the whole company, from directors to telephonists
S	Strategic	Probing analysis of the market and your competitors leading to a winning strategy
E	Effectively executed	Strong and disciplined teamwork in carrying the strategy through effectively

Table 1.1 POISE (source: adapted from *Even More Offensive Marketing*, H. Davidson, Penguin Books)

It is easy to see that software publisher King Digital showed all these features in its brilliant development and marketing of the Candy Crush saga. Launched in November 2012, by early 2014 it had the highest daily usage of any mobile app in the world. It was also grossing an estimated $900,000 a day. King had a long track record of successful games for Facebook, but was one of the first to see the scope for mobile gaming. Candy Crush proved a clever combination of enticing free play plus some irresistible 69p upgrades. King showed every element within the POISE acronym.

Chapters 10–13 show how firms think their strategies through using the **marketing mix**, carefully combining the four main marketing levers: product, price, promotion and place.

1.4 Making sure your marketing is effective

Effective marketing starts with identifying an opportunity, just as King did with its Candy Crush game. Instead of assuming that all games had to target trigger-happy men, King identified other opportunities among girls and older women.

In many small businesses, the owner will come into regular contact with customers. This allows the owner to hear first-hand about the needs and wants of the target market. In large businesses, formal market research is undertaken because head office managers cannot feel sure that they know what customers think and want. Once consumer wants have been identified, products and services will need to be designed to match consumer preferences. Finally, a launch marketing mix must be decided. This involves decisions such as setting price, choosing an appropriate distribution channel and setting a promotional strategy.

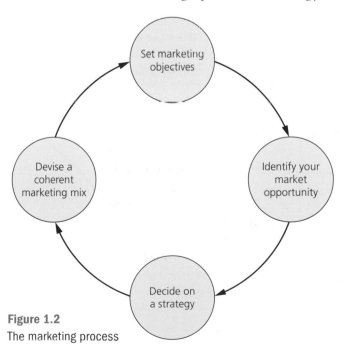

Figure 1.2
The marketing process

1.5 Why is effective marketing important?

Consumers tend to be quite rational. They will seek out fairly priced products that satisfy their needs. In a competitive market, firms stand or fall according to their ability to satisfy the needs of the consumer. Generally, firms that fail will lack customer loyalty and be punished automatically by the market. These firms will lose market share and profit. Firms with products and services that offer genuine consumer benefits will attract revenue and profit.

Consumer tastes do not tend to stay the same for very long. Therefore, a key aspect of effective marketing is the ability to respond, quickly, to any change in consumer tastes. Firms that fail to adapt their business model, at a time when consumer tastes are changing, are normally forced out of business. In recent years, retail chains such as HMV, Jessops and Blockbuster have collapsed.

Real business

Sensations

Launched in 2002 with celebrity backing from Victoria Beckham and Gary Neville, Walkers Sensations once had annual sales of over £100 million in the premium crisps market. But by 2009 sales had flagged seriously, hit by newer, more premium brands such as Kettle Chips. Instead of watching sales continue to drift, Walkers responded by relaunching the brand in early 2010, giving it more striking packaging and launching a wider range of flavours. By 2012 and 2013, the success of this relaunch won the brand new distribution outlets in supermarkets and elsewhere. A well-executed marketing strategy brought the brand back to health (see Figure 1.3).

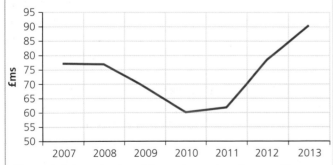

Figure 1.3 Annual sales of Sensations crisps (source: *The Grocer* Top Products Survey)

1.6 The characteristics of effective marketing

Identifying the target market

When a business creates a new market (as Richard Branson is attempting currently with space tourism), it can aim its product at everyone who can afford the product. Some time later competitors will arrive, and usually focus on one segment of the market. In space tourism, perhaps some firms will focus on thrill-seekers, while others will target wealthy, older travellers seeking a super-safe, luxury version of the same thrill.

> '**Everyone is not your customer.**'
>
> Seth Godin, American entrepreneur

To succeed at marketing, you need to know and understand the customers within your target market: what do they *really* want from your product? Is it the satisfaction of using/having the product, or the satisfaction of showing it off to friends? What are their interests and lifestyle? Having a clear idea of the age, sex and personality of the target market enables the business to do the following things.

Focus your market research

A business may focus market research by interviewing only those who make up the target market. This should make the findings far more reliable. If the target market is clearly defined, the firm's market research budget can be spent with greater effect.

Focus your advertising spending

A business may focus advertising spending on the people most likely to buy the product. One national TV commercial can cost £500,000; it will reach millions of people, but how many are really in the target market? Men do not need to know that 'Maybe it's Maybelline'. A product targeting young women would be advertised far more cost-effectively in magazines such as *Look* or *New!*

Segment your markets

Most markets are not made up of identikit consumers who all want exactly the same product. In practice, consumer preferences can vary greatly. Firms that market their products effectively in this situation produce a range of products, each targeted at specific market segments.

A good example of a company that has used **market segmentation** to great effect is British Sky Broadcasting (BSkyB); in 2013, the company made an operating profit of £1,330 million. Before Sky joined the market, the choice of what to watch on TV was limited. BBC, ITV and Channel 4 tried in vain to produce a range of programmes to cover every taste. Sky offered subscribers a choice of over 800 different channels. Among the target segments are kids, sports fans, ethnic minorities and fans of different music types: for example, MTV Base and Performance (classical music). The output of each channel is carefully matched to a particular consumer interest or hobby. Many of these channels attract additional charges, which has helped BSkyB to increase its monthly income (see Figure 1.4).

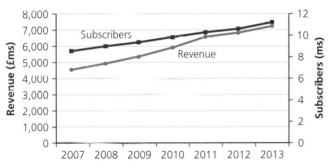

Figure 1.4 BSkyB growth, 2007–2013

A coherent brand image through a coherent marketing mix

Firms that market their products successfully use the marketing mix in an integrated manner to create a coherent and attractive brand image that appeals to the target market. Marketing success depends upon getting all four marketing mix decisions right. A good product that is properly priced and promoted will still fail if distribution is poor. Firms use the marketing mix to create an attractive and coherent brand image for each of the products that they sell. Creating the right brand image is important. If the brand image created by the marketing mix appeals to the target market, there should be an increased chance that the product will succeed.

The most important thing to remember is that all four elements of the mix must be co-ordinated. If the marketing mix is not co-ordinated, mixed product messages will be sent out to the target market. This could create confusion, leading to disappointing sales. The key, then, is to think through the brand image that you want to create *before* making any other decisions on

your product: how you might want to price it, promote it and distribute it.

> 'Word-of-mouth marketing has always been important. Today it's more important than ever because of the power of the internet.'

Joe Pulizzi, business author

1.7 Short-termist marketing = ineffective marketing

Short-termism describes a business philosophy whereby a firm pursues strategies that could boost profit in the short run, even if these strategies damage the firm's long-run profitability. Some examples of short-termist marketing strategies are given below.

High prices designed to exploit consumer loyalty or a dominant market position

In the short run, firms that operate in a market where there is little competition may be tempted to raise their prices to boost revenues and profits. Over many years, WHSmith boosted profits by increasing prices. This worked very well at first, as it seemed to take a while for customers to realise the changes taking place at the store. By 2012, however, 'like-for-like' sales were falling by 5 per cent a year and in 2013 total sales fell by the same percentage.

A decision to exploit consumers by charging high prices is definitely not a good example of effective marketing. High prices can also encourage new competitors to join the industry.

Short-run sales-driven marketing

Some managers believe that their employees can only be motivated to work hard if they are set targets that are linked to bonuses and other performance-related payments. An over-reliance on targets and performance-related pay can create a ruthless and dishonest culture that can affect a firm's marketing. For example, a recent BBC investigation suggested that staff at a high-street bank were encouraged by their supervisors to lie to the bank's customers, in order to hit their personal sales targets. Mis-selling inappropriate financial products to customers can improve a bank's profitability in the short run; however, if the unethical marketing practices are exposed, the resulting wave of bad publicity may hit demand for the firm's products.

Five whys and a how

Questions	Answers
Why is it so hard for large firms to launch new products successfully (fewer than one in five succeeds)?	Because modern markets are so crowded with rival products that it's hard to carve out a profitable new segment.
Why is Apple so successful? Is it down to marketing?	Yes, they have managed to focus the whole business on the young, image-orientated consumer who can make a product 'cool'.
Why do firms set marketing objectives?	Because they clarify the goals that the marketing strategy must achieve.
Why is it a mistake to 'segment a segment'?	If you slice the market up into tiny fragments, it may be impossible to make a profit. Aim at 25–35 year olds, OK; but not just 25–35-year-old women who play snooker.
Why do only 50 per cent of Japanese companies have a marketing department?	They focus on engineering the right product and then hire advertising agencies to advise on marketing, i.e. they are product-led.
How do firms decide how much to spend on marketing?	With difficulty, but often by reference to rivals; if Pepsi is spending £10 million, Coke will want to spend £20 million.

1.8 Introduction to marketing – evaluation

Marketing guru Philip Kotler says that 'marketing only takes a day to learn, but a lifetime to master'. It seems easy to learn what customers want – and sell it to them. In fact, new product launches by big UK companies such as Mars and Heinz have a success rate of less than 20 per cent. So marketing is harder than it looks – largely because it is easy to ask questions, but harder to interpret the results.

All that is certain about marketing is that there is a wrong way to do it. A short-termist approach based on cynicism will backfire. There may be lots of money to be made before it backfires, but backfire it will. To give one more famous quote, from iconic US President

Abraham Lincoln: 'You can fool all the people some of the time, and some of the people all of the time, but you cannot fool all the people all the time.'

Key terms

Marketing mix: the plan for getting the right blend of product, price, promotion and place (the 4Ps).

Marketing objectives: the targets the marketing department must achieve, such as increasing sales by 15 per cent within 12 months.

Market segmentation: dividing a market up by customers' age, gender or income to find areas that are under-served, e.g. bikes for older people.

Marketing strategy: the medium-to-long-term plan for meeting the marketing objectives, delivered through the marketing mix.

1.9 Workbook

Revision questions

(25 marks; 25 minutes)

1 In your own words, explain the meaning of the term 'marketing'. (3)

2 Why do you think most firms decide to review their marketing strategy at fairly regular intervals? (3)

3 What is meant by the phrase 'target market'? (2)

4 Outline two reasons why it is important for firms to be able to identify their target market. (4)

5 Outline one possible marketing objective for each of these companies:
   a) Manchester United FC
   b) easyJet
   c) Topshop. (6)

6 Explain how market segmentation has helped companies such as BSkyB to improve their profitability. (3)

7 Explain how online advertising might help a business to focus its advertising spending on its target market. (4)

Data response 1

The role of chance/luck

Effective marketing usually comes about as a result of careful planning. However, in some cases, firms stumble across a successful marketing strategy. Morgan cars is a conservatively run private business. The production methods used by the company have hardly changed in 50 years. Cars are still made largely by hand. Morgan's best-selling cars are based on designs that have not been changed for decades. In most industries, this approach would be a recipe for disaster. Fortunately for Morgan, the cars continue to sell well within a tiny segment comprised of middle-aged men who want a hand-built British sports car. Morgan has not deliberately engineered its successful use of segmentation, it has happened accidentally; the company has been fortunate.

Figure 1.5 A Morgan car

Questions (30 marks; 30 minutes)

1 From your reading of the text, assess whether Morgan's success is all down to luck. (10)

2 Evaluate the marketing problems Morgan cars could face if it attempts to expand. (20)

New product brand name	Product description	Pre-trial purchase	Post-trial purchase	Better than what's out there	New and different	Overall score
Müllerlight Frultopolls Strawberry	Greek-style yoghurt with strawberry topping 75p each	58%	77%	73%	57%	47/50
Marks & Spencer White tea & Raspberry	An 'infusion' speciality tea £1 for 50 g	26%	21%	19%	55%	27/50
Butterkist Pop'n Pour Chocolate Popcorn	Microwaveable popcorn £1.50 for 2 × 50 g bags	32%	51%	40%	89%	39/50

Table 1.2 Research measurement of sales potential of new brands

Data response 2

Figure 1.6 KitKat Chunky Double Caramel bar

Nestlé Confectionery's flagship brand KitKat, which has annual retail sales of £184 million (year to 21 June 2014; source: IRI), announced what the company called 'our most significant launch for its Chunky format in fifteen years' – KitKat Chunky Double Caramel.

The new bar offers consumers what Nestlé describes as 'a unique concept in chocolate singles' – two portionable halves, each containing a contrasting texture of caramel. One half features a smooth runny caramel inside, while the other half contains a crunchy caramel filling. Each caramel texture sits on top of crispy wafer and is covered in thick milk chocolate. The bar, which is aimed at 25–35 year olds, has a recommended retail price (RRP) of 58p, with stock available from 25 August 2014.

Nestlé UK and Ireland spokesperson James Maxton says: 'Consumer research has shown that a huge 71 per cent of consumers would either probably or definitely buy Double Caramel compared to the typical new product propensity to buy of 54 per cent.' This form of market research is widely used to judge whether or not a new product will succeed. Table 1.2 shows some examples from September 2014 *Grocer* magazines.

The new KitKat bar was supported by a digital and social media campaign set to reach 23 million people. A viral film designed for YouTube launched in September and was amplified through social media and digital channels, including Facebook and Google.

Addressing retailers, Nestlé's James Maxton said:

> 'KitKat has over one million fans on Facebook who will be keen to try this major new launch for themselves. Retailers should therefore expect a high level of trial. In order to capitalise, be sure to stock up from launch and create as high impact off-shelf displays as possible so shoppers cannot miss them.'

Source: adapted from www.wholesalenews.co.uk

Questions (30 marks; 35 minutes)

1 Nestlé is targeting the 25–35-year-old segment of the market with KitKat Double Caramel. Assess two advantages there may be in targeting KitKat Double Caramel at this segment. (8)

2 Look at Table 1.2. Based on the figures, explain why Fruitopolis yoghurt gets such a better overall score than the Butterkist popcorn. (4)

3 Evaluate the factors likely to be the most important in determining how well KitKat Double Caramel sells. (18)

Extended writing

1 In November 2014, 'Share Radio' was launched in the UK. A digital-only radio station, its focus is personal finance. Its founder/owner is especially keen to help teenagers learn more about money. Evaluate how best to market this new station effectively. (20)

2 Several lower-league football clubs have found attendance figures slipping in recent years. Evaluate the best way to build attendance figures at a local sports club of your choice. (20)

2 The market

Linked to: Market research, Ch 3; Market positioning, Ch 4; Pricing strategies, Ch 12; Marketing strategy, Ch 15.

2.1 Mass marketing

Mass marketing is the attempt to create products or services that have universal appeal. Rather than targeting a specific type of customer, mass marketing aims the product at the whole market. The intention is that everyone should be a consumer of the product. Coca-Cola is a good example of a firm that uses mass marketing techniques. The company aims its product at young and old alike. Its goal has always been to be the market leader and remains the same today. The ultimate prize of mass marketing is the creation of **generic brands**. These are brands that are so totally associated with the product that customers treat the brand name as if it was a product category. Examples include 'Coke' (cola) and 'Bacardi' (white rum).

Figure 2.1 Mass marketing

As shown in Figure 2.1, when mass marketing is carried out successfully, it can be highly profitable. Firms such as Ryanair set out to be high-volume, mass market operators and achieve handsome profits. However, it is important to note that mass marketing does not have to go hand in hand with low prices. For example, Nintendo, when it launched the DS, decided to become *the* handheld games console. Superb launch advertising and excellent games software development meant that it achieved mass market sales while keeping its prices high. Even now, with its sales entering the decline phase of its product life cycle (see Figure 2.2), it remains the dominant brand in its market. Mass marketing does not have to aim at the lowest common denominator.

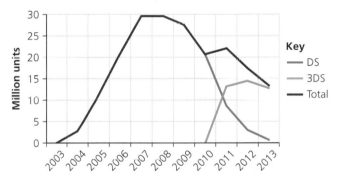

Figure 2.2 Worldwide annual sales of Nintendo handheld consoles (2003–2013) (source: VGChartz.com)

2.2 Niche marketing

A niche market is a very small segment of a much larger market. Niche marketing involves identifying the needs of the consumers that make up the niche. A specialised product or service is then designed to meet the distinctive needs of these consumers. A niche market product sells their prices are in relatively low volumes. As a result, their prices are usually higher than the mass market alternative. Niche market operators often distribute their products through specialist retailers, or directly to the consumer via the internet.

An entrepreneur wanting to set up a niche market business must first identify a group of people who share a taste for a product or service that is currently unsatisfied. A product or a service must then be designed that is capable of meeting this unsatisfied need. It's not that a Bounty bar is better than a Mars bar, but only the Bounty bar gives a hit of coconut sweetness. Finally, the niche must be large enough to support a profitable business. Many new niche market businesses fail because the revenue generated from their niche market business is not high enough to cover the costs of operating.

Small niche operators lack the **economies of scale** required to compete on price with larger, established operators. Instead, the small firm could try to find a small, profitable niche. The amount of profit generated by this niche needs to be high enough for the small firm, but too trivial for the big business. *Rubicon Exotic* has just a 0.6 per cent share of the £2.5 billion UK market for fizzy drinks. Happily, sales of £14 million are profitable enough to satisfy the requirements of Rubicon Drinks, with its low overheads. Small, niche market businesses survive on the basis that they occupy a relatively unimportant market niche. Larger firms operating in the mass market are happy to ignore the niche businesses because they represent too small an opportunity to be worth their while.

Mass v. niche

Let no-one doubt it. Every business would love to have the central, mass market positioning of Wrigley (92 per cent share of UK chewing gum market) or Pampers (63 per cent of UK market for disposable nappies). Better still might be Colgate, with its 45 per cent share of the world market for toothpaste. Unfortunately, for the vast majority of businesses, this glorious position is not an option. Yes, Branston can take on Heinz's mass market positioning in the baked bean market, but who would expect this to be profitable?

The conclusion is clear: if someone else has already 'captured' the mass market, you would be wiser to find your own, profitable niche. Then, who knows, in the long term you may be able to move from a strong niche positioning to chip away at the mass market leader. This is what happened to Twinings tea, which – many years ago – was a tiny, upmarket tea brand in a market dominated by PG Tips and Tetley. In 2014, Twinings toppled Tetley to take second place in the sector – and not too far short of market leader PG Tips (Figure 2.3).

'**Most large markets evolve from niche markets.**'

R. McKenna, businessman

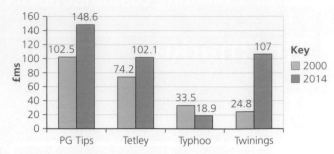

Figure 2.3 UK tea sales (2000–2014) (source: *The Grocer* Top Products Survey)

When choosing a niche positioning, the key issues are authenticity and the ability to gain a true understanding of the niche (Figure 2.4). In its sector, Alpro has proved masterful at understanding the consumers who believe that dairy products are bad for them. In a completely different sector, the German company Haribo started in a small niche which has grown to become the heart of the UK's sugar confectionery market.

Figure 2.4 Logic chain: growing your niche

'**Increasingly, the mass market is turning into a mass of niches.**'

Chris Anderson, author of *The Long Tail*

Mass markets	Niche markets
Long-lasting, wide appeal that spans age groups and gender, e.g. Heinz Ketchup	Strong appeal to a limited audience, e.g. Mars Bounty or Irn-Bru soda
The breadth of appeal comes from the smoothness of the product or service; it has no rough edges or things to dislike, e.g. Coca-Cola or Cadbury Dairy Milk	May be a 'Marmite' characteristic that some love and others hate; Bounty bars divide opinion; those who love may be especially loyal
Usually a successful mass market product will be the market leader, but will not charge too high a price premium	A niche market product probably has higher unit costs than a mass market one, but is able to charge a price premium because of its distinctiveness

Table 2.1 Characteristics of successful products in mass and niche markets

2.3 Market size

If a business has a large share of a market, it may worry that boosting sales further may bring investigations from the Competition and Markets Authority. Therefore, its best way to achieve further growth is by encouraging growth in the market sector as a whole. In the UK, Wrigley has a 90 per cent share of chewing gum sales. So anything it could do to boost the size of the market would help boost its own sales.

In these circumstances, businesses might sponsor research by academics into the health-giving properties of the product. Ocean Spray has a 66 per cent share of the UK market for cranberry juice. So research into the supposed benefits of 'cranberries – the superfruit' could boost sales in the market as a whole, from which Ocean Spray would get 66 per cent of the benefit. Needless to say, for a company with a 25 per cent market share, boosting the market as a whole would make little sense, as 75 per cent of the benefit would be enjoyed by competitors.

2.4 Market share

Nothing is more important to a marketing department than the **market share** of its key brands. External factors largely control market size – for example, the weather or the state of the economy. Market share, by contrast, is largely the product of the marketing department's successes or failures. In 2013, UK sales of Galaxy fell by 5.3 per cent, while sales of Cadbury Dairy Milk rose by 14 per cent. Perhaps Mars (Galaxy) focused too much on a slick new TV advertising campaign with the copy line 'Why have cotton when you can have silk?' Cadbury, by contrast, focused on new product development, such as the launch of Dairy Milk with Oreo cookies.

In setting a market share objective, a company would need to be cautiously optimistic – for example, aiming to push a brand such as Snickers from its 2.5 per cent share of the £3.6 billion UK chocolate market to 3 per cent within the next two years. This would be ambitious, but conceivable. Note that a 3 per cent market share would generate annual sales of £108 million, making it perfectly possible to afford a marketing budget of perhaps £10 million – allowing for a substantial TV advertising campaign as well as a significant budget for social media advertising.

2.5 Brands

Faces can just merge into a crowd and disappear. Products would be the same without branding. A brand can be given a 'personality', which helps it to be recognised and remembered. Think of the different personalities of brands such as Peperami, BMW, Ryanair and Nespresso. Effective branding is a key aspect to establishing a successful niche market brand. It is also at the heart of achieving **product differentiation**.

The subject of branding is covered fully in Chapter 11.

2.6 Dynamic markets

Companies such as Cadbury and Heinz are lucky enough to operate in very long-lived, stable markets. Many others have to operate in a situation of competitive or market turmoil in which yesterday's grower is today's loser. At the time of writing, Sony's ten-month-old PS4 had outsold Microsoft's One by more than 2:1. But Microsoft has just spent $2.5 billion on software sensation Minecraft. This might mean that future versions of the game will be launched for One but not the PS4. This could hit the PS4 hard. Games software is a dynamic market indeed.

There are four key factors to consider in dynamic markets:

1 Online retailing. This distribution channel is dynamic and quite unpredictable. According to research group IGD, in 2014 online grocery sales accounted for just 4.4 per cent of the UK grocery market. As the market is so huge (£175 billion), it still comes to a tidy sum – £7.7 billion – but that is less than the UK sales of Aldi and Lidl combined. IGD forecasts that by 2017 online grocery sales will have a 6 per cent market share. Is that dynamic?

By contrast ASOS plc has grown its online sales from £8.3 million in 2003 to £975 million in 2014 and a planned £2,500 million by 2020. That's dynamic! Another way of measuring the dynamism of online is to look at the retailers who have been broken by online competition, such as Game, HMV and Phones4U.

2 How markets change. Even physical (as opposed to digital/online) markets change significantly over time. A key factor is changing affluence levels. In the last 20 years, Britons have doubled the amount of their income they spend on eating out. This has created huge new business opportunities for independent restaurants and for chains such as Gourmet Burger Kitchen and Strada. Another change has occurred in grocery purchasing, where sales of 'ethical' food and drink rose from £1.35 billion in 2000 to £7.7 billion by 2012. The big gainers were Fairtrade Foods – which more than quadrupled their sales – and Rainforest Alliance.

3 Innovation and market growth. Innovation means bringing a new idea to life, such as launching a new product or service onto the market. Innovation can help a business gain market share, but can also spur market growth. When Coca-Cola launched 'Life' in 2014, the company's head of marketing said: 'One of the driving factors behind our category's success is the relentless pace of innovation. Last year innovation (i.e. new products) added £241m in terms of value to the category.' In other words, new products encourage customers to try something new and therefore boost market growth.

4 Adapting to change. The case of Coca-Cola Life is a classic of adapting to change. With clear evidence that consumers were buying fewer cans of full-sugar fizzy drinks, Coca-Cola brought out a product with 89 calories instead of the 139 in the red can, in the hope of winning customers back. Heinz did something similar in the £580 million 'table sauce' category of the grocery trade. Spotting growing sales for chilli sauces, they introduced Mexican Chilli Ketchup and Sweet Chilli Ketchup to the UK in 2013. As consumer tastes change, and fashion changes, and competitors come and go, every business needs to be clever about adapting rather than waiting and then be forced to change.

2.7 How competition affects the market

In most markets, competition is a key factor, and potential competition is equally important. Wrigley, in 2006, had a 94 per cent share of the UK market for chewing gum. Then Cadbury launched Trident gum in a blaze of TV advertising. Trident quickly achieved sales of £25 million, taking sales from Wrigley. By 2014, Wrigley had seen Trident off (sales had slumped to under £4 million)

and Wrigley's share had recovered to 92 per cent. But managers at Wrigley won't have forgotten the huge shock caused by Cadbury. Potential competition can keep companies on their toes as much as actual competition.

Competition is the pressure that keeps businesses from getting careless and complacent. Try travelling on Virgin West Coast (the sole operator of trains from London to Manchester) and you quickly learn this. A standard class open return ticket for 19 December 2014 was £321! Careful research could have uncovered a return to New York for that sum of money. Virgin has no competition and therefore it can charge high prices and give no more than the minimum service level agreed in its monopoly contract with the government.

For most companies, competition, not monopoly, is the norm. This makes it hard to charge high prices unless customers perceive the business as offering an outstanding product or service. This encourages companies to try their best to be innovative and creative about how to improve their product range and service level. From a customer point of view, that means important things such as cars today being hugely more reliable than they once were and much wider consumer choice across markets from magazines to cosmetics to chocolate bars.

2.8 The difference between risk and uncertainty

Between 2009 and 2014, Jaguar Land Rover enjoyed a sales boom based largely on success in China and Russia. Then, with little warning, a collapse in the price of the Russian rouble meant that Russians would face a doubled Range Rover price in 2015. Sales in Russia at the end of 2014 were already falling sharply; no-one knew how bad it would be in 2015.

So, was this a problem of risk or uncertainty? The difference is that risk can be quantified whereas uncertainty cannot. No economist foresaw the collapse in the oil price that led to a halving in the value of the rouble – so it was impossible to quantify this risk. At the start of 2014, if Jaguar Land Rover managers had brainstormed 'biggest risks we face this year', a halving of the value of the rouble would not have come up.

Uncertainty such as that caused by the rouble collapse is part of business life. Whether it is Sainsbury's lurching from 32 quarters of successive growth to a sales downturn caused by Lidl/Aldi, or ASOS hit by a stronger pound, uncertainty is a constant.

So what exactly is risk? This is best answered with statistics. Data from America shows that only 40 per cent of new, independent restaurants survive until the end of year three. So their failure rate is 60 per cent and therefore the risk of failure can be quantified at 60 per cent. Assuming the same is true in Britain and elsewhere, does that mean that no-one in their right mind should start their own restaurant? Well, no. But it does mean three things:

1 No-one should risk their life savings opening a new, independent restaurant.

2 It may be worth considering a lower-risk proposition, such as buying a **franchise** to operate a successful restaurant brand such as TGI Fridays.

3 It can only be worth opening a high-risk independent restaurant if there are big profit margins, allowing the chance of big profits if the business succeeds (pizza falls into this category, because £1 of ingredients can be sold for £10).

In business, risks are assessed and – where possible – quantified, to help managers make better decisions. Whatever decision is made, factors causing uncertainty (including simple bad luck) will then affect whether the decision turns out well or badly.

Five whys and a how

Questions	Answers
Why might a mass market producer struggle to make a profit?	If the competition is fierce, the battle may have to be on the basis of price, making it almost impossible to make satisfactory profits.
Why might it be beneficial to target an older customer niche?	Demographic trends are boosting the over-60s, so it could be very profitable to get into the Stena/Tena/Saga market.
Why might a large firm benefit from targeting small niches?	With modern, flexible production, it is possible to produce small batches tailored to different customer groups – without forcing costs up.
Why might a brand-new firm benefit from developing a brand-new niche?	The first into any market can develop an image for authenticity that can add value in the long term.
Why might it be hard for an established business to adapt to disruptive change?	Because the 'established' products may be making good profits, making it hard to justify changes that risk a short-term profit downturn.
How difficult would it be to switch from a niche market to a mass market positioning?	It would require a complete rethink of the marketing mix, perhaps including new pack designs and a lower pricing point. Difficult, yes, but Twinings has shown it is not impossible

2.9 The market – evaluation

Which is better? Is it mass or niche marketing? The answer is that it depends. In the bulk ice cream market, large packs of vanilla ice cream have become so cheap that little profit can be made. It is better by far, then, to be in a separate niche, whether regional, such as Mackie's Scottish ice cream, or upmarket, such as Rocombe Farm or Häagen-Dazs. The latter can charge ten times as much per litre as the mass market own-label bulk packs.

Yet would a film company prefer to sell a critic's favourite or a blockbuster smash hit? The answer is the latter, of course. In other words, the mass market is great, if you can succeed there. Businesses such as Heinz, Kellogg's and even Chanel show that mass marketing can be successful and profitable in the long term.

Key terms

Economies of scale: factors that cause costs per unit to fall when a firm operates at a higher level of production.

Franchise: a business that sells the rights to the use of its name and trading methods to local businesses.

Generic brands: brands that are so well known that customers say the brand when they mean the product (for example, 'I'll hoover the floor').

Product differentiation: the extent to which consumers perceive your brand as being different from others.

2.10 Workbook

Revision questions

(30 marks; 30 minutes)

1 Identify two advantages of niche marketing over mass marketing. (3)

2 Give three reasons why a large firm may wish to enter a niche market. (3)

3 Why may small firms be better at spotting and then reacting to new niche-market opportunities? (3)

4 Give two reasons why average prices in niche markets tend to be higher than those charged in most mass markets. (2)

5 Outline two reasons why information technology has made niche marketing a more viable option for large firms. (4)

6 Explain why it is important for a large firm to be flexible if it is to successfully operate in niche markets. (2)

7 In your own words, explain why niche market products may generate higher profit margins than mass market products. (3)

8 A new chairman sets the chief executive of Tesco the corporate objective of restoring Tesco's UK market share to 32 per cent from its current figure of 28.5 per cent. Outline two possible marketing objectives that might help achieve this target. (4)

9 a) If a company operating in a stable market sees its market share fall from 5 per cent to 4 per cent, what would be the percentage impact on its sales revenue? (2)

   b) How might the business respond to such slippage in its market share? (4)

Data response 1

The return of mass marketing to the car industry

For many years, car manufacturers such as Toyota and Nissan have sought out market niches in an attempt to improve profitability. Cars such as the Toyota Prius, a hybrid electric-powered vehicle, are not intended to sell in high volumes. Instead, niche market cars sell for high prices, delivering a higher profit margin per car than more conventional mass market models.

However, in the last couple of years, there are signs that car manufacturers have sought a return to conventional mass marketing, particularly in Asia where rapid rates of economic growth have created a growing middle class. At present both the Indian and the Chinese car markets are unsaturated. For example, only 4 per cent of households in India have a car, whereas the corresponding figure in the US is 88 per cent. Income per head, while increasing rapidly, is still low by American and European standards, and so far this has limited the demand for new cars in India.

The car market in India is dominated by Suzuki Maruti, a joint venture between a Japanese and an Indian company. In early 2014, its top seller was the Alto 800 model, with prices starting at £2,600 for a new car.

This mass market car has seen off the unsuccessful attempt by Indian rival Tata to introduce a £1,500 car, the Nano. Indian car buyers are willing to accept compromises with western safety standards, but still want a degree of comfort and, especially, reliability. Suzuki Maruti, with a market share of more than 40 per cent, provides exactly this.

Environmentalists have expressed their concerns that cheap, mass market cars such as the Alto add to the problem of global warming and climate change. In 2014, Suzuki Maruti estimated they would sell nearly one million cars in India.

Questions (40 marks; 45 minutes)

1 a) What is meant by a niche market product? (2)

   b) Explain why the Toyota Prius is a good example of a niche market product. (4)

2 Explain two reasons why the Indian car market has grown. (4)

3 a) What is meant by a mass market product? (2)

   b) Explain why the Tata Motor's 'People's car' is a good example of a mass market product. (4)

4 Assess two advantages and two disadvantages for European car manufacturers, such as Renault, of mass marketing £2,000 cars in India. (8)

5 £2,000 cars can be profitably made in India. Explain why UK consumers are unlikely to benefit from similar low prices. (4)

6 Evaluate whether companies such as Tata Motors should take into account the concerns of environmentalists when making their business decisions. (12)

Data response 2

Winter melon tea

Mass market soft drinks like Coca-Cola and Pepsi are very popular in countries such as Hong Kong and Singapore. In an attempt to survive against the imported competition, local producers of soft drinks have managed to establish a flourishing niche market for traditional Asian drinks sold in 33cl cans. Sales of these niche market products have been rising but from a very low level.

Consumers that make up this niche market are encouraged to believe, through advertising, that traditional drinks such as winter melon tea and grass jelly drink are healthier than their mass market alternatives. Other firms use economic nationalism to sell their drinks, using slogans such as 'Asian heritage' in their advertising.

However, producers of traditional drinks could now become a victim of their own success. Foreign multinationals have noticed the rapid growth of this market niche, and in response they have launched their own range of traditional drinks.

Questions (30 marks; 35 minutes)

1 **a)** What is meant by a mass market product? (2)

  b) Explain why Asian traditional drinks are examples of niche market products. (4)

2 Assess two ways in which the producers of traditional drinks, such as winter melon tea and grass jelly drink, created product differentiation. (8)

3 Niche market products are normally more expensive than most mass market products. Using the example of traditional Asian drinks, explain why this is so. (4)

4 Evaluate whether the local producers of Asian traditional drinks will be able to survive in the long term given that their products now have to compete against me-too brands produced by foreign multinationals such as Coca-Cola and Pepsi. (12)

Extended writing

1 Choose one of the following markets: women's fashion retailing; computer console software; chocolate bars. For the market of your choice, evaluate whether sales are dominated by mass market or niche market products/brands. (20)

2 Evaluate the view held by some commentators that it is virtually impossible to succeed when trying to turn a niche market into a mass market product. (20)

3 Market research

Linked to: The market, Ch 2; Market positioning, Ch 4; Demand Ch 5; Price elasticity of demand, Ch 8; Product and service design, Ch 10; Pricing strategies, Ch 12.

3.1 Product and market orientation

Effective marketing is usually based around an approach that is market-orientated, rather than product-orientated. In a market-orientated business, managers take into account the needs of the consumer before making any decision. They put the customer at the heart of the decision-making process.

> 'The aim of marketing is to know and understand the customer so well the product or service fits him and sells itself.'

Peter Drucker, business author/guru

Some firms still use a product-orientated approach to marketing. This leads managers to focus on what the firm does best; internal efficiency comes before consumer preferences. Product orientation may lead the business towards the following approaches.

- The hard sell: employing a large sales force to go out and convince consumers that they should buy your product. Individualised sales targets, low basic salaries and high rates of commission ensure that sales staff will be incentivised to hit their targets, enabling the firm to sell the products that it has already produced.

- Cutting costs and prices: if a product-orientated firm's products are not selling very well, managers tend to respond to this crisis by cutting costs. If costs can be cut, retail prices can also be cut without any loss of profit margin.

The problem with the above approaches is that they keep the business doing what it traditionally does, without anticipating customers' changing needs. That is what happened to Sony, who once dominated the world market for personal, portable music. When the iPod arrived, Sony kept on trying to tweak their 'Walkman' product instead of accepting that the digital world had arrived.

On the other hand, there are some weaknesses in market orientation. The death of Rover Cars (once one of the world's biggest car producers) was partly due to this. Rover management thought customers could be attracted by marketing gimmicks such as 'special edition' cars, or cars with angular steering wheels. A greater focus on the quality and reliability of the product would have been far more effective. Fortunately, the Land Rover part of the business was sold off and in recent years has flourished in Britain under the leadership of Tata Motors of India.

Real business

Gap

Figure 3.1 Gap

By 2011, Gap's chief executive, Glenn Murphy, had seen sales fall steadily since his appointment in 2007, and the American clothes retailer had been overtaken by Zara as the world's number one clothing retailer.

Gap suffered from falling sales and market share because it failed to keep up to date with changes in fashion. It built its reputation around selling 'preppy' clothes. Consumer tastes had moved on, but Gap did not. In 2011, Murphy switched the business towards a more market-orientated approach. Qualitative market research was used to help develop a new strategy. In early 2012, Gap introduced new ranges of more brightly coloured clothing, livelier store designs and designer collaborations. In 2013, for the first time in many years, Gap announced that sales were above target and that profits were ahead of expectations. In the second quarter of 2013, its profits were 25 per cent higher than in 2012.

3.2 Primary and secondary market research

One of the biggest causes of business failure is poor market understanding. This is why market research has the potential to be valuable to every business. For a business start-up, finding out the market size and competitors' strengths and weaknesses are all-important. For an established business, market research can reveal where customers are starting to lose faith in a particular product or brand – perhaps opening up an opportunity for an innovative new product.

So how can firms find out this type of information? The starting point is **secondary research**: unearthing data that already exists.

Methods of secondary research

Internet

Most people start by 'Googling' the topic. This can provide invaluable information, though online providers of market research information will want to charge for the service. With luck, Google will identify a relevant article that can provide useful information.

Trade press

Each week, *The Grocer* magazine provides a full analysis of a market. For example 22 November 2014 showed that annual sales of chilled pies amount to £240 million,

with beef outselling chicken 3:1. Every major market is served by one or more magazines written for people who work within that trade. Spending £3 on an issue of *The Grocer* provides lots of statistical and other information. Many trade magazines are available for reference in bigger public libraries.

Government-produced data

The government-funded National Statistics produces valuable reports, such as the 'Annual Abstract of Statistics' and 'Labour Market Trends'. These provide data on population trends and forecasts; for example, someone starting a hair and beauty salon may find out how many 16–20-year-old women there will be in the year 2020.

Having obtained background data, further research is likely to be tailored specifically to the company's needs, such as carrying out a survey among 16–20-year-old women about their favourite haircare brands. This type of first-hand research gathers primary data. Some of the pros and cons of primary and secondary research are given in Table 3.1.

	Secondary research	Primary research
Pros	• often obtained without cost • good overview of a market • usually based on actual sales figures or research on large samples	• can aim questions directly at your research objectives • latest information from the marketplace • can assess the psychology of the customer
Cons	• data may not be updated regularly • not tailored to your own needs • expensive to buy reports on many different marketplaces	• expensive, £10,000+ per survey • risk of questionnaire and interviewer bias • research findings may only be usable if comparable *back data* exist

Table 3.1 The pros and cons of primary and secondary research

Methods of primary research

The process of gathering information directly from people within your target market is known as **primary research** (or field research). When carried out by market research companies it is expensive, but there is much that firms can do for themselves.

For a company that is up and running, a regular survey of customer satisfaction is an important way of measuring the quality of customer service. When investigating a new market, there are various measures that can be taken by a small firm with a limited budget.

- Retailer research: the people closest to a market are those who serve customers directly – the retailers. They are likely to know the up-and-coming brands, the degree of brand loyalty and the importance of price and packaging, all of which is crucial information.
- Observation: when starting up a service business in which location is an all-important factor, it is invaluable to measure the rate of pedestrian (and possibly traffic) flow past your potential site compared with that of rivals. A sweet shop or dry cleaners near a busy bus stop may generate twice the sales of a rival 50 yards down the road.

For a large company, primary research will be used extensively in new product development. For example, if we consider the possibility of launching Orange Chocolate Buttons, the development stages, plus research, would probably be as shown in Table 3.2.

Development stage	Primary research
1 The product idea (probably one of several)	**1** Group discussions among regular chocolate buyers (some young, some old)
2 Product test (testing different recipes, different sweetness, orangeyness, etc.)	**2** A taste test on 200+ chocolate buyers (on street corners, or in a hall)
3 Brand name research (testing several different names and perhaps logos)	**3** Quantitative research using a questionnaire on a sample of 200+
4 Packaging research	**4** Quantitative research as in item 3
5 Advertising research	**5** Group discussions run by psychologists to discover which advertisement has the strongest effect on product image and recall
6 Total proposition test: testing the level of purchase interest, to help make sales forecasts	**6** Quantitative research using a questionnaire and product samples on at least 200+ consumers

Table 3.2 Primary research used in new product development (Orange Chocolate Buttons)

3.3 Qualitative research

This is in-depth research into the motivations behind the attitudes and buying habits of consumers. It does not produce statistics such as '52 per cent of chocolate buyers like orange chocolate'; instead it gives clues as to why they like it (is it really because it's orange, or because it's different/a change?). Qualitative research is usually conducted by psychologists, who learn to interpret the way people say things, as well as what they say.

'Eighty to ninety percent of our behaviour is determined by our subconscious mind. The problem market researchers face is that they communicate with the conscious mind of consumers.'

Robert Poldervaart, researcher

Qualitative research takes two main forms, as described below.

Group discussions (also known as focus groups)

These are free-ranging discussions led by psychologists among groups of six to eight consumers. The group leader will have a list of topics that need discussion, but will be free to follow up any point made by a group member. Among the advantages of group discussions are that they:

- may reveal a problem or opportunity the company had not anticipated
- reveal consumer psychology, such as the importance of image and peer pressure.

Selling luxury in China

A 2013 quantitative study showed that Louis Vuitton, Hermes and Chanel are the luxury brands with the highest reputation in China. But do they share the same image characteristics? To find out, a qualitative study was carried out, depth interviewing people from three groups: the 'nouveau (super) riche', 'gifters' and 'middle class luxury'. The study found that the first two groups were price insensitive; indeed, high prices were in some ways attractive. However, the third group was very price sensitive within a restricted number of acceptable western brands. These groups could be targeted quite differently – for example, online.

Depth interviews

These are informal, in-depth interviews that take place between a psychologist and a consumer. They have the same function as group discussions, but avoid the risk that the group opinion will be swayed by one influential person. Typical research questions are shown in Table 3.3.

Qualitative research	Quantitative research
• Why do people *really* buy Nikes?	• Which pack design do you prefer?
• Who in the household *really* decides which brand of shampoo is bought?	• Have you heard of any of the following brands? (Ariel, Daz, Persil, etc.)
• What mood makes you feel like buying Häagen-Dazs ice cream?	• How likely are you to buy this product regularly?
• When you buy your children Frosties, how do you feel?	• How many newspapers have you bought in the past seven days?

Table 3.3 Typical research questions

3.4 Quantitative research

This asks pre-set questions on a large enough sample of people to provide statistically valid data. Questionnaires can answer factual questions, such as 'How many 16–20 year olds have heard of Chanel No 5?' There are three key aspects to quantitative research:

- sampling, ensuring that the research results are typical of the whole population, though only a sample of the population has been interviewed
- writing a questionnaire that is unbiased and meets the research objectives
- assessing the validity of the results.

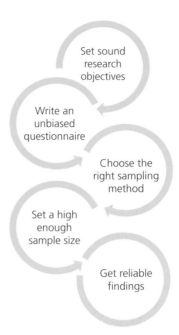

Figure 3.2 Logic chain: getting research right

3.5 Limitations of market research, sample size and bias

Although the most obvious limitation of market research is its accuracy (dealt with below), a more important problem may be its validity – that is, whether the findings tell you anything meaningful. Market research can uncover consumer views on minor things, such as the level of interest in a new Cadbury Dairy Milk bar with cashew nuts. But Steve Jobs always claimed that market research was incapable of seeing potential in real leaps forward. So the Apple iPod, iPhone and iPad received no market research backing. Not that he was the first to think this way. Henry Ford, in the 1920s, said that if he had asked customers, 'they'd have asked for a faster horse' (rather than a car).

'**Running a company on market research is like driving while looking in the rear view mirror.**'

Anita Roddick, founder of Body Shop

Sample size

A key consideration is to determine how many interviews should be conducted. Should 10, 100, or 1,000 people be interviewed? The most high-profile surveys conducted in Britain are the opinion polls asking adults about their voting intentions in a general election. These samples of between 1,000 and 1,500 respondents are considered large enough to reflect the opinions of the electorate of 45 million. How is this possible?

Of course, if you only interviewed ten people, the chances are slim that the views of this sample would match those of the whole population. Of these ten, seven may say they would definitely buy Chocolate Orange Buttons. If you asked another ten, however, only three may say the same. A sample of ten is so small that chance variations make the results meaningless. In other words, a researcher can have no statistical confidence in the findings from a sample of ten.

A sample of 100 is far more meaningful. It is not enough to feel confident about marginal decisions (for example, 53 per cent like the red pack design and 47 per cent like the blue one), but is quite enough if the result is clear-cut (such as, 65 per cent like the name 'Spark'; 35 per cent prefer 'Valencia'). Many major product launches have proceeded following research on as low a sample as 100.

With a sample of 1,000, a high level of confidence is possible. Even small differences would be statistically significant with such a large sample. So why doesn't everyone use samples of 1,000? The answer is because of the cost of doing so. Hiring a market research agency to undertake a survey on 100 people would cost approximately £10,000. A sample of 1,000 people would cost three times that amount, which is good value if you can afford it but not everyone can. As shown in the earlier example of launching Orange Buttons, a company might require six surveys before launching a new product. So the amount spent on research alone might reach £180,000 if samples of 1,000 were used.

Sample bias

Even with a large **sample size**, it is possible to get inaccurate findings due to sample bias. In 1936, an American magazine made the wrong forecast of a Presidential election despite a sample of 2.4 million potential voters. The magazine announced that the Republican candidate would win with 55 per cent of the poll. When Democrat F.D. Roosevelt won a landslide, commentators laughed at the 'useless' new science of sampling. Yet a sample of just 3,000 by the Gallup Poll predicted the result correctly. This proved that the size of a sample is no guarantee of accuracy. The magazine had a huge sample, but it had drawn it from telephone directories and car owners – both affluent populations in the 1930s. Dr Gallup had made sure to find a sample that was truly representative of ordinary Americans. Sampling, then, is more about accuracy than size – though size still matters.

3.6 Use of IT to support market research

Websites

Many websites automatically generate customer questionnaires. They might target everyone through the home page or focus on a subgroup, such as browsers of John Lewis online interested in baby products. Although this seems a great way to get 'free' research data, there are many negatives. Setting up the programme and the automated data collection takes man hours, and there are important questions to ask about the reliability of the findings. Who answers web questionnaires? There could be a bias towards those with time on their hands (pensioners?) or towards those who think particularly highly of the product/company.

The use of social media

Social media provide the interactivity that may help create some bonding between consumer and brand. This may lead to richer market research findings. Social media can provide a way to gain a fuller understanding of what customers really love about the brand and the product range. It can help gain a fuller understanding of customers and the market you are serving. In the past, this was attempted through market research, but the interactions between company and customer have the potential to be much richer. When Innocent Drinks recently introduced their first grass-covered van to Ireland, they asked blog followers to suggest a name. 'LamborGreeny' was one of many suggestions.

Figure 3.3 Innocent Drinks is known for their smoothies

The second benefit is derived from the first. Stronger relationships between consumer and brand can cement brand loyalty – and, in the long run, there are few more valuable attributes than that.

Databases

In May 2014, 74 per cent of UK grocery shopping was done with the use of so-called loyalty cards, such as Tesco's Clubcard. This provides the retailer with a multi-million user database, which can be interrogated to find out answers to quantitative questions, such as what percentage of purchases of Lynx are among households with boys under 12? Classic research on a small sample of the population can never beat finding out facts from a huge database.

▌ 3.7 Market segmentation

Segmentation means finding ways to divide a market up to identify untapped opportunities, perhaps among older consumers, or among those who believe they are wheat intolerant. Market segmentation is the acknowledgement by companies that customers are not all the same. 'The market' can be broken down into smaller sections in which customers share common characteristics, from the same age group to a shared love of Manchester United. Successful segmentation can increase customer satisfaction (if you love shopping and 'celebs', how wonderful that *Look* magazine is for you!) and provide scope for increasing company profits. After all, customers may be willing to pay a higher price for a magazine focused purely on the subjects they love, instead of buying a general magazine in which most of the articles stay unread.

For new, small companies, segmentation is a valuable strategy for breaking in to an established market. For large companies, market segmentation involves two possibilities:

1 Simply to add one niche product to a portfolio otherwise dominated by the mass market.

2 **Multiple segmentation**, in which a wide portfolio of niche brands can add up to a market-leading position. This approach would have risked being only marginally profitable in the past, but flexible, high-tech manufacturing systems can make it cost-effective to produce differently targeted products on the same production line. A good example is Ella's Organic – a baby food company which has enjoyed sales growth from £2 million a year in 2009 to £30 million in 2014 by spreading the idea of food good for babies across a series of different sectors (and 15 countries overseas).

To successfully segment a market, the steps are as follows.

1 Research into the different types of customer within a marketplace – for example, different age groups, gender, regions and personality types.

2 See if they have common tastes/habits; for example, younger readers may be more focused on fashion and celebrities than older ones.

3 Identify the segment you wish to focus on, then conduct some qualitative research into customer motivations and psychology.

4 Devise a product designed not for the whole market but for a particular segment; this may only achieve a 1 per cent market share, but if the total market is big enough, that could be highly profitable.

Real business

In 2003, Camilla Stephens started a pie business that struggled to become profitable. It needed to be refinanced and downscaled in 2004, but from a smaller base it began to grow. Before starting the business, Camilla had been Head of Food at Starbucks UK and also Deputy Editor of Good Housekeeping magazine, so she had a terrific understanding of food trends. Seeing the success of Innocent Drinks and Green & Black's, she focused clearly on hand-made, very high-quality, high-priced pies. Think Chicken and Red Pepper rather than Chicken Balti.

In the early years, the pie business supplied local cafés and caterers, but in 2006 Camilla (with new partner/husband James Footit) developed the Higgidy brand. This proved an incredible turning point. Within 18 months, Higgidy was stocked in Sainsbury's, Booths and Waitrose supermarkets, giving national distribution and a big boost to sales. By taking their time to understand the market segment for posh pies, Higgidy was put on track to achieve success in the static market for pies and pastries. In Figure 3.4, Higgidy's success is contrasted with the flat sales position for mass-market Pukka Pies.

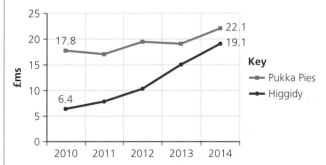

Figure 3.4 Higgidy sales growth (source: *The Grocer* magazine, 2010-2014)

Five whys and a how

Questions	Answers
Why may start-up companies struggle to get accurate market research data?	They lack a base of existing customers who can be interviewed, e.g. to find out about changing tastes.
Why is secondary data a first step, but not a sufficient step?	Because it only gives general information; for data tailored to your own needs, you need to commission primary research.
Why may small samples be dangerous?	Because their findings are subject to high statistical variability, making them unreliable.
Why may qualitative research sometimes prove especially important?	Because sometimes the issues involved are psychological, such as whether a logo strays slightly beyond distinctive towards vulgar.
Will Big Data mean that commissioning primary research becomes a thing of the past? Why?	No. However much data is captured and analysed, it can only be based on past information (such as sales figures); primary research can ask important hypothetical questions about the future.
How might a company set up primary research when the findings relate to a make-or-break corporate decision?	The objectives must be agreed at a high level; the questions need careful scrutiny and to be trialled to make sure they are unbiased; the sample size would have to be very high.

3.8 Market research – evaluation

In large firms, it is rare for any significant marketing decision to be made without market research. Even an apparently minor change to a pack design will only be carried out after testing in research. Is this overkill? Surely marketing executives are employed to make judgements, not merely do what surveys tell them?

The first issue here is the strong desire to make business decisions as scientifically as possible; in other words, to act on evidence, not on feelings. Quantitative research, especially, fits in with the desire to act on science not hunch. Yet this can be criticised, such as by John Scully, former head of Apple Inc, who once said: 'No great marketing decision has ever been made on the basis of quantitative data.' He was pointing out that true innovations, such as the Apple iPad, were the product of creativity and hunch, not science.

The second issue concerns the management culture. In some firms, mistakes lead to inquests, blame and even dismissal. This makes managers keen to find a let–out. When the new product flops, the manager can point an accusing finger at the positive research results: 'It wasn't my fault. We need a new research agency.' In other firms, mistakes are seen as an inevitable part of learning. For every Sinclair C5 (unresearched flop), there may be an iPod (unresearched moneyspinner). In firms with a positive, risk–taking approach to business, qualitative insights are likely to be preferred to quantitative data.

Key terms

Bias: a factor that causes research findings to be unrepresentative of the whole population – for example, bubbly interviewers or misleading survey questions.

Primary research: finding out information first-hand – for example, Coca-Cola designing a questionnaire to obtain information from people who regularly buy diet products.

Secondary research: finding out information that has already been gathered – for example, the government's estimates of the number of 14–16 year olds in Wales.

Sample size: the number of people interviewed; this should be large enough to give confidence that the findings are representative of the whole population.

3.9 Workbook

Revision questions

(35 marks; 35 minutes)

1 State three ways in which a cosmetics firm could use market research. (3)

2 Outline three reasons why market research information may prove inaccurate. (6)

3 Distinguish between primary and secondary research. (3)

4 What advantages are there in using secondary research rather than primary? (3)

5 State three key factors to take into account when writing a questionnaire. (3)

6 Explain two aspects of marketing in which consumer psychology is important. (6)

7 Outline the pros and cons of using a large sample size. (4)

8 Identify three possible sources of bias in primary market research. (3)

9 Explain why street interviewing may become less common in the future. (4)

Data response

Each year, more than £1,500 million is spent on pet food in the UK. All the growth within the market has been for luxury pet foods and for healthier products. Seeing these trends, in early 2014 Town & Country Petfoods launched 'HiLife Just Desserts', a range of pudding treats for dogs. They contain Omega-3 but no added sugar and therefore have no more than 100 calories per tin.

Sales began well, especially of the apple and cranberry version. Now sales have flattened out at around £1 million a year and the company thinks it is time to launch some new flavours. They commissioned some primary research that was carried out using an online survey linked to pet care websites. The sample size was 150.

The main findings of the online survey are shown below.

1 Have you ever bought your dog a pet food pudding?

Never (%)	Just once but no longer (%)	Yes, in past (%)	Yes, still do (%)
61	13	12	14

2 Which of these flavours might you buy for your dog?

	Never (%)	May try (%)	May buy monthly (%)	May buy once a week + (%)
Muesli yoghurt	61	19	15	5
Rhubarb crumble	43	33	22	2
Apples and custard	52	34	12	2

The marketing director is slightly disappointed that none of the new product ideas has done brilliantly, but happy that there's one clear winner. She plans a short qualitative research exercise among existing HiLife customers and hopes to launch two new flavours in time for the annual Crufts Dog Show in three months' time.

Questions (30 marks; 35 minutes)

1 Explain whether the sample size of 150 was appropriate in this case. (4)

2 Explain one possible drawback of using an online survey. (4)

2 Assess the marketing director's conclusion that 'none of the new product ideas has done brilliantly', but that she is 'happy that there's one clear winner'. (10)

3 a) Explain one method of qualitative research that could be used in this case. (4)

  b) Assess two ways in which qualitative research may help the marketing director. (8)

Extended writing

1 'Market research is like an insurance policy. You pay a premium to reduce your marketing risks.' Evaluate this statement. (20)

2 Steve Jobs, boss of Apple, once said that he ignored market research in the early stages of the iPad. He believes that research is useful in relation to existing products, but does not work with innovative new products.

  a) Why might this be?

  b) How could research be used to best effect for assessing new innovations? (20)

4 Market positioning

Linked to: The market, Ch 2; Market research, Ch 3; Demand, Ch 5; Product and service design, Ch 10; Pricing strategies, Ch 12.

4.1 Market mapping

Market mapping is carried out in two stages.

1 Identify the key features that characterise consumers within a market; examples in the market for women's clothes would be: young/old and high fashion/conservative.

2 Having identified the key characteristics, place every brand on a grid such as that shown in Figure 4.1; this will reveal where the competition is concentrated, and may highlight gaps in the market.

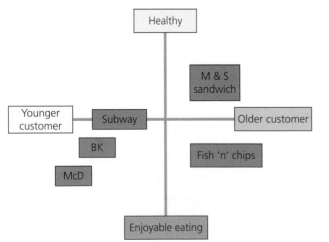

Figure 4.1 Example of a market map for fast food

Using this approach could help in identifying a product or market niche that has not yet been filled. In the **market map** shown in Figure 4.1, there appears to be an available niche for healthy eating for younger customers within the

fast food sector. The market map points to the possibility of this positioning, but then it would be up to the entrepreneur to investigate further. There may be a niche, but too small to provide an opportunity for a profitable business.

A great example of positioning is Aldi's position within the UK's price-motivated segment of the grocery market. With Asda, Lidl and Iceland as its direct competitors, Aldi has seen its sales boom as a result of persuading middle-Britain that shopping at Aldi is sensible rather than cheapskate. Its slogan 'Spend a little. Live a lot' is about having a good time – not about 'low, low prices'. Figure 4.2 shows the value to Aldi of astute positioning.

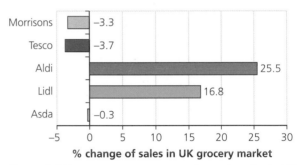

Figure 4.2 Year-on-year percentage change in sales in UK grocery market, 12 weeks to November 2014 (source: Kantar Worldpanel)

4.2 Competitive advantage of a good or service

Figure 4.2 shows the success of Aldi and Lidl within the UK grocery market in 2014. Both had carved out a competitive advantage based on cost. They had chosen to offer a limited range of products and to only accept brands willing to compromise on price. Tesco or Sainsbury's offer customers a full shopping basket; Heinz Ketchup will be there, as will Marmite and Maltesers. Lidl and Aldi work to a different model: they offer shoppers a valuable, low-cost shopping basket of good quality – but they don't promise a full range. So an Aldi shopper may leave feeling a bit disappointed not to have got Maltesers, but there would be no sense of surprise. Because of this approach, brands have to work hard to get stocked by Aldi or Lidl; they have to offer good deals or else they know they won't be stocked at all. This allows Aldi and Lidl to charge lower prices than their competitors, which is why customers seek out the stores.

> **'Competitive advantage is a company's ability to perform in one or more ways that competitors cannot or will not match.'**

Philip Kotler, marketing guru

Competitive advantage can also be achieved by differentiation – that is, setting yourself apart from your rivals. BMW achieves this in the UK car market; Apple achieves it in the market for mobile phones. It may be a result of great design or advanced technology – or simply a consequence of great marketing, as in the case of Coca-Cola. The great strength of this market positioning, though, is that the competitive advantage enables the producer to (within reason) set the price without worrying about the competition.

Figure 4.3 shows the position of supermarkets in the market on a continuum from lowest cost to most highly differentiated. Perhaps the fact that Morrisons and Tesco appear in the middle of the continuum is the reason for their recent trading problems (see Figure 4.2).

Lowest cost		Highest differentiation
Aldi and Lidl	Morrisons and Tesco	Waitrose and M & S Food

Figure 4.3 Competitive advantage in the UK grocery market: avoid being the piggy in the middle

> **'If you don't have a competitive advantage, don't compete.'**

Jack Welch, former boss of the US giant General Electric

4.3 The purpose of product differentiation

Product differentiation is the degree to which consumers perceive that your brand is different from its competitors. A highly differentiated product is one that is viewed as having unique features, such as Marmite or the iPhone. A highly differentiated product may have substitutes. However, if differentiation is strong enough, consumers will not even bother looking at these other brands when making their purchasing decisions. The substitutes available are not acceptable to the consumer. A product's point of differentiation is often described as a **unique selling point**, or USP.

Creating product differentiation

Product differentiation can be created in two ways. One is actual differentiation that creates genuine consumer benefits. Actual product differentiation can be created by:

- a unique design that is aesthetically pleasing to the eye (for example, Scandinavian furniture from IKEA)
- a unique product function (for example, a mobile phone with a unique new feature)
- a unique taste (for example, Dr Pepper)
- ergonomic factors (for example, a product that is easier to use than its rivals)
- superior performance (for example, a Dyson vacuum cleaner).

The second type of differentiation involves creating differences that exist only in the mind of the consumer. A product can be differentiated by psychological factors, despite the fact that it is not physically different from a similar product produced by the competition. Imaginary product differentiation can be created via persuasive advertising, celebrity endorsements and sponsorship. When a product is consumed, it is not just the product itself that is consumed; buyers also enjoy 'consuming' the brand's image too. Many people are prepared to pay a price premium for a product that has a brand image that appeals to them.

The purpose behind product differentiation is two-fold:

1. To insulate the product or service from the competitive market. Marmite is 'spread' that goes on bread or toast; but if there's a cut in the price of rival spreads, honey or jam, sales of Marmite will hardly register a blip. And this is what companies seek: a world in which they control their market position and, therefore, their sales. No company wants fierce, direct competition.

2. To enable the business to increase its prices if costs go up, in order to protect its profit margins. As is discussed in Chapter 8, this suggests that the higher the product differentiation, the lower the **price elasticity**.

> **'There is no such thing as a commodity. It is simply a product waiting to be differentiated.'**

Philip Kotler, marketing guru

Figure 4.4 Logic link: boosting product differentiation

4.4 Adding value to products or services

Adding value means stretching the difference between the cost of bought-in goods and services and the price that a company can get for its goods. In some cases, the added value may be huge, such as the difference between the price of a Starbuck's coffee and the cost of the coffee beans, milk and sugar. In other cases, the added value may be quite slim, as in the case of a Ford Focus, which is assembled by Ford from lots of parts bought-in from other suppliers.

Traditionally, in the catering trade, the rule-of-thumb has been to charge customers four times the cost of ingredients. So a £5 piece of steak is priced at £20. The remaining £15 is far from profit, of course. It is needed to pay the wage bill, the rent, the bills, the advertising and so on.

So how can value be added to a product or service? The most common ways are:

1 To create an image that is so attractive or quirky that people are willing to pay more to be associated with the brand. At the time of writing, lots of people want jackets or jumpers that shout *Jack Wills* or *SuperDry*. Wonderfully for the producer, customers are paying a price premium to advertise the company's brand.

2 To create a truly fantastic product or service. The Taj hotel chain has a wonderful reputation for good customer service – travellers will pay a premium for that.

3 To wrap the product up in a way that makes it seem remarkably clever (and perhaps costly to produce). There is a reluctance to spend a lot on an English breakfast because we all know how to cook it. But although it may be no cleverer to make waffles and maple syrup, customers may be more impressed. So a waffle with 20p of ingredients sells for £3, while a £2 breakfast sells for £4.

Five whys and a how

Questions	Answers
Why might market positioning be more important than the marketing mix?	If the positioning strategy is wrong, the product is wrong, so it can't be saved – even by a clever mix.
Why might product differentiation be harder to achieve with a service than a product?	A service may be less specifically designed than a product, making it malleable and therefore less well differentiated.
Why might the wrong advertisement create negative value added?	A bad ad can detract from the product's image, making customers willing to pay less for it.
Why may Jack Welch be right in saying that 'An organisation's ability to learn is the ultimate competitive advantage'?	Because companies need to respond to changes in the economy or the actions of competitors and adapt their positioning accordingly.
Why might excessive product differentiation prove a problem?	It might lead to the Cadbury 2014 mistake: Dairy Milk Banana Caramel Crisp; it is too niche to have a profitable future.
How does Chanel differentiate its perfumes from those of its rivals?	By lavish advertising featuring global names, such as Nicole Kidman – backed by authenticity from the company's illustrious past.

4.5 Market positioning – evaluation

In recent decades, Real Madrid and Manchester United have both tried to position themselves as the most glamorous football club in the world. At the time of writing, Real Madrid has achieved this. Barcelona might play the best football and Bayern Munich might be the best team, but Real's point of differentiation is glamour. The clever thing is that this point of differentiation adds value – people will pay more for a glamorous shirt.

This, then, is the key message behind market positioning: choose a position that customers find acceptable, while the company finds it profitable, then work out how to secure it. Advertising, packaging and all other forms of promotion must focus on making customers believe in that market position.

4.6 Workbook

Revision questions

(30 marks; 30 minutes)

1 Identify three markets where age is a crucial factor in drawing up a market map. (3)

2 The UK population is growing older, with a rising proportion of over 60s. Outline two business opportunities that may arise as the population gets older. (4)

3 Give three possible sources of competitive advantage for an independent clothes shop. (3)

4 Why might it be difficult to differentiate a mass market brand? (4)

5 What would you say is the USP of each of the following:
   a) Maltesers
   b) the latest iPhone
   c) Marmite? (6)

6 Suggest four ways in which value could be added to a plank of wood. (4)

7 Explain how your school or college differentiates itself. (6)

Data response

Galaxy chocolate at 15p – head for India

Around the globe, the $100 billion chocolate market is a battle between three multinationals: Mars, Nestlé and Mondelēz (the Kraft subsidiary that includes Cadbury). An exception is India, where Mars has no significant foothold. Given that India is the world's fastest-growing market for chocolate, it should be no surprise that Mars was determined to tackle this issue. In November 2013, it launched Galaxy 'Premium' chocolate to take on the might of Cadbury Dairy Milk.

Its approach to the launch showed all the signs of desperation. Although the Galaxy launch was supported by a glossy advertising campaign featuring Bollywood actor Arjun Rampal and model Sapna Pabbi, Mars priced Galaxy extremely competitively. In the middle of the market, Cadbury Dairy Milk had a 38 gram 'value' pack priced at 22p and a 60 gram Dairy Milk 'Silk' pack for 55p. Mars priced a 40 gram pack of Galaxy at 15p.

Mr Natarajan, general manager of Mars India, said:

'India is the world's fastest growing chocolate market and the moulded chocolate segment is the fastest growing sector. India is a very important market for Mars. With this launch we are entering an extremely dynamic segment with our business objective of growing our product range in India.'

The market for chocolate in India has a value of just £555 million at the moment. It is this small because Indians currently eat less than a sixtieth of the amount of chocolate eaten in Britain (0.165 kg per person per year, compared with our 10.2 kg!). But the market is forecast by Cadbury to grow at 23 per cent a year between 2013 and 2018, which will take it towards the UK's market size.

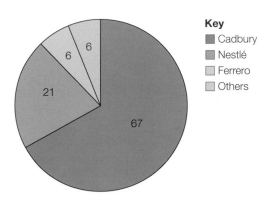

Figure 4.5 Chocolate market share percentage, India 2013

Mr Natarajan's marketing strategy has two further elements to it. There is a marketing plan targeting the 0–18 age category, based on free distribution of sweets twice a year, on Independence Day and again on Republic Day. The 19–35s are also targeted using a tie-up with Facebook. One week before a friend's birthday, Facebook sends the message 'Do you want to send chocolates on your friend's birthday?' There can be no doubt that Mars is determined to succeed.

Questions (30 marks; 35 minutes)

1 Assess two possible reasons why Mars wants to build a market share in India. (8)

2 From the text, assess how well Mars has used market positioning in its launch of Mars Premium chocolate in India? (10)

3 Evaluate how Mars, India, might add more value to its Galaxy brand to enable it to charge a higher price. (12)

Extended writing

1 Choose one of these products/services: Burger King, Domino's Pizza, Topshop, Pepsi. Evaluate whether their current market positioning is right for the brand. (20)

2 To what extent is there effective product differentiation within the market of your choice? Evaluate how that differentiation has been achieved. (20)

5 Demand

> **Definition**
>
> 'Demand' measures the level of interest customers have in buying a product. To be effective, that interest must be backed by the ability to pay.

Linked to: The market, Ch 2; Supply, Ch 6; Markets and equilibrium, Ch 7; Pricing strategies, Ch 12; Moving from entrepreneur to leader, Ch 28.

5.1 Introduction

Managers and owners seek control over the day-to-day events affecting their business. Ice cream entrepreneurs hate the fact that – however great their ice cream – the weather is the single biggest determinant of daily demand. There are many factors that affect the demand for different products and services. Business people try, as much as possible, to bring the factors within their influence and ideally control. Even if the weather cannot be controlled, businesses try to combat its effects. In central London, Italian ice cream parlour Amorino also specialises in 15 different flavours of hot chocolate – to keep customers coming even when the weather is poor.

> '**What the customer demands is last year's model, cheaper. To find out what the customer needs you have to understand the customer.**'
>
> Edna St Vincent Millay, 1920s poet and playwright

5.2 Main factors affecting demand for a product or service

Price

Price affects demand in three ways.

1 You may want an £80,000 Mercedes convertible, but you cannot afford it; the price puts it beyond your income level. The higher the price, the more people there are who cannot afford to buy.

2 The higher the price, the less good value the item will seem compared with other ways of spending the money. For example, a Chelsea home ticket costing £48 is the equivalent of going to the movies six times. Is it worth it? The higher the price of an item, the more there will be people who say no.

3 It should be remembered that the price tag put on an item gives a message about its 'value'. A ring priced at 99p will inevitably be seen as 'cheap', whether or not it is value for money; so although lower prices should boost sales, firms must beware of ruining their image for quality.

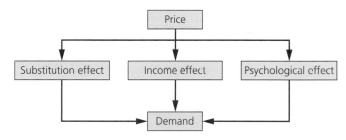

Figure 5.1 Logic chain: impact of price on demand

Prices of other goods

The demand for PS4s is affected not only by the price Sony sets for its console, but also prices set by others. In May 2014, Microsoft cut the price of its 'One' console by $100, boosting its demand at the (temporary) expense of the PS4. This shows that the two products are **substitutes** for each other. In other words, they are competitors, where the success of one is at the expense of the other.

Another factor affecting sales of the PS4 is the price set by software producers for PS4 games. If these rose from £40 each to £50, this would have an effect on sales of Sony PS4 hardware. Some potential customers would stick with their PS3 and others might look towards the Microsoft product. So PS4 software and PS4 hardware are **complementary goods**, where sales of one have a positive effect on sales of the other. See Table 5.1 for more detail on this.

	Substitute	Complement	Substitute
	Microsoft One console sales	PS4 software sales	PS4 console sales
Microsoft One price cut	Up	Down	Down
Microsoft One price increase	Down	Up	Up
PS4 software price cut	Down	Up	Up
PS4 software price increase	Up	Down	Down

Table 5.1 Impact on PS4 console sales of price changes by other products

Changes in consumer incomes

The British economy usually grows at a rate of about 2.25 per cent a year. This means that average income levels double every 30 years. Broadly, when your children are aged about 16–18, you are likely to be twice as well off as your parents are today. Economic growth means we all get richer over time (and spend more time in traffic jams).

The demand for most products and services grows as the economy grows. Goods like cars and cinema tickets are **normal goods**, for which demand rises broadly in line with incomes. In some cases, it grows even faster; for example, if the economy grows by 3 per cent in a year, the amount spent on foreign holidays can easily rise by 6 per cent. This type of product is known as a **luxury good**.

Other goods behave differently, with sales falling when people are better off. These products are known as **inferior goods**. In their case, rising incomes mean falling sales. For example, the richer we get, the more Tropicana we buy and the less Tesco orange squash. As orange squash is an inferior good, a couple of years of economic struggle (and perhaps more people out of work) would mean sales would increase as people switch from expensive Tropicana to cheap squash.

Fashion, tastes and preferences

This category contains some quite different influences upon demand. Fashion is difficult to manage because, by definition, the term implies that what goes up must come down. Very few brands stay in fashion for ever. It was the huge height of the fashion for FCUK that made the logo unwearable once consumer taste had moved on. French Connection suffered seven lean years after that happened.

Yet some brands do seem to be eternally fashionable, such as Chanel, Jack Daniels and Nike. This adds value to the brand and therefore allows higher prices to be charged, and higher profits to be made.

'The customer is never wrong.'

Cezar Ritz, hotelier

Consumer tastes and preferences can be fickle, but in many markets there is a core of stability that helps companies feel confident about ongoing demand. A good example is the demand for fitness club/gym membership. Yes, it may suffer a bit during a recession, but the ongoing consumer preference for this expenditure has been proven over several decades.

For an example of the fickle consumer, one need look no further than food and drink. Egged on by TV programmes and social media wanting 'a story', tastes lurch from 'no carb diets' to 'low-cal foods' and back again. Meat can be good (protein) or bad (fat) and orange juice has a similarly schizophrenic existence. For the producer, stable demand is the desirable state of affairs, but oh-so hard to achieve.

'There is only one boss. The customer. And he can fire everybody in the company from the chairman on down, simply by spending his money somewhere else.'

Sam Walton, founder of Walmart

Real business

In 2014, the value of the UK market for chocolate was unchanged from 2013 at £2.5 billion, though sales volumes slipped by 2.5 per cent. Given the static nature of the market as a whole, some of the shifts in brand sales were startling. See Figure 5.2 for some shockers.

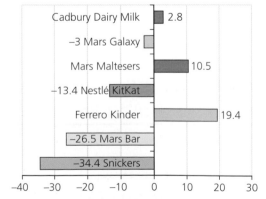

Figure 5.2 Percentage change in sales volume since 2013 for chocolate bars in the UK market (year to 16 August 2014) (source: IRI Infoscan)

Advertising and branding

In 2013, ice cream bar Magnum was backed by £4 million of advertising support. That was much more than any other UK ice cream brand. In fact, Magnum advertising represented more than 40 per cent of all ice cream advertising that year. Perhaps as a result, Magnum's sales rose by 17.6 per cent to £102.8 million. Unsurprisingly, advertising spending can boost demand.

In the long run, branding is more important than advertising. If the brand is one that the consumer finds memorable, can identify with and may even be proud to be associated with, the payback to the brand owner can be huge. In its 2014 rankings of global brands, *Forbes* magazine placed Google as Number 1, with a brand value of $159 billion (Table 5.2). The value of a brand is its ability to command a higher price for products and to achieve high levels of customer loyalty.

2014 global rank	Brand	Category	Brand value
1	Google	Tech	$159 bn
2	Apple	Tech	$148 bn
3	IBM	Tech	$108 bn
4	Microsoft	Tech	$90 bn
5	McDonald's	Fast food	$86 bn
6	Coca-Cola	Soft drinks	$81 bn
7	Visa	Credit cards	$79 bn
8	AT&T	Telecoms	$78 bn
9	Marlboro	Tobacco	$67 bn
10	Amazon	Retail	$64 bn

Table 5.2 Ranking of global brands, 2014

Demographics

Demographics breaks down population data – for example, by age, ethnic origin or gender. In the UK market for yoghurt, two of the top ten brands are focused on children: Petits Filous (sales of £98 million in 2013) and Munch Bunch (£54.4 million in 2013). Demographically based brands such as these transformed demand in the yoghurt market. In 1970, the UK market consisted solely of plain, unsweetened yogurt in glass jars – and sales were just £5 million. Today's UK market is worth more than £2,000 million (figures from *The Grocer*, 21 December 2013).

Today, the most exciting area for demographic opportunity is old people. Figure 5.3 shows the growth to come in this age group. A glance at daytime TV shows the huge range of products and services in this category.

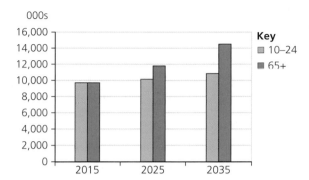

Figure 5.3 UK population by age category (source: ONS projections for England)

External shocks

In May 1996, the EU banned all exports of beef from the UK. The reason was 'mad cow disease', which could be passed on to humans in the form of a ghastly disease (CJD) that rotted the brain and could kill you. The ban would only be lifted in 2006, giving ten years of a massive reduction in beef exports and a collapse in the market price of beef in the UK. For beef farmers, this was a devastating shock.

Although not as dramatic, most businesses will have to face some kind of external shock on a fairly regular basis. In south Nottingham in 2014/2015, work building a new tram system closed down a series of roads for months. Some shop owners in the Clifton district suffered falls in demand as high as 40 per cent for a six-month period. Some boarded-up shops show the impact of this on cash flow. In fact, businesses that survive this period may find trade improves as a result of a glossy new tram system. But if you run out of cash, the future becomes irrelevant.

Among many potential causes of external shock are:

- natural disasters, such as flooding (UK) or earthquakes (many other parts of the world)
- a change in the law, such as the August 2014 ban on vacuum cleaners with more than 1,600 watts of power
- an unexpected change of mind by a major customer or supplier.
  Some small firms may sell more than 50 per cent of their output to Tesco; a sudden cancellation would devastate the business. In September 2014, Phones4U closed itself down because Vodafone decided to stop

selling its phones through the retail outlet. This was a devastating shock for Phones4U's 5,500 staff, though less of one, perhaps, for the company's private equity owner BC Capital, which had managed to pay itself enough in 2013 to make a profit on its investment in the now-to-be-liquidated business.

Seasonal factors

Most firms experience significant variations in sales through the year. Some markets, such as ice cream, soft drinks, lager and seaside hotels, boom in the summer and slump in the winter. Other markets, such as sales of perfume, liqueurs, greetings cards and toys, boom at Christmas. Other products with less obvious **seasonal variations** in demand include cars, cat food, carpets, furniture, TVs and newspapers. The variation is caused by patterns of customer behaviour and nothing can be done about that. A well-run business makes sure that it understands and can predict the seasonal variations in demand; and then has a plan for coping.

5.3 Demand risks

There are two situations that every manager should beware of: undiversified demand and overtrading.

Undiversified demand

When Andrew and Debbie Keeble won a £5 million order from Tesco for their Heck sausages, they were thrilled. But it meant that Tesco accounted for 75 per cent of all the brand's sales. This put the small business in a very vulnerable position. It had to create the production capacity to meet the orders, but that might leave them with impossibly high costs if Tesco decided to cancel. Similar problems of undiversified demand occur when a business is dependent on just one product (think 'loom bands' as a craze that came and went).

The answer is to try to diversify – that is, to spread risk by finding new sources of demand and therefore being less reliant upon any single source.

Overtrading

Sometimes small businesses grow so fast that they struggle to generate enough cash to meet rising bills due to rising production levels. The problem is that meeting next month's higher demand levels requires extra cash spent today (more materials and components, more staff and so on). Overtrading means running so fast that the

cash position is on a knife edge, probably at the overdraft limit. That is risky. The topic of overtrading is dealt with in more depth in Chapter 28.

Five whys and a how

Questions	Answers
Why may there be risks involved in demand rising too fast?	Because it could result in overtrading and therefore an excessive strain on the firm's cash position.
Why may managers worry about the pricing decisions made by firms selling complementary goods?	Because a price rise by a complementary good can damage the sales of its partner good/product.
Why might a buy one get one free (BOGOF) promotion be a foolish way to boost demand?	Because it creates a temporary leap in sales at the possible cost of the long-term credibility of the product or brand.
Why might a boost to demand be at the cost of the company's profit?	A price cut will boost demand, but may eat into the profit margins so sharply that overall profit falls.
Why might it be risky for a young firm to focus on high-fashion markets?	Because sales of high-fashion items may slump when fashion moves on.
How might a fall in consumer incomes affect demand for an inferior good/service, such as shopping at Lidl?	People being worse off is usually good news for inferior goods, so sales should grow.

5.4 Demand – evaluation

The cleverest judgements to be made in business come from the ability to separate what is from what could be. For 20 years, Britain's *Financial Times* (business) newspaper was priced at £1 – a small premium to the other 'quality' papers, *The Times* and *The Guardian*. Then, between 2007 and 2010, the price of the *Financial Times* was increased until – at £2.50 – it became treble the price of its rivals. Astonishingly, sales were virtually unaffected. Those who wanted an economics and business-focused paper had nowhere else to go. A clever executive had spotted the opportunity to make considerably more profit from the paper. Such good judgement is based upon sound understanding of market demand; that is, a really fine understanding of what customers think, feel and want.

Key terms

Complementary goods: these are bought in conjunction with each other, such as eggs and bacon or cars and petrol.

Inferior goods: ones for which sales *fall* when people are better off, but rise when consumers are struggling financially.

Luxury goods: ones for which sales rise rapidly when people are better off, but may fall rapidly in hard times.

Normal goods: ones for which sales move in line with changes in consumer incomes, e.g. sales at dry cleaning outlets.

Seasonal variation: change in the value of a variable (for example, sales) that is related to the seasons.

Substitutes: products or services in competition with each other, so customers will substitute one for the other (e.g. Dairy Milk and Galaxy).

5.5 Workbook

Revision questions

(35 marks; 35 minutes)

1 Demand up or down?

   a) When a substitute good cuts its prices. (1)

   b) When a complementary good increases its prices. (1)

2 The giant Procter & Gamble cut its 2014 spend on UK advertising by 9 per cent and switched spending away from TV towards social media. UK sales in 2014 were flat, meaning a slight fall in volume terms. What does this imply about the effect of marketing spending upon demand? (5)

3 In your own words, explain the term 'inferior good' and give your own example. (3)

4 How might demand for UK hotel rooms be affected by a sharp economic downturn in America? (4)

5 Outline three conclusions the chief executive of Tesco might draw from the following United Nations' population forecasts. (6)

	2015	2050	2100
United Kingdom	64 million	74 million	77 million
Nigeria	183 million	440 million	900 million

6 Use your knowledge of *one* of the following to explain the two factors you believe are the most important in determining the demand for:

   a) Arsenal season tickets

   b) Vittel bottled water

   c) *Vogue* magazine

   d) KitKat four-finger pack. (4)

7 Suggest one way in which a business could try to estimate the future demand for its brand new product. (3)

8 Examine two possible reasons for the boost to demand outlined in the following quote from Dundee FC website in 2014: (8)

'The Club has been bowled over with the sales of season tickets to date, with an incredible increase of 150 per cent on the same period last year. The Manager and Board of Directors have been delighted by the level of both renewals and new sales ... with 40 per cent of sales being either previously lapsed season ticket holders or supporters buying for the first time.'

Data response

Factors affecting demand for breakfast cereals

Over recent years, many factors have affected the UK market for breakfast cereals. The single most important is probably health – or the perception of health. Between 2007 and 2013, the market grew £240 million by value – with almost all the gains going to existing and new brands perceived to be healthy. In 2007, Kellogg's Special K's focus on dieters made it seem healthy. In 2013, Weetabix, oat-based products and mueslis such as Alpen had the winning formula.

A second influence was the decision by the last government, in 2008, to prevent cereal producers from advertising children's brands in children's TV slots. This had little immediate effect on sales, but slowly it seems to have hurt brands such as Sugar Puffs and Frosties. (NB 'healthy' Alpen has more calories per 100 grams than Frosties, but marketing is about perceptions, not realities.) Despite the general strengths of 'healthy' cereals, Kellogg's has achieved success with Krave – a chocolate-based, indulgent cereal supposedly aimed at young men.

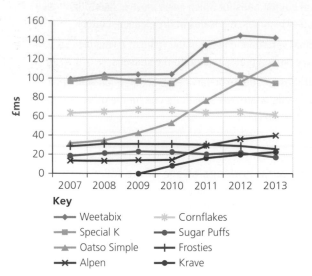

Key

- ◆ Weetabix
- ✳ Cornflakes
- ■ Special K
- ● Sugar Puffs
- ▲ Oatso Simple
- ✚ Frosties
- ✖ Alpen
- ● Krave

Figure 5.4 Annual UK breakfast cereal sales (source: *The Grocer* magazine)

One other factor has been hugely important to this market – the continuing move away from sit-down breakfasts towards breakfasts on-the-go. In some ways, the producers can capture this change through cereal bars, but once out of the house, school children in particular may end up buying crisps and an energy drink rather than cereal. In 2013, the market for breakfast cereal grew 2.7 per cent by value, but fell 2.8 per cent by volume.

The final issue has been the recession. This has hit manufacturers in two ways: first, it has forced them to fight harder with promotional pricing, thereby lowering profit margins. In 2012, half of all breakfast cereal was bought on special offer. Second, and at least as important, there has been a switch to supermarket own-label cereals. In 2007, 18.9 per cent of sales were supermarket brands. By 2013, this figure had risen to 21.5 per cent.

Table 5.3 shows the actual UK sales figures recorded each year by *The Grocer* magazine. Weetabix is number 1 and Quaker's Oatso Simple has overtaken Special K to become number 2.

Questions (30 marks; 35 minutes)

1 Following a decline in its sales in 2009 and 2010, Special K had a great year in 2011. Explain two factors that may have caused this. (4)

2 Assess two factors that may have affected the demand for Alpen between 2007 and 2013. (8)

3 a) Calculate the market share for Frosties (to two decimal points) in 2007 and again for 2013. (2)

   b) Explain why this information might be important to Kellogg's, owners of the Frosties brand. (4)

4 From the information provided and your wider knowledge, evaluate two factors that might affect the total market size for cereals over the coming 12 months. (12)

Figs in £ms*	2007	2008	2009	2010	2011	2012	2013
Weetabix	99.3	103.7	104.6	104.4	135.1	145.8	143
Special K	96.5	101.2	97.4	94.6	119.4	103.5	94.5
Oatso Simple	31.5	35.2	42.7	53.1	76.7	95.9	116
Alpen	13.2	13.5	13.6	14.5	29.6	36	39.8
Cornflakes	63.7	65.2	66.9	66.7	63.4	64.7	61.7
Sugar Puffs	18.6	21.7	23.4	22.9	20.3	21.4	16.9
Frosties	28.6	31	31.3	31.4	30.9	29	25.7
Krave			0	8.5	16.1	19.5	22.5
Total market	1,334.80	1,378.10	1,458.30	1,465	1,451	1,532.10	1,573.5

*The figures are in current prices, i.e. they have not been adjusted for inflation.

Table 5.3 UK sales figures: cereals

Extended writing

1 In late 2014, the global price of oil collapsed – partly because of a fall in demand in countries such as the UK. Evaluate the key factors that might lead to a recovery in UK demand for oil in the future. (20)

2 In a declining market for boxed chocolate assortments (such as Quality Street), Lindt Lindor has been enjoying sharply rising sales. Evaluate how a business might set about boosting sales of its brands despite a decline in the market as a whole. (20)

6 Supply

> **Definition**
>
> 'Supply' is the quantity of a product that producers are able to deliver within a specific time period.

Linked to: Markets and equilibrium, Ch 7; Product and service design, Ch 10; Distribution, Ch 13; Approaches to staffing, Ch 17; Capacity utilisation, Ch 42; Stock control, Ch 43.

6.1 Introduction

If demand can be visualised as customers filling up their supermarket trolleys, supply is the huge truck unloading at the back of the store. If the truck is from Warburtons, the delivery is the end of a **supply chain** that started with raisins drying in Turkish fields and flour milled in Canada. From the customer's point of view, they probably do not care about the complexities of sourcing the ingredients and producing the goods. They just want the right quantities of the right products to turn up on time – and with the right prices on the bill. Not many people think about supply.

> **'Only recently have people begun to recognise that working with suppliers is just as important as listening to customers.'**
>
> Barry Nalebuff, US business author

Figure 6.1 Logic chain: benefits of buoyant supply

6.2 What should firms supply?

In some cases, this is an easy question to answer. When Fulham play Stoke, the 26,000 seats will provide more than enough supply. The ticket office will sell to whoever is willing to pay the price. The available supply will be 26,000; the demand may be around 20,000, leaving a surplus of 6,000.

In other cases, the supply may be harder to plan for. A farmer planting a field with apple trees knows that the first fruit crop will begin in two to five years' time. So the actual supply in three years' time is very uncertain. This is important because the big supermarket chains will only deal with suppliers who promise to deliver the right quantity at the right time.

Profit-focused firms will want to supply at the level that makes as a high a profit as possible. This is known as the profit-maximising point. In the example shown in Table 6.1, the profit-maximising point occurs when the business supplies 40,000 units per week.

Supply	Profit per unit	Total profit
10,000	£3.20	£32,000
20,000	£3.60	£72,000
30,000	£3.50	£105,000
40,000	£3.20	£128,000
50,000	£2.50	£125,000

Table 6.1 Example to show the profit maximising point for a business

6.3 Factors leading to a change in supply

Changes in costs of production

Changes in costs of production include the cost of materials, rent, fuel, salaries and advertising. The higher the costs, the lower the incentive to supply. This is because the higher the costs, the lower the profit per unit. Of course, if all your competitors face the same cost increases, you may not worry. You may simply assume that if everyone puts their prices up, market share figures should remain unchanged.

Introduction of new technology

This could have a significant effect on production costs and efficiencies. Figure 6.2 shows the dramatic rise in recent business purchases of industrial robots (especially from China). Robots can have a direct impact on labour productivity and therefore costs per unit. A big increase in the supply of robots can lower production costs and also help to boost production capacity. Therefore, supply is not only cheaper but also more plentiful.

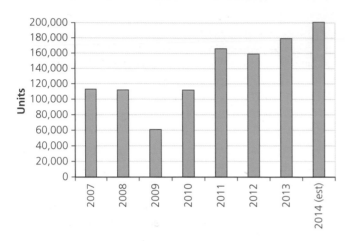

Figure 6.2 Global sales of industrial robots (source: World Robotics Report, IFR Statistical Department)

Indirect taxes

Indirect taxes are taxes levied by government onto goods and services. The most widespread one in the UK is the 20 per cent rate of VAT put onto most goods and services (though not food). Another indirect tax is 'duty' – special taxes put onto things the government believes to be socially undesirable, such as alcohol and petrol. If the government decided to increase the duty on petrol, this would add to the cost of supply. Therefore, oil companies would wish to supply less petrol to the market. This would push the price up.

Government subsidies

The reverse of taxation is subsidy. This is when the government wants to promote supply and therefore gives businesses a financial contribution towards supply. In March 2013, the BBC reported on a Nottinghamshire farmer who received a £50,000 grant each year for running his 585 acres. Later in the year, the government offered subsidies worth perhaps £17 billion to encourage the building of four new nuclear power plants. Subsidies encourage extra supply.

External shocks

Cars are made of steel and aluminium, but also use a lot of copper. These metals are commodities with prices governed by the world market. Figure 6.3 shows the world copper price between 2000 and 2014, varying from a low of $1,377 to a high of $9,881. For car producers, getting used to a price per tonne of around $8,000 in 2006–2008, the world recession that hit in late 2008 saw the copper price crash to $3,105. Any car company that bought stockpiles of copper at $8,000 would suffer significant losses when the **market price** fell in that way.

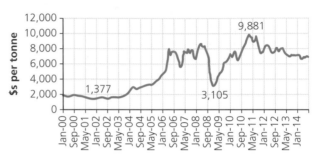

Figure 6.3 Copper, price per tonne (source: www.indexmundi.com)

Other possible external shocks

A natural disaster, such as a flood or earthquake, can disrupt supply lines, causing particular problems for manufacturers or retailers who choose to carry very low stocks; inevitably a supply shortfall leads to price rises.

In September 2014, Vodafone told retailer Phones4U that it would no longer supply it with phones. The owners of Phones4U responded by closing down the business. It said that without supply the business would have nothing to do; therefore, closure was the only option.

Physical constraints

In the short term, businesses may not be able to change one or more of the key factors determining supply. Between January 2004 and August 2008, the world price for copper rose from $2,500 to $8,000 per tonne. Despite the huge opportunity to make profits, copper mining companies struggled to increase supply. The mines were working to full capacity and no new copper mines were discovered and opened during this time. By 2014, though, new copper mines started to open, such as the Totten mine in Canada. This extra supply eased the copper price down to $6,600 by April 2014.

'When you went into a Boston Chicken and ordered a quarter chicken, white, with mash and corn, when that was rung up it would signal all the way along the supply chain the need for more potatoes to be put on a truck a thousand miles away.'

Stephen Elop, Vice President, Microsoft

6.4 Drawing a supply curve

A **supply curve** can be drawn to show how supply increases when customers are willing to pay more for the product. In the example shown in Figure 6.4, companies are willing to supply 20,000 tonnes when the price is $4,000. If the price were to rise further, to $6,000, suppliers would be delighted to offer 30,000 tonnes of supply.

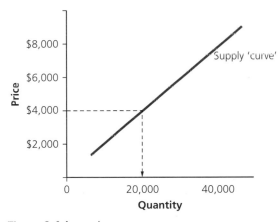

Figure 6.4 A supply curve

The supply curve is drawn on the assumption that suppliers can respond quickly to changes in demand. This would be possible if plenty of the product was kept in storage, or if the production process is speedy and flexible enough to be increased at will.

Five whys and a how

Questions	Answers
Why might a supply shortfall cause prices to rise?	Customers bid more to try to get the amount they want from the limited supply.
Why would a rise in production costs make a company less willing to supply?	The more it costs to produce, the less profit there is in supplying it.
Why might frost in Brazil affect coffee supplies in Britain?	Frost in Brazil hits the coffee harvest so there is less coffee for Nescafé or Costa.
Why might it be hard for a company to increase supply by 10 per cent?	If it is operating to the maximum, its factories won't do more.
Why is Britain unable to supply all the raw materials businesses want?	Oranges and mangoes won't grow; gold can't be found.
How can a retail chain be sure that its supplies are ethically sound?	It can insist on inspecting every part of the supply chain.

6.5 Supply – evaluation

When considering supply factors, timescale is a hugely important issue. In the short term, companies can vary supply only up to the limit of their maximum production capacity. In the longer term, they can build new factories or buy in new, faster machinery, but only if they are sure that demand will stay high. One of the reasons the UK recovered so slowly from the 2009 recession was that company investment spending stayed exceptionally low. Companies were not convinced that there was any purpose in investing in extra supply. At a time of austerity, where was the extra demand going to come from? So when there is a question on supply, every answer should clarify the timescale involved – short term or long term.

Key terms

Market price: the price of a commodity that has been established by the market – that is, where supply equals demand.

Supply chain: the whole path from suppliers of raw materials through production and storage on to customer delivery.

Supply curve: a line showing the quantity of goods firms want to supply at different price levels (the higher the price, the more enthusiastic the supply).

6.6 Workbook

Revision questions

(30 marks; 30 minutes)

1 Explain why a fall in supply increases price. (4)

2 How might a rise in the national minimum wage affect the supply of goods in the UK? (3)

3 Identify two possible physical constraints that could stop a railway company from completing engineering works on time. (2)

4 Consider the following.
   a) Draw a supply curve for Cadbury Creme Eggs, based on the data shown in Table 6.2. (5)
   b) Why might Cadburys be unwilling to supply any Creme Eggs at a price of 20p each? (2)

5 Use your knowledge of one of the following to explain the two factors you believe are the most important in determining the supply of:

Price	Supply
20p	0
25p	1m
30p	6m
35p	15m
40p	32m
45p	65m
50p	80m

Table 6.2 Data for Cadbury Creme Eggs

   a) Arsenal season tickets
   b) Vittel bottled water
   c) *Vogue* magazine
   d) KitKat four-finger pack. (6)

6 China produces half the world's steel. Explain the implications of this for suppliers of iron ore to China. (4)

7 Explain how a government fish subsidy might affect the supply of cod to UK consumers. (4)

Data response

In 2014, potato prices were 75 per cent lower than their peak the previous year. Early 2013 had seen dreadful weather in the UK, with exceptionally high rainfall leading to flooding. Potato crops struggled to get established so the harvest was late and small. As a result of this supply shortfall, the price of potatoes shot up, reaching a peak of £390 a tonne – literally ten times the price potatoes had been five years before.

In 2014, good weather across the UK and the EU made the summer a good one for potato supplies. In the UK, the planted area for potatoes was unchanged at 120,000 hectares, but the crop was 20 per cent higher. By mid-September, the UK potato price was £98 a tonne. In other western European markets, potato prices were as low as £54 a tonne, as supply outstripped demand.

For British fish and chip shops, the outcome was a significant boost to profit margins. Chip shops serve nearly half a kilogram of potatoes in a portion of chips (three times more than McDonald's fries), so the high supply price in 2013 was quite a burden. And because UK households were still struggling financially from the effects of the weak economic recovery, chip shops kept their retail prices unchanged. The 2014 fall in the cost of potatoes came as a blessed relief.

Questions (20 marks; 25 minutes)

1 Construct a labelled diagram to show the impact of the bad weather on the 2013 UK supply of potatoes. Briefly explain what it shows. (8)

2 Explain why the potato price fell in 2014. (4)

3 Explain in your own words how the change in the price of potatoes would have affected fish and chip shop profits in 2013. (8)

Extended writing

1 Some farmers specialise in a single crop; others have a mixed farm with different crops plus livestock. Evaluate the strengths and weaknesses of each in a world where market prices are affected by changing supply conditions globally. (20)

2 Evaluate the possible effects on the supply of commodities of a continuing sharp rise in global temperatures as a result of climate change. (20)

7 Markets and equilibrium

> **Definition**
>
> Equilibrium is the point where there is a balance between supply and demand; this makes the price stable (though, if demand was high enough, the equilibrium point might be at a very high price).

Linked to: Demand, Ch 5; Supply, Ch 6; Pricing strategies, Ch 12; Stock control, Ch 43.

7.1 Introduction

In markets where products are differentiated from each other, perhaps by branding, prices are set by producers. The price of Chanel No 5 perfume (£91.50 for a tiny 7.5ml bottle) is set by Chanel. But in some important markets there is no product differentiation. Food and drink producers around the world need to buy sugar and coffee. They buy it by the tonne at the world's **market price**. At the time of writing, sugar is about 10p per pound weight, whereas coffee is about £1.30 per pound. In **commodity markets**, the price is determined by market forces – that is, supply and demand. The price that pulls demand to the same point as supply is the equilibrium price.

> **'Markets reduce everything, including human beings and nature, to commodities.'**
>
> George Soros, billionaire financier

7.2 Drawing a demand curve

A **demand curve** can only be drawn after gathering evidence about the likely level of sales at different prices. If you had the rights to a one-off 'Evening with J.K. Rowling', in which Harry Potter's creator was to speak for the first time about 'Harry's Greatest Adventure', what would you charge for the tickets? Ideally, you would try to work out what the demand would be at different prices (see the demand curve shown in Figure 7.1). Then you could find out the cost of hiring differently sized venues, to create a supply curve. From that, you would

be able to work out the most profitable combination of price and demand.

Price	Demand for tickets (in Manchester)
£40	40,000
£50	38,000
£60	36,000
£70	34,000
£80	32,000

Table 7.1 Research findings of demand for tickets

Figure 7.1 Demand curve for J.K. Rowling tickets

The graph shown in Figure 7.1 is based on (assumed) research findings given in Table 7.1.

Once the curve has been drawn up, you can use it to work out, for instance, the right price to charge if you hire the City of Manchester Stadium, which would be able to seat 35,000 people for the evening 'show'.

> **'Buy land, they ain't making any more of it.'**
>
> Will Rogers, early twentieth-century Hollywood legend

7.3 Interaction of supply and demand

In the above example, if you found that there were three venues in Manchester capable of holding this level of audience (including Manchester United football stadium, which could easily take 40,000), you could draw a supply curve on the same graph as the demand curve.

Figure 7.2 Supply and demand curves for a one-off evening with J.K. Rowling

Figure 7.2 shows that the most sensible outcome would be to hire the City of Manchester stadium and price the tickets at £68 in order to fill the 35,000 seats. The price at which supply equals demand is known as the market price.

The interaction of supply and demand is an important factor in many business decisions. In this case, the focus is on the price of tickets. Globally, the world oil price has an enormous effect on firms. This is also determined by supply and demand. In early 2008, tight oil supplies plus booming demand from China pushed the world oil price up to $120 per barrel (quadruple the figure from three years before). By 2010, a rise in supply and (recession-influenced) slippage in demand allowed the oil price to fall back to $65 per barrel. When global economic recovery arrived in early 2014, the oil price rose to $100 a barrel, before rising supply pushed the price down to $50.

'The market has no morality.'

Michael Heseltine, businessman and Conservative politician

Table 7.2 shows the impacts of different supply and demand conditions on the price of oil (or any other commodity).

	The impact of supply upon price		
	Supply down	Supply the same	Supply up
Demand up	Price up sharply	Price up	Price unchanged
Demand stays the same	Price up	Price stays the same	Price down
Demand down	Price stays the same	Price down	Price down sharply

Table 7.2 The impacts of different supply and demand conditions on price

Real business

A torn 50 p ticket to see the Rolling Stones at Reading Town Hall in 1963 had been gathering dust in the back of a drawer. Turning it over, the owner saw (and had forgotten) the signatures of the five original band members. It was put up for auction at Bonhams in June 2014. Demand was high enough for this rare item to be sold for £850.

Figure 7.3 The Rolling Stones in concert in the 60s

7.4 Supply and demand in practice

A well-run business is sensitive to demand. Its managers realise that demand is a complex, ever-changing factor. Running a hotel is a good example. Demand for hotel rooms is weakest on a Sunday night, so room rates are at their lowest. For city centre hotels, Saturday night may be a good night for bringing in wealthy night-clubbers, but business customers from Monday to Thursday are the biggest 'money-spinners'. Look at the room rates shown in Table 7.3 for a Leeds hotel in October 2014.

Date	Executive room (for two)
Tuesday 5 October	£119
Wednesday 6 October	£119
Thursday 7 October	£109
Friday 8 October	£59
Saturday 9 October	£99
Sunday 10 October	£59
Monday 11 October	£79

Table 7.3 Room rates for a Leeds hotel in October 2014 (source: www.laterooms.com. Hotel: Hilton, Leeds City)

What the room prices show is a business that is tuned into its customers well enough to know that the rates need to be different on different days.

Most businesses not only face daily sales variations but also seasonal ones. Carpet and furniture sales rise in the spring, as people see the wear and tear more clearly in the spring sunshine. Swimwear and holiday sales peak in the summer, while toy and perfume businesses can take 50 per cent of their year's sales in the five weeks leading up to Christmas. Businesses that are close to their customers make sure that seasonal sales cause no surprise.

The key to meeting varying demand is to anticipate it by varying supply. The toy shop buys in extra supplies and hires extra, temporary staff in September. The stock is in place and the staff are trained comfortably before the Christmas rush. Cadbury starts making pre-Easter Creme Eggs from the summer of the previous year to ensure that plenty of stock is available for the amazing peak sales of this major UK brand.

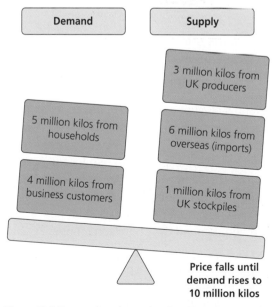

Figure 7.4 Demand and supply of apples

Five whys and a how

Questions	Answers
Why does price slip back if there is more supply than demand?	Because suppliers get a bit desperate to get rid of the excess stock.
Why, when a product becomes fashionable, do suppliers increase prices?	Because the opportunity is there, and because 'fashionable' means higher demand.
Why doesn't every consumer market work this way?	For branded products, company bosses want control over pricing; there's no free market equilibrium in Marmite.
Why might it be true to say that 'markets have no morality'?	Because they allocate commodities not on the basis of need, but on the ability to pay.
Why are hotel rooms cheapest on Sunday nights?	Because the supply of rooms is the same but the demand is lower (very few business travellers and relatively few leisure ones).
How do you know when a market is in equilibrium?	Prices hold stable, as do commodity stockpiles.

7.5 Markets and equilibrium – evaluation

In theory, markets stabilise at an equilibrium price. High prices pull forward more supply, which brings price back down again. And when prices are low, demand rises (and supply falls), which pulls prices back up again. This is why government should not need to intervene if the price of wheat or pork shoots up – the market will sort it out.

Unfortunately, there is an exception to this – and that is the human factor. Markets are governed by people's decisions, and when prices rise, speculators see opportunities. Some of those speculators are wealthy householders, seeing opportunity in rising house prices and therefore trying to buy a second house. Others are professional traders, wanting to make a profit today from a possible price rise in wheat tomorrow. When speculators get involved, high prices can attract more demand rather than less. There is then a risk of a speculative bubble, which can ultimately lead to a crash when the bubble bursts. That was the problem in 1929, in 1999 and in 2007. History suggests that the phenomenon will inevitably happen again – but it doesn't point to *when*.

Key terms

Commodity markets: these cover undifferentiated products such as rice, oil or gold. The principle is that every kilo is the same as every other kilo, so traders can buy and sell without needing to worry which kilo they are dealing in.

Demand curve: a line showing the demand for a product at different prices (the higher the price, the lower the demand).

Market price: the price of a commodity that has been established by the market – that is, where supply equals demand.

7.6 Workbook

Revision questions

(35 marks; 35 minutes)

1 Choose one of the following terms, and explain what it means:

   a) stock market

   b) labour market

   c) foreign exchange market. (4)

2 State the probable impact on price of:

   a) falling demand, while supply remains unchanged

   b) rising supply at a time when demand is unchanged

   c) rising demand at a time of falling supply. (3)

3 When a shortage of Ed Sheeran tickets allows touts to charge £400, only wealthy people can get to the concerts. Most people would not worry about this. But why might people be concerned about a high 'market price' if there was a shortage of water at a time of drought? (4)

4 Explain why the price of a hotel room might be high on a Wednesday night. (4)

5 Consider the following.

   a) Draw supply and demand curves for oranges, based on the data shown in Table 7.4. (5)

Price	Demand	Supply
20p	900,000	100,000
25p	800,000	300,000
30p	700,000	500,000
35p	600,000	700,000
40p	500,000	900,000
45p	400,000	1,100,000
50p	300,000	1,300,000

Table 7.4 Market data for oranges

   b) Why may orange growers be unwilling to supply any oranges at 10p each? (2)

6 Explain how market movements might ensure that a sharp rise in the price of apples proves temporary. (4)

7 Examine Figure 7.2 (supply and demand for J.K. Rowling in Manchester) on page 40 and answer the following:

   a) Why is £68 the right price to charge for the tickets? (4)

   b) What would the effect be of setting a price of £80 for the tickets? (5)

Data response 1

The market for rice

Rice output in India is set to climb to a record in 2013, according to Bloomberg. The crop should increase by 2.4 per cent to 95 million tonnes. There are two main reasons for this within the world's second-largest rice producer: first, an early monsoon will have encouraged a bigger area to be planted for rice in 2013 than 2012; and second, the Indian Agriculture Ministry has been encouraging farmers to use higher yielding 'hybrid' seeds. These can boost yields by one tonne per hectare; in 2012, there were 39 million hectares of rice planted in India.

India is the world's biggest exporter of rice, so its extra output will have an impact on world supply levels. This might put pressure upon the price of rice as global commodity stockpiles are expected to rise for the seventh year in a row. The US Department of Agriculture expects stockpiles to rise 2.7 per cent to 108.6 metric tonnes in 2013/2014. World output of 480 million tonnes is forecast to exceed demand by 2.8 million tonnes.

The situation is a far cry from 2008, when the price of rice topped $1,000 a tonne, sparking food riots in many parts of the developing world. A US government report later concluded that the 2008 'price increase was not due to crop failure or a particularly tight

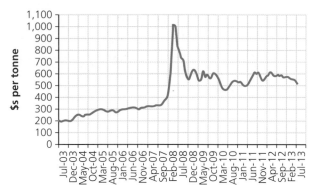

$s per tonne (y-axis): 0, 100, 200, 300, 400, 500, 600, 700, 800, 900, 1,000, 1,100

x-axis: Jul-03, Dec-03, May-04, Oct-04, Mar-05, Aug-05, Jan-06, Jun-06, Nov-06, Apr-07, Sep-07, Feb-08, Jul-08, Dec-08, May-09, Oct-09, Mar-10, Aug-10, Jan-11, Jun-11, Nov-11, Apr-12, Sep-12, Feb-13, Jul-13

Figure 7.5 World commodity price: rice (source: www. indexmundi.com)

global rice supply situation. Instead, trade restrictions by major suppliers, panic buying by several large importers and a weak dollar were the immediate cause of the rise in rice prices.' Speculative buying by market traders was almost certainly a further explanation of the trebling of prices within six months.

Questions (30 marks; 35 minutes)

1 Explain why production of rice in India may be significant for the world market price. (4)

2 Assess two implications for the market price of rice of 'world output of 480 million tonnes forecast to exceed demand by 2.8 million tonnes'. (8)

3 Construct a labelled graph of the changes in the supply and demand for rice in India in 2013. (6)

4 Assess the possible impact of 'speculative buying by market traders' on the market for rice. (12)

Data response 2

Supply, demand and the entrepreneur

By the edge of Lake Victoria, Tanzania, is a village with 2,000 people. It is poor, but has its own fishing boats, boatbuilder, vegetable field and (tiny) street market. The villagers work together, but individuals can keep any money they make. One villager, Pembo, noticed that – year after year – the villagers planted tomatoes in the ideal growing conditions of the rainy season.

But when the tomatoes were ripe, the price in the local market town was too low to make a profit. Fewer people wanted to buy them (they grew their own) and far more growers brought tomatoes to the marketplace.

In August 2014, Pembo marked out a large patch of sandy earth by the side of the lake and sowed tomato seeds. As the rainy season was over, he had to water by hand. Every day he spent hours collecting water in a bucket from the lake and watering each plant. He marked his patch out carefully and replanted each seedling to give it the space to grow. He tied them, tended them and eventually was able to harvest them and take them to the market.

Whereas the villagers' tomatoes usually fetched $2 per bushel, Pembo's made $5. As he had done all the work himself, the villagers accepted that he kept all the money: this proved to be just over $100 for two months' work (about six times the average income). He used the $100 to buy a second-hand motorbike with a trailer.

Others in the village soon copied the method for growing tomatoes, though Pembo was already onto his next idea. He paid two 12 year olds to look after his own patch, while he talked to a hotel in the Serengeti National Park about supplying all their fruit and vegetables.

Questions (40 marks; 40 minutes)

1 Assess two possible motives for Pembo's business start-up. (8)

2 Assess the understanding of supply and demand shown in Pembo's start-up of his tomato patch. Use a diagram to aid your answer. (10)

3 Assess whether this business idea of out-of-season tomato growing will continue to succeed. (10)

4 Assess whether Pembo is likely to prove a really successful businessman in the longer term. (12)

Extended writing

1 Look at the 'Real business' box on page 40. How can an old 50p concert ticket be worth £850? Explain your reasoning. (20)

2 China is the world's biggest purchaser of almost every commodity and the world's biggest producer of most industrial items. Evaluate how a sharp economic downturn in China might affect the equilibrium of markets worldwide. (20)

8 Price elasticity of demand

> **Definition**
>
> Price elasticity measures the extent to which demand for a product changes when its price is changed.

Linked to: Demand, Ch 5; Income elasticity of demand, Ch 9; Branding and promotion, Ch 11; Pricing strategies, Ch 12.

■ 8.1 Introduction

When a company increases the price of a product, it expects to lose some sales. Some customers will switch to a rival supplier; others may decide they do not want (or cannot afford) the product at all. Economists use the term 'the law of demand' to suggest that, almost invariably:

Figure 8.1 The law of demand

Price elasticity looks beyond the law of demand to ask the more subtle question: 'When the price goes up, by how much do sales fall?' Elasticity measures the extent to which price changes affect demand.

■ 8.2 Price elasticity of demand

In the short term, the most important factor affecting demand is price. When the price of the *Independent* newspaper increased from £1.20 to £1.40 in 2013, sales fell by 9 per cent between May and October, whereas the *Telegraph's* price rise from £1 to £1.20 (the year before) cut sales by just 4 per cent. Readers of the *Independent* proved more price sensitive than readers of the *Telegraph*. Therefore, the owners of the *Telegraph* could feel delighted with their pricing decision. Selling 4 per cent fewer papers but receiving 20 per cent more

for each one sold meant a significant boost to revenue and profits.

The crucial business question is: how much will demand change when we change the price? Will demand rise by 1 per cent, 5 per cent or 25 per cent following a 10 per cent price cut?

Some products are far more price sensitive than others. Following a 5 per cent increase in price, the demand for some products may fall sharply, say by more than 20 per cent. The demand for another type of product may fall by less than 1 per cent.

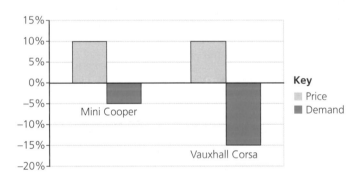

Figure 8.2 The impact of a 10 per cent price rise on sales

Price elasticity can be calculated using the formula shown below:

$$\text{Price elasticity} = \frac{\% \text{ change in quantity demanded}}{\% \text{ change in price}}$$

Price elasticity measures the percentage effect on demand of each 1 per cent change in price. So if a 10 per cent increase in price led to demand falling by 20 per cent, the price elasticity would be 2. Strictly speaking, price elasticities are always negative and therefore the actual figure is −2. This is because a price rise pushes demand down, and a price cut pushes demand up. The figure of −2 indicates that, for every 1 per cent change in price, demand will move by 2 per cent in the opposite direction.

8.3 Determinants of price elasticity of demand

Why do some products, services or brands have low price elasticity of demand and some high elasticity? Why is the price elasticity of demand for Branston Baked Beans higher than that of Heinz Baked Beans? Or the price elasticity of demand for the *Financial Times* as low as −0.05 while the price elasticity of demand for *Look* magazine is as high as −2.0 (that is, 40 times higher)?

Figure 8.3 Choice of newspapers and magazines

The main determinants of price elasticity are as follows.

The degree of product differentiation

This is the extent to which customers view the product as being distinctive from its rivals. *Look* may be an excellent magazine, but it is offering the same mix of fashion, shopping and 'celebs' as many other magazines aimed at young women. So if the cover price is increased, it is easy for readers to switch to an alternative, whereas readers of the *Financial Times* do not have any other options. Therefore, the higher the product differentiation, the lower the price elasticity of demand.

The availability of substitutes

Customers may see 7 Up and Sprite as very similar drinks. In a supermarket, they may buy the cheaper of the two. At a cinema, though, only Sprite may be available. At a train station vending machine, almost certainly Sprite will be the only lemonade. This is because it is a Coca-Cola brand and the company's distribution strength places Sprite in locations where 7 Up never goes. When Sprite has no direct competition, its price elasticity is much lower; therefore, the brand owner (Coca-Cola) can push the price up without losing too many customers.

Branding and brand loyalty

Products with low price elasticity of demand are those that consumers buy without thinking about the price tag. Some reach for Coca-Cola without checking its price compared with Pepsi, or buy a Harley-Davidson motorcycle even though a Honda superbike may be £4,000 cheaper. Strong brand names with strong brand images create customers who buy out of loyalty.

Real business

Boosting revenue

When the *Telegraph* newspaper increased its price from £1 to £1.20, its daily sales fell by 4 per cent, from 604,000 to 579,000 copies per day. This caused the following effect on daily revenue:

- Before price rise: price £1 x sales volume 604,000
  = £604,000.
- After price rise: price £1.20 x sales volume 579,000
  = £694,800.

That is, sales revenue rose by £90,800 per day, a 15 per cent increase. As the slight fall in sales volume would reduce total variable costs, the impact on profit would have been even greater.

8.4 Classifying price elasticity

Price-elastic demand

A product with **price-elastic** demand has a price elasticity of above 1. This means that the percentage change in demand is greater than the percentage change in price that created it. For example, if a firm increased prices by 5 per cent and as a result demand fell by 15 per cent, price elasticity would be:

$$\frac{-15\%}{+5\%} \times 100 = -3$$

The higher the price elasticity figure, the more price elastic the demand. Cutting price on a product with price-elastic demand will boost total revenue. This is because the extra revenue gained from the increased sales volume more than offsets the revenue lost from the price cut. On the other hand, a price increase on a product with price-elastic demand will lead to a fall in total revenue.

Price-inelastic demand

Products with **price-inelastic** demand have price elasticities below 1. This means the percentage change in demand is less than the percentage change in price. In other words, price changes have hardly any effect on demand, perhaps because consumers feel they must have the product or brand in question: the stunning dress, the trendiest designer label or – less interestingly – gas for central heating. Customers feel they must have it, either because it really is a necessity or because it is fashionable. Firms with products with price-inelastic demand will be tempted to push the prices up. A price increase will boost revenue because the price rise creates a relatively small fall in sales volume. This means the majority of customers will continue to purchase the brand but at a higher, revenue-boosting price.

	Product with price-elastic demand	Product with price-inelastic demand
Characteristics	• Undifferentiated • Many competitors	• Differentiated • Few competitors
Impact of a price cut	Sales rise sharply... ...so revenue rises	Sales rise, but not much... ...so revenue falls
Numerically	Between −1 and −5 or more	Between −0.1 and −0.99
Impact of a price rise	Sales fall sharply... ...so revenue falls	Sales fall, but not much... ...so revenue rises

Table 8.1 Summary of price elasticity of demand

8.5 The value of price elasticity to decision makers

Being able to estimate a product's price elasticity of demand is a hugely valuable aid to marketing decision making. At West Ham United, ticket prices for under-16s vary, from £70 in top seats for top games such as Manchester United, all the way down to £1 when trying to fill the stadium against less attractive opposition on midweek winter evenings. Unusually for a business, the objective is to fill the stadium rather than maximise revenue. Understanding the price elasticity of demand (PED) for junior tickets helps West Ham achieve an average capacity utilisation of 95 per cent or more. A business that knows its price elasticity can make better decisions than one that is in ignorance.

Data on a product's price elasticity of demand can be used for two purposes, as outlined below.

Sales forecasting

A firm considering a price rise will want to know the effect the price change is likely to have on demand. Producing a sales forecast will make possible accurate production, personnel and purchasing decisions. For example, in September 2013, Nintendo cut the price of its Wii U in America by 15 per cent, from $350 to $299. In October–November 2013, sales rose by 150 per cent. At that time, the price elasticity of the Wii U proved to be:

$$\frac{+75\%}{-15\%} = -5.$$

Nintendo could then use that knowledge to predict the likely impact of future price changes. Another price cut of 10 per cent could lead to a sales increase of 50 per cent ($-10\% \times -5 = +50$ per cent). This information can be passed on to operations and HR, to get the staff in place to produce 50 per cent more stock.

Pricing strategy

There are many external factors that determine a product's demand, and therefore its profitability. For example, a soft drinks manufacturer can do nothing about a wet, cold summer that causes sales and profits to fall. However, the price the firm decides to charge is within its control, and it can be a crucial factor in determining demand and profitability. Price elasticity information can be used in conjunction with internal cost data to forecast the implications of a price change on revenue.

Example

A second-hand car dealer currently sells 60 cars each year at an average price of £2,500 per car. This means a revenue of:

Total revenue = £2,500 × 60 = £150,000

From past experience, the salesman believes the price elasticity of his cars is approximately −0.75. The dealer is thinking about increasing his prices to £3,000 per car, an increase of 20 per cent. Using the price elasticity information, a quick calculation would reveal the impact on sales:

$$\% \text{ change in price} \times \text{PED} = \% \text{ change in demand}$$

$$+20\% \times -0.75 = -15\%$$

That is, a sales decline of 9, causing car sales to slip from 60 to 51.

On the basis of these figures, the new revenue would be:

$$\text{Total revenue} = \text{new price} \times \text{new sales volume}$$

$$= £3,000 \times 51 \text{ cars}$$

$$= £153,000$$

So, even though the price rise cuts sales to 51 cars, the revenue actually increases.

8.6 Strategies to reduce price elasticity

All businesses prefer to sell products with price-inelastic demand. Charging more for a price-inelastic product guarantees an increase in short-term profit. If a firm has price-elastic products, it will always feel vulnerable, as a rise in costs may be impossible to pass on to customers. And if a firm is tempted to cut the price of a product with price elastic demand, sales will probably rise so sharply that competitors will be forced to respond. A price war may result.

It is important to realise that a product's price elasticity of demand is not set in stone. Price elasticity is not an **external constraint**. The most important influence on a brand's price elasticity of demand is substitutability. If consumers have other brands available that they think deliver the same benefits, price elasticity will be high. So, to reduce a brand's price elasticity of demand, the firm has to find ways of reducing the number of substitutes available (or acceptable). How can this be done?

Increasing product differentiation

Product differentiation is the degree to which consumers perceive that a product is different (and preferably better) than its rivals. Some products are truly different from others, such as Cadbury Dairy Milk, with its distinctive taste. Others are successfully differentiated by image, such as Versace Jeans or Coca-Cola. Wearing Versace Jeans makes a statement about the wearer, even if the cloth itself is no different from that used by Levi's or Wrangler.

Reducing the competition

One way to reduce price elasticity is to eliminate competition. This might be done through **predatory pricing**: a deliberate attempt to force a competitor out of a market by charging a low, loss-making price. The reduction in the number of substitutes available allows the predator to raise its prices. If there are no cheaper substitutes available, the customer is forced to pay the higher prices or go without. The same effect can be achieved by takeover bids (for example, the purchase by Adidas of Reebok footwear).

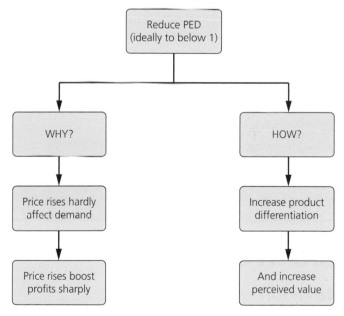

Figure 8.4 Logic chain: lowering price elasticity

Five whys and a how

Questions	Answers
Why might a company care more about its price elasticity of demand than its sales figures?	Because extra sales do not necessarily boost profit, but control over pricing can transform a firm's profits and prospects.
Why might it be a mistake to cut the price of a product with high price elasticity of demand?	As demand will jump ahead following the price cut, this might hit competitors so hard that they have to respond – risking a price war.
Why might a product's price elasticity of demand change over time?	Because the degree of competition may change, as may the level of differentiation established by advertising.
Why are consumers better off buying price-elastic products (and services)?	Because the close rivalry between suppliers ensures efficient, value-for-money products.
Why might a product's price elasticity of demand vary over its life cycle?	If innovative, it would be low at birth, but increase as rivals catch up; then rise more when it falls out of fashion and into decline.
How might a retail dry cleaner reduce its price elasticity of demand?	By finding a USP or strong point of differentiation, e.g. free local collection and delivery.

8.7 Price elasticity of demand – evaluation

For examiners, elasticity is a convenient concept. It is hard to understand, but very easy to write exam questions on! But how useful is it in the real world? Would the average marketing director know the price elasticities of his or her products?

In many cases, the answer is no. Examiners and textbooks exaggerate the precision that is possible with such a concept. The fact that the price elasticity of the *Telegraph* proved to be -0.2 in 2012 does not mean it will always be that low. Price elasticities change over time, as competition changes and consumer tastes change.

Even though elasticities can vary over time, certain features tend to remain constant. Strong brands such as BMW and Coca-Cola have relatively low price elasticity. This gives them the power over market pricing that ensures strong profitability year after year. For less established firms, these brands are the role models: everyone wants to be the Coca-Cola of their own market or market niche.

Key terms

External constraint: something outside the firm's control that can prevent it achieving its objectives.

Predatory pricing: pricing low with the deliberate intention of driving a competitor out of business.

Price-elastic: a product with demand that is highly price sensitive, so price elasticity is above 1 (strictly speaking, from *minus* 1 to *minus* infinity).

Price-inelastic: a product with demand that is not very price sensitive, so price elasticity is below 1 (strictly speaking, between *minus* 0.01 and *minus* 0.99).

8.8 Workbook

Revision questions

(35 marks; 35 minutes)

1 a) If a product's sales have fallen by 21 per cent since a price rise from £2 to £2.07, what is its price elasticity of demand? (4)

   b) Is the demand for the product price elastic or price inelastic? (1)

2 Outline two ways in which Nestlé could try to reduce the price elasticity of its Aero chocolate bars. (4)

3 A firm selling 20,000 units at £8 is considering a 4 per cent price increase. It believes its price elasticity is -0.5.

   a) Calculate the effect on revenue. (6)

   b) Outline two reasons why the revenue may prove to be different from the firm's expectations. (4)

4 Explain three ways a firm could make use of information about the price elasticity of demand of its brands. (6)

5 Identify three external factors that could increase the price elasticity of demand of a brand of chocolate. (3)

6 A firm has a sales target of 60,000 units per month. Current sales are 50,000 per month at a price of £1.50. If its products have a price elasticity of demand of −2, what price should the firm charge to meet the target sales volume? (5)

7 Why is price elasticity always negative? (2)

Data response 1

A firm selling Manchester United pillow cases for £10 currently generates an annual turnover of £500,000. The marketing director is considering a price increase of 10 per cent.

Questions (15 marks; 20 minutes)

1 Given that the price elasticity of demand of the product is believed to be −0.4, calculate:

a) the old and the new sales volume

b) the new revenue. (7)

2 If the firm started producing mass-market white pillow cases, would their price elasticity of demand be higher or lower than the Manchester United ones? Explain your reasoning. (8)

Data response 2

Sauces and sources

Heinz Tomato Ketchup is an iconic brand, more than 100 years old. It dominates the market for ketchup with annual sales of £125 million in the UK. It has a share of UK tomato sauce sales believed to be over 75 per cent. It has no effective branded competition, though sales of supermarket own-label ketchups can be considerable.

In 2013, it took a risk by increasing its prices by 10 per cent, even though the average price increase for 'table sauces' was only 3.5 per cent. The result was a 5 per cent fall in Heinz sales volumes.

Heinz says that the major growth stories in table sauces come from more exotic flavours, such as Mexican Chilli and Heinz Sweet Chilli. Perhaps this increased competition explains the collapse in sales of Levi Roots' Reggae Reggae Barbeque Sauce, which suffered a 17 per cent fall in 2013 sales volumes following a price rise of 8.5 per cent. Table 8.2 sets out the full story (sources for the whole story: *The Grocer* and Mysupermarket.com).

Figure 8.5 Heinz Tomato Ketchup

Figure 8.6 Reggae Reggae Sauce

	2012	2013
Selling price	£1.55	£1.68
Sales volume (bottles)	3.1 million	2.56 million
Sales revenue (£ millions)	£4.8 m	£4.3 m

Table 8.2 Reggae Reggae Sauce sales, 2012 and 2013 (source: *The Grocer* magazine)

Questions (34 marks; 35 minutes)

1 a) Calculate the price elasticity of demand for Heinz Tomato Ketchup in 2013. (4)

  b) Assess two reasons why this product may have this degree of price elasticity of demand. (8)

2 a) Calculate the price elasticity of demand for Reggae Reggae Sauce in 2013. (4)

  b) It is believed that the price elasticity of demand for Reggae Reggae Sauce is higher now than in the past. Explain two possible reasons why this might have occurred. (8)

3 The figures suggest that Heinz Tomato Ketchup has a significantly lower price elasticity of demand than that of Reggae Reggae Sauce. Assess the implications of that for Heinz. (10)

Extended writing

1 You have been appointed marketing director of Topshop and set the goal of reducing the price elasticity of its retail sales. Evaluate how you might go about achieving this objective. (20)

2 Evaluate how the price elasticity of demand for a product such as the iPhone 6 might change over the four phases of its life cycle: birth, growth, maturity and decline. (20)

9 Income elasticity of demand

> **Definition**
>
> Income elasticity measures the extent to which demand for a product changes when there is a change in consumers' real incomes. The shorthand YED is often used for income elasticity of demand.

Linked to: Price elasticity of demand, Ch 8; Economic influences, Ch 45.

9.1 Introduction

Price elasticity focuses on what the business can do to maximise its revenue and profit given the products it has, their differentiation and competitors. Income elasticity starts from a different point. It looks at how a company's sales will be affected by changes in the economy – that is, changes that are totally outside the company's control. As shown in Figure 9.1, falling household incomes and confidence at the start of the **recession** hit UK car sales sharply in 2008 and 2009. A 5 per cent fall in real incomes pushed new car sales down by 15 per cent between 2007 and 2009. This was nothing compared with Italy and Greece when austerity measures hit them between 2010 and 2012. Car sales in Italy halved, while in Greece they fell by 75 per cent. All car companies could do to survive was to cut production and cut costs (and look to China where car sales were still booming).

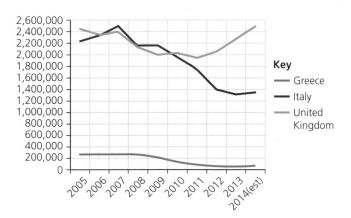

Figure 9.1 New car sales and the economy

Income elasticity is important because it shows the direction and the extent to which sales change when real incomes change.

9.2 What is meant by *real* incomes?

The government's Office for National Statistics (ONS) provides data each month on the rate of change in average earnings. This is the amount the average employee receives before any deductions for tax or pension contributions. That is their gross income. In July 2014, this figure for average pay was 0.6 per cent higher than the previous year. So people were 0.6 per cent better off.

Or were they, because in that same period prices (the rate of inflation) rose by 1.6 per cent. So consumers had 0.6 per cent more income, but had to pay 1.6 per cent more for their shopping basket. In effect, then, they were 1 per cent worse off.

Real incomes are measured, then, by the formula:

% rise in average earnings *minus* % rise in prices
= % change in real income

Another way of expressing this is to say that real incomes are incomes after allowing for inflation.

9.3 Calculating income elasticity of demand

In the recession year of 2009, UK car sales fell by 6 per cent. More expensive, luxury cars were especially hard hit. BMW sales fell 12 per cent, Lexus by 28 per cent and Bentley by 50 per cent! Some cheaper cars actually enjoyed sales increases, with Skoda sales up by 1 per cent and Fiat by 9 per cent. These changes in sales were a consequence of the different income elasticities of demand for these different brands.

Income elasticity is calculated using the formula shown below:

$$\text{Income elasticity} = \frac{\% \text{ change in quantity demanded}}{\% \text{ change in real incomes}}$$

For example, in 2009 real incomes in the UK fell by 6 per cent. Therefore, the income elasticity of demand for the car market as a whole was:

$$\frac{\% \text{ change in quantity demanded}}{\% \text{ change in real incomes}} = -\frac{-6\%}{-6\%} = 1$$

So the UK car market proved to have an income elasticity of 1 (meaning a one-for-one relationship between changes in income and changes in demand). The car brands mentioned above had the income elasticities shown in Table 9.1.

	% change in real incomes	% change in sales	Income elasticity
Bentley	−6	−50	+8.3
Lexus	−6	−28	+4.7
BMW	−6	−12	+2
Market average	−6	−6	1.0
Skoda	−6	+1	−0.17
Fiat	−6	+9	−1.5

Table 9.1 UK car income elasticities of demand calculated from the 2009 recession year

9.4 Interpreting numerical values for income elasticity

There are three categories a product can be put into:

- a 'normal good', with **positive income elasticity** of demand, and a YED of between 0.1 and 1.5
- a 'luxury' good, with very positive income elasticity of demand more than 1.5
- an 'inferior' good – that is, one with **negative income elasticity** of demand (so, as people get better off, they buy less of it, perhaps including orange squash or Asda Value Milk Chocolate).

In the case of the data in Table 9.1 you can see that BMW, Lexus and Bentley are luxury car brands because they each have an income elasticity of demand of more than +1.5. And, clearly, if BMW is a luxury, Lexus is a greater luxury and Bentley is a huge self-indulgence! Note that Bentley's figure of +8.3 implies that in a year when real incomes rise by 3 per cent, Bentley sales should jump by 3 × 8.3 = 25%. In the first eight months of 2014, with the UK economy growing at 3 per cent, Bentley sales were up by 21 per cent.

Table 9.1 also shows two 'inferior' goods: Skoda and Fiat. Both enjoyed rising sales when the economy worsened. Note here that the term inferior is not a comment on the quality of the item. It is simply a technical term for a product or service that has negative income elasticity.

9.5 Factors influencing income elasticity of demand

Why do some products, services or brands have positive and others have negative income elasticity of demand? And why is the income elasticity for some items strongly positive and for others only slightly positive? The main factors influencing income elasticity are as follows.

Whether the product is a necessity or a self-indulgence

When incomes are rising, people feel happier to splash out on luxuries. Therefore, posh hotels, business–class travel and champagne all enjoy sales booms in good times, but suffer sharp sales declines when real incomes are falling. During the global recession year of 2009, champagne exports from France fell by 28 per cent. So, for luxury products, income elasticities are strongly positive, such as +4. It is important, then, to remember that a figure as high as +4 is wonderful when the economy is healthy, but a huge burden when times are tough.

> 'In the affluent society, no useful distinction can be made between luxuries and necessities.'
>
> J.K. Galbraith, great economist and author (*The Affluent Society*)

By contrast, necessity goods will have low (but, usually, positive) income elasticities of demand. Toilet paper, shampoo and petrol will all tend to have advancing sales when real incomes are rising, but not by much. Sales of toilet paper, for example, seem to have an income elasticity of demand of about +0.5. If households are 2 per cent better off, they spend an extra 1 per cent on toilet paper.

Who buys the product

Some luxury products are bought only by the super-rich. Their incomes may not be affected by a change in 'average' real incomes. So although a time of recession may hit sales of £800 handbags from Mulberry, the demand for Hermes or Chanel bags may be unaffected. It is important to measure income elasticity of demand for each individual brand rather than assume that all posh bags are the same.

> 'You do not build brand value by saying how cheap you are. You do build brand value by reinforcing how special you are.'

Larry Light, brand consultant

Positive and negative elasticity

When measuring income elasticity, it is crucial to state whether the answer is positive or negative. Between 2008 and 2013, the UK economy was struggling more than at any time since the 1930s. Yet Poundland's sales trebled between 2008 and 2014 and grocery discounters Lidl and Aldi enjoyed a sales and profit boom. When real incomes are falling, consumers trade down to where they can find the right value and the right prices for their slimmed-down wallets. When falling incomes lead to a sales boom, the product or service has negative income elasticity.

By contrast, the majority of products and services have positive income elasticity of demand – that is, the better off we feel, the more we spend and buy. Most goods are 'normal', in that their income elasticity is about +1, meaning that a 3 per cent rise in real incomes would cause a 3 per cent rise in sales.

9.6 The significance of income elasticity to businesses

Knowing the income elasticity of a product is vital in order to develop a well-balanced product portfolio. Because inferior goods sell well during recessions, it is helpful for a company to have inferior goods as well as luxury goods. Nevertheless, as the UK economy tends to grow at around 2.5 per cent a year in the long term, normal and luxury goods are the most important part of a long-term strategy.

Data on a product's income elasticity can be used for two purposes, as outlined below.

Sales forecasting

In November 2008, Poundland had 200 stores. By December 2014, the number had risen to 550.

By the end of 2014, with the worst of the recession over, how many shops should it plan to open in the coming years? A clear starting point was to look at forecasts of economic growth in the UK, together with forecasts of likely changes in real incomes. If and when the forecasts turned strongly positive, it would probably forecast that Poundland sales would be flattening off and therefore store-opening plans should be put on hold.

For a company such as Jaguar Land Rover, a quite different sales forecast would be made. Rising real incomes would mean higher sales and, therefore, at some stage, higher production capacity and hiring and training new staff.

Financial planning

Once a business can forecast its future sales level, it can start to plan for the financial implications. If sales are likely to boom, higher production will be needed and probably a significant amount of extra funding, perhaps requiring a bank loan or a rights issue (asking existing shareholders to buy extra shares at a discount). If sales look likely to fall, a finance director will know that a trip to the bank would be a mistake. The business will try to find a plan to cut its cash outgoings in order to survive the problem period.

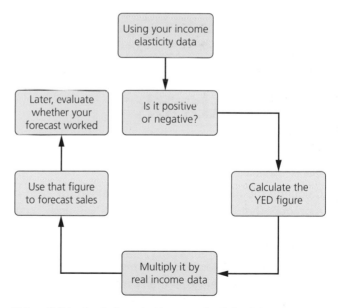

Figure 9.2 Logic chain: using income elasticity data

Five whys and a how

Questions	Answers
Why may normal goods be better than inferior goods in the long run?	Because recessions are unusual; in any year, the economy grows in real terms ten times as often as it shrinks.
Why may it be a good thing if your product has negative income elasticity of demand?	Because it gives your company some protection against periods when people are getting worse off (such as recessions).
Why do products with high price elasticity not necessarily have high income elasticity of demand?	Price elasticity is about competition and differentiation; income elasticity is about luxury; so a Bentley has low price elasticity but high income elasticity.
Why might a product's income elasticity of demand rise over time, say from +1.5 to +3.0?	Because customers are treating it as more of a luxury item (perhaps because its price has been pushed up significantly).
Why might it be hard to forecast next year's sales using income elasticity data?	Because economic forecasting is such an inexact science that you can't really trust the forecast of economic growth.
How do you know that a product is an 'inferior good'?	It has negative income elasticity.

9.7 Income elasticity of demand – evaluation

Income elasticity is a hugely important concept because it acknowledges how vulnerable companies can be to changes in the economy. When economic growth is steady, some chief executives forget that bad times can arrive suddenly and unexpectedly. By the time a recession has started, it may be too late to try to find a new product with negative income elasticity. So much cleverer to be Volkswagen, having already acquired Skoda, or Renault, with its low-priced Dacia brand.

Success in business is largely about thinking and planning ahead, allowing long-term strategies to be developed.

Just focusing on price elasticity can deceive a boss into thinking s/he has more control over demand than is really the case. Income elasticity is the reminder that demand is, at least in part, a function of forces outside the firm's control.

Key terms

Negative income elasticity: a product for which sales fall when people are better off (but rise when people are worse off).

Positive income elasticity: a product for which sales rise when people are better off (but fall in recessions).

Recession: two or more quarters of negative economic growth.

9.8 Workbook

Revision questions

(30 marks; 30 minutes)

1 Calculate the income elasticity of demand for a product that sold 20,000 units in 2008, and 22,400 in 2009, when real incomes in the UK fell by 6 per cent. (4)

2 For each of the following, explain whether you think the product/service is a normal, a luxury or an inferior good. Make your reasoning clear.

   a) a railway commuter's return ticket

   b) a trip for the family to Disneyland Paris

   c) a can of Tesco Value tomato soup. (9)

3 Are these products normal, luxury or inferior?

   a) Product A: income elasticity −1.5

   b) Product B: income elasticity +4.5

   c) Product C: income elasticity +0.9. (3)

4 See the quote by Larry Light on page 53. Explain the implications of the quote for the income elasticity of demand for a product or service of your choice. (5)

5 Explain the circumstances that might lead a product that is a normal good to become an inferior good over a period of two or three years. (3)

6 Pol Roger champagne sells 10,000 bottles a month in the UK at £30 a time. Its PED is −0.4 and its YED is +6.

a) Calculate the value of its UK sales next year if real incomes rise by 2.5 per cent. (3)

b) Briefly explain how Pol Roger might use the data on its price elasticity of demand. (3)

Data response

Income elasticity

Figure 9.3 shows the difference between the rise in wages and the rise in prices between 2001 and 2014 – and therefore shows the trends in real wages. In the period from January 2010 to July 2014, Aldi's share of the UK grocery market rose from 2.8 per cent to 4.8 per cent, while Tesco's share fell from 30.3 per cent to 28.9 per cent. Look at Figure 9.3 and answer the questions below.

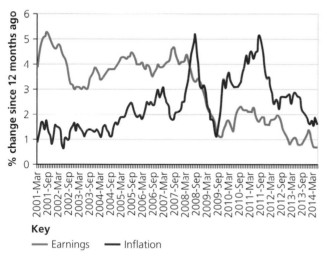

Key
— Earnings   — Inflation

Figure 9.3 Percentage change in earnings compared with prices (Consumer Prices Index) (source: ONS, September 2014)

Questions

(25 marks; 30 minutes)

1 Explain what the graph is showing about real wages in the UK between 2001 and 2014. (5)

2 Assess what the text and diagram imply about the income elasticity of:

a) Tesco

b) Aldi (no need for calculations). (8)

3 In mid-2013, UK households were suffering a 2 per cent fall in real incomes. In that period, sales at Aldi rose by 18 per cent.

a) Calculate the implied income elasticity figure for Aldi. (4)

b) Assess two possible factors that may be distorting the apparent correlation between Aldi's sales and consumers' real incomes. (8)

Extended writing

1 A young designer of women's shoes wants to create a top-end luxury shoe brand. Evaluate how this might be achieved and the advantages and disadvantages of achieving it. (20)

2 Evaluate the possible difficulties of determining the income elasticity of demand for a brand such as the Samsung Galaxy, given the ever-changing nature of the mobile phone market. (20)

10 Product and service design

> **Definition**
>
> Design means finding the right balance between creating something that people desire to have, that they can afford to buy and that works reliably.

Linked to: Market research Ch3; Market positioning, Ch4; Price elasticity of demand, Ch8; Branding and promotion, Ch11; Quality management, Ch44.

10.1 Introduction to design

The design of a product is not just about its appearance and shape. It is also about the product's function, quality and durability. Designers work to a design brief, which tells them the criteria for looks, cost and quality. All must be considered in designing the finished product. Larger firms have their own design teams on the payroll. Smaller firms may rely on design consultants to turn a product idea or requirement into a finished product.

Good design adds value to products and can be the key differentiator that marks one brand out from its competitors. No other UK firm has been quite as successful at this as Dyson Ltd. Famously, James Dyson created 5,127 prototypes of his first vacuum cleaner before he was satisfied that he had perfected the cleaning mechanism. The modern Dyson empire, though, with global sales of £6 billion and profits of £800 million a year, owes a huge amount to visual (aesthetic) design. The patent on Dyson's 'dual cyclone' vacuum mechanism expired in 2001. Yet the distinctiveness of the products has continued to generate huge sales success even though Dyson prices are often double those of its competitors.

10.2 The design mix

> 'When you say 'design,' everybody thinks of magazine pages. So it's an emotive word. Everybody thinks it's how something looks, whereas for me, design is pretty much everything involved in making something.'

James Dyson, vacuum design billionaire

A useful way to consider design is through the design mix. Every designer must consider the following three factors.

1 *Aesthetics*: the look, feel, smell or taste (that is, the appeal to the senses).

2 *Function*: does it work? Is it reliable? Is it strong enough or light enough for the customer's purpose?

Figure 10.1 James Dyson

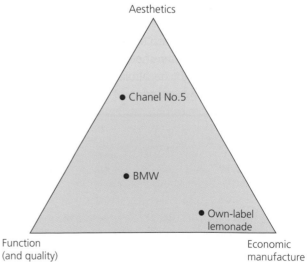

Figure 10.2 The design mix

3 *Economic manufacture*: is the design simple enough for it to be made quickly and efficiently and therefore relatively cheaply?

In some cases, all three factors will be of equal importance. In most, there will be a clear priority. As Figure 10.2 shows, with own-label lemonade, cheap production would be the overwhelming priority. So design will focus on simplicity, using a standard plastic bottle shape and low-cost materials that are easy to manufacture. For BMW, design for function would be important, as would the car's appearance. Production costs will be a lower priority. Firms decide on their design mix after careful market research to identify the purchasing motivations of existing and potential customers. Table 10.1 gives some indications of other design priorities for businesses.

	Aesthetics	Function	Economic manufacture
Dacia Sandero (UK's cheapest car: £5,950)	3	2	1
Hermes 'Birkin' bag (price: upwards from £7,500)	1	2	3
An online, home-delivery dry-cleaning business	2=	1	2=
Box of Cadbury 'Indulgence' chocolates	1	2	3

Table 10.1 Design priorities for different products and services

Real business

Design disaster

In early 2014, Adam Pritchard, boss of £8 million juice brand 'Pomegreat', relaunched the brand as 'Simply Great' with a new pack design featuring 'superhero' brand mascots. Pomegreat had built up sales steadily since its launch in 2000, securing supermarket listings and a 'loyal, middle-aged customer base'. Pritchard believed that a new, younger market could be attracted by the superhero logos and a new range of 'superfruits', including mango and cranberry.

The result was a sales disaster. Within six months. sales had halved. Old-time customers walked away while very few new ones were attracted. Pritchard bit the bullet, brought out a new-but-like-the-old design in early November 2014 and within weeks sales were jumping ahead.

Design matters.

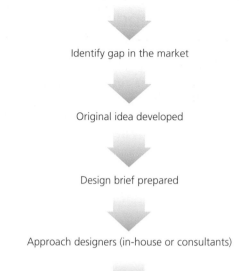
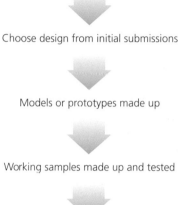

Market research on consumer's needs and state of the market

⬇

Identify gap in the market

⬇

Original idea developed

⬇

Design brief prepared

⬇

Approach designers (in-house or consultants)

⬇

Choose design from initial submissions

⬇

Models or prototypes made up

⬇

Working samples made up and tested

⬇

Consumer trials on target group

⬇

Tooling up for manufacture

⬇

Organise supplies of raw materials

⬇

Full scale production

Figure 10.3 The design process

10.3 Changes in the mix to reflect social trends

Concern over resource depletion

With the global population forecast to grow from seven to eleven billion by the end of the century, people worry that key resources such as fresh water will not be able to keep up. They may be depleted to the point that there is not enough to go round. The same could be true of any other resource that is finite – that is, in limited supply. By definition, that is true of minerals such as iron ore and gold, as we have only one planet. Other resources that are a concern include fish stocks, crops that like cool climates (if the planet continues to get warmer) and essentials such as oil and wood.

Sustainability means that the purchase you make will not affect long-term supplies of the product because it is automatically replenished. For example, although cod is an endangered fish, with a serious risk that supplies will dry up, there are plenty of supplies of other fish available, such as pollock. Birds Eye has given in to pressure to reduce the amount of cod in its fish fingers, using pollock instead. Pollock and chips, anyone?

As resources deplete, their price will rise. This will be the signal for designers to try to find alternative solutions based on different materials. Oil is the basis for all plastics. If oil starts to run out, there may need to be a switch back from plastic bottles to glass. Fortunately, that may be aesthetically pleasing.

Designing for waste minimisation and re-use

A well-designed product can be manufactured with minimal wastage. This process starts with computer-aided design (CAD) software, which enables the designer to work out the wastage implications of the production process. Waste minimisation keeps production costs down and helps reduce the environmental footprint of the business. This, in turn, might be used as a marketing message to convey to customers: 'We are serious about every aspect of the environment.'

Re-usage is also potentially important. Economic growth in the twentieth century was associated with an increasingly disposable society. Disposable lighters, razors, torches and even clothes became fashionable.

Recycling

Waste materials can be disposed of in one of only three ways: burn them, bury them or reuse them. Burning them directly increases greenhouse gas emissions and burying them is not only destructive of the environment, but can also cause air pollution. The ideal solution is therefore recycling, which means re-using as much as possible of the original materials. There are simple solutions to this that shoppers seem uninterested in: for instance, getting milk from a milkman who collects, washes and refills glass milk bottles; people are sufficiently ill-focused to make a fuss about recycled plastic when there is a much better solution available. Nevertheless, individual businesses cannot concern themselves with re-educating the public; their duty is to attract custom.

> **'A common mistake that people make when trying to design something completely foolproof is to underestimate the ingenuity of complete fools.'**
>
> Douglas Adams, author of *Hitchhiker's Guide to the Galaxy*

In 2014, Colgate–Palmolive announced their intention that by 2020 they would switch to using environmentally friendly toothpaste tubes made from a mixture of paper pulp and recyclable plastic. This may have an impact on the aesthetics of the toothpaste tube (drabber colours, perhaps, or less comfortable to hold). But there will also be a functional benefit that can translate into a new marketing proposition: good for your teeth; good for the planet.

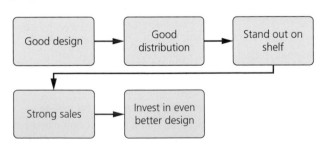

Figure 10.4 Logic chain: design matters

10.4 Ethical sourcing

The Ethical Sourcing Forum (ESF) has been operating since 2002 to try to give western companies an idea about the reality of working conditions and practices in different parts of the world. In January 2014, they published a report on Bangladesh – doubtless in the aftermath of the 2013 Rana Plaza industrial disaster in which 1,130 garment workers were crushed to death. ESF carried out their research in 400 factories in Bangladesh and found huge inconsistencies within this little-regulated business environment. In 40 per cent of footwear factories, there were too few emergency evacuation exits. The same industry was the worst on a series of measures: wages, excessive working hours and many others. One of the most striking findings was that in 80 per cent of cases in the footwear sector, inspectors were unable to find evidence that workers were allowed a day off a week (as is required by local laws).

For western retailers of clothing and footwear, the working conditions in countries such as Bangladesh, India and Cambodia have become an important issue. Not, in reality, due to the ethical and moral values of the company directors, but because several embarrassing TV and newspaper revelations in the past have made them wary of bad publicity. For 'ethical sourcing', it is better to assume 'sourcing based on fear of ethical revelations'. These are not the same thing.

The term ethical sourcing can be taken in two ways:

1 Sourcing based on the manufacturer or retailer's ethical values: this might include buying supplies from known businesses or farms, where the customer knows the supplier treats staff, animals and the environment with respect. Implicitly, for this to be based on ethics, the customer must be prepared to sacrifice some profit in this buying process.

2 'Ethical sourcing' may also be a buzz-term, almost a cliché within a business. In 2009, Cadbury announced that its Dairy Milk brand would 'go Fairtrade'. It remains so, yet most Cadbury brands based on Dairy Milk chocolate are not Fairtrade. This surely suggests that Cadbury took that purchasing decision on the grounds of consumer image and profit maximisation, not through principle. Does this matter? Well, yes, because it would be nice to trust that a company is genuinely concerned about ethical sourcing; in most cases, you have to read the packaging with great care to be sure of how the supplies have been obtained.

Recent years of recession have made it look as if the British consumer takes 'premium' sourcing seriously only in good times. When the 2009 recession arrived, sales of organic food reversed a longstanding upwards sales trend (see Figure 10.5). The slight economic recovery in 2013 presaged a slight improvement in sales of organics. During that same period, sales of Fairtrade produce rose sharply, but that may have been mainly due to supply decisions (Cadbury and Dairy Milk, and Nestlé and Fairtrade KitKat) rather than demand ones.

And what is the relevance of all this to design? In some companies, there will be little or none. Designers at Apple have a critical job to do – but they are not involved at all in the process of getting the products made. Many would have no idea of where key components are made – or the conditions for the workers involved. In other companies, designers would have a greater overall responsibility for the coherence of the product. There is not much point in a beautifully designed dress being made from sustainably sourced cotton if the silk lining is made by child labour in south-east Asia.

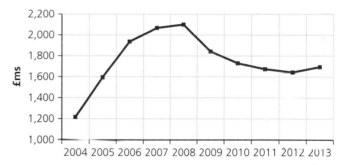

Figure 10.5 Sales value of organic food in the UK (source: Soil Association Annual Reports)

Five whys and a how

Questions	Answers
Why is design important in services as well as products?	Design is vital in the underlying systems, such as the work-flow in a McDonald's, and also matters in terms of how bright and friendly an outlet looks.
Why does design add value?	Good design can turn cheap-to-produce materials into lively, quirky and even classy-looking products that command high prices.
Why might design need graduates from engineering schools rather than art colleges?	Because a lot of design is scientific and technical, such as the design behind Toyota's 'Hybrid Synergy Drive' cars like the Prius.
Why might designers need to think about ethical sourcing?	Because design coherence is important; the design of a posh sofa might be undermined if the wood is not from sustainable sources.
Why might a product be positioned at the extreme tip of 'economic manufacture' on the design mix?	Because the planned target market is lower-income groups.
How might Tesco benefit from better design input?	Better designed stores could use less energy and perhaps fewer staff, making them cheaper to run – and could also look and flow better for customers.

10.5 Product and service design – evaluation

The fundamental theme for evaluating any question involving design is the contrast between long- and short-term thinking. Part of the brilliance of Mercedes engineering is that, although the cars develop year by year, there are design themes that keep a Mercedes completely recognisable. Companies whose objective is short-term profit maximisation are unlikely to think in this way. The key is to take a long-term view, then stick to it. This is what Pilkington did with its self-cleaning glass, which took ten years to perfect. The Toyota Prius took more than ten years to become profitable. As a past Guinness advertisement once said: 'Good things come to those who wait.'

> 'Design can be art. Design can be aesthetics. Design is so simple, that's why it is so complicated.'
>
> Paul Rand, art director and logo designer

Key terms

Prototype: a test model of a planned design, used to see if it functions properly, with durability, reliability and safety.

Sustainability: making something using materials that will still be around for future generations, perhaps because you are planting a tree for every one you fell.

10.6 Workbook

Revision questions

(30 marks; 30 minutes)

1 Explain how resource depletion might affect the future design of motor cars. (4)

2 Explain where you would plot the following on Figure 10.2. Give your reasoning:

   a) the latest iPhone

   b) the packaging of a Cadbury £5 Easter egg

   c) a new double-decker bus for London. (9)

3 Explain two marketing advantages that good design could bring to a business of your choice. (8)

4 How are the concepts of short-termism and design linked? (3)

5 Briefly state and explain whether ethical sourcing would be important to customers in the following circumstances:

   a) the sourcing of a meat pie at Charlton FC's snack bar

b) the sourcing of a meat pie at Dundonald Primary School

c) the sourcing of a silk scarf sold at a department store. (6)

Data response

General Atomics: making a killing from drones

Drones are unmanned aircraft that are used for military and surveillance purposes. The market for drones is dominated by four American companies: Boeing, Grummand Northrop, Lockheed Martin and General Atomics. The biggest buyer of drones is the American government. They have been used in Afghanistan and Pakistan to kill locals who were terrorist suspects. From the government's point of view, the main advantage of drones over boots on the ground is that they enable a government to kill its enemies without risking the lives of its service personnel. There is a huge amount of profit to be made from supplying the government with military equipment such as drones. According to the Stockholm International Peace Research Institute, the American government's military budget in 2013 was $640 billion, which is more than the rest of the world's military spending put together.

The MQ-9 Reaper is an armed drone that fires Hellfire missiles. It was developed by General Atomics for the US government at a cost of $2.8 billion. Unsurprisingly, the research and development programme that led to the creation of the MQ-9 Reaper was kept secret to ensure that competitors to General Atomics were unable to design a 'me-too' product. The $2.8 billion investment made by General Atomics has paid off. By 2013, the American government had bought 106 Reapers at a cost of over $6 billion. Now General Atomics has a new drone to sell – the Avenger. As the photo shows, even though drones may never be seen by the enemy, the design features matter – a warplane should look aggressive; the Avenger certainly does.

Questions (40 marks; 45 minutes)

1 Use the design mix to assess the right combination of function, aesthetics and economics when designing a plane such as the Avenger. (10)

2 Look at the James Dyson quote on page 56. Assess how well his thoughts relate to the world of General Atomics and drone bombers. (10)

3 Evaluate the importance of design to the profitability of a business such as General Atomics. (20)

Extended writing

1 Evaluate the extent to which success is guaranteed for a producer with a brilliantly designed new product. (20)

2 The Co-op, Waitrose and Sainsbury's all boast about their ethical sourcing. Yet, in 2014, annual sales growth at each company was −1.3 per cent, +5.6 per cent and −2.5 per cent, respectively. Evaluate whether consumers really care about ethical sourcing. (20)

11 Branding and promotion

Definition

Branding is the skill of giving a product or service distinctiveness – even personality. Promotion is the part of the marketing mix that focuses on persuading people to buy the product or service.

Linked to: Market research, Ch 3; Product and service design, Ch 10; Marketing strategy, Ch 15.

11.1 Introduction to branding

Branding is the process of creating a distinctive and lasting identity in the minds of consumers. Establishing a brand can take considerable time and marketing effort, but once a brand is established it becomes its own means of promotion. The brand name is recognised and this makes it more likely that the customer will buy the product for the first time. If the experience is satisfactory, the customer is very likely to continue to choose the brand. Once established, branding has many advantages, such as the following:

- It enables the business to reduce the amount spent on promotion.
- Customers are more likely to purchase the product again (repeat purchase).
- It is easier to persuade retailers to put the products in their stores.
- Other products can be promoted using the same brand name.

'The best advertising is done by satisfied customers.'

Philip Kotler, marketing guru

Real business

In June 2014, in the streets of Uruguay, only one brand mattered: Adidas, as worn by Luis Suarez. His two goals against England when half-fit, plus what was taken as European Suarez persecution when he was banned from the World Cup, made him a super-hero. Adidas boots went from being desirable to being essential. Elsewhere in 2014, Nike won the sales battle with Adidas. Not in Uruguay.

11.2 Types of branding

Individual brand

Some brands are so powerful and distinctive that they stand on their own, such as Marmite. Do you know who makes Marmite? Probably not. Unilever is keen to have its **corporate brand** on many other products, but with Marmite you have to read the small print at the back of the label. The manufacturer has no interest in you associating Marmite with other Unilever brands such as Persil or Wall's (Marmite ice cream, anyone?). A huge benefit of keeping brands individual is that a publicity disaster for one has no effect on the others. At the time of writing, Tesco is getting a daily hammering by news media, which must have a dampening effect on the image and sales throughput at Tesco Extra (hypermarkets), Tesco Online, Tesco Metro and so on.

Brand family

Cadbury is now one division of the huge, American-owned Mondelez International. Cadbury itself is perhaps the ultimate British brand family. Whether you buy a Twirl, a Wispa or a bar of Dairy Milk, the Cadbury logo is prominent. It adds value, it adds acceptability ('I'll try that, it's from Cadbury') and it adds a comforting familiarity – we know we'll like the chocolate taste and texture because we've known it since childhood. A good brand has emotional qualities (even if they're largely subconscious). Even if you know that Cadbury is now owned by an American multinational, it makes no difference to the warmth of the association with the brand.

Corporate brand

In the global food business, there are three mighty corporations: Nestlé, Unilever and Mondelez. Of those, only Nestlé feels the need to put its logo on everything. So it's Nestlé KitKat, Nestlé Cheerios and Nestlé Munch

Bunch yoghurt. Nestlé wants to reinforce its corporate brand – clearly believing that it adds credibility to the individual brand names. From a UK perspective, this may not really be true; but if you went into a shop in Thailand and saw a Nestlé branded ice cream, it might provide the reassurance you need.

Branding became important in Britain in the nineteenth century as a way to reassure customers of quality and reliability in a world where shopkeepers regularly added (cheaper) powdered chalk to flour and sawdust to tobacco. Today we have consumer protection laws, but occasional scares such as the 2012 horsemeat scandal remind us of why it is nice to have a brand to trust.

'**The art of marketing is the art of brand building. If you are not a brand you are a commodity.**'

Philip Kotler, marketing guru

Among the benefits of strong branding are:

- Added value: a strong brand gives reassurance and may provide aspirational benefits; some men grow up aspiring to own a BMW or a Ferrari. The brand sums up all the benefits consumers see in the product (or service) and therefore adds value to the purchase.
- Charging premium prices: a recent report showed that the UK market leader in instant coffee (Nescafé) can charge customers £19.52 per kilo, while supermarket own-label coffees average £12.25. That premium of £7.27 per kilo means Nescafé is priced nearly 60 per cent higher than own-label coffees. This added value gives huge scope for making Nescafé a very profitable brand.
- Reduced price elasticity: strong branding can be placed somewhere on the spectrum from brand loyalty to brand obsession. People willing to queue 24 hours for a new phone must come into the obsession category. But there are others: football club supporters, players of Grand Theft Auto and those who have to be dressed in a particular fashion brand. Brand loyalty lowers price elasticity, enabling the producer to push prices up with little damage to sales volumes. Brand obsession makes this passport to profit even easier.
- Combatting the discounters: at a time when Lidl, Aldi and Poundland are among our most successful retailers, weak brands are being squeezed out. In 2013, a remarkable thing happened: a £100 million brand, number two in its market (disposable nappies), withdrew from the UK market (see Figure 11.1). Huggies gave up in its battle against Pampers. The

owner of Huggies (Kimberley Clark) said it couldn't make a profit when up against the strength of Procter & Gamble's Pampers. A strong brand gives you the power to hold firm against discount retailers. Weaker brands have to cut their prices to £1 (for Poundland) or accept marginally profitable orders from other retailers. Weak brands always struggle to survive.

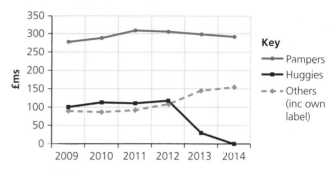

Figure 11.1 UK market for disposable nappies (source: *The Grocer*, 2009–2014)

'**Authentic brands don't emerge from marketing cubicles or advertising agencies. They emanate from everything the company does...**'

Howard Schultz, founder of Starbucks

11.3 Ways to build a brand

Building a brand has a timescale that matches the phases of a product life cycle. Heinz has built a brand in the UK based on more than a hundred years of beans, soup and ketchup. By contrast, Snapchat built a brand in months rather than decades. Possibly that makes Snapchat's brand quite brittle, whereas Heinz could cope with the odd flash of bad publicity.

Ways to build a brand include the following:

- Unique selling points (USPs) are an extreme version of product differentiation. Coca-Cola's USP is that it was the original cola drink; no-one can match that. In many cases, though, a USP is a temporary benefit because it can be copied. Most of the iPhone's original features have been copied by rivals; often its main differentiator is simply the brand name.
- Advertising: in 2014, Nestlé backed its superstar £425 million brand Nescafé with £10 million of advertising (mainly on TV). The previous year it did much the same. When a brand is as profitable as Nescafé, it would be foolish to do anything else. Partly the advertising is

to keep reinforcing messages about the superiority of the product, and partly it is to encourage new, younger buyers to tap into the mainstream consumer decision. In the UK, coffee means Nescafé.

- Sponsorship: this is an attempt at long-term brand-building that, when done cleverly, can help give a brand a 'personality'. Over the years, Richard Branson's Virgin has been clever at this. More recently, Red Bull has taken some beating. It supports its £250 million UK brand with its backing for extreme sports and Formula 1 motor racing. The cool image established by this helps it fight Coca-Cola's energy drink brands: Monster and Relentless.
- Use of digital media: not everyone can afford to sponsor an F1 team (its sponsorship costs Red Bull £80–£100 million a year). So social media offer interesting alternatives. Adwords (bought from Google) allows an advertiser to spend a fixed maximum. Soft drink producer AG Barr could promote its Rockstar energy drink by 'buying' Red Bull. It might pay Google 50p for listing Rockstar above Red Bull, whenever anyone 'Googles' Red Bull. If it set a maximum spend of £40,000, then after 80,000 Red Bull Googles its money would run out. In the meantime, AG Barr would hope to have attracted lots of energy drink fans to consider the Rockstar brand.

> **'Your premium brand had better be delivering something special, or it's not going to get the business.'**
>
> Warren Buffett, multi-billionaire investor

11.4 Changes in branding and promotion to reflect social trends

Viral marketing

For more than 30 years, marketing companies have been fascinated by the thought that brand messages can spread like a virus, from mouth to mouth. Many premium products were launched into highly selected retail outlets and promoted only in selected magazines, in the hope that word would spread. This is how Häagen-Dazs ice cream began and how Jimmy Choo developed (more than 20 years ago). Today's social media add a huge extra dimension to viral marketing – speed. One tweet from Ronaldo (32 million followers) about a great restaurant could book the place out for months to come. Inevitably, then, companies try to find ways to manipulate supposedly 'social' media for their own commercial benefit.

> **'Focus on how to be social, not how to do social.'**
>
> Jay Baer, US marketing consultant and author

Social media

This has become a serious alternative to standard press or TV advertising. There are three important benefits to firms from this form of digital marketing:

- The targeting can be especially tightly targeted at the precise tastes and habits of each individual, including noting changes in their behaviour, such as when they move from home to university.
- Traditional advertising was a one-way process from company to customer; social media provide the interactivity that may help create some bonding between consumer and brand.
- The success of **crowdfunding** sites such as KickStarter show that people are interested in getting involved in businesses, as long as they share the apparent aspirations of the proprietors. This, again, helps create a two-way bond.

Real business

At Christmas 2014, there was an advertising battle for hearts and minds between John Lewis, Sainsbury's and Marks & Spencer. John Lewis featured a tearjerker based on penguins, Marks & Spencer went for fairies and 'magic sparkle', and Sainsbury's focused on the famous Christmas football match on the First World War frontline. All three spent millions on making the TV advertisements and buying the airtime.

But what about the social media impact of the three campaigns? *Retail Week* magazine reported (12 December 2014) that the campaigns could be measured on 'Buzz' (blogs, forums and tweets), on Reach (how many accessed the commercials through social media) and Hashtag use. The social media results are shown in Table 11.1.

	John Lewis	Sainsbury's	Marks & Spencer
Buzz	14,702	24,401	534
Reach	47.4 million	83.7 million	3.7 million
Hashtag use	6,675	8,042	188

Table 11.1 Social media results of three Christmas advertising campaigns

Understandably, *Retail Week* declared Sainsbury's the winner.

For companies, the ultimate question is whether spending on social media provides a sufficient return on the money spent. Although this question cannot be answered satisfactorily by most companies, they feel that they are better off being in than out. The company that ignores the digital, online world may become the Morrisons of its own sector.

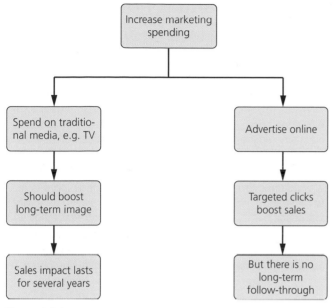

Figure 11.2 Logic chain: traditional v. online advertising

Emotional branding

Like viral marketing, this is nothing new. The Andrex puppy arrived in 1972, and since then has appeared in countless commercials, all trying to create an emotional connection with the brand. All that may prove to be different is the ease with which a two-way connection can be created and – perhaps even more powerfully – a community of followers can be established that becomes self-sustaining. This, in theory, should be a bunch of fans who post emotional commitments to the brand, be it a fashionable restaurant or a pop group. The reality, though, is often that for every fan there is another disillusioned fan, keen to break the emotional bonds. In business, there are rarely any easy ways of marketing your product.

■ 11.5 What is promotion?

Promotion is a general term that covers all the marketing activity that informs customers about a product and persuades them to buy it. The different elements of promotion can be grouped into two broad categories: those that stimulate short-term sales and those that build sales for the long term. This distinction provides the basis for analysis of most business situations and questions.

Types of promotion for building long-term sales include those described below.

Persuasive advertising

Persuasive advertising is designed to create a distinctive image. A good example is BMW, which has spent decades persuading us that it produces not a car but a 'Driving Machine'. Advertising of this kind has also helped to create clear consumer images for firms such as Tesco and L'Oréal (see Table 11.2).

Company	Slogan	Meaning
Innocent Drinks	'Chain of good: tastes good, does good'	'Our smoothies are good for you (whatever the anti-fruit juice folk say) and we give 10 per cent of our profits to charity (please forget we're now owned by Coca-Cola).'
L'Oréal	'Because you're worth it'	'Go on, spoil yourself; you can afford that bit extra, so buy our products, not those of our competitors.'
McDonald's	'I'm lovin' it'	'Our food may be unhealthy, but it tastes great.'

Table 11.2 Examples of persuasive advertising

Public relations

This is the attempt to affect consumers' image of a product without spending on media advertising. It includes making contacts with journalists to try to get favourable mentions or articles about your product. It would also include activities such as sponsorship of sport or the arts (see Figure 11.3). In 2014, Waitrose decided to sponsor the England cricket team. The upmarket image of cricket would be the perfect match for the posh image of Waitrose stores.

Figure 11.3 Sports sponsorship can boost a brand's image

Types of promotion for sparking short-term sales include those described below.

Buy one get one free (BOGOF)

This type of offer is a desperate, highly short-sighted way to generate sales. It will boost demand, but at the cost of short-term profit margins and at the risk of undermining the credibility of the brand. Would BMW do it (buy one BMW get another free)? Would Apple? No. Nor should anyone else.

Seasonal price promotion

After the summer, seaside hotels face months of empty rooms. Sensible, then, to promote price promotions on your website, or on hotel websites such as Laterooms. com. This can be an effective way to boost **capacity utilisation** and cash flow.

Five whys and a how

Questions	Answers
Why do brands matter?	Because, at their most successful, they give products/services a name, a 'face' and perhaps a personality.
Why does price elasticity reduce when branding is strengthened?	Because stronger branding makes customers less price sensitive. They want *that* brand and therefore take their eye off the price tag.
Why do firms love to think about viral marketing?	Because the business ideal is a cheap (even free) way to generate lots of customer interest followed by product trial.
Why may a large company be reluctant to rely on social media for its brand images?	It is easy to influence but very hard to control social media, so companies like the certainties involved in running their own TV advertisements/propaganda.
Why may short-term promotions be a mistake in the long term?	No serious business sees short-term sales maximisation as a proper objective; to build for the long term, image has to be built, not exploited.
How important is branding for a business-to-business company?	Even business customers like the promise of quality and consistency, which is the appeal at the heart of many brands.

11.6 Branding and promotion – evaluation

Successful branding is one way to ensure good distribution and good in-store display. Shopkeepers want to show off the latest and the classiest brands. The big question in business is, how can you make a brand desirable? It isn't enough simply to make a high-quality product and charge a lot for it. Customers desire authenticity, distinctiveness and aesthetic quality in their brands; this can be hard to achieve. The US chocolate giant Hershey has all of these things, but repeated research has shown that the British won't accept the Hershey brand.

Whenever writing about branding and promotion, there are two central lines of thought: one, branding success is hugely difficult and may sometimes be partly a matter of luck (right time, right place); and two, promotion always needs to be rooted in long-term strategy; short-term sales fixes risk damaging the brand.

11.7 Workbook

Revision questions

(45 marks; 45 minutes)

1 Read the quote by Howard Schultz on page 63. What implications does that have for running a business? (4)

2 a) Analyse one of the following brands, examining what you think its qualities are: Galaxy chocolate, TGI Fridays, Nike footwear, Nintendo. (4)

  b) For the brand you analysed, explain how its qualities add value. (4)

3 a) Give two examples of a brand family. (2)

  b) Give two examples of individual brands. (2)

4 In your own words, explain what is meant by viral marketing. (3)

5 Outline how your school might promote itself through social media. (4)

6 Explain what form of promotion you think would work best for marketing:

  a) a new football game for the PS4

  b) a small, family-focused seaside hotel

  c) organic cosmetics for women. (9)

7 Why is it important for businesses to monitor the effect of their promotional activity? (4)

8 What is meant by the phrase 'promotion needs to be effective'? (4)

9 Explain why promotion is essential for new businesses. (5)

Data response

Getting started in business – the cronut craze

It's 5 am, Soho, Manhattan, and dozens of people are already in line. Only three hours until the Dominique Ansel bakery opens. Are they looking for work? No, they're queuing for New York's food craze of 2013: the cronut. And when the shop opens, they'll happily hand over $10 for a box containing just two of the pastries. It is said that they can be resold at ten times the retail price, but as each customer is allowed just one box, this would be a hard way to make a living.

Figure 11.4 The cronut craze

The cronut craze started in mid-May 2013 when bloggers spread the word about the new combination of donut and croissant at this new bakery. Baker-proprietor Ansel makes the flaky layers of a croissant into a ring shape, deep-fries it, then inserts patisserie cream and tops it off with a swirl of icing. Only 200 are made each day, so they sell out by just after 9.00 each morning. Ansel is trying to find a way to manufacture the cronut to meet demand throughout America. Until he does, the queues will persist.

Remarkably, Ansel has been allowed to trademark the name 'cronut', so although he has many imitators already, the 'doissant', the 'zonut' and the 'dosant' have not been able to convince customers that they are the real thing. This has helped him keep the price at more than double the typical price for a New York pastry.

But are the cronuts any good? College students Danielle Owens and Camara Lewis clearly think so, as they've succeeded six times in queueing and eating the cakes. Each month, Dominique Ansel changes the flavour of the pastry crème filling, to encourage repeat purchase. *The Financial Times* reports that 'The deeply buttery pastry is wonderful, crispy and stacked high with greedy, messy-to-eat layers; the lemon-maple cream is pleasingly sickly.' Visitors from around the US make a beeline for the bakery. Ansel has made a brilliant start so far to his business career. But can he turn the cronut into a nationwide success?

Questions

(30 marks; 30 minutes)

1 Explain any evidence here of viral marketing.   (4)

2 Assess the importance of social media in the development of the cronut business.   (10)

3 Examine three factors that may determine whether Ansel succeeds in making cronuts a successful brand in the long term. Explain which one you believe will prove the most important.   (16)

Extended writing

1 Evaluate whether it is time for a brand such as Cadbury Dairy Milk to abandon traditional TV and press media to spend their whole advertising budget on digital and social media.   (20)

2 Heinz has found that its famous brand limits it from expanding its product portfolio, as people won't accept Heinz chilled ready meals or Heinz pizzas. Evaluate how it might try to overcome this consumer resistance.   (20)

12 Pricing strategies

Linked to: Market research Ch 3; Market positioning, Ch 4; Price elasticity of demand, Ch 8; Marketing strategy, Ch 15.

12.1 How important are decisions about price?

Price is one of the main links between the customer (demand) and the producer (supply). It gives messages to consumers about product quality and is fundamental to a firm's revenues and profit margins. As part of the marketing mix, it is fundamental to most consumer buying decisions. The importance of price to the customer will depend on several factors, as discussed below.

Customer sensitivity to price

Consumers have an idea of the correct price for a product (see Figure 12.1). They balance price with other considerations. These include the factors set out below.

The quality of the product

Products seen as having higher quality can carry a price premium; this may be real or perceived quality.

How much consumers want the product

All purchases are personal; customers will pay more for goods they need or want.

Consumers' income

Customers buy products within their income range; consumers with more disposable income are less concerned about price. Uncertainty about future income will have the same effect as lower income. If interest rates are high, hard-pressed home-buyers will be much more sensitive to price; they need to save money and so they check prices more carefully and avoid high-priced items.

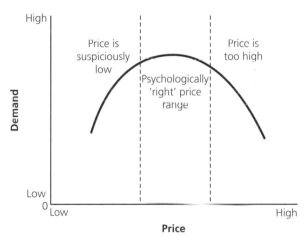

Figure 12.1 The 'right' price

Price sensitive	Not very price sensitive
No-frills air travel	Business-class air travel
Fiat and Ford cars	BMW and Mercedes cars
Children's white school shirts	Babies' disposable nappies
Monday-night cinema tickets	Saturday-night cinema tickets

Table 12.1 Price sensitivity in practice

12.2 Types of pricing strategy

A pricing strategy is a company's plan for setting its prices over the medium-to-long term. In other words, it is not about deals such as 'This week's special: 40 per cent off!' Short-term offers are known as **pricing tactics**.

For new products, firms must choose between two main pricing strategies:

1 Skimming

2 Penetration.

The main advantages of each are shown in Table 12.2.

Skimming

This is used when the product is innovative. As the product is new, there will be no competition. The price can therefore be set at a high level. Customers interested in the new product will pay this high price. The business recovers some of the development costs, making sure that enthusiasts who really want the product pay the high price they expect to pay. For example, the first DVD players came onto the UK market at a price of around £1,000. Firms use the initial sales period to assess the market reaction. If sales become stagnant, the price can be lowered to attract customers who were unwilling to pay the initial price. The price can also be lowered if competitors enter the market.

Penetration

Penetration pricing is used when launching a product into a market where there are similar products. The price is set lower to gain market share. Once the product is established, the price can be increased. It is hoped that high levels of initial sales will recover development costs and lead to lower average costs as the business benefits from bulk–buying benefits.

Figure 12.2 Logic chain: pros and cons of penetration pricing

	Price skimming	Price penetration
Advantages	High prices for a new item such as the iPhone help establish the product as a must-have item.	Low-priced new products may attract high sales volumes, which makes it very hard for a competitor to break into the market.
	Early adopters of a product usually want exclusivity and are willing to pay high prices, so skimming makes sense for them and for the supplier.	High sales volumes help to cut production costs per unit, as the producer can buy in bulk and therefore get purchasing costs down.
	Innovation can be expensive, so it makes sense to charge high prices to recover the investment cost.	Achieving high sales volumes ensures that shops will provide high distribution levels and good in-store displays.
Disadvantages	Some customers may be put off totally by 'rip-off pricing' at the start of a product's life.	Pricing low may affect the brand image, making the product appear 'cheap'.
	When the firm decides to cut its prices, its image may suffer. Buyers who bought early (at high prices) may be annoyed that prices fell soon afterwards.	It may be hard to gain distribution in more upmarket retail outlets, due to mass-market pricing.
		Pricing on the basis of value for money can cause customers (and therefore competitors) to be very price sensitive.

Table 12.2 Advantages and disadvantages of price skimming and price penetration

After years of dominance by Nike and Adidas, local sports footwear manufacturers made inroads into the Chinese market in 2010. Local brand Li Ning pulled alongside Adidas as the industry number two (market share by volume). The head of JWT China (advertising agency) said, 'The moment that a local brand can command the same price as a multinational brand is the day that a breakthrough has been made.'

To push further, Li Ning announced a new, higher-priced product range to sit 15 per cent below its foreign rivals. But by 2013, Li Ning was reporting sales slumping by 25 per cent and more than 1,000 store closures. At the same time, Nike sales in China slipped by just 3 per cent. The price breakthrough hasn't happened yet.

Figure 12.3 Li Ning brand

Pricing strategies for existing products

Cost-plus

For existing products, the key is to be clear about where your brand is positioned in the market. Pricing strategy on the latest Mercedes sports car will be based on the confidence of the company in the strength of its brand name. Mercedes will not worry about what Ford or Mazda charge for a sports car, or even the prices of its BMW or Lexus rivals. Mercedes can price a sports car on the basis of cost-plus. That means calculating the production costs per car, then adding a percentage mark-up that reflects the profit level the company wants from the product. Naturally, every business would like to be able to use this method. It virtually guarantees making a profit – and perhaps a large profit. But few businesses are in a position to ignore competitors' prices. In autumn 2014, a new Mercedes SL sports car carried a price tag of £72,500.

To calculate a price based on cost-plus:

Cost–plus formula: Unit cost + (% mark-up)

Step 1 – calculate unit cost:

$$\frac{\text{Total costs}}{\text{Number of units}} = \text{Unit cost}$$

Step 2 – add your desired mark-up (clothes shops typically add a 100 per cent mark-up; small grocers add around 25 per cent).

For example: a business manufactures educational DVDs. Fixed costs are £40,000 a month and variable costs are £5 per DVD. The business produces 20,000 a month.

Total costs are:

$$£40,000 + (£5 \times 20,000) = £140,000$$

Unit costs are therefore:

$$\frac{£140,000}{20,000} = £7 \text{ each}$$

Assuming a 200 per cent mark up, the selling price is:

$$£7 + (200\% \text{ of } £7 = £14) = £21$$

'If you're starting a service business, markup is more difficult to calculate because variable costs are hard to work out.'

Competitive

This is when the price is set at the market level or at a discount to the market. This happens in highly competitive markets, or in markets where one brand dominates. When Branston Baked Beans were launched in 2006, they were priced at 41p, compared to the 44p charged by the price leader, Heinz. By 2014, the Asda price of Branston was 50p to the 68p of Heinz, implying that Branston is still a price taker, but in a significantly weaker position now than then. Every business would like to set its own prices based on cost-plus. Mercedes can and Heinz can. Those that cannot use competitive pricing, which means that they have no real control over their future revenues.

'The moment you make a mistake in pricing, you're eating into your reputation or your profits.'

Katharine Paine, business executive

Predatory

Predatory pricing means pricing low enough to drive a rival or rivals out of business. Typically, the predator would be hoping that, having eliminated the competition, prices can then be set much higher. Clearly this approach can only work if:

- the predator is strong financially, perhaps because the product or service involved in the price war is not an important part of the overall business; at present, Cadbury and Mars are fighting hard for a share of the small but growing share of the chocolate market in India. Cadbury sell their chocolate bars at a unit price of 10p; even if this caused losses to Cadbury in the attempt to 'kill off' Mars, it wouldn't be a big problem as sales in India represent less than 5 per cent of Cadbury sales.

- the other company or companies are weak financially; if, for example, a huge outsourcing company such as Serco chose to undercut a small local competitor in one part of the country, it might be very easy to drive it out of business; this would be illegal, but only if it can be proved that the price cutting had the intention of driving a rival out of business. Generally, price cutting rarely gets a bad press from consumers or the media.

Psychological

This is perhaps more of a tactic than a strategy. At the time of writing, all the UK's big five supermarkets are charging 49p for a pint of milk. They are all concerned about pushing the price to or beyond 50p because they think 50p is a psychological price barrier. In other words they believe that **price elasticity** will be higher in changing from 49p to 50p than it was when the price rose from 48p to 49p.

So producers and retailers believe that consumers have certain psychological price barriers that are hard to cross without losing sales. In the car market, £9,999 seems quite a bit less than £10,499. In Primark, £9.99 seems quite a bit less than £10.99 and so on.

Choosing a pricing strategy

The choice of pricing strategy will depend on the competitive environment. Figure 12.4 shows how the choice of pricing strategy will vary according to the level of competition.

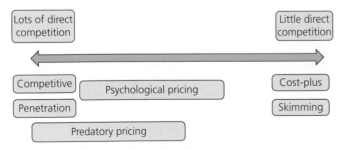

Figure 12.4 Factors affecting choice of pricing strategy

12.3 Factors that determine the appropriate pricing strategy

Many companies conduct regular market research into pricing. They use monthly 'retail audits' to get regular feedback on whether customers see their prices as value for money. If there is a slippage in this rating, there would be serious thought given to cutting prices or to trying to rebuild 'value' by more advertising or perhaps a packaging or product revamp. Companies know that pricing is the key to sales revenue and therefore keep a constant eye on it.

Product differentiation

However much competition there is in the market, a well-differentiated product can stand apart. In the crowded UK market for chocolate bars, Bounty is wonderfully differentiated. In fact it could be said to have a unique selling point – that unbelievably sweet coconut filling. Some are hooked on that; others avoid it. Generally, if people feel strongly for or against a product, it is probably in a good position to withstand competition. Highly differentiated products can think in terms of cost-plus pricing.

Strength of the brand

Few methods of differentiation are as effective as strong branding. A coconut filling can be copied by a rival producer tomorrow; but no-one else can call it a Bounty bar. Super-strong brands such as Wrigley (92 per cent market share) or Pampers (63 per cent market share) can use cost-plus pricing and launch new products on the basis of skimming the market.

Amount of competition

The fiercer the competition in a market, the more important price becomes. Customers have more choice, so they take more care to buy the best-value item, whereas a business with a strongly differentiated position is able to charge higher prices. The more direct the competition, the more likely it is that competitive pricing will be required. Predatory pricing is an absolute last resort.

Price elasticity of demand

The three above factors (differentiation, branding and competition) can all be summed up in a single figure: price elasticity. A highly differentiated, strong brand will have low price elasticity of demand and therefore be able to set its price without too much concern about sales volumes – ideal for cost-plus pricing.

For a product or service with high price elasticity of demand, competitive pricing is inevitable, but may make it very hard to generate a profit. These are the circumstances in which a large business might be tempted to take predatory action – to eliminate weaker competitors and thereby remove some of the pressure to cut prices.

Stage in the product life cycle

At certain times during a product's life cycle, pricing is especially important. Incorrect pricing when the product is launched could cause the product to fail. At other stages in the product's life, pricing may be used to revive interest in the brand.

There are two basic pricing decisions: pricing a new product and managing prices throughout the product life. Both decisions require a good understanding of the market: consumers and competitors. Many businesses launch at relatively good value prices and hold prices down in the early growth phase of the business. When growth develops further, prices are steadily increased and remain high during the maturity and early decline phases. Only when decline becomes entrenched may prices be cut to try to keep the business going for longer.

Real business

London's Hoxton Hotel

To build up its business, for its first ten years of trading, London's Hoxton Hotel promised to sell five rooms per night at £1 and another five at £29. The other 190 were at the 'normal' rate of £249! The Hoxton used this device to get customers to register as members of the Hoxton Fan Club. Only they were told when the sale was taking place of the £1 rooms. So this pricing trick gave the Hoxton a terrific email list of people interested in London hotel rooms. Today, you have to get used to weekday prices starting at £249.

Costs and the need to make a profit

Pricing is critical because, unlike the other ingredients in the marketing mix, it is related directly to revenue through the formula:

revenue = price × units sold

Pricing involves a balance between being competitive and being profitable. An important part of that is a good understanding of costs. These costs must include

purchasing, manufacturing, distribution, administration and marketing. Cost information should be available from the company's management accounting systems.

The lowest price a firm can consider charging is set by costs. Except as a temporary promotional tactic (a **loss leader**), businesses must charge more for the product than the variable cost. This ensures that every product sold contributes towards the fixed costs of the business.

12.4 Changes in price to reflect social trends

Online sales

The growth of Amazon.com has been a classic in pricing strategy. Boss Jeff Bezos wanted to build Amazon into the world's biggest online shop and used pricing quite ruthlessly as part of this programme. In the phenomenon that was the publishing of Harry Potter books, Amazon slashed prices to half price or less, threatening the survival of independent book shops. Indeed many called its actions 'predatory'. The number of independent book shops in the UK fell from 1,535 in 2005 to 987 by the beginning of 2014.

Without doubt, buying online makes it easier to compare prices and to buy from the cheapest. This is great for consumers, for as long as there is competition to the giants such as Amazon. As shown in Figure 12.5, UK shoppers are especially inclined to shop online.

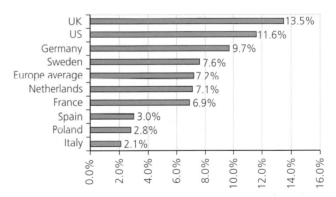

Figure 12.5 Online retail shares of home market, 2014 (estimate) (source: Centre for Retail Research)

Price comparison sites

Useful though online shopping is for consumers, price comparison sites suffer from conflicts of interest, which lead to a lack of clarity about what they are. These sites are not necessarily designed to find you the best deal; they may be designed to get the best deal for the site. In other words, they may propose a 'best deal' that is not the cheapest, but gives the site the highest rate of commission. Despite these doubts, usage of the sites seems to grow steadily, backed by huge investments in advertising.

> **'With the advent of the internet, customers are able to compare prices easily and this has raised the importance of pricing among the 4Ps.'**
>
> Philip Kotler, marketing guru

Five whys and a how

Questions	Answers
Why should companies be wary of tactical, low pricing, e.g. special offers?	Because of the potential damage to image. Can you imagine a 'special offer' BMW? Or, indeed, buy one BMW, get one free?
Why is price cutting a risk to profits even when it helps increase revenue?	If a 10 per cent price cut boosts demand by 15 per cent, revenue rises; but the price cut hits the profit margin, which may mean that profits actually fall.
Why may firms set lower prices in the growth phase than in the decline phase of the life cycle?	In the growth phase, prices may be kept low to attract a large number of potential loyalists; in decline, there are few new customers to attract, so prices may be kept high to exploit customer inertia/loyalty.
Why may skimming the market prove the wrong pricing strategy for a new product?	Skimming may generate a good image plus strong profits in the short term, but allow space in the market for new rivals to step in.
Why don't music acts price their tickets high enough to make ticket touting irrelevant?	Because the groups worry that their fans will feel they are being 'ripped off'; much better to blame the touts.
How should a new, independent pizza business set its prices?	It should find out customer reactions to the brand and the product – and set prices accordingly.

12.5 Pricing strategies – evaluation

Economists think of price as a neutral factor within a marketplace. Many businesses would disagree, especially those selling consumer goods and services. The reason is that consumer psychology can be heavily influenced by price. A '3p off' sticker makes people reach for the Mars bars, but '50% off' might make people wonder whether they are old stock or have suffered in the sun; they are *too* cheap.

When deciding on the price of a brand new product, marketing managers have many options. Pricing high may generate too few sales to keep retailers happy to stock the product. Yet, pricing too low carries even more dangers. Large companies know there are no safe livings to be made selling cheap jeans, cheap cosmetics or cheap perfumes.

If there is a key to successful pricing, it is to keep it in line with the overall marketing strategy. When Häagen-Dazs launched in the UK at prices more than double those of its competitors, many predicted failure. In fact, the pricing was in line with the image of adult, luxury indulgence and Häagen-Dazs soon outsold all other premium ice creams (though today Ben & Jerry's is number one). The worst pricing approach would be to develop an attractively packaged, well-made product and then sell it at a discount to the leading brands. In research, people would welcome it, but deep down they would not trust the product quality. Because psychology is so important to successful pricing, many firms use qualitative research, rather than quantitative, to obtain the necessary psychological insights.

Key terms

Loss leader: pricing a product below cost in order to attract further, profitable business. Sony did this at the launch of the PS3 and the PS4 – bring customers in who will then buy accessories and software.

Price elasticity: a measurement of the extent to which a product's demand changes when its price is changed.

Price sensitive: when customer demand for a product reacts sharply to a price change (that is, demand is highly price elastic).

Pricing tactics: short-term pricing responses to opportunities or threats.

12.6 Workbook

Revision questions

(35 marks; 35 minutes)

1 Explain why price is fundamental to a firm's revenues. (3)

2 Look at Figure 12.1. Outline two factors that would affect the 'psychologically right price range' for a new Samsung phone. (4)

3 Explain how the actions of Nike could affect the footwear prices set by Adidas. (3)

4 Look at Table 12.1, on the price sensitivity of products, brands and services. Think of two more examples of highly price-sensitive and two examples of not-very-price-sensitive products, services or brands. (4)

5 Explain the difference between pricing strategy and pricing tactics. (2)

6 For each of the following, decide whether the pricing strategy should be skimming or penetration. Briefly explain your reasoning.

   a) Richard Branson's Virgin group launches the world's first space tourism service (you are launched in a rocket, spend time weightless in space, watch the world go round, then come back to earth). (4)

   b) Kellogg's launches a new range of sliced breads for families who are in a hurry. (4)

   c) The first robotic washing machine is launched. It washes, dries and irons the clothes – and places them in neat piles. (4)

7 Is a price-elastic product likely to be priced competitively or on a cost-plus basis? Explain your reasoning. (3)

8 Outline two circumstances in which a business may decide to use predatory pricing. (4)

Data response 1

On 1 February 2014, Tesco Price Check provided the information given in Table 12.3 on the prices of shampoo brands. Study the table and then answer the questions that follow.

Product description	Tesco price (£)	Asda price (£)
Tresemmé Instant Refresh Dry Shampoo 200 ml	4.99	5.00
Pantene Volume & Body 250 ml	2.89	2.68
Head & Shoulders Classic 250 ml	2.99	2.79
Vosene Original 250 ml	1.79	2.00
John Frieda Full Repair 250 ml	5.89	5.89
Own-label* Baby 500 ml	1.00	1.00
Own-label* Budget Shampoo 1000 ml	0.40	0.40
Bob Martin Dog Shampoo 250 ml	–	3.48

*Own-label means the supermarket's own brand.

Table 12.3 Prices of shampoo brands in January 2014

Questions (30 marks; 30 minutes)

1 Explain why it may be fair to describe Vosene shampoo as a price-taker. (4)

2 John Frieda shampoo is priced at more than 40 times the level of supermarket budget shampoos (per ml). Assess two reasons why customers may be willing to pay such a high price. (8)

3 Examine the position of the long-established brand Head & Shoulders within the UK market for shampoo. What pricing strategy does it seem to be using and why may it be possible to use this approach? (6)

4 Assess whether dogs should have 'better' shampoo than kids. (12)

Data response 2

New product pricing strategy

Before the October 2012 launch of Maruti Suzuki's new Alto 800, the company set itself a target unprecedented in the history of the Indian automobile industry. Maruti called it the '50/20/10 target'. It meant aiming for 50,000 test drives and 20,000 deliveries – all within the first 10 days.

To make it harder to achieve, the car market was slipping backwards in autumn 2012 as the Indian economy grappled with 10 per cent inflation and high interest rates. With such high inflation, it would have been understandable if Maruti had priced their new Alto model 10 per cent higher than the previous one. Instead it made headlines by launching at 2 per cent below – even though the specification had been upgraded. Prices for the Alto started at £2,500, with £3,400 for the highest spec.

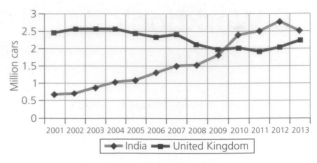

Figure 12.7 Market for new cars: India v. UK (source: www.oica.net)

Figure 12.6 The Maruti Alto 800

On the morning of the tenth day, Maruti Suzuki's Managing Executive Officer for marketing and sales announced: 'We crossed all three targets. We launched in 821 cities and 1,130 outlets.' That morning, the new Alto had crossed 27,000 bookings and 10,200 deliveries.

Getting the pricing right was critical because Maruti, for so long the dominant force in India with a 45 per cent market share, had lost three percentage points in the previous year. This was partly because the Alto model, which had once sold 35,000 cars a month, had seen its sales slip to 18,000 by early 2012. And with small cars such as this taking 70 per cent of the Indian car market, the Alto launch was vital.

When asked whether this pricing might spark a price war, Maruti suggested that it was simply making use of its competitive advantage. An independent auto analyst confirmed that 'Maruti enjoys huge economies of scale, even at lower margins. No other company can do that.'

The reduced price is intensifying competition in the market in what Abdul Majeed, Partner at PwC, calls the 'volume game'. He explains that Maruti's pricing may initially spark a price war, but it is important to develop the market three or four years down the line, as it would generate high volumes. 'If you can't sell 200,000 to 300,000 cars, you can't make money', he says. In the short term, margins will feel the pinch, but in the long run the move will be beneficial, as small cars still make up 70 per cent of the Indian car market. 'Car makers will have to take the risk', says Majeed.

A year on, in September 2013, the Alto was India's top-selling car and Maruti's market share had recovered from 41 to 43.5 per cent since the same month in 2012.

Questions (25 marks, 30 minutes)

1 Examine one way in which market trends in new car sales in India (see Figure 12.7) might have influenced the pricing decision for the new Alto 800. (5)

2 Assess two possible implications for the Indian car market if Maruti's pricing does 'spark a price war'. (8)

3 Assess whether Maruti was wise to adopt a penetration pricing strategy for its new Alto model. (12)

Extended writing

1 At a supermarket, a Mars Bar is priced at 79p and a pack of three at £1. From the point of view of the consumer and the producer, evaluate whether both these prices can be right. (20)

2 Research the launch prices and sales of Sony's PS4 and the Microsoft One in 2013/2014. Evaluate whether pricing was the key reason for Sony's sales success. (20)

13 Distribution

> **Definition**
>
> Distribution is about availability (how to get the product to the right place for customers to make their purchases). It includes physical or online distribution availability and visibility.

Linked to: The market, Ch 2; Branding and promotion, Ch 11; Pricing strategies, Ch 12; Marketing strategy, Ch 15.

13.1 Introduction to distribution

Within the framework of the marketing mix, distribution is known as 'place'. This can be unhelpful because it suggests that manufacturers can place their products where they like (for example, at the entrance of a Waitrose store). The real world is not like that. Obtaining distribution in Waitrose is a dream for most small producers, and a very hard dream to turn into reality. For new firms in particular, place is the toughest of the 4Ps.

Persuading retailers to stock a product is never easy. For the retailer, the key issues are **opportunity cost** and risk. As shelf space is limited, stocking a particular chocolate bar probably means scrapping another; but which one should the retailer choose? What revenue will be lost? The other consideration is risk. A new, low-calorie chocolate bar may be a slimmer's delight, but high initial sales might slip, leaving the shopkeeper with boxes of slow-moving stock.

For the manufacturer, an important aspect of distribution strategy is whether your product is a planned purchase or whether it is bought on impulse. **Impulse purchasing** implies the need to maximise distribution – and to make sure of great displays, such as close to the till. So if you are selling Tic Tac mints or strawberry lip balm, you incentivise the retailers by offering them fat profit margins, and help them by giving out display units to show off the product to its best advantage. With a planned purchase, distribution and display become less important because the customer will come to look for the item they want. Therefore, the supplier doesn't need to offer such generous retail profit margins; in a sense, the product is selling itself. A good example might be a Flymo lawnmower or BaByliss hair straighteners.

13.2 Choosing appropriate distributors

When a new business wants to launch its first product, a key question to consider is the distribution channel: in other words, how the product passes from producer to consumer. Should the product be sold directly, as with pick-your-own strawberries? Or via a **wholesaler**, then a retailer, as with crisps bought from your local shop? This decision will affect every aspect of the business in the future, especially its profit.

Manufacturers must decide on the right outlets for their own product. If Chanel chooses to launch a new perfume, 'Alexa', backed by Alexa Chan, priced at £69.99, controlling distribution is vital. The company wants it to be sold in a smart location where elegant sales staff can persuade customers of its wonderful scent and gorgeous packaging. If Superdrug or Morrisons want to stock the brand, Chanel will try hard to find reasons to say no.

Yet the control is often in the hands not of the producer, but of the retailer. If you come up with a wonderful idea for a brand new ice cream, how would you get distribution for it? The freezers in corner shops are usually owned by Wall's and Mars, so they frown upon independent products being stocked in 'their' space. To the retailer, every foot of shop floor space has an actual cost (the rental value) and an opportunity cost (the cost of missing out on the profits that could be generated by selling other goods). In effect, then, your brand new ice cream is likely to stay on the drawing board because obtaining distribution will be too large a **barrier to entry** to this market.

> **'Establish channels for different target markets and aim for efficiency, control and adaptability.'**
>
> Philip Kotler, marketing guru

13.3 Distribution channels

There are five main channels of distribution.

Traditional physical channel

Small producers find it hard to achieve distribution in big chains such as B&Q or Sainsbury's, so they usually sell to wholesalers who, in turn, sell to small independent shops. The profit mark-up applied by the 'middleman' adds to the final retail price, but a small producer cannot afford to deliver individually to lots of small shops.

Direct to retailer

Larger producers cut out the middleman (the wholesaler) and sell directly to retail chains, from Boots to Tesco. This is more cost-effective, but exposes the seller to tough negotiation from the retail chains on prices and credit terms. Large retailers also demand that manufacturers pay for special offers and price promotions, from BOGOFs (buy one get one free) to boxes of Maltesers for £1.

Be your own retailer

Although Apple, Chanel and Burberry are known for iconic product design, they also love to control their distribution, display and sales by running their own shops. In China, Burberry decided to buy out its retail partner so that it could get closer to the market.

> **'Get closer than ever to your customers. So close that you tell them what they need well before they realise it themselves.'**
>
> Steve Jobs, founder of Apple Inc.

Direct online

Using this channel of distribution, the producer sells directly to the consumer. Manufacturers can do this through mail order or – far more likely today – through a website. This ensures that the producer keeps 100 per cent of the product's selling price. The benefit of the direct distribution channel is that the producer's higher profits can finance more spending on advertising, website development or new product development.

Online retail

Small firms often lack the ability and/or the finance to build a successful **e-commerce** sales platform. So it can make sense to piggy-back on an established platform such as eBay in the West or the amazingly successful TaoBao in China. TaoBao has more than two million businesses using the site to sell to the hundreds of millions of China's online shoppers. TaoBao is one part of Jack Ma's Alibaba business that had sales, in 2014, of $420 billion – dwarfing Amazon and eBay combined.

Real business

In 2013, internet sales of groceries rose by 19 per cent according to market research agency Kantar. By comparison, sales from grocery shops only rose by 2 per cent. This trend towards online shopping has been developing for ten years and may be accelerating. In the four days leading up to Christmas 2013, 15 per cent of all grocery sales were online. No wonder that Morrisons, the only UK grocery chain with no online presence, was rapidly losing market share. In (belated) response, Morrisons started its first online deliveries in a test market in Warwickshire in January 2014. The same company proved extraordinarily slow to spot the success of smaller, urban grocery outlets such as Tesco Metro.

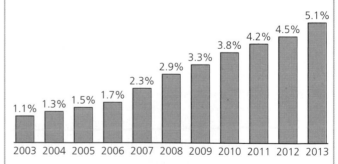

Figure 13.1 E-commerce share of UK grocery spending, 2003–2013 (source: Kantar Worldpanel, 'Shopping for Groceries', 6 August 2013)

13.4 Changes in distribution to reflect social trends

Online distribution

A company such as Supergroup plc (owner of the Superdry brand) has retail outlets in many countries but not all. They might sell 100 jackets to a South American wholesaler, who then sells them to shops in Rio and Caracas. If the retail price is to be the equivalent of £100, they may need to sell to the wholesaler for £35. This will create the chain:

Figure 13.2 Prices charged at each stage of the distribution chain

So although it is a Superdry product with the intellectual property owned by Supergroup plc, the company only gets £35 per jacket, while the wholesaler makes £15 and the retailer gets £50 (clothing retailers usually work on a 100 per cent mark-up). How much better, then, for Supergroup if a shopper in Rio simply buys the item from the Superdry website. They can get £100 for the jacket instead of £35.

From the consumer's point of view, there are also huge benefits from purchasing online. Most shops stock a relatively narrow range of sizes, aimed at the 'average' 65 per cent of the market. People bigger or smaller than that will struggle in the high street. This is understandable because the wider the range of sizes you keep on the shelves or in the stockroom, the fewer the number of items you'll have the room to display or store: a classic issue of opportunity cost. For an online seller with a warehouse in a cheap-rent part of town, it's not an issue. The same goes for customers with a quirky taste in music, or books or vintage clothes: these days there is a long tail of small firms, each specialising in minority tastes too small to make a profit in the high street.

> 'Distribution has really changed. You can make a record with a laptop in the morning and have it up on YouTube in the afternoon and be a star overnight.'

Bonnie Raitt, singer

Changing from product to service

Is there a difference between distributing a service compared with distributing a product? Largely the answer is no. Your grandparents bought insurance from 'The Man from the Pru', who knocked on doors monthly to collect insurance premiums from clients. Your parents (when younger) bought insurance directly over the phone or by going into a Prudential Insurance high street shop. Today they buy insurance from a combination of online (direct with the company or via the 'retailers': Moneysupermarket.com, Comparethemarket.com and so on) and by phone. In other words, selling services has been affected by modern online trends as much as anything else.

Of course there are some services that may never be affected significantly by online distribution because they are about physical experiences. So it's hard to see how clubbing, staying at a hotel, going on holiday or taking your partner to a restaurant can change much over time. The only change is to the way such experiences are booked, and much of that is already online.

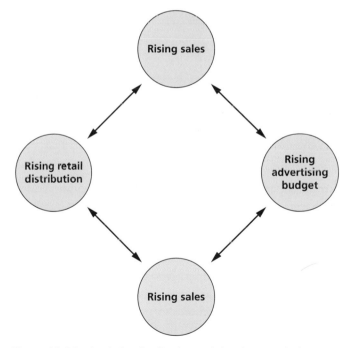

Figure 13.3 Logic chain: distribution and the virtuous circle

Five whys and a how

Questions	Answers
Why is it hard for a new company to achieve retail distribution for its products?	No retailers have gaps in their shelves, so accepting a new product means dropping an existing one, risking lost revenue.
Why might it be a mistake for a company to seek 100 per cent distribution for its products?	Long-term sales success relies on having a clear, positive image. Nike doesn't want its latest sportswear sold cheaply at Sports Direct; the short-term sales would be at a long-term cost.
Why do most modern firms pursue multi-channel distribution strategies?	Because today's consumers sometimes want traditional, browsing shopping and sometimes want speedy online purchasing from home.
Why may it be a profitable strategy for a producer to offer extra-high profit margins to retailers?	The bigger the slice of a sale taken by the retailer, the less there is for the producer, but high margins attract higher distribution levels and better display at the point-of-sale (e.g. right by the cash till); so sales volumes are boosted.
Why are online grocery sales still so low (with a market share of well below 10 per cent)?	The problem is probably not on the supply side, as Ocado, Sainsbury's and others are efficient and easy-to-use; it must be that most people still want to go and look and feel before buying.
How might a brand new producer of hair straighteners gain retail distribution?	They would have to persuade shops that there is something innovative about the product and therefore worth stocking (or offer higher profit margins than rivals).

13.5 Distribution – evaluation

Place is of particular importance in business because it can represent a major barrier to entry, especially for new small firms. The practical constraint on the amount of shop-floor space makes it hard for new products to gain acceptance, unless they are genuinely innovative. Therefore, existing producers of branded goods can become quite complacent, with little serious threat from new competition.

Famously, in the nineteenth century, Ralph Waldo Emerson said: 'If a man can make a better mousetrap, though he builds his house in the woods the world will make a beaten path to his door.' In other words, if the product is good enough, customers will come and find you. In a modern competitive world, though, the vast majority of products are not that exciting or different from others. So it is crucial to provide customers with convenient access to your products and/or shelf space in an eye-catching location. Getting products into the right place should not be taken for granted.

Key terms

Barrier to entry: factors that make it hard for new firms to break into an existing market (for example, strong brand loyalty to the current market leaders).

E-commerce: literally, electronic commerce – carried out online.

Impulse purchasing: buying in an unplanned way (for example, going to a shop to buy a paper, but coming out with a Mars bar and a Diet Coke).

Long tail: the huge number of tiny businesses appealing to minority tastes that can find a profitable existence online because they can target the whole planet, not just the local area.

Opportunity cost: the cost of missing out on the next best alternative when making a decision (or when committing resources).

Wholesaler: the middleman between the producer and retailers, who breaks bulk down from container lorry-loads into manageable parcels, such as a case of 12.

13.6 Workbook

Revision questions

(30 marks; 30 minutes)

1 Outline the meaning of the term 'place'. (2)

2 Explain in your own words why it may be that 'place is the toughest of the 4Ps'. (4)

3 Outline what you think are appropriate distribution channels for:

   a) a new F1 racing game for mobiles and tablets

   b) a new adventure holiday company focusing on wealthy 19–32 year olds. (6)

4 Retailers such as WHSmith charge manufacturers a rent on prime store space, such as the shelving near to the cash tills.

   a) How might a firm work out whether it is worthwhile to pay the extra? (3)

   b) Why may new small firms find it hard to pay rents such as these? (3)

5 Explain in your own words what is meant by the phrase 'a better mousetrap'. (3)

6 Outline three reasons for the success of direct online distribution in recent years. (5)

7 Explain why modern businesses seek 'multi-channel distribution'. (4)

Data response 1

Getting distribution right

Secondary data can be hugely helpful to new companies looking for distribution of their first products. A company launching the first 'Kitten Milk' product has to decide where to focus its efforts. Where does cat food sell? Is it in pet shops, in corner shops or in supermarkets? Desk research company BMRB reports that, whereas 65 per cent of dog owners shop for pet food at supermarkets, 81 per cent of cat owners do the same. A different source (TNS) puts the cat food market size at £829 million. TNS also shows that the market is rising in value by around 2.5 per cent a year.

Further secondary data shows that pet food shoppers spend only 80 per cent of the amount they intend to when they go to a shop. This is because poor distribution stops them finding what they want. And 50 per cent of shoppers will not return to the same store after being let down twice by poor availability.

Questions (20 marks; 25 minutes)

1 What is meant by the term 'market size'? (2)

2 a) The year 1 sales target for Kitten Milk is £5 million. Calculate what share of the total market for cat food that would represent. (4)

   b) Explain why it might be hard to persuade retailers to stock a product with that level of market share. (4)

3 The marketing manager for Kitten Milk is planning to focus distribution efforts on getting the brand placed in pet shops. Assess whether this seems wise. (10)

Data response 2

An arm's length from desire

From its origins in America in 1886, Coca-Cola has been a marketing phenomenon. It was the world's first truly global brand; it virtually invented the red, jolly Christmas Santa, and its bottle design (1919) was the first great piece of packaging design.

Yet a 1950 *Time* magazine article quoted another piece of marketing genius: 'Always within an arm's length of desire.' The marketing experts at Atlanta (home of Coca-Cola) realised nearly 60 years ago that sales of Coca-Cola were limited mainly by availability. Especially on a hot day, a cold Coke would be desired by almost anyone who had it an arm's length away.

This led the company to develop a distribution strategy based on maximum availability, maximum in-store visibility and therefore maximum impulse purchase.

From then on, Coca-Cola targeted four main types of distribution:

1 in supermarkets and grocers

2 in any kiosk in a location based on entertainment (for example, a bowling alley or a cinema)

3 in any canteen, bar or restaurant

4 in a vending machine near you; automatic vending proved one of the most valuable ways of building the market until worries about healthy

eating saw them banned in schools; a vending machine is the ultimate barrier to entry.

Overall, though, the Coca-Cola approach to distribution set out in 1950 is what most companies still try to do today.

Questions (30 marks; 35 minutes)

1 What is meant by the term 'distribution'? (2)

2 Explain how a vending machine can be a 'barrier to entry' to new competitors. (4)

3 Explain what the text means by the difference between 'maximum availability' and 'maximum visibility'. (4)

4 From all that you know about today's Coke, Diet Coke and Coke Zero, evaluate whether Coca-Cola's distribution strategy was the single most important factor in the firm's marketing success. (20)

Extended writing

1 Evaluate the proposition that 'internet retailing will mean the death of the high street'. (20)

2 You have just developed a new console game that combines the appeal of Candy Crush with the force of Call of Duty. Evaluate how to achieve strong enough distribution to make this product a hit in the UK. (20)

14 Product life cycle and portfolio

Definition

The product life cycle is the theory that all products follow a similar pattern over time, of development, birth, growth, maturity and decline. The product portfolio places brands into a matrix based on market share and market growth.

Linked to: Market research, Ch 3; Pricing strategies, Ch 12; The market, Ch 2; Capacity utilisation, Ch 42.

14.1 What is the product life cycle?

The product life cycle shows the sales of a product over time. When a new product is first launched, sales will usually be slow. This is because the product is not yet known or proven in the market. Retailers may be reluctant to stock the product because it means giving up valuable shelf space to products that may or may not sell. Customers may also be hesitant, waiting until someone else has tried it before they purchase it themselves.

If the product does succeed, then it enters the growth phase of the product life cycle, with new customers buying and existing customers making repeat purchases. However, at some point sales are likely to stabilise; this is known as the maturity phase. This slowing down of the growth of sales might be because competitors have introduced similar products or because the market has now become saturated. Everyone who wants one has bought one, so sales fall back to replacement purchases only.

At some point sales are likely to decline, perhaps because customer tastes have become more sophisticated. So orange squash sales decline as people buy more fresh orange juice. A decline in sales may also be because competitors have launched a more successful model or the original creator has improved its own product; for example, the iPad drawing sales from the iPhone.

The five key stages of a product's life cycle are known as: development, introduction, growth, maturity and decline. These can be illustrated on a product life cycle diagram. The typical stages in a product's life are shown in Figure 14.1.

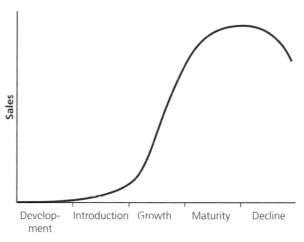

Figure 14.1 The product life cycle

14.2 What is the value of the product life cycle?

The product life cycle model helps managers to plan their marketing activities. Marketing managers will need to adjust their marketing mix at different stages of the product life cycle, as outlined below.

- In the introduction phase, the promotion may focus on making customers aware that a new product exists; in the maturity phase, it may focus more on highlighting the difference between your product and competitors that have arrived since its introduction.
- At the beginning of the life cycle, a technologically advanced product may be launched with a high price (think of the iPhone); over time the price may fall as

newer models are being launched. By considering the requirements of each stage of the life cycle, marketing managers may adjust their marketing activities accordingly.

Managers know that the length of the phases of the life cycle cannot easily be predicted. They will vary from one product to another and this means the marketing mix will need to be altered at different times. For example, a product may be a fad and therefore the overall life of the product will be quite short. Many fashions are popular only for one season and some films are popular only for a matter of weeks. Other products have very long life cycles. The first manufactured cigarettes went on sale in Britain in 1873. By chance, sales hit their peak (120 billion) exactly 100 years later. Since 1973 sales have gently declined.

It is also important to distinguish between the life cycle of a product category and the life cycle of a particular brand. Sales of wine are growing, but a brand that was once the biggest seller (Hirondelle) has virtually disappeared as wine buyers have become more sophisticated. Similarly, confectionery is a mature market but particular brands are at different stages in their life cycles: Mars bars are in maturity while Maltesers are in the growth stage, even though the brand is 80 years old!

▌14.3 Extension strategies

The aim of an **extension strategy** is to prevent a decline in the product's sales in the medium-to-long term. The two main variables for basing a new extension strategy are the product itself and the way it is promoted.

	Development	Introduction	Growth	Maturity	Decline
Sales	Zero	Low	Increasing	Growth is slowing	Falling
Costs per unit	High investment in product development but only a few prototypes and test products being produced	High; sales are relatively low but launch costs are high and overheads are spread over very few units	Falling as overheads are spread over more units	Falling as sales are still growing	Low as development costs have been covered and promotional costs are being cut
Product	Prototypes	Likely to be basic	May be modified given initial customer feedback; range may be increased	Depends – may focus on core products and remove poor sellers; may extend brand to new items	Focus on most profitable items
Promotion	As development is nearly finished it may be used to alert customers of the launch	Mainly to raise awareness	Building loyalty	May focus on highlighting the differences with competitors' products	Probably no spending at all
Distribution	Early discussions with retailers will help in finalising the product packaging	May be limited as distributors wait to see customers' reactions	Increasing as more distributors willing to stock and product is rolled out to more markets	May focus on key outlets and more profitable channels	Lower budgets to keep costs down
Price	Not needed	Depends on pricing approach, e.g. high if skimming is adopted; low if penetration is adopted to gain market share	Depends on demand conditions and strategy; e.g. with a skimming strategy, the price may now be lowered to target more segments	May have to drop to maintain competitiveness	Likely to discount to maintain sales

Table 14.1 Examples of how the marketing mix may vary at different stages of the product life cycle

Product

Over the years, detergents such as Persil have had innumerable 'New Improved!' formulations and relaunches. In the past, these offered 'Whiter than ever!' washes, though more recently the trend has been for smaller pack sizes (more concentrated) or presenting the product in tablet rather than loose form. The point is to incorporate new product technology and therefore fight off new brand challengers.

Successful product-based extension strategies include:

- McDonald's, in 2007, relaunching itself with different design (greens rather than red) and a menu featuring more salads, more fruit and coming clean about calories per item
- Innocent Drinks, facing falling sales for their smoothies in 2013/2014, launching 'Super Smoothies' with product claims about their health-giving properties
- Maltesers, stretching the brand by launching Malteaster bunnies and Teasers chocolate bars.

Promotion

Simply running a new advertising campaign or switching from traditional to social media does not comprise an extension strategy. Something more substantial and long term is required. Good examples include the following:

- By targeting a new segment of the market: when sales of Johnson & Johnson's baby powder matured, the company repositioned the product towards adults; sales boomed.
- By developing new uses for the product: the basic technology in hot-air paint strippers, for example, is no different from that in a hairdryer.
- By increasing the usage of a product: Actimel's 'challenge' was for consumers to eat one pot a day for a fortnight – a wonderful way to encourage increased consumption.

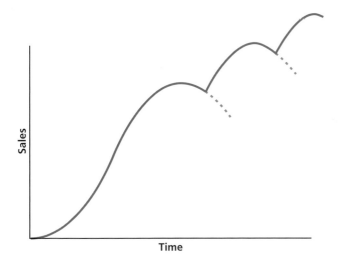

Figure 14.2 The effect of extension strategies

The continued success of products such as Coca-Cola and Kellogg's cornflakes is not just due to luck; it is down to sophisticated marketing techniques that have managed to maintain sales over many years despite fierce competition. The Kellogg's logo is regularly updated, new pack sizes are often introduced, and various competitions and offers are used on a regular basis to keep sales high.

Given the fact that developing a product can involve high costs and that there is a high failure rate of new products, it is not surprising that, if a product is successful, managers will try to prolong its sales for as long as it is profitable. Who would have thought, in the 1880s, that a frothy drink would still be a huge seller more than 125 years later? Clever Coke.

14.4 New product development (NPD)

New product development includes the people and processes involved in turning new ideas into products (or services) ready for launch. It is likely to involve research and development (R&D), market research, product engineering and design, plus expertise in packaging, advertising, pricing and branding. It represents all the activities categorised as 'development' in the product life cycle. Some examples of NPD are so excellent (think iPhone, the PS4 or Snapchat) that their life cycles have a remarkably easy start.

Unfortunately, even consumer giants such as Cadbury and PepsiCo have poor success rates with new product launches. The statistics are hard to find, but it seems that fewer than one in five new products becomes a commercial success. Clearly there must be many reasons why it is hard to create a successful new product, though the single most important is the cautious consumer who would rather buy a trusted product than a new one.

Key influences on successful NPD include:

- a clear understanding of the consumers within a certain market segment, with a special focus on their future needs or wants
- the creativity to be able to see how an everyday problem or issue can be solved innovatively
- enough resources (money and manpower) to be able to develop an idea effectively and market it persuasively.

When a new product succeeds, the consequences can be transformational. Nintendo's Wii U was looking down and out before the launch of Mario Kart 8 saw sales of the hardware rise by 600 per cent in June 2014. So the value of NPD cannot be doubted. A successful new product can create its own new life cycle – giving an entire business a morale and profit boost.

14.5 The product portfolio

Product **portfolio analysis** examines the existing position of a firm's products. This allows the firm to consider its existing position and plan what to do next. There are several different methods of portfolio analysis. One of the best known was developed by the Boston Consulting Group, a management consultancy; it is known as the Boston Matrix.

The Boston Matrix shows the market share of each of the firm's products and the rate of growth of the markets in which they operate. By highlighting the position of each product in terms of market share and market growth, a business can analyse its existing situation and decide what to do next and where to direct its marketing efforts. This model has four categories, as described in Figure 14.3.

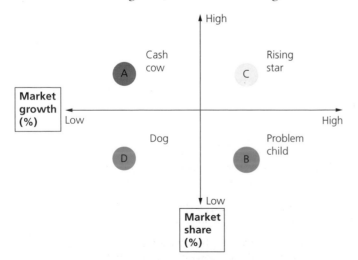

Figure 14.3 Product portfolio: the Boston Matrix

Cash cow: a high share of a slow-growing market

In Figure 14.3, product A has a high market share of a low-growth market. The size of the circle depends on the turnover of the product. This type of product is known as a **cash cow**. An example of a cash cow might be Heinz Baked Beans. The overall market for baked beans is mature and therefore slow growing. Within this market, the Heinz brand has a market share of more than 50 per cent. This type of product generates high profits and cash for the company because sales are relatively high, while the promotional cost per unit is quite low. Heinz can therefore 'milk' cash from baked beans to invest in newer products, such as Heinz Organic Ketchup.

Problem child: a low share of a fast-growing market

Product B, by comparison, is in a high-growth market but has a low market share. This type of product is known as a **problem child** (also called a 'question mark'). A problem child may well provide high profits in the future; the market itself is attractive because it is growing fast and the product could provide high returns if it manages to gain a greater market share. However, the success of such products is by no means certain and that is why they are like problem children: they may grow and prosper or things may go wrong. These products usually need a relatively high level of investment to promote them, get them distributed and keep them going.

Rising star: a high share of a growing market

Rising stars such as product C have a high market share and are selling in a fast-growing market. These products are obviously attractive; they are doing well in a successful market. However, they may well need protecting from competitors' products. Once again, the profits of the cash cows can be used to keep the sales growing. Heinz Organic Soups are in this category. They are very successful, with fast-growing sales, but still need heavy promotion to ensure their success.

Dogs: a low share of a stable or declining market

The fourth category of products is known as **dogs**. These products (like product D in Figure 14.3) have a low share of a low-growth market. They hold little appeal for a firm unless they can be revived. The product or brand will be killed off once its sales slip below the break-even point.

The purpose of product portfolio analysis

Product portfolio analysis aims to examine the existing position of the firm's products. Once this has been done, the managers can plan what to do next. Typically, this will involve four strategies.

1 Building: this involves investment in promotion and distribution to boost sales and is often used with problem children (question marks).

2 Holding: this involves marketing spending to maintain sales and is used with rising star products.

3 Milking: this means taking whatever profits you can without much more new investment and is often used with cash cow products.

4 Divesting: this involves selling off the product and is common with dogs or problem children.

The various strategies chosen will depend on the firm's portfolio of products. If most of the firm's products are cash cows, for example, it needs to develop new products for future growth. If, however, the majority are problem children, then it is in quite a high-risk situation; it needs to try to ensure some products do become stars. If it has too many dogs, then it needs to invest in product development or acquire new brands.

▌Five whys and a how

14.6 Product life cycle and portfolio – evaluation

The product life cycle model and portfolio analysis are important in assessing the firm's current position within the market. They make up an important step in the planning process. However, simply gathering data does not in itself guarantee success. A manager has to interpret the information effectively and then make the right decision. The models show where a business is at the moment; the difficult decisions relate to where the business will be in the future.

Product portfolio analysis is especially useful for larger businesses with many products. It helps a manager to look critically at the firm's product range. Then decisions can be made on how the firm's marketing spending should be divided up between different products. By contrast, the product life cycle is of more help to a small firm with one or two products.

Key terms

Cash cow: a product that has a high share of a low-growth market.

Dog: a product that has a low share of a low-growth market.

Extension strategy: marketing activities used to prevent sales from declining.

Portfolio analysis: an analysis of the market position of the firm's existing products; it is used as part of the marketing planning process.

Problem child: a product that has a small share of a fast-growing market.

Rising star: a product that has a high share of a fast-growing market.

Questions	Answers
Why does growth slide back towards maturity?	Market saturation is one reason (everyone who wants the product has already bought it); the arrival of competition is another.
Why do many extension strategies fail?	Because the business has failed to find a new market position for a new type of customer.
Why do new product launches have such a low success rate?	Because many consumers are locked into patterns of repeat behaviour, such as always buying Cadbury Dairy Milk.
Why may firms struggle to manage their cash flow when their products have short life cycles?	Short life cycles imply a constant need to invest heavily in NPD to develop the next winner to take over from today's fading products.
Why do firms find it useful to use both product life cycle and portfolio analysis?	Because product life cycle helps analyse the progress of a single product, while portfolio analysis looks at all of a firm's products.
How does R&D differ from market research?	R&D is about scientific research and technical development of products or processes; market research is about consumer habits and tastes.

14.7 Workbook

Revision questions

(40 marks; 40 minutes)

1 Identify the different stages of the product life cycle. Give an example of one product or service you consider to be at each stage of the life cycle. (4)

2 Explain what is meant by an 'extension strategy'. (4)

3 'Without new product development every business must die.' Is this true? (6)

4 How is it possible for products such as Barbie to apparently defy the decline phase of the product cycle? (7)

5 What is meant by 'product portfolio analysis'? (3)

6 Distinguish between a cash cow and a rising star in the Boston Matrix. (4)

7 Explain how the Boston Matrix could be used by a business such as Cadbury. (5)

8 Firms should never take decline (or growth) for granted. Therefore, they should never take success (or failure) for granted. Explain why this advice is important if firms are to make the best use of product life cycle theory. (7)

Data response

Monster life cycle

The market for energy drinks is dominated by Red Bull. First launched in 1987, its UK sales have grown steadily to reach £248 million in 2013. With the market for energy drinks still rising at 10–15 per cent per year, many other companies are determined to take their share of this success. The attractions are obvious. Not only are sales rising faster than for soft drinks as a whole, but the price per litre is much higher. On 30 December 2013, Tesco charged 49p for a 330ml can of Coca-Cola and £1.58 for 330ml can of Red Bull.

As Coca-Cola observed the growth of Red Bull during the 'noughties', it resolved to launch its own rivals. First came 'Relentless' in late 2006, which received its first serious promotional push by being given away at the 2007 Reading and Leeds Music Festivals. Since then, it has focused on sponsoring 'extreme' sports. As shown in Figure 14.4, Relentless has achieved significant sales, though sales fell by £5 million between 2011 and 2013.

Perhaps sensing that Relentless was not the answer, in 2010 Coca-Cola took over the distribution of a US energy drink called Monster. The brand holds a 35 per cent share of the $30 billion US market for energy drinks, though there have been questions raised in

Congress about the safety of the product. Energy drinks are heavy in three ingredients: caffeine, taurine and sugar. In fact, the caffeine level is no higher than in coffee, but the combination of ingredients is thought by some to place it in between alcoholic and soft drinks.

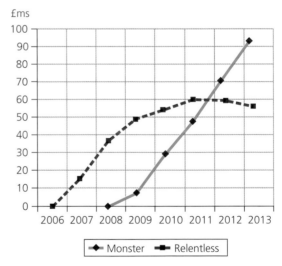

Figure 14.4 Energy drink life cycles

Is Monster a real challenger to Red Bull in the UK? With a sales increase of 30 per cent in 2013 compared with 6 per cent for Red Bull, Coca-Cola can hope. But the risk must remain that the Monster life cycle will end up following that of Relentless. Time will tell.

Questions (25 marks; 30 minutes)

1 Briefly explain the meaning of the term product life cycle. (3)

2 Give the stage of the product life cycle for each of the following in 2013:

   a) Relentless

   b) Monster. (2)

3 Assess two possible extension strategies Coca-Cola might use with Relentless in coming years. (8)

4 Assess the factors that will influence the future life cycle of Monster in the UK. (12)

Extended writing

1 After many decades of success in the UK, breakfast cereal manufacturers are suffering from a decline in the market size as consumers want to eat breakfast on the move instead of in the kitchen. Evaluate a suitable extension strategy for a cereal producer such as Kellogg's. (20)

2 Cadbury has a wide range of chocolate brands including Dairy Milk, Flake, Crunchie, Twirl and Fudge. It wishes to push its UK market share from 34 per cent to 38 per cent within the next two years. Evaluate the extent to which the Boston Matrix might help in achieving this goal. (20)

15 Marketing strategy

Definition

Marketing strategy is a carefully evaluated plan for future marketing activity that balances company objectives, available resources and market opportunities. It is implemented through the marketing mix.

Linked to: Market research, Ch 3; Market positioning, Ch 4; Product and service design, Ch 10; Pricing strategies, Ch 12.

15.1 What are the keys to a successful marketing strategy?

A strategy is the plan of the medium-to-long-term actions required to achieve the company goals or targets. Selecting the best marketing strategy means finding a fit between the company objectives, customer requirements and the activities of competitors.

The aim of this planning is to shape the company's activities and products to generate the best returns for the business. Marketing strategy is about adding value. It takes advantage of any unique selling points. It helps the business to identify the right mix between design, function, image and service.

Strategy is about the future

The term 'strategy' implies looking to the future. It is important not to look at what is working well now but at what the future prospects are. Toyota recognised that there was a growing interest in environmental issues. It started to invest in the production of hybrid cars. Although requiring significant investment with no sure return, Toyota executives felt that this was the way forward. The move was highly successful, with global sales of more than four million cars by the end of 2014.

Strategy must be achievable

Strategy is concerned with what is possible, not just desirable. It must take into account market potential and company resources. The company needs to recognise its own limitations and potential. It also needs to consider economic and social circumstances. If the world economy is weakening, firms will be much more cautious about entering new export markets. If the home market is stagnating, businesses may well concentrate on lower-priced 'value' products.

Strategy is company specific

Each company will have a different marketing strategy. The strategy selected will reflect the individual circumstances of the business. Within the same industry, one company may be aiming to increase market share while another looks for cost reductions in order to compete on price. The tyre industry is a good example of this. The market leaders were faced with increasing price competition from developing countries. They had to develop new marketing strategies. Their responses differed: Goodyear reduced costs; Michelin put its effort into innovation and widened its product range; Pirelli decided to concentrate on the market for luxury and speed.

Marketing strategy is the marketing plan of action that:

- contributes to the achievement of company objectives
- finds the best fit between company objectives, available resources and market possibilities
- looks to the future
- is carefully thought out
- is realistic.

Real business

New strategy at Morrisons

Faced with a 7 per cent decline in like-for-like sales in the early months of 2014, supermarket chain Morrisons announced a major switch in marketing strategy. For several years leading up to May 2014, Morrisons had focused TV advertising on its concept of 'Market Street' – focusing on the fresh food stalls at the entrance to the stores. Presented by TV stars Ant and Dec, this advertising campaign was suddenly thrown to one side. Now the focus was to be 'I'm cheaper', with the new slogan backed by the media announcement of 'biggest ever' price cuts.

Cynics regarded the announcement of this new marketing strategy as a desperate attempt by Chief Executive Dalton Phillips to keep his job. Others saw it as a logical response to the market share gains achieved by the German discounters Aldi and Lidl. Phillips told the press: 'We are confident that these meaningful and permanent reductions in our prices will resonate strongly with consumers.'

15.2 Marketing strategy for mass markets

To succeed in a mass market, a brand needs to be differentiated in a way that makes it interesting but not niche. In the UK chocolate market, Cadbury Dairy Milk is the dominant force, with annual sales of £500 million. But Galaxy is also a mass market force, with sales of just over £200 million. Cadbury's marketing strategy is easy: it simply promotes Dairy Milk as an iconic brand – everyone knows where it sits at the heart of the chocolate market. Mars (owners of Galaxy) positions Galaxy as special and smooth, but has to beware of making it a special-occasion-only brand (lots of prestige, but much lower sales than a brand for everyday).

If a brand succeeds in the mass market, it can enjoy:

- distribution levels of close to 100 per cent (i.e. all shops want to stock it)
- control over advertising and promotion (retailers cannot force the market leader's hand); in the year to 30 June 2014, Cadbury spent nothing on Dairy Milk, while Galaxy had a spend of more than £10 million; Dairy Milk sales rose 5.5 per cent by value during that period
- a degree of control over pricing, though it can never get too greedy – because it is the mass market.

'There is no victory at bargain basement prices.'

Dwight D. Eisenhower, US General, then President

15.3 Marketing strategy for niche markets

A niche within the confectionery market is for chewing gum. Some niches have several brands competing on equal terms, but the £300 million UK chewing gum market is dominated by Wrigley. In the year to June 2014, Wrigley (owned by Mars) had a 92.5 per cent market share! When Cadbury decided to break into this niche, it launched a range of different flavours under the brand name Trident. Cadbury boasted that it would be looking for £20 million of sales growth each year for the first five years. As you can see in Figure 15.1, the launch year of 2007 was a success, but if Cadbury looked back at this venture they would realise that it was a waste of their money and time.

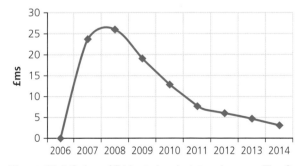

Figure 15.1 Sales of Trident chewing gum (source: *The Grocer* magazines, 2007-2014)

Often, marketing within niche markets needs a patient approach. Customers within niches are often experts on the product category and may be very choosy. So a great deal of marketing focuses on reinforcing the distinctive characteristics of each product. In the super-premium sector of the ice cream market, Ben & Jerry's combination of quirky flavours and social responsibility has helped it win a battle against Häagen-Dazs.

15.4 Marketing strategy for business to consumer markets (B2C)

The key to successful marketing is that every element in the mix should be co-ordinated towards delivering a marketing strategy that fits in with the marketing objectives. This is relatively easy to think through in relation to a business that targets the consumer (B2C). Whether it is a product or service, the consumer expects a reality that conforms to the image and therefore delivers value for money. In many cases, the image itself may be at the heart of the proposition. If so, keeping that image vibrant and distinctive may be a critical focus of the marketing mix.

> **'Don't sell the steak, sell the sizzle.'**

Advice on advertising from Elmer Wheeler, US business writer

15.5 Marketing strategy for business to business markets (B2B)

B2B means selling to other businesses, be they retail distributors or businesses that have no direct connection with the public, such as a chemical refinery or a sawmill. The key aspect of B2B marketing strategy is that there tend to be different priorities. Consumers buy with a lot of emotion. We love Cadbury because it was a big treat as a kid; we love Apple because it makes us look cool (and wealthy!). Businesses try to buy with no emotion whatever. They want to buy the best product for the best price with the best and most reliable service. So glossy advertising becomes less important. The key is understanding the business customer's needs – and meeting them.

A producer of sandwiches for the consumer market might gain a huge order to feed the staff daily at a nearby sawmill employing 800 people. This B2B order carries the financial disadvantage that the customer will want to pay on credit (perhaps 60 days), which hurts the supplier's cash flow. It also switches the marketing priorities. Instead of smiley customer service being a priority, the sandwiches have to be delivered by a certain time, to a specified quality – and there will be no acceptable excuses for failure.

B2B and the marketing mix

- In some cases companies will be selling **homogenous goods** to other businesses, e.g. 10 litres of white paint or 5,000 light switches. This will make price the most important element in the mix.
- A business such as Rolls-Royce Motors needs thick, blemish-free soft leather for making the car seats; in this case, product will be the key to successful sales.
- Nissan UK wants its most important suppliers right next to its Sunderland car factory, so that they can deliver on a just-in-time basis (see Chapter 43). This makes place the most important part of the mix.
- Unless you are an iconic brand, such as Marmite, to keep shelf space in big supermarket chains requires producer/suppliers to fund regular price or 'BOGOF' promotions. In this case, promotion is the key.

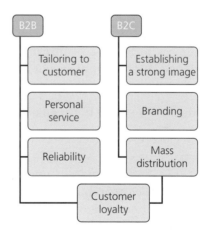

Figure 15.2 Logic chain: *B2B* v. *B2C*

15.6 How businesses develop customer loyalty

Customer loyalty implies more than repeat purchase. It suggests a real emotional connection, as a football supporter might have with his or her team. That connection may be based on something like love, or on faith, as in 'I trust Colgate'. Other connections may be a bit looser, but still important, as with liking to wear Nike or eat Nando's.

The heart of this connection has to be the product/service itself. Going to Nando's is partly about the menu, partly about the quality of the food and partly about the relaxed, youthful but efficient service. You go out feeling better than when you went in. So you come back. The starting point, therefore, is to really study your customers – and make sure that every aspect of the customer experience works for them.

> **'The first step in exceeding your customer's expectations is to know those expectations.'**

Roy H. Williams, author and marketing consultant

Yet customer loyalty is about much more than the product. It is often said that, in blind tests, people prefer Pepsi to Coke. Yet Coke outsells Pepsi 5–1 in the UK. In this case, the emotional connection is probably one established in childhood: Coke manages to persuade kids that Coke is associated with Christmas, summer holidays, special occasions and happiness generally. That is highly skilful (if manipulative) advertising and promotion.

In the short term, marketing may be about shifting products; in the long term, it is usually rooted in creating the right image to appeal to the right target market. This is why qualitative research is so widely used by firms.

> **'There is only one boss. The customer. And he can fire everyone in the company from the chairman on down, simply by spending his money somewhere else.'**

Sam Walton, founder of Walmart

15.7 Marketing strategy – evaluation

The most important marketing strategies are the long-lived ones. 'Have a break, have a KitKat' started in the early 1990s and served well for 20 years. It not only became a promotional strategy but also influenced the product as well, making multi-packs more relevant, as people could hand out KitKats to co-workers or kids. Even longer lived is Audi's phrase, used worldwide, 'Vorsprung durch Technik' ('advancement through technology'), which was first used in 1982 in UK advertising. In 1982, Audi was just a producer of mass market cars; brand owner Volkswagen's 1990s decision to push the brand upmarket fitted in with the positive imagery created by the advertising.

Brand owners and their advertising agencies are always looking for a strategy 'with legs' – that can last decades rather than years. Weak exam answers see marketing as a series of quick fixes; marketing strategy should always be seen as a key part of far-sighted business practice.

> ### Key terms
>
> **Homogenous goods:** these have no points of differentiation and therefore each one is the same as every other (making competition focus on price).
>
> **Product differentiation:** the extent to which consumers perceive your brand as being different from others.

Five whys and a how

Questions	Answers
Why is the marketing mix such an important part of marketing strategy?	Whereas the strategy is the background thinking, the mix is how you put those thoughts into a plan of action through product, price, promotion and place.
Why is strategy always about the future?	Because it is a thinking process about what needs to happen next. It may draw lessons from the past, but its direction is the future.
Why is strategy always 'company specific'?	Because every company is different, with a different culture and different customer expectations.
Why may Trident gum disappear from shops fairly soon (see Figure 15.1)?	Its sales path is so dismal that it will surely soon be withdrawn from sale (it's a 'dog').
Why may marketing B2B require a different strategy to B2C?	Because business customers care less about brands/images and more about reliability and good service.
How might Aldi or Lidl act to build long-term customer loyalty?	Keep working frantically on having the lowest prices yet good quality; switching strategy to posher, carpeted stores would be a big mistake.

15.8 Workbook

Revision questions

(35 marks; 35 minutes)

1 What is marketing strategy? (2)

2 What is a unique selling point? Give two examples. (4)

3 Explain how one of the following products is differentiated from its rivals:

   a) Marathon chocolate bar

   b) Microsoft Xbox One

   c) Heinz Tomato Ketchup. (4)

4 Outline two pieces of quantitative data that might help a business develop its marketing strategy. (4)

5 Why is it important for a firm to examine its internal resources before deciding on a strategy? (3)

6 How does marketing strategy relate to the objectives of a business? (4)

7 Outline two advantages of niche marketing over mass marketing. (4)

8 Give three reasons why a large firm may wish to enter a niche market. (3)

9 Explain why small firms may be better at spotting and reacting to new niche-market opportunities? (3)

10 Outline two reasons why average prices in niche markets tend to be higher than those charged in most mass markets. (4)

Data response 1

Morrisons' marketing strategy

In the 12 weeks to 30 March 2014, sales at UK grocery discounter Aldi rose by 35.3 per cent, while at rival Morrisons they fell by 3.8 per cent. This compounded a wretched two-year period for Morrisons – the worst since Dalton Phillips took over as chief executive in January 2010 (see Figure 15.3). On 8 May 2014, the *Daily Telegraph* reported that:

> 'The supermarket chain slashed the price of 1,200 lines by 17 per cent last week to counter the rise of the discounters and to reignite its two-year attempt to report like-for-like sales growth. "I'm very confident we are doing the right things," Mr Philips said. "My job is to make big, bold decisions. The proof will be when there are more items in more baskets; how could it not be the right strategy to tackle this on price?"
>
> Sainsbury's outgoing chief executive, Justin King, accused Morrisons of "playing catch-up" in lowering prices and said customers were enticed by ethically sourced products rather than simply price.'

Later, Phillips said that shareholders would 'hold our feet in the fire' if the price-cutting strategy proved unsuccessful, but he was convinced that this was the right long-term positioning for Morrisons.

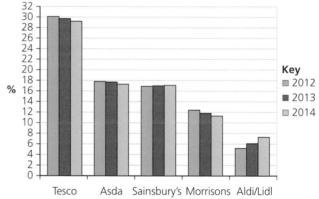

Figure 15.3 UK grocery market share, 2012–2014 (source: Kantar Worldpanel)

Questions (25 marks; 30 minutes)

1 Explain why price cutting in this case can be called a strategy rather than a tactic. (4)

2 Outline two factors that may determine whether Morrisons' 2014 strategy proves successful. (5)

3 Explain one possible weakness in the strategy as outlined in the data provided. (4)

4 In Morrisons' circumstances, assess the probable effectiveness of its new marketing strategy. (12)

Data response 2

Apple's cash machine

The Apple iPod was launched in 2001, into a market dominated by Sony. For a company based on computers, the move into personal music appeared risky. As the graph in Figure 15.4 shows, sales grew slowly; iTunes was launched in 2002 but only in late 2004 did iPod sales move ahead dramatically. This was partly due to the launch of the iPod Mini, but also coincided with the start of the brilliant 'silhouette' advertising campaign. In fact, Apple has handled iPod's marketing strategy very cleverly.

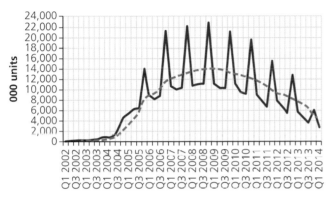

Figure 15.4 Worldwide iPod sales volume (three-monthly periods) (source: Apple Inc accounts)

iPod marketing mix

- *Product:* quick product development, from iPod 2001 to iPod Mini 2003, iPod Photo 2004 to iPod Shuffle 2005, and the iPod Touch in late 2007 and iPod Touch 4g in late 2010. As with all its competitors, the iPod is made (very cheaply) in China, so the key to its success is the stylish design, not high-quality manufacture.
- *Price:* always startlingly high; at launch, the iPod was over £200; even in 2014 prices for the iPod Touch were as high as £329, whereas other MP3 players cost as little as £20. Apple has managed the business dream of achieving market penetration at prices that skim the market.
- *Place:* nothing new here; Apple has distributed the iPod through the normal mixture of department stores, electrical shops and online retailers.
- *Promotion:* brilliant and lavish use of posters and TV, featuring one of the all-time great images, the 'silhouette'.

The key to the strategy has always been to achieve high credibility through brilliant design and a non-corporate image. Consumers have tended not to notice that the iPod is an amazing cash machine. In the year to March 2014, the revenues generated by iPod and iTunes came to $19,960 million.

Questions (40 marks; 50 minutes)

1 a) What is meant by the term 'product life cycle'? (2)

Figure 15.5 iPod

b) Assess what Figure 15.4 shows about iPod's product life cycle. (8)

2 Assess which of the elements of iPod's marketing mix have been the most important in its sales success. (10)

3 Given the business's success with the iPod, iPhone and iPad, evaluate whether Apple should now make a move towards the games console business, competing with Nintendo, Sony and Microsoft. (20)

Extended writing

1 Evaluate the quote by former President Eisenhower: 'There is no victory at bargain basement prices.' (20)

2 Evaluate the proposition that 'Marketing strategy can be successful only if a firm has set the right objectives.' (20)

16 Introduction to managing people

> **Definition**
>
> Managing people is the task of every manager – and usually their most important one. The business department known as 'Personnel' (or human resource management) manages the process of recruiting, training and incentivising staff.

Linked to: Approaches to staffing, Ch 17; Recruitment, selection and training, Ch 18; Organisational design, Ch 19; Motivation in practice, Ch 21; Leadership, Ch 22.

16.1 People are our most important asset

In company accounts, including those of Center Parcs and Churchill China plc, the business cliché is set out: 'Our people are our most important asset.' In the case of Center Parcs, this probably isn't true. The biggest assets of the business are probably the brand name plus the market positioning: safe, healthy, outdoor holidays for the whole family. Yet the company makes the claim because managers want staff to feel appreciated; and, of course, holidaymaker satisfaction does depend on the friendliness and efficiency of staff. But does it have to be *this* staff and *these* people? Or could the current staff all be replaced tomorrow by younger, cheaper people? In which case, the 'important asset' claim would be a hollow one.

Contrast the situation at Center Parcs with that at Churchill China. Churchill employs people with the skill to make the tableware you would eat from at the Ritz hotel or the finest Michelin-starred restaurants: skilfully made and beautifully decorated. Churchill is the market leader in supplying china plates, cups, etc. to the UK's hospitality industry. The company's annual report for 2014 highlights the company's 200 years of manufacturing in Stoke-on-Trent and the 'talented, dedicated team' that makes the company what it is today. These skilled staff really are a vital asset, which is why Churchill never followed the practice of others who 'outsourced' production to the Far East.

'Employees are a company's greatest asset – they're your competitive advantage. You want to attract and retain the best; provide them with encouragement, stimulus, and make them feel that they are an integral part of the company's mission.'

Anne Mulcahy, former chief executive, Xerox Corporation

Although few Personnel Directors would admit it, some companies regard their staff as costs rather than assets. As such, they seize every opportunity to cut these costs, perhaps by **outsourcing** tasks or by changing employment contracts from permanent and full-time towards the insecure world of **zero-hours contracts**. When unemployment is high, it is easy to see that companies can get away with such indifference towards their employees' security and morale. Well-run companies with sights on long-term success would do everything they can to avoid breaking the bond of trust that should exist between management and staff.

'Everyone talks about building a relationship with your customer. I think you build one with your employees first.'

Angela Ahrendts, former chief executive, Burberry plc

> **Real business**
>
> In November 2014, Airbus won a £9 billion order for 50 wide-bodied jet planes from Delta Airlines. This was a huge success for the European plane maker because Delta is an American airline that usually buys from Boeing. Boeing and Airbus each have around 50 per cent of the world market for manufacturing passenger planes, but most US airlines buy from US Boeing. The reason for the Airbus success was largely down to production capabilities. Airbus was able to promise delivery dates of 2017 for 25 of the planes and 2019 for the remainder. Boeing has struggled to increase production levels, and couldn't promise delivery until 2021! In the past, Boeing responded to downturns in orders by making staff redundant and outsourcing production

of aircraft parts to Japan, Malaysia and other parts of the world. Now, in its production base in Seattle, on America's west coast, it no longer has enough skilled, experienced staff to take on extra orders. Perhaps staff were their biggest asset after all.

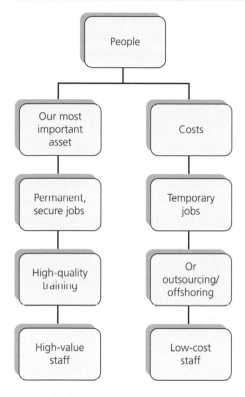

Figure 16.1 Different ways of viewing people in a business

16.2 Keys to effective people management

Fundamentally, there are two key goals when managing people:

- making sure you have the right number of staff, with the right skills and experience and in the right places, to meet all production and customer service requirements

- making sure those staff understand the business culture ('the way we do things round here') and are motivated in the right way, to ensure that quality standards match or beat customer expectations.

It is important to realise that neither of those goals need be met by a personnel department. In small businesses, it will often be the case that one director has responsibility for personnel issues, but this might be one among several duties. Therefore, hiring and training staff may be carried out by a director with no professional background or training in personnel. But such people can sometimes be fantastic in the role. A small building business may hire a fresh-from-college bricklayer and do a terrific job in instilling the company's attitude to quality standards, in how to deal with customers and in the pace and productivity of the working day.

> 'Your employees come first. And if you treat your employees right, guess what? Your customers come back, and that makes your shareholders happy. Start with employees and the rest follows from that.'

Herb Kelleher, co-founder of South West Airlines

Despite this, exam questions tend to assume that personnel tasks such as recruitment are carried out by personnel departments. These can be central parts of an organisation or end up semi-detached, regarded by most managers as a bureaucratic weight on the firm's shoulders. The key is to keep the personnel department fresh, by regularly placing staff into other departments so that they really understand the business: two weeks on the road, selling products; four weeks in the factory, learning every process and skill and so on.

If the personnel department is acknowledged internally to be a valuable part of the whole, managers from other departments will come to discuss their needs. Personnel managers can then work on solving the people problems of others. See Table 16.1 for more detail.

Department	Requirement/problem	Personnel solution
Marketing	Department needs to hire a new, young team of super-bright, creative minds to run a new digital/social media department.	Personnel staff will run recruitment fairs at four key universities, inviting candidates to a 'Mud Weekend' of quad biking, paintballing and more.
Finance	All department staff need to be trained on new financial software to be introduced in three months' time.	Personnel staff hire a software consultant to run training sessions every Thursday, with finance staff attending on a rota basis.
Resource management	New paintshop robots are to replace 100 skilled jobs next year.	Extra jobs should arise in other skilled functions, so a once-a-week retraining programme can start for all those who wish to stay with the company.

Table 16.1 Personnel problem solving

16.3 Planning your staffing needs

Personnel planning is about thinking ahead so that staff have the right balance of the right skills in each year into the future. In 2013, Fulham FC started the season with the oldest squad in the Premier League (by far). At the season end, the club was relegated. A succession of managers had failed to develop an effective personnel plan. The key components of such a plan are set out below.

1 Audit what you have at the moment: how many staff and what are their skills; ideally, this audit would include aspirations (for example, staff who say 'I'd love to travel' or 'I've always wanted to learn a foreign language').

2 Analyse the business plan to turn plans into people. For example, if Lidl's corporate plan says '20 new stores to be opened in Britain in the next two years', the workforce plan can be set: 20 new stores, each staffed by 120 people = 2,400 new staff needed.

3 Take into account the changes on the way from here to there. How many will leave to retire, have kids or a career change? Some football teams age together; eleven 29-year-olds may be great, but four years later there will be a problem.

4 Calculate the gaps that need to be filled between now and two years' time.

An example of a human resource (HR) plan by UK grocery chain Tesco is given in Table 16.2. Having completed this process (which should be done carefully, with full consultation with every senior manager), it is time to put it into practice. The process of human resource planning includes recruitment and selection, training and development, **redeployment** and sometimes planned redundancies.

16.4 Instilling staff culture and motivation

It isn't enough to have the right number of people in the right places. These people must give their best and do so in a manner that fits in with the overall company style and ethos. The sandwich chain Pret a Manger has been brilliant at this. They recruit on the basis of personality, not skill, then train people with care. The result is that every branch of Pret seems to be staffed by friendly, helpful but energetic/quick staff – exactly what an office worker wants at lunchtime.

When new recruits have been appointed, they should begin with an induction training programme that focuses on the company traditions and culture. At Harrods, the vast store is a maze, so every member of staff asks every customer whether they need help finding their next destination. At Aldi, customers expect no more than efficient, speedy service.

When it comes to motivation, though, there are big issues to consider. Personnel departments love to get involved with incentivising staff – that is, creating rewards systems that are intended to encourage the behaviours the company wants from staff. In furniture retailing, a 2 per cent commission rate is common for shop-floor sales staff. So a £1,200 leather sofa is worth an extra £24 in the wage packet. This should prove a good incentive to sell effectively, without being such a fantastic sum of money that staff oversell or mis-sell to people who may later regret their purchase (and complain bitterly online).

The important thing here is to learn the difference between incentivisation and motivation. Yes, incentives may sometimes be useful, but they are not a way to motivate staff. Motivated staff give their best in every

Component of a human resource plan	Example: UK grocery chain Tesco, investigating opening stores in India
1 Audit current staff, to find out their skills	How many current staff speak Hindi, and how many have significant, recent local knowledge?
2 Identify the workforce needs in two years' time, based on the corporate plan	How many staff will be needed in the UK in two years' time, broken down by skill and seniority; and how many will be needed in India?
3 Estimate employee loss through natural wastage	Research HR records to find how many of the 500,000 staff will be retiring; if the labour turnover is 10 per cent, 50,000 people need to be recruited just to maintain the present situation.
4 Calculate the gaps between what exists now and what is needed in two years' time – then plan to fill them	If Tesco plans ten new store openings in the UK plus ten in India, it may need 8,000 new staff in addition to the 50,000 needed to replace leavers. These 58,000 must be divided up to plan for how many Hindi speakers, how many butchers, bakers, accountants etc. are needed.

Table 16.2 Components of a human resource plan for Tesco

way they can, such as the Business teacher who always gets work marked and returned for the next lesson. No-one's paying a bonus for this; it is simply motivation. Incentives never get people to give their best, only to get people to do more of the most important job function, e.g. paying a striker £1,000 per goal they score. But the problem with incentives is the unintended consequences. Suddenly your team is scoring fewer goals because the striker is too greedy in the penalty box. Chapters 20 and 21 cover this issue with care.

> **'The factory of the future will have only two employees, a man and a dog. The man will be there to feed the dog. The dog will be there to keep the man from touching the equipment.'**
>
> Warren Bennis, business author

Five whys and a how

Questions	Answers
Why may it be hard to ensure that the personnel plan fits with a new business strategy?	Because staff develop ways of thinking and working that can be hard to change; can Marks & Spencer staff change to become more like those at Pret a Manger? Hm.
Why should companies take plenty of time deciding on their staff recruitment – even for shop-floor workers?	Because customers are more likely to come into contact with 'ordinary' staff than with managers, so the attitude and competence of shop-floor staff is vital to competitiveness.
Why might some recruitment managers be more interested in skills than in staff attitudes?	The job may not be customer-facing, so a smile may be irrelevant – and the skills may be all-important, such as a software engineer.
Why may staff redeployment prove more expensive than redundancy plus fresh recruitment?	Redeployment from teaching German to teaching Economics may cost more in training than the cost of redundancy plus recruiting a new, young economist.
Why may incentives not motivate?	An incentive focuses behaviour on one aspect of a job; motivated staff give their best in general and because they enjoy doing so.
How might Tesco improve its personnel planning?	By clarifying its overall business plan, making it easier for personnel staff to decide what skills and attitudes are needed from future recruits.

16.5 Introduction to managing people – evaluation

Some firms talk about staff being an important asset without seeming to believe it. But there's every reason to think that, for the majority of firms, staff really *are* that important. Currently Jaguar Land Rover (JLR) is one of Britain's most successful businesses. It needed huge investment from owner Tata Motors, but Tata would not have invested without the brilliantly successful Evoque car, designed and manufactured by some highly motivated British engineers. (Between 2010 and 2014, JLR sales to China rose fivefold, from 26,000 to 130,000, largely due to sales of the Evoque.) When management and the workforce really believe that they can succeed together, the results can be fantastic. Labour turnover at JLR is less than 2 per cent as staff want to carry on being part of this great success.

As a rule, then, it is reasonable to think that wise organisations make sure that staff feel wanted, trusted and secure, give them regular training and make sure that the job they do is stimulating and motivating.

> ### Key terms
>
> **Labour turnover:** the number of staff leaving a company as a percentage of the number employed.
>
> **Outsourcing:** taking a task traditionally run by your own staff (such as Security) and putting it out to tender, with the lowest bid winning the contract.
>
> **Redeployment:** retraining a staff member to give the skills required to take on a new job role.
>
> **Zero-hours contracts:** employment contracts that agree employee duties and hourly pay rates, yet offer no guarantee of any work (and therefore income) in any specific week.

16.6 Workbook

Revision questions

(30 marks; 30 minutes)

1 Give three reasons why managing people is important to a business such as a low-cost airline. (3)

2 Outline two possible reasons why an employee might prefer a full-time job to a zero-hours contract. (4)

3 Pret a Manger recruits a high proportion of its staff from overseas. Explain why it may choose to do that. (4)

4 Explain one situation in which a clothing chain such as Topshop might need to:

   a) redeploy 20 staff

   b) outsource a job function. (8)

5 Do you agree with Angela Ahrendts (see page 96)? Explain your reasoning. (5)

6 Explain one advantage and one disadvantage to a firm of having a high proportion of staff who have been with the business for 20+ years. (6)

Data response

Churchill China

Churchill China plc is a pottery company based in Stoke-on-Trent. It is shortly coming up to its 200th anniversary and is relatively rare in Stoke (once the world's leading pottery region) for still manufacturing locally. On the face of it, the company is going nowhere. Sales revenue is lower today than in 2006, and exports have changed little in the last ten years.

Yet there has been an interesting shift in strategy. In 2006, revenue came in a 55:45 ratio of B2B sales to B2C sales. In the first half of 2014, the ratio was 80:20. Churchill has switched to becoming overwhelmingly a supplier of china plates, cups, etc. to hotels, restaurants and the catering trade generally. Indeed it is now the UK's market leader in supplying to the 'hospitality industry'. This is a nice niche position to be in because it is more to do with small-scale, tailored production than the mass market. This keeps Churchill's trade business away from direct competition from the Far East. It also may give rise to a real growth path in the future, given that eating out remains a growth trend in Britain (and elsewhere in the west).

Even prior to 2006, Churchill had largely given up producing china for the retail market. Instead it designed 'tableware' in the UK, but had it made in the Far East. So the fall-away in retail sales has quite a few economic positives. Churchill is now focusing on producing in the UK for the UK market – though it is also developing stronger export sales within the hospitality trade. In the first half of 2014, Churchill's B2B sales to continental Europe rose by 20 per cent.

Throughout recent years, Churchill has invested in new technology, especially in robotic kiln-loading and unloading. That means that there are fewer low-skilled jobs in the factory today than in 2006. Fortunately, the jobs that remain are extremely highly skilled, making it hard for others to copy the quality and variety of Churchill's output. Hence its status as market leader.

	2006	2007	2008	2009	2010	2011	2012	2013	2014
Revenue, £000s	45,930	46,930	41,969	41,705	43,746	42,296	41,435	43,157	45,700
Operating profit, £000s	2,795	3,230	2,804	2,288	2,287	2,713	2,830	3,371	4,000
No. of staff	596	635	599	510	555	540	535	520	N/A
Staff cost, £000s	13,991	16,592	15,817	14,258	14,421	15,128	14,991	15,844	N/A

Table 16.3 Overall operational performance of Churchill China, 2006–2014 (for 2014, first half figures doubled up)

Questions (40 marks; 45 minutes)

1 Explain the difference between B2B and B2C.   (4)

2 a) Calculate the cost of staff as a percentage
      of sales revenue in 2007 and again in 2013.   (4)

   b) Explain one conclusion you can draw from
      the figures you have calculated.   (4)

3 Assess two reasons why small-scale, tailored
   production might suit a company with highly
   skilled staff.   (8)

4 Evaluate whether it would be right to say
   that Churchill China's staff are its greatest
   asset.   (20)

Extended writing

1 For one of its Christmas TV commercials,
   Waitrose boasted that 'people who own the
   business care more'. Yet regular surveys by *The
   Grocer* magazine suggest that customer service
   at Waitrose is significantly worse than at Asda
   or Morrisons. Evaluate the possible factors that
   might make staff at one supermarket care more
   about customers than the staff at another.   (20)

2 Your friend the Emir of Bhutan has just
   bought Birmingham FC and appointed you as
   manager. All the staff have been sacked so
   that you can start afresh (with a £200 million
   budget). Evaluate the key principles that would
   influence your people management plan.   (20)

17 Approaches to staffing

> **Definition**
>
> Staffing is the thinking behind the broad approach to staff (asset or cost?) and the specifics of how many people are needed in each role.

Linked to: Introduction to managing people, Ch 16; Recruitment, selection and training, Ch 18; Motivation in practice, Ch 21.

17.1 Staff as an asset; staff as a cost

Some companies manage to be consistently good employers over time. They pay pensions, they do all they can to avoid redundancies and they invest in staff training. They say, with some substance: 'Staff are our most important asset.'

Other firms treat staff consistently meanly, paying the lowest wages they can get away with, perhaps holding them to **zero-hours contracts**. Billionaire Mike Ashley's Sports Direct business has 20,000 staff on a particularly severe zero-hours contract that means the employee is not allowed to work for anyone else. So even if Sports Direct says 'zero' for next week's working hours, the employee is not allowed to work for anyone else. Mr Ashley appears to regard his staff as a cost, not an asset.

17.2 Flexible workforce

During the 2009 recession, British engineer JCB found, at one point, that UK demand for its construction vehicles had fallen by 90 per cent. That's extreme, but it indicates that businesses need flexibility within their operations. In addition to economic factors, this need may have increased for a number of reasons.

- Ever-improving technology means that the marketplace is subject to frequent and often rapid change. Firms need to be able to anticipate these changes and respond to them quickly in order to maintain a competitive edge.

- Many consumers want more customised goods and services (that is, better tailored to smaller segments of the population); firms have to adapt the production process in order to meet demand, while still operating efficiently and keeping costs down.

- Increasing competition, especially from overseas firms, has forced businesses faced with fluctuating or seasonal demand to introduce greater operational flexibility, in order to eliminate any unnecessary costs.

To succeed in modern markets that are often fragmented into relatively small niches, and where customer tastes are ever-changing, many firms have adopted lean production. This approach implies the use of machinery that can quickly be reprogrammed to carry out a range of tasks, and the creation of a multi-skilled and flexible workforce that can quickly adapt – and be adapted – to meet a firm's changing requirements.

> **Real business**
>
> **Benefits of flexible working**
>
> As part of its pitch to get top graduates to apply for a job, Lloyds Bank makes this statement about its flexible work practices: 'To help you strike the right balance between work and your personal life, we'll consider flexible working arrangements. These include the potential for part-time, job sharing, variable daily hours and a "compressed working week".' Lloyds believes that both it and its staff can benefit from non-traditional work flexibility.
>
> Source: www.lloydsbankinggroup-careers.com, 2014

17.3 Achieving greater flexibility within the workforce

There are a number of ways in which firms can attempt to increase the level of workforce flexibility, some of which are described below.

Multi-skilling

This occurs when workers are given the scope and ability to carry out a variety of tasks, rather than specialising in completion of one particular area. This can be encouraged through the use of job rotation, in which workers carry out an increased number of tasks at the same level of difficulty. In a hotel, for instance, the people who are usually on reception could spend time organising wedding parties, giving them a wider understanding of the business. In Japan, this is known as horizontal promotion, as it implies that the company has enough faith in the individual to invest time and money in training him or her for an extra job.

Multi-skilling the workforce should mean that a firm's human resources can be used more effectively. It ensures that employees are equipped with the skills needed to cover for staff absences, minimising any disruption or loss of production that this may otherwise have caused. Individual workers may respond positively to the increased variety and new challenges provided, improving motivation and productivity. However, firms may be unwilling to bear the costs of additional training unless the benefits of adopting a new approach are obvious and immediate. See Table 17.1.

Benefits	Drawbacks
Increases in productivity from greater utilisation of employees	Potential loss of production as workers switch between different tasks
Reduction in disruption to production caused by staff absence	Greater training requirements and cost as individual workers acquire a wider range of skills, increasing costs
Greater employee motivation created by more varied and challenging tasks at work	Workers may be reluctant to acquire new skills, especially if there is no corresponding increase in pay

Table 17.1 Multi-skilling: benefits and drawbacks

Part-time and temporary

In recent years, there has been a significant increase in the number of part-time employees. Figure 17.1 shows that around a third of all employees in Britain work part-time.

Employers love part-time workers because they give flexibility, such as to have extra transport staff during rush hours. There is some doubt, though, about whether part-time work is what employees want – or simply have to accept. A May 2014 *Financial Times* report suggested that 40 per cent of the part-timers want more working hours. Other research suggests that 20–25 per cent want full-time work.

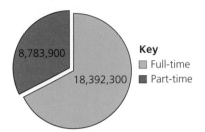

Figure 17.1 Employment in Britain, December 2013 (source: ONS)

Temporary work operates in a similar way. Giving staff short-term contracts makes it easy for the company to cut staff without getting criticism; all they need to do is allow the contract to lapse, and the staff member has gone.

With short-term contracts and all the other forms of employee flexibility, the problem for the employee is: a) am I earning enough and regularly enough to feed my kids and b) how can I possibly get a bank or building society to trust me with a mortgage?

Flexible hours and home-working

Greater flexibility can also be created by moving away from the traditional 9–5 working day and 38-hour working week, in order to respond more effectively to customer demands. There are a number of methods used by firms to vary the pattern of working, including the use of part-time work, job sharing, annualised hours contracts and flexitime. For example, banks, insurance companies and mobile phone operators make extensive use of flexitime systems to provide 24-hour employee cover via the telephone and internet, in order to provide customers with greater convenience. Introducing greater time flexibility can also have a number of benefits for employees who may have family or other commitments during normal working hours. Providing staff with more flexible working arrangements can help to improve recruitment, increase motivation and reduce labour turnover, leading to reduced costs and boosts to productivity.

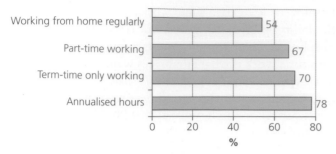

Figure 17.2 Flexible working arrangements offered by large firms (source: DTI, CIPD and industry estimates)

A particular type of time flexibility comes from zero-hours contracts. In April 2014, government statistics showed that 1.4 million zero-hours contracts were in use in the UK. Only two years before, the estimate had been just 200,000. A zero-hours contract is an employment contract like any other, except that whereas a full-time teacher contract might state a minimum of 35 hours a week, a zero-hours one states a minimum of zero. In other words, the employer guarantees nothing. The reality might be that workers are told on a Thursday what work they are being offered for the following week. If it is zero hours, a family could go hungry. The prospects of getting a mortgage are also zero. These contracts are especially common among jobs taken by younger workers and in poorly paid sectors. In hotels and catering, 26 per cent of staff have zero-hours contracts. For employers, it is wonderful to turn a fixed cost into a variable one. For the staff, flexibility becomes insecurity.

Another type of flexible worker is the home-worker. This is someone who works at home, probably on a laptop connected permanently to the main office. In some cases, it can be that a full-time employee does two days a week at home – with fewer distractions from the phone, from meetings and from gossipy staff. In other cases, the business may want as few people as possible at head office, to keep overhead costs down, so they encourage staff to work at home, and perhaps occasionally come in and 'hot-desk'.

Figure 17.3 Working at home

Some really enjoy this arrangement, whereas it makes others feel insecure. Ideally, an employee would have this as an option; it would be much less satisfactory if it were forced upon the worker.

Real business

Home-working eases stress levels

Working from home reduces stress in office workers, but leads to fears about career progression, according to research. A survey of 749 staff in managerial or professional positions conducted by Durham Business School showed that home-workers worried about missing out on 'water-cooler networking', where potential opportunities for moving up the ladder are discussed informally in the office.

Despite these concerns, the study also found that working from home generally had a positive effect on an employee's work–life balance, giving them more time with the family, and leading to less stress and less chance of burnout.

Source: www.PersonnelToday.com

Outsourcing

Outsourcing involves a firm finding an external business to carry out part of the production process, in order to cut costs or achieve a better level of service. For example, it may involve hiring cleaning or catering services from other companies. All firms need enough workers to respond to sudden increases in customer demand, without having to bear the cost of employing unnecessary staff should sales decline temporarily. One way is through the use of temporary contracts, agency staff and **subcontracting** or outsourcing certain operations to other firms. Flexible temporary staff enable firms to respond to a sudden rise in sales by increasing the workforce quickly – and then reducing its size just as quickly, should the sales increase prove to be temporary. However, while a reliance on temporary staff and external organisations may help to reduce costs and improve reaction to change, productivity may be harmed by a lack of expertise and worker loyalty to the firm.

'Businesses are no longer receiving the cost savings from outsourcing that they once did.'

Gerald Chertavian, US social entrepreneur

17.4 Distinction between dismissal and redundancy

There are three main circumstances when companies need to dispense with the services of staff:

1 When individual staff members lack the competence to carry out their duties effectively – or are too disruptive.

2 When economic or other factors depress demand throughout an industry, forcing companies to cut costs in order to stay above their break-even level of operation.

3 When competitive or other factors cause the business to lose market share in a way that forces management to cut staff. In 2013, Blackberry cut 40 per cent of its staff (4,500 people) to try to stay alive.

In the latter two cases, the requirement to cut staff is about posts not people; supervisor jobs may be cut from 200 to 120. This is redundancy. From the firm's point of view, it isn't making people redundant; it is accepting that the job is redundant. In the UK, large firms that are planning redundancies have to give staff three months' notice that this is about to happen. That period is for consulting with employees or their trade unions, but usually there is no changing the mind of the company. Having decided on the redundancies, there are legal requirements for the minimum redundancy payments, as long as staff have been employed for at least two years. These are:

- half a week's pay for each full year of working when you were under 22
- one week's pay for each full year of working when you were 22–40
- one and a half week's pay for each full year of working when you were 41 or older.

Whereas redundancy is about the job, dismissal is about the individual. An employee can be dismissed on the spot for 'gross misconduct', such as being violent or stealing. An employee can also be dismissed fairly, just for lack of competence, as long as the management can demonstrate fairness in giving warnings and in offering retraining or a switch to an easier job. Dismissal comes with no payments at all.

> **'You do not get good people if you lay off half your workforce just because one year the economy isn't very good and then you hire them back.'**
>
> Kenneth Iverson, chairman, Nucor Corporation

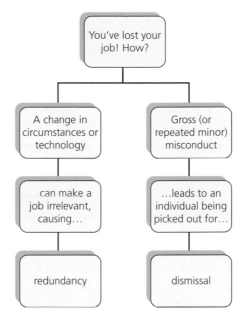

Figure 17.4 Logic chain: *redundancy v. dismissal*

17.5 Employer–employee relationships

Intelligent bosses realise that success depends on the full participation of as many staff as possible. Football managers typically use the club captain as the representative of the players. Small firms may have an informal group consisting of one person from each department; monthly meetings are used as a way to raise issues and problems, and discuss future plans. In larger firms, more formal methods are used to ensure that there is a structure to allow an element of workplace democracy. Alternatively, the organisation's staff may belong to a trade union that represents their interests through collective bargaining.

Trade unions and collective bargaining

A trade union is an organisation that employees pay to join in order to gain greater power and security at work. The phrase 'unity is strength' is part of the trade union tradition. One individual worker has little or no power when discussing pay or pensions with his or her employer; union membership provides greater influence collectively in relations with employers than workers have as separate individuals.

Some people assume that union membership is only for people in low-status jobs. In fact, although trade unions are in decline in Britain, some powerful groups of 'workers' remain committed to membership. For example, the PFA (Professional Footballers' Association) includes almost all Premiership players, and more than 75 per cent of airline pilots belong to their union, BALPA.

Traditionally, unions concerned themselves solely with obtaining satisfactory rates of pay for a fair amount of work in reasonable and safe working conditions. Today the most important aspect of the work of a trade union is protecting workers' rights under the law. Far more time is spent on health and safety, on discrimination and bullying, on unfair dismissal and other legal matters than on pay negotiations. One other important matter today is negotiations over pension rights. Recently, many companies have cut back on the pension benefits available to staff; the unions fight these cutbacks as hard as they can.

Traditionally, the key function of a union was 'collective bargaining'. This means that the union bargains with the employers on behalf of all the workers (for example, that all nurses should get a 2.4 per cent pay rise). In April 2014, a one-year wrangle between the Post Office and the Communication Workers' Union resulted in agreement to pay rises of up to 7.3 per cent.

Real business

Unite

In March 2013, workers at Greencore's cake factory in Hull voted overwhelmingly to accept management's offer to restore pay and conditions to their original levels. This was the culmination of an 18-month dispute. In October 2011, Greencore (supplier of cakes to Tesco and other supermarkets) gained agreement from its staff and trade union to a temporary cut in payments for overtime and bank holiday working. A year later, though, when the 'temporary' period was over, the company refused to reinstate the original terms. Staff who were mainly paid minimum wage levels stood to lose £40 a week (according to Unite, their trade union). Legal appeals and a one-day strike followed – eventually leading to the company's climb-down.

'The two sides of industry have traditionally always regarded each other in Britain with the greatest possible loathing, mistrust and contempt. They are both absolutely right.'

Auberon Waugh, writer

Individual bargaining

Most employers are in favour of individual rather than collective bargaining. Quite simply, it puts the boss in a stronger position. This situation may be presented as a matter of 'freedoms', but at heart it is a matter of power. The huge decline in union membership in America and Britain in the past 30 years has coincided with a significant reduction in income equality. Individuals' weak bargaining power has meant that workers today are far worse off compared with their managers than would have been the case 30 years ago.

Five whys and a how

Questions	Answers
Why do managers love labour flexibility?	Because it can transform a fixed cost into a variable one – and if used sparingly, that lower variable cost makes the business more competitive.
Why do staff have mixed feelings about flexibility?	Flexibility is great if you need to pick kids up from school or not work in the holidays, but awful if it condemns you to underemployment and poverty.
Why have trade unions declined in recent years?	Tougher laws and privatisation have made it harder for strikes to succeed, and that weakens union power.
Why is there no shame in being made redundant?	It is not the individual but the job that is no longer needed.
Why did personnel departments start calling themselves HR?	Largely in an attempt to make their role seem less administrative and more strategic and managerial; has it worked? Not really – there are still very few HR directors on UK boards.
How might trade unions rebuild their memberships?	Hm, that's tough. Perhaps by making themselves important in people's careers, e.g. by funding outstanding training programmes.

17.6 Approaches to staffing – evaluation

The adoption of a **flexible approach** and a more flexible workforce can, in principle, be an attractive prospect for any modern business, offering a number of benefits, including reduced costs and an increased ability to respond to changing customer demands. The separation of employees into highly valued **core workers** and an easily dispensable periphery may allow a business to 'pick and mix' skills and obtain the exact combination required within the market at that particular moment in time.

However, it can also lead to a number of problems in the long term, especially if it creates insecurity among **peripheral workers** that leads to high levels of staff turnover. The ability to cut labour costs quickly and easily in the face of a downturn in the market has obvious attractions. However, in the long term, the establishment of a multi-skilled and loyal workforce, able to adapt and diversify into new markets, may lead to even greater success.

Key terms

Core workers: employees who are essential to the operations of a business, supporting whatever makes it distinctive or unique. Such workers are likely to receive attractive salaries and working conditions, and enjoy a high degree of job security.

Flexible approach: an approach to operations that implies a move away from mass production to batch production, the use of machinery that can be quickly reprogrammed to carry out a range of tasks, and the creation of a multi-skilled and flexible workforce that can quickly adapt to meet a firm's changing requirements.

Hot-desk: an approach that provides a temporary desk for home-workers to use when they come to the main office; they are not allowed to leave any of their own possessions there.

Outsourcing: taking a task traditionally run by your own staff (such as Security) and putting it out to tender, with the lowest bid winning the contract.

Peripheral workers: those workers who are not seen as being central to a firm's operations. They may carry out necessary tasks, but may be required only on a temporary basis and may be easily replaced.

Subcontracting: where another business is used to perform or supply certain aspects of a firm's operations (see 'Outsourcing').

Zero-hours contracts: employment contracts that agree employee duties and hourly pay rates, yet offer no guarantee of any work (and therefore income) in any specific week.

17.7 Workbook

Revision questions

(40 marks; 40 minutes)

1 Why could increased market change have an effect on the way people are employed today? (3)

2 Outline two reasons why firms may have chosen to adopt a more flexible approach to workforce arrangements. (4)

3 Briefly explain what is meant by the term 'lean production'. (3)

4 Explain, using examples, what is meant by the term 'multi-skilling'. (4)

5 Why might a company encourage its staff to work from home rather than in a central office? (3)

6 In 2013, a newspaper said that '100 workers have been dismissed (at a local factory) because of weak trading'. Explain why the paper was incorrect. (3)

7 State two ways in which a bank offering telephone and internet services to customers would benefit from introducing greater time flexibility. (4)

8 Outline one advantage and one disadvantage to joining a trade union when you start your first job. (6)

9 Outline two reasons why a firm's employees may welcome the decision to move towards increased labour flexibility. (4)

10 Examine two reasons why the move towards greater flexibility might lead to increased insecurity within the workforce. (6)

Data response 1

Flexible working at First Direct

First Direct is one of the UK's leading commercial banks, providing a wide range of financial services via telephone and the internet to 1.2 million customers. When First Direct began, high street banks opened only between 9.00am and 3.00pm, Monday to Friday. However, the company set out to create a different business model, based on the customer need for greater convenience. Since its establishment, First Direct's reputation has rested on the fact that it is the bank that never closes. It ignores weekends and bank holidays. Operators in the company's call centres handle approximately 235,000 calls each week, with more than 13,000 daily coming outside normal working hours.

The company's operations have required it to develop a working culture that is very different from the traditional model. This has included longer shifts, a high proportion of part-time and home-based workers, and reliance on so-called 'mushrooming' – a term used to describe workers employed to work night-time shifts.

First Direct appears to have succeeded on a number of levels. The quality of its customer service has resulted in high rates of customer retention. Employees also appear to approve of the company's approach to flexible working; labour turnover, at 14 per cent, is far below the average for call centres, and 90 per cent of female staff return to their jobs after maternity leave.

Questions (30 marks; 35 minutes)

1 Give two examples of flexible working practices used by First Direct. (2)

2 Assess two possible benefits for a business such as First Direct of creating a more flexible workforce. (8)

3 Evaluate whether the creation of a more flexible workforce is crucial to the continuing success of a company such as First Direct. (20)

Data response 2

Life on zero-hours contracts

Chris Morrison: I'm 28, single and work in retail. One week I can have 30-plus hours, the next I'll have less than 15. It's next to impossible to maintain a decent standard of living when your wages are so unpredictable. I struggle to pay bills sometimes. The company I work for has cut back to a bare essential crew but still expects the same level of service, which is next to impossible to do. I often leave work feeling very stressed, which is not good for my health.

Harry Thompson: I'm a student and have had a few zero-hours contracts, from working in factories wrapping cheese in cling film to picking out spare parts in a vending machine factory. Zero-hours contracts were useful occasionally, but I'd support any attempts to regulate them. I worked on zero hours during the summer and, when I was on a week-long placement, I was told that part of the factory had a technical problem so its contracted employees couldn't work – so they sent home the people on zero-hours contracts and replaced us with the contracted employees. It is not a nightmare for a student, but you can't plan a life on zero hours. I can't imagine being on low pay living on the brink and then just being told to go home when there isn't any work. If zero-hours contracts were regulated, they'd almost certainly have hired people to do the work anyway, but with proper rights and stability.

Source: *The Guardian*, 30 April 2014

Questions (30 marks; 35 minutes)

1 Give two complaints about zero-hours contracts made by both Chris and Harry. (2)

2 For firms, an alternative to zero-hours contracts is to outsource the work to specialist companies. Assess two possible downsides to outsourcing a job such as nursing. (8)

3 The move to zero-hours contracts is said to be a way to adapt the organisational structure to improve competitiveness. Using the evidence and your wider knowledge, evaluate how likely it is to achieve this effect. (20)

Extended writing

1 Management guru Robert Townsend urged companies to dismantle their personnel departments and make sure that every manager felt responsible for training and motivating their own staff. Evaluate whether that idea would work in a big, modern business such as McDonald's. (20)

2 Evaluate the possible impact of adopting more flexible working practices on the international competitiveness of a firm such as Cadbury. (20)

18 Recruitment, selection and training

> **Definition**
>
> Recruitment (and selection) means filling job vacancies by defining the job, attracting suitable candidates and selecting those best suited to fill it. Training means work-related education, where employees learn new skills or develop the skills they already possess.

Linked to: Introduction to managing people, Ch 16; Approaches to staffing, Ch 17; Production, productivity and efficiency, Ch 41.

18.1 The need for effective recruitment

Every service business relies on its staff to present the face of the organisation to the customer. It can be a gloomy, perhaps bored face, or it can be lively and smiling. Many factors are involved in this stark difference, but it certainly helps if you recruit bright, enthusiastic staff in the first place.

Real business

Ryanair and easyJet compete for qualified pilots

The rapid growth of low-cost airlines has forced Ryanair and easyJet to compete fiercely for the scarcest resource: qualified pilots. Table 18.1 shows what each airline was offering in summer 2014 to attract potential recruits.

	easyJet	Ryanair
Annual salary	£93,821	£75,000
Days off a year	137 days	162 days
Extra remuneration	7 per cent pension contribution	Share option scheme
Extra attractions	Share options	Home every night

Table 18.1 Terms and conditions of employment (source: easyJet.com and ryanair.com)

18.2 The recruitment process

The recruitment process may be triggered by a number of events. For example, an existing employee may have chosen to leave his or her job, perhaps as a result of retirement or after finding employment elsewhere. At this point, it would be worth analysing the vacant job role. Do all of the responsibilities associated with the vacant job still need to be carried out or are some redundant? Could the remaining duties be reorganised among the existing employees? Alternatively, additional workers may need to be recruited in order to support a firm's expansion strategies, or employees with new skills may be required to help develop new products or new markets.

Once the firm has established its human resources requirements, the next step is to consider the nature of work and workers required in order to draw up a job description and a person specification.

Both documents have an important influence on recruitment and selection; they can be used not only to draw up job adverts, but also to assess the suitability of candidates' applications and may also form the basis of any interview questions.

Job description

A job description relates directly to the nature of the position itself, rather than the person required to fill it. Typically, a job description would contain the following information:

- the title of the post
- details of the main duties and tasks involved
- the person to whom the job holder reports and any employees for whom the job holder is responsible.

Person specification

A person specification identifies the abilities, qualifications and qualities required of the job holder in order to carry out the job successfully. The main features of a person specification include:

- any educational or professional qualifications required
- necessary skills or experience
- suitable personality or character – for example, ability to work under pressure or as part of a team.

Real business

By 2014, recovery from recession and policies such as near-zero interest rates had created a recruitment boom in the City of London. KPMG is one of the biggest employers of graduates, hiring approximately 1,000 university leavers each year. The accountancy firm goes to great lengths to ensure that they hire the best possible people. Their recruitment begins with an online application form. After the form has been completed, applicants are sent a hyperlink to a Situational Judgement Test (SJT). The test asks candidates how they would respond to a series of challenging work-based situations. Those who pass the SJT are then invited to sit another online test, designed to assess the candidates' numerical and verbal reasoning. If this test is also passed, applicants are interviewed over the telephone to see whether they have the right 'behavioural capabilities'.

The next hurdle is the Immersive Assessment Centre – a one-day visit to KPMG's offices in central London where prospective employees' communication and decision-making skills are assessed. Candidates are required to respond to emails and voicemails sent from fake clients. The day ends with two simulated meetings. Pass this and you are through to the sixth and final stage of the process: an interview.

18.3 Internal recruitment

A business may choose to fill a vacancy internally – that is, from the existing workforce. This could be done either by redeploying or by promoting a worker from elsewhere in the business. Although internal recruitment can have a number of benefits, it also has a number of disadvantages and is obviously of no use when a business needs to expand its workforce in order to respond to an increase in demand. See Table 18.2.

Advantages	Disadvantages
• It is likely to be quicker and cheaper than external recruitment. • Greater variety and promotion opportunities may motivate employees. • It avoids the need (and cost) of **induction training**. • The firm will already be aware of the employee's skills and attitude to work.	• Existing workers may not have the skills required, especially if the business wants to develop new products or markets. • Relying on existing employees may lead to a stagnation of ideas and approaches within the business. • It may create a vacancy elsewhere, postponing external recruitment, rather than avoiding it.

Table 18.2 Internal recruitment: advantages and disadvantages

18.4 Recruiting external candidates

Firms can choose from a range of methods to attract external candidates to fill a job vacancy. The advantages and disadvantages of external recruitment are set out in Table 18.3.

Advantages	Disadvantages
• It should result in a wider range of candidates than internal recruitment. • Candidates may already have the skills required to carry out the job in question, avoiding the need for (and cost of) training.	• It can be an expensive and time-consuming process, using up valuable resources. • It can have a demotivating effect on members of the existing workforce, who may have missed out on promotion.

Table 18.3 External recruitment: advantages and disadvantages

Methods of recruitment

Methods of recruiting external candidates include those set out below.

Media advertising

Firms may place job adverts in newspapers or specialist magazines, on the radio or TV or by using dedicated employment websites, such as www.monster.co.uk.

Job centres

These are government-run organisations which offer a free service to firms and tend to focus on vacancies for less-skilled manual and administrative jobs.

Commercial recruitment agencies

Examples of commercial recruitment agencies include Alfred Marks or Reed, which will carry a number of human resources functions, including recruitment, on behalf of firms in return for a fee.

Executive search consultants

Executive search consultants are paid to directly approach individuals – usually those in relatively senior positions. (This is known as poaching or headhunting.)

Firm's own website

In addition, many businesses have careers pages on their own websites, which are used to advertise vacancies.

Factors influencing choice of method

The choice of recruitment method or methods used by a business will depend on a number of factors, including the:

- cost of the recruitment method
- size of the recruitment budget
- location and characteristics of the likely candidates.

18.5 The selection process

Once a number of suitable candidates have applied for the vacancy, the selection process can begin. This will involve choosing the applicant who most closely matches the criteria set out in the person specification for the job. A number of selection techniques exist, including those set out below.

Interviews

This is still the most frequently used selection technique; an interview may consist of one interviewer or a panel. Interviews are relatively cheap to conduct and allow a wide variety of information to be obtained by both sides, but are often susceptible to interviewer bias or prejudice. They are, therefore, considered to be an unreliable indicator on their own of how well a candidate will carry out the job in question.

Testing and profiling

Aptitude tests measure the level of ability of a candidate such as, for example, the level of ICT skills. Psychometric profiling examines personality and attitudes – for example, whether the candidate works well under pressure or is an effective team player. Profiling is commonly used as part of management and sales consultancy recruitment, but it is questionable as to whether recruiting a 'personality type' for a particular job is desirable. Recruiting a wider range of personalities may lead to a more interesting and creative environment.

Assessment centres

These allow for a more in-depth assessment of a candidate's suitability by subjecting them to 'real-life'

role plays and simulations, often over a number of days. Although assessment centres are considered to be an effective selection method, they can be expensive and tend, therefore, to be reserved for filling more senior management positions. See Figure 18.1 for an illustration of the stages in the recruitment process.

Figure 18.1 Stages in the recruitment process

Although a firm can only be certain that the right person has been recruited once he or she starts work, effective recruitment and selection will reduce the risk involved. There are a number of methods that can be used to evaluate the process, including calculating the cost and time involved in filling a vacancy, the percentage of candidates who actually accept job offers and the rate of retention of staff once employed.

Real business

Do employers still want graduates?

According to research published by the IPPR (Institute of Public Policy Research) in June 2014, the UK economy is expected to create an additional 14.4 million jobs over the next decade. The study claims that two-thirds of these new jobs will be in medium and low-skilled industries, such as building, administration and social care. In response to their own report, the IPPR have called for more students to consider vocational courses, rather than university degrees. More than a quarter of graduates suffer from 'low-earner anxiety' and are less likely to be happy with their pay than non-graduates. According to the IPPR, this suggests that a degree can promote 'a false sense of earnings capability'.

18.6 Costs of recruitment and selection

Recent research puts the average cost for recruiting new staff at around £1,850 per employee. This is only a small part of the overall loss to the business, which includes hiring temporary workers before the employee starts and the 28 weeks it takes for new workers to reach their optimum productivity level. The overall loss is important because it emphasises that companies must get their recruitment and selection methods right. Spending thousands to hire someone, then having to do it all again when they leave, is really costly.

Among the main direct costs of recruitment and selection are management time spent interviewing candidates (perhaps £800), recruitment agency fees (£450), advertising (£400) and HR time spent administering the process (£200). Some of these costs will change over time, especially advertising, as firms switch to cheaper digital communication. Overall, though, the cost is not huge in relation to the potential losses from high **labour turnover** if the recruitment and selection process is bungled.

18.7 Training

The purpose of training is to help employees to develop existing skills or gain new ones. The benefits and costs of training are given in Table 18.4. Types of training include those set out below.

Benefits	Costs
• It increases the level and range of skills available to the business, leading to improvements in productivity and quality. • It increases the degree of flexibility within a business, allowing it to respond quickly to changes in technology or demand. • It can lead to a more motivated workforce by creating opportunities for development and promotion.	• It can be expensive, in terms of both providing the training itself and the cost of evaluating its effectiveness. • Production may be disrupted while training is taking place, leading to lost output. • Newly trained workers may be persuaded to leave and take up new jobs elsewhere.

Table 18.4 Training: benefits and costs

Induction training

Induction training aims to make newly appointed workers fully productive as soon as possible by familiarising them with the key aspects of the business. Induction would typically include:

- information on important policies and procedures, such as health and safety
- a tour of the organisation and an introduction to colleagues
- details of employment; for example, payment arrangements, holiday entitlement, and so on, and basic duties.

On-the-job training

For this method of training, employees are not required to leave their workplace but actually receive instruction while still carrying out their job. This means that workers can receive training while remaining productive to some extent. Common methods include mentoring and coaching. A key benefit of **on-the-job training** is that it is specific to the particular workplace. Instead of being taught in general about stock control systems, Sainsbury's staff learn about the Sainsbury's stock control software and stock management. A government survey of employers published in January 2014 found that 52 per cent of staff had received on-the-job training in the previous year. This is compared with 49 per cent of staff taking off-the-job training.

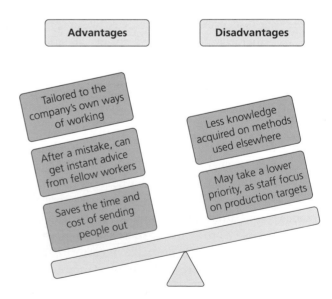

Figure 18.2 Logic balance: on-the-job training

Off-the-job training

For **off-the-job training**, employees leave their workplace in order to receive instruction. This may involve using training facilities within the firm – for example, seminar rooms, or those provided by another organisation, such as a university, college or private training agency. Although this will inevitably involve a temporary loss of production, it should allow the trainee to concentrate fully on learning and perhaps allow access to more experienced instructors than those available within the workplace.

18.8 Costs of training

The costs involved in training staff *should* be accepted as a valuable and responsible part of the role of an employer. Not all companies see things that way. Among small firms employing 2–4 people, 48 per cent provide no staff training at all. This figure declines to 7 per cent as the company size increases to 25–99 staff and falls to zero for those employing 100+. As shown in Figure 18.3, the average spend on training amounted to £2,550 per employee in 2013. Note that this figure includes everything, including the salaries of the human resource staff involved in organising the training, and the salaries of the staff being trained! The average staff member would struggle to believe that they had received £2,550 worth of training in a year.

According to government data, between 2011 and 2013, there was a significant fall in the amount employers spent on staff training. This is surprising given that this was a period of quite sharply improving company profitability, with rising dividends being paid out to shareholders. Furthermore it was a period of rising employee numbers. Figure 18.3 shows the severity of the decline, with the amount being spent per employee falling by 17 per cent between 2011 and 2013.

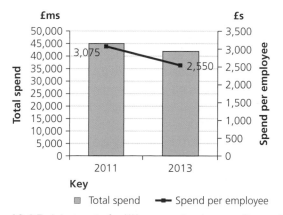

Figure 18.3 Training costs for UK companies (source: figures from UK Commission's Employer Skills Survey 81, January 2014)

Five whys and a how

Questions	Answers
Why do some companies offer holiday jobs to university students?	Because it gives the company a good long look at the individual, allowing better recruitment decisions to be made later on.
Why might a company try to avoid getting a lot of applicants for a job?	Shortlisting, assessing and interviewing take a lot of staff time; if the role is not critical for the business, managers may prefer fewer candidates.
Why might a company include someone from personnel on a selection panel?	Mainly to make sure that no rules are broken in the process, e.g. regarding discrimination.
Why might one retailer use mainly on-the-job training while another prefer off-the-job training?	Some firms want to serve customers in a distinctive style, in which case on-the-job training would be the most appropriate.
Why do some firms go on providing staff training, even for those over 60?	There are always new things to learn, most obviously things to do with technology; but also it is important that older staff should be as effective and involved as younger ones.
How might a large business such as Tesco recruit a new chief executive?	Probably by getting a headhunter to provide a shortlist, then getting members of the Board of Directors to be on the interview panel.

18.9 Recruitment, selection and training – evaluation

Recruitment and training are key aspects of human resources management (HRM) and the importance of effective HR strategies in helping a firm – however large or small – to achieve its objectives cannot be overstated. 'Having the right person with the right skills in the right job at the right time' will allow a business to maintain or improve its competitiveness; having the wrong person is likely to lead to a deterioration in performance and an increase in costs. Many organisations continue to view training in particular as an avoidable expense, choosing to cut training budgets when under pressure to cut costs, or to poach employees already equipped with the necessary skills from other firms. New employees can bring a number of benefits, including fresh ideas and approaches to work. However, such an approach may fail to weigh up the possible long-term impact on the quality and motivation of the workforce, and the implications of this for productivity and competitiveness.

Key terms

Induction training: familiarises newly appointed workers with key aspects of their jobs and their employer, such as health and safety policies, holiday entitlement and payment arrangements. The aim is to make employees fully productive as soon as possible.

Labour turnover: the number of staff leaving a company as a percentage of the number employed.

Off-the-job training: where employees leave their normal place of work in order to receive instruction, either within the firm or by using an external organisation such as a college or university.

On-the-job training: where employees acquire or develop skills without leaving their usual workplace, perhaps by being guided through an activity by a more experienced member of staff.

18.10 Workbook

Revision questions

(40 marks; 40 minutes)

1 Outline two reasons why a business may need to recruit new employees. (4)

2 Briefly explain the difference between a job description and a person specification. (4)

3 Outline two factors that would influence the method of recruitment used by a business. (4)

4 Suggest two reasons why internal recruitment may not be a suitable means of filling vacancies for a rapidly expanding business. (2)

5 Outline one advantage and one disadvantage of external recruitment. (4)

6 Examine one suitable method for recruiting applicants to each of the following job roles:

   a) a caretaker for a local school

   b) a temporary sales assistant for a high street retailer over the Christmas period

   c) a marketing director for a multinational company. (12)

7 Outline one advantage and one disadvantage of using interviewing as a method of selecting candidates for a job vacancy. (4)

8 Suggest two methods that a firm could use to evaluate the effectiveness of its recruitment and selection procedure. (2)

9 Outline two reasons why a firm should provide induction training for newly recruited employees. (4)

Data response 1

Etsy

Etsy is an American-based e-commerce business that competes against eBay by specialising in selling vintage and handmade bags, furniture, jewellery and toys.

In 2012, Chief Technical Officer (CTO) Kellan Elliot-McCrea realised that the company had a problem: 80 per cent of their customers were female. However, only three out of their 110 website engineers were women. Elliot-McCrea saw this as a problem because she believed that there was a danger that the engineers who designed the website might become disengaged with the company's customers. She responded by launching a recruitment drive that was designed to hire more women in order to create a better gender balance.

Etsy decided against lowering their standards. Female applicants were expected to have the same qualifications, skills and experience as their male counterparts. However, the company did decide to change its aggressive style of interviewing that placed greater emphasis on speed and bluster, rather than on technical knowledge. They also offered $5,000 grants that were paid selectively to women programmers in return for attending a three-month Hacker School set up by Etsy in New York City.

The programme is working; by 2013, 20 out of the company's team of 110 engineers were women.

Source: adapted from *Business Insider*, 11 February 2013

Questions (25 marks; 30 minutes)

1 Outline one possible reason why most of Etsy's team of engineers were men. (3)

2 Assess how businesses like Etsy might benefit from employing a more diverse workforce. (10)

3 Assess the pros and cons of on-the-job and off-the-job training for companies like Etsy. (12)

Data response 2

Are butlers born, not made?

Butlers, the discreet mainstays of high society in the nineteenth and early twentieth centuries, are enjoying a renaissance. While middle classes in the US and Europe have suffered during the five years of economic crisis, the ultra-rich have fared far better during and since the recession. Amid growing demand, butler training courses have flourished. For recent training offered by the Italian Butlers Association, 70 people applied for ten places. Candidates were selected through written applications and an interview. Aspiring butlers met in Rome's Empire Palace Hotel. They were taught how to polish silver and set the table for brunch on a boat, and were lectured on the subtle art of escaping from a talkative guest. They were also taught the basics of wine tasting and serving.

Some scoff at the idea that butlering can be taught in a classroom. 'They're taking anybody, including somebody who might have been a truck driver for 20 years who decides he want to be a butler', says John Pettman, a former butler who now recruits staff for families on the Forbes Billionaires List.

Source: *Reuters*, 16 May 2014

Questions (25 marks, 25 minutes)

1 Outline two personal qualities to be expected of a butler to a billionaire. (5)

2 Assess two possible benefits of training prospective butlers in the classroom. (8)

3 Assess what might be included in a programme of induction training for a new butler. (12)

Extended writing

1 Stamford Software Solutions, a medium-sized IT company based in the south-east of England, needs to recruit a new sales manager. Evaluate how the company should do this. (20)

2 According to the Leitch Report, UK employers spend an estimated £33 billion in total each year on training, yet one third of employers provide no training at all. Evaluate the most likely consequences for firms who choose not to train their staff. (20)

19 Organisational design

> **Definition**
>
> Organisational design means creating the formal hierarchy that establishes who is answerable to whom throughout the organisation. When presented as a diagram, it shows the departmental functions plus the vertical and horizontal links that represent the formal communications system.

Linked to: Motivation in theory, Ch 20; Motivation in practice, Ch 21; Leadership, Ch 22.

19.1 Introduction

As organisations became larger and more complex, early management thinkers such as F.W. Taylor and H. Fayol considered how to structure an organisation. Both saw the function of organisations as converting inputs, such as money, materials, machines and people, into output. Therefore, designing an organisation was like designing a machine, the objective being to maximise efficiency.

Taylor and Fayol based their thoughts largely on the way an army is organised. The key features of the hierarchy would be as follows:

- To break the organisation up into divisions with a common purpose: in business, this would usually be the business functions: marketing, finance, people and resource management.
- Every individual would answer to one person: their **line manager**.
- No manager would be overloaded with too many subordinates, so the **span of control** would be kept low.
- To achieve low spans of control, it would be necessary to have many management layers. Examples of management layers are shown in Table 19.1.

Military	Business
Captain	Senior manager
Lieutenant	Manager
Sergeant	Team leader
Corporal	Supervisor
Foot-soldier	Shop-floor worker

Table 19.1 Examples of management layers

19.2 The growing business

In the early stages of a new business, there are often only one or two people involved. When the business is so small, the day-to-day tasks are carried out by the owner/s; no formal organisation is needed as communication and co-ordination will be carried out on an informal, face-to-face basis. However, as the business grows and more people become involved, the firm will need to develop a more formal organisational structure. This will show the roles, responsibilities and relationships of each member of the firm. This is often illustrated through an organisational chart. This is a diagram that shows the links between people and departments within the firm. It also shows communication flows/channels, lines of authority and layers of hierarchy. Each of these terms will be explained later in the chapter.

When Matteo Pantani founded Scoop ice cream in Covent Garden in 2007, he employed only part-time staff at the counter to serve the ice cream and take the money. Matteo made the ice cream and ran the business. He did not need to think about a 'hierarchy' or a 'structure'; the organisational structure that existed in 2007 is shown in Figure 19.1.

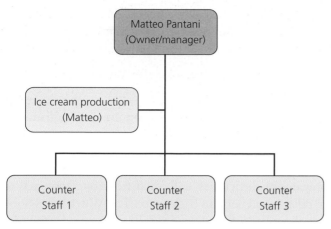

Figure 19.1 Scoop: old organisational structure

As the business grew, he opened a second outlet in 2010, in Brewer Street, Soho, and a third in South Kensington in 2012. This meant he needed managers to run the other outlets, while Matteo was largely at Covent Garden. By mid-2014, the organisational hierarchy looked like the one shown in Figure 19.2.

The point, of course, is to appreciate how much more complex a hierarchy becomes as the business grows.

19.3 Organisational structure

This section will examine the main areas of theory associated with organisational structure and how it is designed. To help clarify, references will be made to the organisational structure in Figure 19.2.

Levels of hierarchy

These show the number of different supervisory and management levels between the bottom of the chart and the top of the hierarchy. Figure 19.2 shows that at Scoop there are now four levels of hierarchy. In an organisation such as Tesco plc, which employs more than 500,000 staff, it is easy to see how there might be 25 levels of hierarchy. This will cause problems with extremely slow (and unreliable) communications between top and bottom of the organisation. TV programmes such as *Undercover Boss* show consistently how hard it is for the chief executive to understand the problems faced by those on the shop floor.

Span of control

This describes the number of people directly under the supervision of a manager. Matteo has the widest span of control, as he has four staff under him directly. If managers have very wide spans of control, they are directly responsible for many staff. In this case, they may find that there are communication problems, or the workers may feel that they are not being given enough guidance. The ideal span of control will depend upon the nature of the tasks and the skills and attitude of the workforce and manager. (See Table 19.2.)

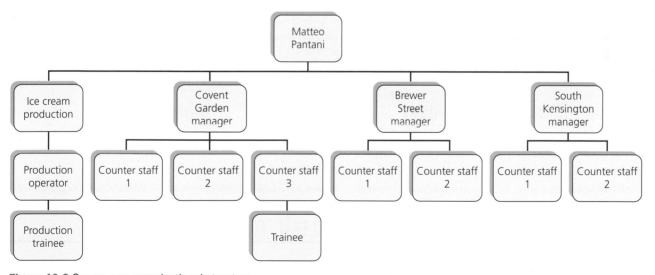

Figure 19.2 Scoop: new organisational structure

Advantages	Disadvantages
Allows close management supervision; this is vital if staff are inexperienced, if labour turnover is high or if the task is critical, e.g. manufacturing aircraft engines.	Workers may feel over-supervised and therefore not trusted; this may cause better staff to leave, in search of more personal responsibility.
Communications may be excellent within the small, immediate team, e.g. the boss and three staff.	Communications may suffer within the business as a whole, as a narrow span means more layers of hierarchy, which makes vertical communications harder.
Many layers of hierarchy means many rungs on the career ladder, i.e. promotion chances arise regularly (though each promotion may mean only a slightly different job).	The narrow span usually leads to restricted scope for initiative and experiment; the boss is always looking over your shoulder; this will alienate enterprising staff.

Table 19.2 Advantages and disadvantages of a narrow span of control

Chain of command

This shows the reporting system from the top of the hierarchy to the bottom; that is, the route through which information travels throughout the organisation. In an organisation with several levels of hierarchy, the chain of command will be longer and this could create a gap between workers at the bottom of the organisation and managers at the top. If information has to travel via several people, there is also a chance that it may become distorted.

Centralisation and decentralisation

This describes the extent to which decision-making power and authority is delegated within an organisation. A centralised structure is one in which decision-making power and control remains in the hands of the top management levels. A decentralised structure delegates decision-making power to workers lower down the organisation. Many organisations will use a combination of these approaches, depending upon the nature of the decision involved. For example, in many schools and colleges, the decisions concerning which resources to use will be decentralised – that is, taken by teachers as opposed to the senior management team. Other decisions, concerning future changes in subjects being offered, may be centralised – that is, taken by senior managers.

'It's a paradox that the greater the decentralisation, the greater the need for both leadership and explicit policies from the top management.'

Bruce Henderson, chief executive, Boston Consulting Group

Influences on centralisation v. decentralisation are primarily internal – that is, within the business. Often they represent alternatives that look rosier if the opposite approach has proved disappointing. Therefore, there is a risk that a company in difficulties will lurch from one approach to the other – and perhaps back again. The Waterstones book shop chain has suffered from this. It was set up by founder Tim Waterstone as a decentralised, locally oriented chain of stores. When bought by WHSmith, book buying and store layouts were centralised. Today they are back with a more localised, decentralised approach.

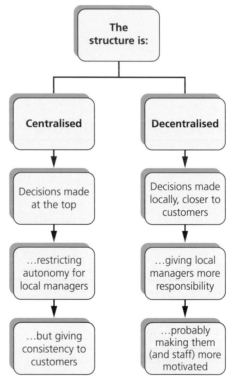

Figure 19.3 Logic chain: centralised v. decentralised organisations

19.4 Types of structure

Tall

A hierarchy is tall when there are lots of layers of management – all responsible for relatively few people. In other words, the span of control is narrow. In Figure 19.4, you can see a relatively tall hierarchy on the left. It takes four layers of management to run 81 shop-floor staff because each manager is directly responsible for only three people. On the right, only two layers of management are needed because the span of control is nine.

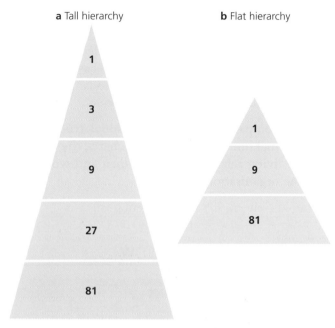

Figure 19.4 Organisational structures with the number of people at each level of the hierarchy

In Figure 19.4, the whole staff remains quite small at around 100. At the time of writing, Tesco plc has over 500,000 staff. Imagine how tall the hierarchy would have to be, especially if Tesco has a narrow span of control throughout the business. That, in turn, would mean too many layers for a message to get successfully and speedily from the shop floor to the chief executive.

> 'If a sufficient number of management layers are superimposed on top of each other, it can be assured that disaster is not left to chance.'

Norman Augustine, US chief executive

So why would any business want a tall hierarchy? If the business wants to avoid mistakes, it will make sure that everyone is carefully supervised. That requires a narrow span of control and therefore a tall hierarchy. If you are a young company needing to make quick, smart decisions, you will want a flat hierarchy in which the boss can really know the thoughts from the shop floor. In a middle-aged company with successful brands, avoiding mistakes may be the priority.

Flat

If the hierarchy is flat, vertical communication should be speedy and perhaps direct (shop-floor worker talking straight to the boss instead of talking through his or her manager). This is a huge help in the service sector, where most shop-floor workers are in daily touch with customers, giving them fantastic insights. There should be nothing to stop the boss sharing these.

> 'Every management layer you can strip away makes you more responsive.'

John Whitney, US academic

So the younger and more dynamic the market, the better it is to have a flat structure. Also, from the worker's point of view, a flat structure implies a wide span of control. That means every boss is in charge of quite a lot of staff, which in turn means that it is impossible to supervise everybody closely. So a wide span will give employees more flexibility to do things their own way, which has the potential to be motivating.

Matrix

Whether a structure is tall or flat, most people at work know who their boss is; in other words, the lines of accountability are clear. I work for you and if I do well you praise me and if I do badly, you know – and act accordingly. You are my 'line manager'.

In a **matrix structure**, it is different. My job description may say I work in marketing, but I may have been put (or volunteered to go) into a project team that is 'cross-functional'. In other words, it may include a design engineer from operations, an accountant and a marketing executive, all working together to find a solution to a problem – or working on an innovative new product.

Advantages	Disadvantages
• Working together should avoid each function trying to 'win' by getting its own ideas at the forefront.	• Above all else, each matrix member will now have two bosses: the project leader and their functional boss…
• Working together should avoid hold-ups (e.g. marketing putting something forward and operations stalling on it), and speed is vital to competitive advantage.	• …but this can cause problems, especially if the functional boss resents the 'distraction' of the matrix-managed project; it can be hard for the employee to resolve priorities.
• It enriches the experience of every team member, as they learn the views of those from other departments.	• Unless the project leader is very experienced, people from four functions may struggle to agree when key decisions are needed.

Table 19.3 Advantages and disadvantages of a matrix structure

19.5 Impact of organisational structure on efficiency and motivation

In the past, some firms had very tall hierarchical structures, which meant there were many layers of management, often with quite narrow spans of control. This made them expensive to run, because of the management salaries that had to be paid. Tall structures also resulted in longer chains of command, which could have a negative impact on communication. More recently, companies have become flatter, meaning fewer layers of management, with each manager having a wider span of control. Although some managers dislike this increased responsibility, workers often thrive with increased independence. Furthermore, the firm will have reduced overhead costs, which means greater business efficiency.

Why is organisational structure so important?

As a firm grows, more people will become involved and, to ensure that the different tasks are fulfilled, it will be vital that every person is clear about what the role involves and who they are answerable/accountable to and responsible for. Poor organisational structures will lack co-ordination, causing the following problems of business efficiency:

- poor communication leading to mistakes
- duplication of tasks
- tasks being overlooked
- departments failing to work together effectively.

In the longer term, these problems will create a sub-standard service and this will have an impact on the firm's sales, revenue and profit. As a firm expands, it must ensure that its organisation structure accommodates the growth.

And what is the impact of different structures on motivation?

Motivation comes from within; it is the desire to push yourself to achieve what you want to achieve (not for an external reason, such as money). Key influences on motivation are scope for initiative and responsibility. Both are extremely unlikely in a tightly supervised role, and therefore a narrow span of control/tall hierarchy is likely to be a hindrance. Much more promising is a less structured, flat hierarchy. This was how Microsoft, Apple, Google and Facebook all started. Individuals were given the freedom to develop their own ideas within a loose, but flat structure. They all did pretty well. The same logic applies to decentralisation (potentially motivating) versus centralisation (little scope for motivation).

It would be wrong, though, to simplify these things. Simply having a flat structure guarantees nothing. At the time of writing, both Asda and Morrisons have removed a whole middle-management layer in their stores. This makes their structures flatter. Yet if all that results is more work for everyone left in post, it is improbable that motivation will improve. For a flat structure to be effective, it needs to be thought through so that everyone has the time to think – and perhaps talk – about the fundamental issues that can help make a success of the business.

> 'Every company has two organisational structures: the formal one is written on the charts; the other is the living relationship of the men and women in the organisation.'
>
> Harold Geneen, US management guru

Five whys and a how

Questions	Answers
Why is organisational structure so important?	Because, however keen and competent the staff, large organisations can operate slowly, frustratingly and bureaucratically if the organisational structure is wrong.
Why might there be benefits from widening an organisation's span of control?	A wider span means fewer layers of hierarchy are needed. This would allow delayering to take place – which saves money and can improve vertical communication.
Why might Asda and Morrisons both have decided (in 2014) to remove a layer of supervisory management from all their stores?	Perhaps both felt the need to cut fixed overhead costs given the market share gains achieved by the discounters Aldi and Lidl.
Why do firms such as Google usually start with an informal management hierarchy, but firm it up when the business has grown?	Because a formal structure is unnecessary when everyone knows/can talk to the boss/bosses. Once Google had 20,000 staff, that was no longer possible.
Why are businesses so scared of the word 'bureaucracy'?	Because it suggests slowness and complacency that firms believe only happens in government departments.
How might a large plc improve its performance by improving its organisational structure?	Usually, the flatter the structure the better the business. This also serves as a warning against growing too big (through take-overs).

19.6 Organisational design – evaluation

There is no 'ideal' organisational structure or span of control. What works for one business may fail in another, even if both are the same size. In exams, there will usually be hints about whether the structure is working. A flat hierarchy may be at the heart of an innovative business, or there may be signs that staff lack direction and morale. A tall hierarchy may be at the centre of a focused, career-orientated workforce, or it may be bureaucratic and incapable of a quick decision. The judgement is yours.

19.7 Workbook

Revision questions

(35 marks; 35 minutes)

1 What is meant by the chain of command? (2)

2 Define span of control. (2)

3 Some theorists believe that the ideal span of control is between three and six. To what extent do you agree with this? (5)

4 Explain two implications of a firm having too wide a span of control. (4)

5 Explain what an organisational chart shows. (4)

6 Why is it important for a growing firm to think carefully about its organisational structure? (5)

7 State three possible problems for a business with many levels of hierarchy. (3)

8 What is meant by the term 'accountable'? (2)

9 What do you think would be the right organisational structure for a hospital? Explain your answer. (4)

10 In your own words, explain the meaning of the term 'matrix management'. (4)

Data response 1

Management changes at ailing Morrisons could see 2,000 jobs axed

Morrisons is set to reveal a management restructuring in its stores within weeks that could lead to as many as 2,000 job losses. The move, resulting from trials of slimmed-down management structures is likely to affect middle-managers overseeing product categories such as fresh food or non-food across the supermarket's 500 UK stores.

The restructuring echoes those by other supermarkets who are also trying to cut costs in stores as grocery sales shift online and prices come under pressure from discounters such as Aldi and Lidl. 'Restructures are going to happen everywhere because sales volumes are going down and aren't coming back, so to keep shareholders happy costs have got to come down', one industry insider said.

Currently each Morrisons store has a manager, a deputy manager and three or four assistant deputy managers who oversee broad product categories such as fresh food. Supervisors for individual departments, such as green groceries, meat or fish, report to them. Under the new structure departments will be merged and these posts would be replaced by team leaders, who will spend most of their time working on the shop floor.

Source: adapted from *The Guardian*, 4 June 2014

Questions (30 marks; 35 minutes)

1 Explain how Morrisons' organisational chart will change following the restructuring. (4)

2 Analyse the probable thinking behind Morrisons' decision to change its management structure. (6)

3 Evaluate whether the changes are guaranteed to improve Morrisons' profitability. (20)

Data response 2

Chicken Little

Peter (known as 'Paxo') Little set up his free-range chicken farm in the early 1990s. At the time, it was an unusual move, especially on the grand scale envisaged by 'Paxo'. His farm had the capacity to produce 250,000 chickens every 45 days; that is, four million birds a year. Since then, the business has grown enormously, to a turnover of £25 million today.

But Paxo is getting concerned that his business is not as efficient as it used to be. As managing director, he finds that he rarely hears from junior staff; not even the quality manager's five staff, who used to see him regularly. As he said recently to the operations director, 'the communication flows seem like treacle today, whereas they used to be like wildfire'.

Fortunately, the boom in demand for free-range and organic produce has helped the business. So even though the team spirit seems to have slipped away, profits have never been higher. Unfortunately, the marketing director repeatedly talks about rumours that a huge Dutch farming business is about to set up poultry farms in Britain. That could 'set the cat among the chickens', in other words, provoke quarrelling and dissention.

Questions (35 marks; 40 minutes)

1 a) From Figure 19.5, give the managing director's span of control. (1)

   b) Assess the strengths and weaknesses of this organisational structure. (10)

   c) Assess the importance of personnel management within this business. (10)

2 Explain why vertical communications may not be as effective today as in the past at Chicken Little. (4)

3 Assess the ways in which the factory manager may benefit or suffer from the organisational structure shown in Figure 19.5. (10)

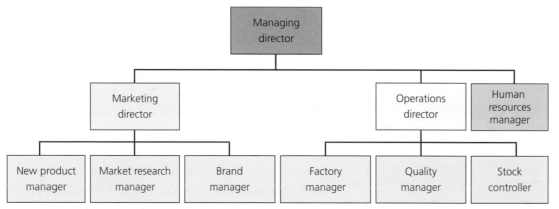

Figure 19.5 Organisational structure of Chicken Little farms

Extended writing

1 For a business of your choice, evaluate why it may be moving towards – or moving away from – a centralised management approach. (20)

2 Organisational hierarchies were originally modelled on the Army, with many ranks and clarity about who was the boss of whom. Evaluate whether this approach is out of date in a business world dominated by online sales and online businesses. (20)

20 Motivation in theory

Definition

According to American psychologist Professor Frederick Herzberg, motivation occurs when people do something because they want to do it; others think of motivation as the desire to achieve a result.

Linked to: Motivation in practice, Ch 21; Leadership, Ch 22; Production, productivity and efficiency, Ch 41.

20.1 Introduction

A study by the Hay Group found that just 15 per cent of UK workers consider themselves 'highly motivated'. As many as 25 per cent say they're 'coasting' and 8 per cent admit to being 'completely demotivated'. In the same survey, employees felt they could be 45 per cent more productive if they were doing a job they loved. Poor management is part of the problem, as 28 per cent say they would be more productive with a better boss.

The Hay Group calculates that if the under-performance was tackled successfully, the value of UK output would rise by more than £350 billion a year. So motivation matters. This is why it merits a unit to itself and is the reason why many consider motivation theory to be the most important topic within Business A level.

20.2 F.W. Taylor and Scientific Management

Although there were earlier pioneers, a good starting point for the study of motivation is F.W. Taylor (1856–1917). As with most of the other influential writers on this subject, Taylor was American. His influence over the twentieth-century world has been massive. Much business practice in America, Europe, Japan and the former Communist countries is still rooted in his writing and work.

A recent biography of Taylor is titled *The One Best Way*; this sums up neatly Taylor's approach to management. He saw it as management's task to decide exactly how every task should be completed, then to devise the tools needed to enable the worker to achieve the task as efficiently as possible. This method is evident today in every McDonald's in the world. Fries are cooked at 175 degrees for exactly three minutes; then a buzzer tells employees to take them out and salt them. Throughout every McDonald's is a series of dedicated, purpose-built machines for producing milkshakes, toasting buns, squirting chocolate sauce, and much else. Today, 120 years after his most active period working in industry, F.W. Taylor would feel very much at home ordering a Big Mac.

> 'In our scheme, we do not ask the initiative of our men. We do not want any initiative. All we want of them is to obey the orders we give them, do what we say, and do it quick.'
>
> F.W. Taylor, *The Principles of Scientific Management*, 1911

So, what was Taylor's view of the underlying motivations of people at work? How did he make sure that the employees worked effectively at following 'the one best way' laid down by managers?

Taylor believed that people work for only one reason: money. He saw it as the task of the manager to devise a system that would maximise efficiency. This would generate the profit to enable the worker to be paid a higher wage. Taylor's view of human nature was that of 'economic man'. In other words, people were motivated only by the economic motive of self-interest. Therefore, a manager could best motivate a worker by offering an incentive (a 'carrot') or a threat (the 'stick'). Taylor can be seen as a manipulator, or even a bully, but he believed his methods were in the best interests of the employees themselves.

Taylor's influence stemmed less from his theories than his activities. He was a trained engineer who acted as a very early management consultant. His methods were as follows.

- Observe workers at work, recording and timing what they do, when they do it and how long they take over it (this became known as time and motion study).
- Identify the most efficient workers and see how they achieve greater efficiency.
- Break the task down into small component parts that can be done quickly and repeatedly.
- Devise equipment specifically to speed up tasks.
- Set out exactly how the work should be done in future; 'each employee', Taylor wrote, 'should receive every day clear-cut, definite instructions as to what he is to do and how he is to do it, and these instructions should be exactly carried out, whether they are right or wrong'.
- Devise a pay scheme to reward those who complete or beat tough output targets, but that penalises those who cannot or will not achieve the **productivity** Taylor believed was possible; this pay scheme was called **piece rate** – no work, no pay.

As an engineer, Taylor was interested in practical outcomes, not in psychology. There is no reason to suppose he thought greatly about the issue of motivation. The effect of his ideas was profound, though. Long before the publication of his 1911 book *The Principles of Scientific Management*, Taylor had spread his managerial practices of careful measurement, monitoring and – above all else – control. Before Taylor, skilled workers chose their own ways of working and had varied, demanding jobs. After Taylor, workers were far more likely to have limited, repetitive tasks, and to be forced to work at the pace set by a manager or consultant engineer.

Among those influenced by Taylor was Henry Ford. His Model T was the world's first mass-produced motor car. By 1911, the Ford factory in Detroit, USA, was already applying Taylor's principles of high **division of labour**, purpose-built machinery and rigid management control. When Ford introduced the conveyor belt in 1913, he achieved the ultimate Taylorite idea: men's pace of work dictated by a mechanical conveyor belt, the speed of which was set by management.

Eventually workers rebelled against being treated like machines. **Trade union** membership thrived in factories run on Taylorite lines, as workers wanted to organise against the suffocating lives they were leading at work. Fortunately, in many western countries, further developments in motivation theory pointed to new, more people-friendly approaches.

> **'Blue collar and white collar call upon the identical phrase: "I'm a robot".'**
>
> Studs Terkel, much-missed US journalist (from his book *Working,* 1974)

Real business

More than 100 years after F.W. Taylor's book was published, 2013 saw a wave of criticism of the working conditions at Amazon.com distribution depots in Britain and Germany.

Many staff work under zero-hours contracts that provide no guaranteed income but they can still have to walk up to 15 miles during a shift, while toilet breaks are monitored and timed. It is also claimed they can be sacked and re-hired.

Former staff at Amazon's warehouse in Rugeley, Staffordshire, told newspaper reporters that they were hired for 12 weeks before being sacked and re-employed so that the company did not have to give them the same rights as full-time employees.

An investigation by Channel 4 News found that employees are tracked using GPS tags while inside the warehouse. A BBC Panorama reporter concluded that the work was much harder physically than seemed reasonable. If staff are found to breach any of the company's rules, such as talking to colleagues or leaving work early, they can be dismissed on a 'three strikes and you are out' basis.

F.W. Taylor would have agreed with Amazon's desire for full control of workers' actions, but would have made more effort to make sure that the job requirement represented a 'fair day's work'.

20.3 Elton Mayo and human relations theory

Elton Mayo (1880–1949) was a medical student who became an academic with a particular interest in people in organisations. Although an Australian, he moved to America in 1923. Early in his career, his methods were heavily influenced by F.W. Taylor. An early investigation of a spinning mill in Pennsylvania identified one department with labour turnover of 250 per cent, compared with 6 per cent elsewhere in the factory. His Taylorite solution was to prescribe work breaks. These had the desired effect.

Mayo moved on to work at the Hawthorne plant of Western Electric Company in Chicago. His investigations there are known as the Hawthorne experiments.

He was called in to Hawthorne to try to explain the findings of a previous test into the effects of lighting upon productivity levels. The lighting conditions for one work group had been varied, while those for another had been held constant. The surprise was that, whatever was done to the lighting, production rose in *both* groups. This proved that there was more to motivation and efficiency than purely economic motives.

Between 1927 and 1932, Mayo conducted a series of experiments at Hawthorne. The first is known as the Relay Assembly Test. Six volunteer female assembly staff were separated from their workmates. A series of experiments was carried out. The results were recorded and discussed with the women. Every 12 weeks, a new working method was tried. The alternatives included different:

- bonus methods, such as individual versus group bonuses
- rest periods
- refreshments
- work layouts.

Before every change, the researchers discussed the new method fully with the operators. Almost without exception productivity increased with every change. At the end, the group returned to the original method (48-hour, 6-day week with no breaks) and output went up to its highest level yet! Not only that, but the women claimed they felt less tired than they had at the start.

The experiments had started rather slowly, with some resistance from the operatives. Progress became much more marked when one member of the group retired. She was replaced by a younger woman who quickly became the unofficial leader of the group.

Mayo's conclusions

Mayo drew the following conclusions from his experiments:

- The women gained satisfaction from the freedom and control over their working environment.
- 'What actually happened was that six individuals became a team and the team gave itself wholeheartedly and spontaneously to co-operation in the experiment' (Mayo, 1949).
- Group norms (expectations of one another) are crucial and may be influenced more by informal than official group leaders.

- Communication between workers and managers influences morale and output.
- Workers are affected by the degree of interest shown in them by their managers; the influence of this upon motivation is known as 'the Hawthorne effect'.

The consequences of Mayo's work were enormous. He influenced many researchers and writers, effectively opening up the fields of industrial psychology and industrial sociology. Many academics followed Mayo's approach in what became known as the human relations school of management.

Businesses also responded to the implications of Mayo's work for company profitability and success. If teamwork, communications and managerial involvement were so important, firms reasoned that they needed an organisational structure to cope. In Taylor's era, the key person was the engineer. The winners from Mayo's work were personnel departments. They grew throughout America and Britain in the 1930s, 1940s and 1950s as companies tried to achieve the Hawthorne effect.

20.4 Maslow and the hierarchy of needs

'Direction and control are of limited value in motivating people whose important needs are social and egotistic.'

Douglas McGregor, author of *The Human Side of Enterprise*

Abraham Maslow (1908–1970) was an American psychologist whose great contribution to motivation theory was the 'hierarchy of needs'. Maslow believed that everyone has the same needs, all of which can be organised as a hierarchy. At the base of the hierarchy are physical needs, such as food, shelter and warmth. When unsatisfied, these are the individual's primary motivations. When employees earn enough to satisfy these needs, however, their motivating power withers away. Maslow said that 'It is quite true that humans live by bread alone – when there is no bread. But what happens to their desires when there is bread?' Instead of physical needs, people become motivated to achieve needs such as security and stability, which Maslow called the safety needs. In full, Maslow's hierarchy consisted of the elements listed in Table 20.1.

Maslow's levels of human need	Business implications
Physical needs, e.g. food, shelter and warmth	Pay levels and working conditions
Safety needs, e.g. security, a safe structured environment, stability, freedom from anxiety	Job security, a clear job role/description, clear lines of accountability (only one boss)
Social needs, e.g. belonging, friendship, contact	Team working, communications, social facilities
Esteem needs, e.g. strength, self-respect, confidence, status and recognition	Status, recognition for achievement, power, trust
Self-actualisation, e.g. self-fulfilment; 'to become everything that one is capable of becoming', wrote Maslow	Scope to develop new skills and meet new challenges, and to develop one's full potential

Table 20.1 Maslow's hierarchy of needs: implications for business

Ever since Maslow first put his theory forward (in 1940), writers have argued about its implications. Among the key issues raised by Maslow are the following.

- Do all humans have the same set of needs? Are there some people who need no more from a job than money?
- Do different people have different degrees of need; for example, are some highly motivated by the need for power, while others are satisfied by social factors? If so, the successful manager would be one who can understand and attempt to meet the differing needs of her/his staff.
- Can anyone's needs ever be said to be fully satisfied? The reason the hierarchy diagram (see Figure 20.1) has an open top is to suggest that the human desire for achievement is limitless.

Figure 20.1 Maslow's hierarchy of needs

Maslow's work had a huge influence on the writers who followed him, especially McGregor and Herzberg. The hierarchy of needs is also used by academics in many subjects beyond Business, notably Psychology and Sociology.

20.5 Herzberg's two-factor theory

The key test of a theory is its analytic usefulness. On this criterion, the work of Professor Fred Herzberg (1923–2000) is the strongest by far.

The theory stems from research conducted in the 1950s into factors affecting workers' **job satisfaction** and dissatisfaction. It was carried out on 200 accountants and engineers in Pennsylvania, USA. Despite the limited nature of this sample, Herzberg's conclusions remain influential to this day.

Herzberg asked employees to describe recent events that had given rise to exceptionally good feelings about their jobs, then probed for the reasons why. 'Five factors stand out as strong determiners of job satisfaction', Herzberg wrote in 1966, 'achievement, recognition for achievement, the work itself, responsibility and advancement – the last three being of greater importance for a lasting change of attitudes'. He pointed out that each of these factors concerned the job itself, rather than issues such as pay or status. Herzberg called these five factors 'the motivators'.

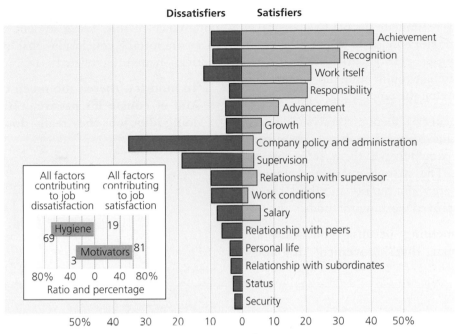

Figure 20.2 Comparison of satisfiers and dissatisfiers

The researchers went on to ask about events giving rise to exceptionally bad feelings about their jobs. This revealed a separate set of five causes. Herzberg stated that 'the major dissatisfiers were company policy and administration, supervision, salary, interpersonal relations and working conditions'. He concluded that the common theme was factors that 'surround the job', rather than the job itself. The name he gave these dissatisfiers was **hygiene factors**; this was because fulfilling them would prevent dissatisfaction, rather than causing positive motivation. Careful hygiene prevents disease; care to fulfil hygiene factors prevents job dissatisfaction.

To summarise: motivators have the power to create positive job satisfaction, but little downward potential; hygiene factors will cause job dissatisfaction unless they are provided for, but do not motivate. Importantly, Herzberg saw pay as a hygiene factor, not a motivator. So a feeling of being underpaid could lead to a grievance; but high pay would soon be taken for granted. This motivator/hygiene factor theory is known as the 'two-factor theory' (see Table 20.2).

> **'Motivators and hygiene factors are equally important, but for different reasons.'**
>
> F. Herzberg

Motivators (can create positive satisfaction)	Hygiene factors (can create job dissatisfaction)
Achievement	Company policy and administration (the rules, paperwork and red tape)
Recognition for achievement	Supervision (especially being over-supervised)
Meaningful, interesting work	Pay
Responsibility	Interpersonal relations (with supervisor, peers, or even customers)
Advancement (psychological, not just a promotion)	Working conditions

Table 20.2 Herzberg's two-factor theory

Movement and motivation

Herzberg was keen to distinguish between movement and motivation. Movement occurs when somebody does something; motivation is when they *want* to do something. This distinction is essential to a full understanding of Herzberg's theory. He did not doubt that financial incentives could be used to boost productivity: 'If you bully or bribe people, they'll give you better than average performance.' His worries about 'bribes' (carrots) were that they would never stimulate people to give of their best; people would do just enough to achieve the bonus. Furthermore, bribing people to work harder at a task they found unsatisfying would build up resentments, which might backfire on the employer.

Herzberg advised against payment methods such as piece rate. They would achieve movement but, by reinforcing worker behaviour, would make them inflexible and resistant to change. The salaried, motivated employee would work hard, care about quality and think about – even welcome – improved working methods.

> 'If you do something because you want a house or a Jaguar, that's movement. It's not motivation.'
>
> F. Herzberg

Job enrichment

The reason why Herzberg's work has had such an impact on businesses is because he not only analysed motivation, he also had a method for improving it. The method is job enrichment, which he defined as 'giving people the opportunity to use their ability'. He suggested that, for a job to be considered enriched, it would have to contain the following.

A complete unit of work

People need to work not on just a small repetitive fragment of a job, but a full challenging task; Herzberg heaped scorn upon the 'idiot jobs' that resulted from Taylor's views on the merits of high division of labour.

Direct feedback

Wherever possible, a job should enable the worker to judge immediately the quality of what she or he has done; direct feedback gives the painter or the actor (or the teacher) the satisfaction of knowing exactly how well they have performed. Herzberg disliked systems that pass quality inspection off onto a supervisor: 'a man must always be held responsible for his own quality'. Worst of all, he felt, was annual appraisal, in which feedback is too long delayed.

Direct communication

For people to feel committed and in control and to gain direct feedback, they should communicate directly – avoiding the delays of communicating via a supervisor or a 'contact person'. In itself, it is hard to see the importance of this. For a student of Business, it leads to an important conclusion: that communication and motivation are inter-related.

> 'In industry, there's too much communication. And of course it's passive... But if people are doing idiot jobs they really don't give a damn.'
>
> F. Herzberg

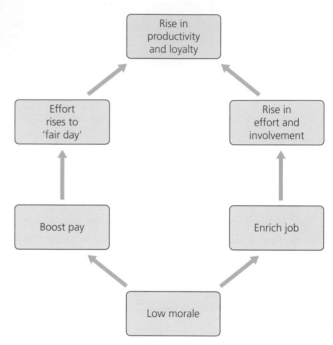

Figure 20.3 Herzberg logic chain: take care of hygiene factors and motivators

Conclusion

Herzberg's original research has been followed up in many different countries, including Japan, Africa and Russia. An article he wrote on the subject in the *Harvard Business Review* in 1968 (called 'Just one more time, how do you motivate employees?') has sold more than one million reprinted copies. His main insight was to show that, unless the job itself was interesting, there was no way to make working life satisfying. This led companies such as Volvo in Sweden and Toyota in Japan to rethink their factory layouts. Instead of individual workers doing simple, repetitive tasks, the drive was to provide more complete units of work. Workers were grouped into teams, focusing on significant parts of the manufacturing process, such as assembling and fitting the gearbox, and then checking the quality of their work. Job enrichment indeed.

Five whys and a how

Questions	Answers
Why did trade unions dislike F.W. Taylor with his financial incentives and 'one best way'?	They disliked the shift in power towards management and hated being 'deskilled': doing the same repetitive task every day.
Why do theorists such as Herzberg distinguish motivation from morale?	Morale can be high if the future looks bright and job security is strong – that doesn't mean that motivation will be high; motivation is doing a good job because you want to.
Why might 'esteem needs' be hard to provide in some workplaces?	It might be hard in some jobs that society rates lowly, such as bin-collecting or roadsweeping.
Why does Herzberg think financial incentives aren't motivating?	He accepts that they incentivise and therefore can generate some 'movement' – but to him, motivation comes from within.
Why may companies find it difficult to provide a 'complete unit of work'?	Some tasks can be completed far more efficiently with high division of labour, so a complete unit of work can seem an indulgence.
How could you increase the motivation of England's national football team?	Recruit players who love playing, give them plenty of responsibility – perhaps to discuss and plan tactics – and let them do the pre- and post-match interviews.

20.6 Motivation in theory – evaluation

Most managers assume they understand human motivation, but they have never studied it. As a result, they may underestimate the potential within their own staff, or unthinkingly cause resentments that fester.

The process of managing people takes place in every part of every organisation. So every manager should be aware of motivation theory. In some cases, ignorance leads managers to ignore motivation altogether; they tell themselves that control and organisation are their only concerns. Other managers may see motivation as important, but fail to understand its subtleties.

For these reasons, there is a case for saying that the concepts within this unit are the most important in the whole subject. Certainly it is true to say that Taylor, Mayo, Maslow and Herzberg are studied from Russia to Japan and Angola to Zimbabwe.

Key terms

Division of labour: subdividing a task into a number of activities, enabling workers to specialise and therefore become very efficient at completing what may be a small, repetitive task.

Hygiene factors: 'everything that surrounds what you do in the job', such as pay, working conditions and social status; all are potential causes of dissatisfaction, according to Herzberg.

Job satisfaction: the sense of well-being and achievement that stems from a satisfying job.

Piece rate: paying workers per piece they produce (for example, £2 per pair of jeans made).

Productivity: output per person (that is, a measure of efficiency).

Trade union: an organisation that represents the interests of staff at the workplace.

20.7 Workbook

Revision questions

(30 marks; 30 minutes)

1 Which features of the organisation of a McDonald's could be described as Taylorite? (3)

2 Explain the meaning of the term 'economic man'. (3)

3 Explain how workers in a bakery may be affected by a change from salary to piece rate. (4)

4 Which two levels of Maslow's hierarchy could be called 'the lower-order needs'? (2)

5 Describe in your own words why Maslow organised the needs into a hierarchy. (3)

6 State three business implications of Maslow's work on human needs. (3)

7 Herzberg believes pay does not motivate, but it is important. Why? (3)

8 How do motivators differ from hygiene factors? (3)

9 What is job enrichment? How is it achieved? (3)

10 If staff absenteeism is increasing, it is likely to be because (choose one answer):

a) hygiene factors are over-rewarded

b) wage increases are outstripping inflation

c) there's too much self-actualisation

d) division of labour is too high. (1)

11 Herzberg's 'hygiene factors' relate best to (choose one answer):

a) Taylor's focus on the 'one best way'

b) Maslow's concept of self-actualisation

c) Taylor's idea of self-actualisation

d) Maslow's physiological needs. (1)

12 Maslow's idea of 'self-actualisation' means (choose one answer):

a) striving to get a promotion

b) finding just what you're capable of

c) getting the money rewards you deserve

d) finally enjoying true self-esteem. (1)

Data response 1

Look back at Figure 20.2. It shows the results of Herzberg's research into the factors that cause positive job satisfaction and those that cause job dissatisfaction. The length of the bars shows the percentage of responses.

Questions (25 marks; 25 minutes)

1 Give the factors that had the least effect on satisfaction or dissatisfaction. (1)

2 Herzberg categorises 'Salary' as a hygiene factor, i.e. underpayment is a source of demotivation. Assess that view based on the evidence in Figure 20.2. (10)

3 Separate research by Herzberg showed that 'responsibility' had the longest-lasting effects on job satisfaction. Explain why this might be so. (4)

4 Assess which of the factors is the most important motivator. (10)

Data response 2

Tania was delighted to get the bakery job and looked forward to her first shift. It would be tiring after a day at college, but £52 for eight hours on a Friday would guarantee good Saturday nights in future.

On arrival, she was surprised to be put straight to work, with no more than a mumbled: 'You'll be working packing machine B.' Fortunately, she was able to watch the previous shift worker before clocking-off time, and could get the hang of what was clearly a very simple task. As the 18.00 bell rang, the workers streamed out, but not many had yet turned up from Tania's shift. The conveyor belt started to roll again at 18.16.

As the evening wore on, machinery breakdowns provided the only, welcome, relief from the tedium and discomfort of Tania's job. Each time a breakdown occurred, a ringing alarm bell was drowned out by a huge cheer from the staff. A few joyful moments followed, with dough fights breaking out. Tania started to feel quite old as she looked at some of her workmates.

At the 22.00 meal break, Tania was made to feel welcome. She enjoyed hearing the sharp, funny

comments made about the shift managers. One was dubbed 'Noman' because he was fat, wore a white coat and never agreed to anything. Another was called 'Turkey' because he strutted around, but if anything went wrong, got into a flap. It was clear that both saw themselves as bosses. They were not there to help or to encourage, only to blame.

Was the bakery always like this, Tania wondered? Or was it simply that these two managers were poor?

Questions (25 marks; 30 minutes)

1 Assess the working lives of the shift workers at the bakery, using Herzberg's two-factor theory. (10)

2 If a managerial follower of Taylor's methods came into the factory, how might she or he try to improve the productivity level? (5)

3 Later on in this (true) story, Tania read in the local paper that the factory was closing. The reason given was 'lower labour productivity than at our other bakeries'. The newspaper grumbled about the poor attitudes of local workers. Assess the extent to which there is justification for this view. (10)

Extended writing

1 Followers of F.W. Taylor and Professor Herzberg each set about increasing the motivation of teachers. Evaluate which would be the most successful. (20)

2 Evaluate the changes that might occur if Tesco's new boss decided to apply Maslow's hierarchy of needs to the whole workforce. (20)

21 Motivation in practice

Definition

Assessing how firms try to motivate their staff and how successful these actions are. In this context, companies take 'motivation' to mean enthusiastic pursuit of the objectives or tasks set out by the firm.

Linked to: Approaches to staffing, Ch 17; Organisational design, Ch 19; Motivation in theory, Ch 20.

21.1 Introduction

There are four main variables that influence the **motivation** of staff in practice:

1 financial incentives

2 empowering the employees: delegation, consultation and empowerment

3 team and flexible working

4 job enlargement: job enrichment and job rotation.

All four will be analysed with reference to the theories outlined in Unit 20.

21.2 Financial reward systems

Piecework

Piecework means working in return for a payment per unit produced. Pieceworkers receive no basic or shift pay, so there is no sick pay, holiday pay or company pension.

Piecework is used extensively in small-scale manufacturing; for example, of jeans or jewellery. Its attraction for managers is that it makes supervision virtually unnecessary. All the manager needs to do is operate a quality control system that ensures the finished product is worth paying for. Day by day, the workers can be relied upon to work fast enough to earn a living wage.

Disadvantages of piecework

Piecework has several disadvantages to firms, however, including the following.

- Scrap levels may be high, if workers are focused entirely on speed of output.

Motivation

Famous sayings

'There is no room for criticism on the training field. For a player – and for any human being – there is nothing better than hearing "well done". Those are the two best words ever invented in sports.'

Sir Alex Ferguson

'Motivation is everything. You can do the work of two people, but you can't be two people. Instead, you have to inspire the next guy down the line and get him to inspire his people.'

Lee Iacocca, successful boss of Chrysler Motors

'I have never found anybody yet who went to work happily on a Monday that had not been paid on a Friday.'

Tom Farmer, Kwik-Fit founder

'Motivating people over a short period is not very difficult. A crisis will often do just that, or a carefully planned special event. Motivating people over a longer period of time, however, is far more difficult. It is also far more important in today's business environment.'

John Kotter, management thinker

'My best friend is the one who brings out the best in me.'

Henry Ford, founder of Ford Motors

Source: Stuart Crainer (1997) *The Ultimate Book of Business Quotations*, Capstone Publishing.

- There is an incentive to provide acceptable quality, but not the best possible quality.
- Workers will work hardest when they want higher earnings (probably before Christmas and before their summer holiday); this may not coincide at all with seasonal patterns of customer demand.
- Worst of all is the problem of change; Herzberg pointed out that 'the worst way to motivate people is piece rate… it reinforces behaviour'; focusing people on maximising their earnings by repeating a task makes them very reluctant to produce something different or in a different way (they worry that they will lose out financially).

Real business

Most football clubs have signed expensive new players who subsequently fail to perform on the pitch. In 2013, Liverpool decided to overcome this problem by offering newly signed players lower basic salaries offset by lucrative performance-related bonuses. Football clubs that link pay to performance pay bonuses for each game won, goals scored, clean sheets and featuring in the starting line-up. According to Managing Director Ian Ayre, 'From the football club's perspective, our view has to be that people are rewarded for contributing towards what we achieve. As long as contracts are structured in that way then everyone wins.' That year, Liverpool went on to enjoy one of their highest finishes in the Premier League.

Commission

Commission is a bonus earned on top of a basic salary, usually in line with a specific achievement, such as meeting a sales target. It might be that a member of staff is expected to generate £80,000 of sales a year, and for every £1,000 above that total a commission will be paid of £50. That 5 per cent rate of commission might enable the individual to boost income considerably by the end of the year.

Commission is used widely to incentivise staff in clothes shops, furniture shops and other outlets where it can take effort and skill to clinch a sale. Note that it would be incorrect to write about commission as a 'motivator'. In Professor Herzberg's terms, commission is simply a hygiene factor.

Bonus

According to Professor Herzberg, 'the best way to pay people is a salary'. He considered every attempt to 'motivate' people through financial incentives doomed to fail – simply because people would be incentivised to do the wrong thing – again and again. This proved true in the 2008/2009 financial crisis, when the mayhem in the financial sector was often the result of faulty bonus structures that encouraged excessive short-term risk-taking. Quite simply, City traders knew that risks that paid off gave them bonuses (measured perhaps in hundreds of thousands of pounds) but risks that failed cost the bank money. Ultimately their risk-taking cost banks so much money that taxpayers had to bail the banks out. In December 2009, the National Audit Office announced that UK banks had been bailed out to the tune of £850 billion (yes, I have checked that extraordinary sum!).

Even after these events, banks in Britain (and many politicians) try to suggest that bonuses are an important, positive part of **remuneration**. In late 2014, British banks were still complaining about an EU ruling that no bank should pay a bonus greater than double a person's salary (a very wise rule).

Relatively small-scale bonuses can act as a nice thank-you for a job done well. When they are large enough to become the focus of an individual's working life, they distort behaviour and potentially turn an employee into a money-seeking robot. Just as paying a striker a huge goal bonus would eliminate team play, the same is true in the ordinary business world.

Profit share

As financial rewards go, this is a relatively sensible one. It gives a sense of involvement to staff, and may affect behaviour favourably. If staff receive some share of the profits, they may be slightly warmer towards customers and a little more likely to turn off the lights when leaving a room. Sainsbury's, in 2014, distributed an £80 million profit share among its 161,000 staff. That makes an average of £500. However, when you check on the customer service rankings of the supermarket chains, Sainsbury's doesn't seem to provide any better a customer experience than Asda or any of the other supermarkets.

An annual profit share is a fine thing, but day by day, if you're not enjoying your job, few would look forward to £500 in a year's time and say: it'll all be worth it. Good employers realise that motivation comes from the satisfaction – pleasure, even – of doing a good job. A profit share is a lovely thank-you, but no more than that.

Performance-related pay

Performance-related pay (PRP) is a financial reward to staff whose work is considered above average. It is used for employees whose work achievements cannot be assessed simply through numerical measures (such as units produced or sold). PRP awards are usually made after an appraisal process has evaluated the performance of staff during the year.

The usual method is outlined below.

1 Establish targets for each member of staff/management at an appraisal interview.

2 At the end of the year, discuss the individual's achievements against those targets.

3 Those with outstanding achievements are given a Merit 1 pay rise or bonus worth perhaps 6 per cent of salary; others receive between 0 per cent and 6 per cent.

Lack of evidence for benefits of PRP

Despite the enthusiasm they have shown for it, employers have rarely been able to provide evidence of the benefits of PRP. Indeed, the Institute of Personnel Management concluded in a report that:

> 'It was not unusual to find that organisations which had introduced merit pay some years ago were less certain now of its continued value... it was time to move on to something more closely reflecting team achievement and how the organisation as a whole was faring.'

This pointed to a fundamental problem with PRP: rewarding individuals does nothing to promote teamwork. Furthermore, it could create unhealthy rivalry between managers, with each going for the same Merit 1 spot.

Other problems for PRP systems

Other problems for PRP systems include the following.

- Perceived fairness/unfairness: staff often suspect that those awarded the maximum are being rewarded not for performance but out of favouritism; this may damage working relations and team spirit.
- Whether they have a sound basis in human psychology: without question, Professor Herzberg would be very critical of any attempt to influence work behaviour by financial incentives; a London School of Economics study of Inland Revenue staff found that only 12 per cent

believed that PRP had raised motivation at work, while 76 per cent said it had not; Herzberg would approve of the researchers' conclusion that: 'The current system has not succeeded in motivating staff to any significant degree, and may well have done the reverse.'

As the last point illustrates, a key assumption behind PRP is that the chance to be paid a bit more than other employees will result in a change in individual behaviour, in increased motivation to work. A survey for the government publication *Employment in Britain* found that 'pay incentives were thought important for hard work by fewer than one in five [employees], and for quality standards by fewer than one in ten'.

Why do firms continue with PRP?

So why do firms continue to pursue PRP systems? There are two possible reasons:

1 to make it easier for managers to manage/control their staff (using a carrot instead of a stick)

2 to reduce the influence of collective bargaining and therefore trade unions.

Real business

Performance-related pay does not encourage performance

The clue ought to be in the name. Performance-related pay is pay for performance, and the better performance you turn in and the harder you work, the more you will get to take home. Except that academics are now suggesting, more often than not, the opposite may be the case.

New research by the London School of Economics (LSE) has argued that, far from encouraging people to strive to reach great heights, performance-related pay often does the opposite and encourages people to work less hard.

An analysis of 51 separate experimental studies of financial incentives in employment relations found what the school has described as 'overwhelming evidence' that these incentives could reduce an employee's natural inclination to complete a task and derive pleasure from doing so.

The findings are, of course, deeply controversial, given the depths of anger still felt by many over the role of performance-related pay in causing or contributing to the current economic crisis.

'We find that financial incentives may indeed reduce intrinsic motivation and diminish ethical or other reasons for complying

---

with workplace social norms such as fairness', argued Dr Bernd Irlenbusch, from the LSE's Department of Management.

'As a consequence, the provision of incentives can result in a negative impact on overall performance', he added.

Companies therefore need to be aware that the provision of performance-related pay could result in a net reduction of motivation across a team or organisation, he suggested.

Source: www.management-issues.com

21.3 Empowering employees

Empowerment

Empowerment is a modern term for delegation. There is only one difference between the two. The empowered worker has not only the authority to manage a task, but also some scope to decide what that task should be. An IKEA store manager has power delegated to him or her, but head office rules may be so rigid that the manager has little scope for individual judgement. An empowered store manager would be one who could choose a range of stock suited to local customers, or a staffing policy that differs from the national store policy.

Empowerment means having more power and control over your working life, and having the scope to make significant decisions about how to allocate your time and how to move forward. It is a practical application of the theories of Maslow and Herzberg. It may lead to greater risks being taken, but can also lead to opportunities being identified and exploited. Above all else, it should aid motivation.

Delegation

Delegation means passing the authority for a task down to junior staff. In theory, the person who has delegated the task remains responsible (to shareholders, perhaps), but the junior manager can decide how to set the process. To be effective, the boss has to:

- trust the junior staff member
- provide extra training, if needed
- provide the resources that will be needed, e.g. a budget
- stay interested, but not intervene or 'micromanage'.

When effective, delegation should be motivating to the staff member, as it is great to be trusted and great to tackle a new challenge. Effective delegation of substantial tasks

is a sign of democratic leadership, as it passes decision making down the hierarchy.

Consultation

Consultation means asking the views of the staff you manage, then taking them into account in the decisions you make. Effective consultation requires that the boss:

- consults on important issues (some bosses take big decisions without discussion, but bring trivial things up in meetings; this irritates staff)
- consults widely and deeply, so that all full-time staff feel they have had their say, no matter how junior (it is very hard to consult with part-timers as they may only be at work in the evenings or weekends)
- takes those views into account when making decisions…
- …and explains how they have been taken into account, including when they have been considered but rejected.

When carried through intelligently, consultation helps boost team working and morale. People want to be able to express their views and – occasionally – find those views have made a difference. Effective consultation is a sign of high-quality paternalistic leadership.

21.4 Team working

Team working is the attempt to maximise staff satisfaction and involvement by organising employees into relatively small teams. These teams may be functional (the 'drive-thru crew' at a McDonald's) or geographic. The key features of such teams are that they should be:

- multi-skilled, so that everyone can do everyone else's job
- working together to meet shared objectives, such as to serve every customer within a minute or produce a fault-free gearbox
- encouraged to think of the future as well as the present, in a spirit of **kaizen** (continuous improvement).

From a theoretical point of view, team working fits in well with Maslow's findings on the importance of social needs. In practical terms, modern managers like team working because of the flexibility it implies. If worker A is absent, there are plenty of others used to dealing with the job. Therefore, there is no disruption. Team working also gives scope for motivating influences, such as job enrichment and **quality circles**.

Professor Charles Handy suggests in his book *Inside Organisations* that 'a good team is a great place to be, exciting, stimulating, supportive, successful. A bad team is horrible, a sort of human prison.' It is true that the business will not benefit if the social norms within the team discourage effort. Nevertheless, team working has proved successful in many companies in recent years.

21.5 Flexible working

Aspects of workforce flexibility that could help staff performance include those that make it possible for talented staff to work effectively, even though they have other issues or responsibilities. **Flexitime** is an example, as it gives parents of small children and employees with disabilities the scope to arrive and leave later or earlier than others. This would allow a wheelchair-bound employee to avoid the rush hour, or a dad to take the kids to school before coming to work. The same positive aspects of flexible working come from methods such as:

- term-time only working
- job sharing
- occasional home-working.

Flexible working is covered fully in Chapter 17.

21.6 Job enlargement

Research into workplace engagement often shows that people feel trapped within the limitations of their job. They are bored. So researchers look for ways to increase the scope of the job. This is called job enlargement.

Job enlargement is a general term for anything that increases the scope of a job. There are two ways of doing this:

1 *Job rotation*: increasing a worker's activities by switching between tasks of a similar level of difficulty. This does not increase the challenge, but may reduce the boredom of a job. This is shown in Figure 21.1. It can be argued that this horizontal job enlargement will do little more than relieve the boredom. The individual is still quite likely to see work as a chore.

2 *Job enrichment*: this enlargement of the scope of the job involves extra responsibilities and challenges, as well as extra activities/workload.

Professor Herzberg defines job enrichment as 'giving people the opportunity to use their ability'. A full explanation of his theory is outlined in Chapter 20. How can job enrichment be put into practice? The key thing is to realise the enormity of the task. It is not cheap, quick or easy to enrich the job of the production line worker or the supermarket checkout operator. The first thought may be to add more variety to the work. The supermarket operator could switch between the checkout, shelf-stacking and working in the warehouse. Known as job rotation, this approach reduces repetition but still provides the employee with little challenge. Herzberg's definition of job enrichment implies giving people 'a range of responsibilities and activities'. Job rotation only provides a range of activities. To provide job enrichment, workers must have a complete unit of work (not a repetitive fragment) and responsibility for quality and for self-checking, and must be given the opportunity to show their abilities. In Figure 21.2, you can see that a supermarket operator could be given responsibility for a section of the store – taking on supervisory as well as mundane tasks. That combination of horizontal and vertical enlargement is job enrichment.

Figure 21.1 Job rotation

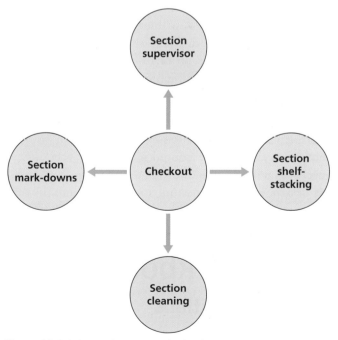

Figure 21.2 Job enrichment: vertical enlargement

Five whys and a how

Questions	Answers
Why might bonus payments fail to motivate?	They provide incentives, but Herzberg says motivation comes from within, i.e. doing something because you want to; if there's a financial incentive, that only achieves movement. (For the difference between movement and motivation, remember the English football team at the 2014 World Cup.)
Why may payment on the basis of piecework make it hard to achieve change in the workplace?	Those with high earnings on the old system will fear change – and all staff will have been conditioned to do one thing repeatedly.
Why is empowerment more powerful than delegation?	Delegation passes down the hierarchy the power to do things; empowerment gives the power to decide what to do.
Why do you think that HR departments love performance-related pay?	Because it gives them a role and a degree or control. Pay everyone a salary, and who needs an HR department?
Why would F.W. Taylor be thrilled to see that performance-related pay is still a powerful force in the twenty-first century?	Taylor believed that workers should be under the tight control of management; PRP can achieve this by forcing staff to do what they're told in order to maximise their pay.
How might performance-related pay for teachers affect lessons in future?	It might make them more formulaic, with all teachers focused solely on maximising grades.

21.7 Motivation in practice – evaluation

When writing about financial incentives, there is a serious risk of over-simplification. The reality is that using money to try to motivate people often proves a dreadful mistake (as Herzberg always made clear). Exaggerated commissions or performance-related pay can lead sales staff to oversell goods or services, such as cosmetic surgery or questionable investments, which may cause customers huge difficulties later on. Also, within the workplace, serious problems can arise: bullying to 'motivate' staff into working harder, or creating a culture of overwork, which leads to stress.

Fortunately, there are many businesses in which the management of motivation is treated with respect: companies which know that quick fixes are not the answer. Successful motivation in the long term is a result of careful job design, employee training and development, honesty and trust. It may be possible to supplement this with an attractive financial reward scheme, but money will never be a substitute for motivation.

> ### Key terms
>
> **Flexitime:** giving staff flexibility over their arrival and leaving times as long as the right numbers of hours are completed (and usually there's a mandatory period, e.g. 10.30–3.30).
>
> **Kaizen:** continuous improvement, usually achieved by workforce engagement and involvement (as opposed to automation).
>
> **Motivation:** to Professor Herzberg, it means doing something because you want to do it; most business leaders think of it as prompting people to work hard.
>
> **Quality circles:** discussion groups in which staff discuss an operational problem with a view to recommending a solution to management.
>
> **Remuneration:** all the financial rewards received by an employee: pay, pension contributions, bonuses and any 'fringe benefits', such as a company car.

21.8 Workbook

Revision questions

(35 marks; 35 minutes)

1 Identify three advantages to an employee of working in a team. (3)

2 Look at the famous saying by Lee Iacocca on page 131. Explain in your own words what he meant by this. (3)

3 How *should* a manager deal with a mistake made by a junior employee? (4)

4 State three reasons why job enrichment should improve staff motivation. (3)

5   Distinguish between job rotation and job
    enrichment.   (4)

6   Explain in your own words how 'empowerment'
    differs from 'delegation'.   (3)

7   State two advantages and two disadvantages
    of offering staff performance-related pay.   (4)

8   What could be the implications of providing a
    profit share to senior managers but not to the
    workforce generally?   (5)

9   What problems may result from a manager
    bullying staff to 'motivate' them?   (6)

Data response 1

Link pay to pupil progress, over half of teachers polled say

Over half of teachers in state schools in England support the government's plan to link pay to pupils' progress and results, suggests a survey. The National Foundation for Educational Research polled over 1,000 teachers for the charity Sutton Trust.

Of those surveyed, 55 per cent of primary teachers and 52 per cent of secondary teachers said incremental pay rises should depend at least in part on performance. But almost half favoured the old system of linking pay to length of service. From September 2014, the government requires schools to link pay progression, for teachers in the first five years of their career, to classroom performance.

Professor Steven Higgins, of Durham University's School of Education, casts doubt on this new policy by referring to research conducted in America. He told the Education Media Centre that:

'The evidence is not convincing that linking teacher pay to the performance of their pupils is effective in improving learning outcomes, either in the short, medium or long term... Attracting the best teachers and retaining them, for which pay may be a significant component, is more important than rewarding teachers on the basis of their pupils' recent test scores or their observed lesson performance.'

Professor Higgins also said research suggested observing lessons is 'not a reliable way of identifying teacher effectiveness, so any system which relies only on observation or test scores or even a combination is likely to be flawed'.

Christine Blower, general secretary of the National Union of Teachers, opposes performance-related pay for teachers on the grounds that it is less transparent and open to biased judgements.

Source: adapted from Sutton Trust press release, 6 June 2014, and other sources

Questions (40 marks; 45 minutes)

1   Explain why the government appears to
    believe that teachers are motivated by money.   (4)

2   Apart from money, assess two other factors
    which might motivate teachers.   (8)

3   Assess two ways the government might
    measure the individual performance of teachers.   (8)

4   Evaluate the benefits of the government's
    proposal to scrap pay increases based on
    length of service in favour of performance-
    related pay.   (20)

Data response 2

An October 2013 study finds 'emotional factors' are strongest motivators in the workplace

Bonuses are not the top motivator for employees, according to a study into what makes workers most productive by the Institute of Leadership and Management (ILM).

The survey of more than 1,000 workers found that only 13 per cent of people agreed that a bonus would have an effect on their motivation; however having a good basic salary and pension was viewed as an important incentive by almost half of the respondents.

In fact, the top motivator was 'job enjoyment' according to 59 per cent of respondents, while other emotional factors such as good working relationships and fair treatment also rated highly in the survey. More than two-fifths of the respondents cited 'getting on with colleagues' as a key motivator, while just over a fifth agreed that 'how well they are treated by their managers' affected motivation, with a further fifth saying that higher levels of autonomy motivated them.

The ILM said the findings suggested that the £36.9 billion spent on performance bonuses in the UK last year had 'no impact on the motivation and commitment levels of the vast majority of recipients'.

The survey highlights how important good managers are to ensuring happy and motivated staff. When asked to identify one thing that would motivate them to do more, 31 per cent of employees said 'better treatment from their employer', 'more praise' and 'a greater sense of being valued'. However, while the majority of managers (69 per cent) said they are 'always giving feedback' to their staff, just 23 per cent of employees agreed.

'Understanding your employees and what makes them tick is vital in having a happy and motivated workforce,' said Charles Elvin, chief executive of the ILM. 'In the past year UK companies have collectively spent an astronomical amount on financial incentives for their staff. But this report is telling us there are far more effective, and cost-effective, ways to motivate people. These include giving regular feedback, allowing people to have autonomy in a role, the opportunity to innovate and improved office environments.'

Source: www.cipd.co.uk

Questions (30 marks; 35 minutes)

1 From the passage:

  a) Outline three points that fit into the category called 'motivators' by Herzberg. (6)

  b) Outline two points that fit into the category called 'hygiene factors' by Herzberg. (4)

2. The ILM implies that the £36.9 billion spent on performance bonuses was a waste of money. Assess two possible reasons why businesses might persist with staff bonuses despite the evidence provided here. (8)

3 Use the evidence provided in the text to assess how a manager might improve the workplace performance of one of the following: a school cleaner; a full-time employee at Tesco; or a bus driver. (12)

Extended writing

1 Evaluate the view that there is no one ideal method to motivate staff, because everyone is different. (20)

2 Evaluate the importance of financial reward systems in the motivation of young, part-time staff at a business such as Nando's, McDonald's or KFC. (20)

22 Leadership

Definition

Leadership, at its best, means inspiring staff to achieve demanding goals.

Linked to: Motivation in theory, Ch 20; Motivation in practice, Ch 21, Moving from entrepreneur to leader, Ch 28.

22.1 Leaders and managers

It is important to understand that the role of the leader is not the same as that of the manager. Management guru Peter Drucker once said that: 'Managers do things right; leaders do the right thing.'

In other words, an effective manager is someone who can put an idea or policy into action, and get the details right. By contrast, the leader is good at identifying the key issues facing the business, setting new objectives, and then deciding what should be done, by when and by whom. It is also argued that a leader needs to inspire staff. This is often confused with charismatic leadership – that is, when the personal charisma of the leader inspires staff to give something extra or work a bit harder. Although some successful leaders such as Ghandi, Churchill and Mandela had charisma, many others had success despite quite dull personalities. The great British Prime Minister Clement Attlee 'had a lot to be modest about', according to Churchill. Liverpool FC's long period as Britain's top club began with the charismatic Bill Shankly; yet the huge haul of trophies came later, under the leadership of the shy, slightly bumbling Bob Paisley.

The main differences between managers and leaders can be summarised as follows:

1 The job role: leaders have to avoid being bogged down in short-term 'fire-fighting' (solving today's problems); they should be looking ahead to see new opportunities as well as threats. So a key difference is the timescale within which they operate. A second aspect of the job role is that the manager will be working within tight resource constraints (e.g. a staffing budget and an expense account). By contrast, the leader is in a position to find the money or resources for whatever is needed, by re-jigging other budgets.

2 The person: leaders need to have steely qualities when needed – for example, to fire someone who is simply not fitting in; a manager may get away with ducking difficult decisions. Although leaders do not need to have natural charisma, they have to have qualities that make people willing to follow them. Roy Hodgson (England manager at the time of writing) has no obvious charisma, but he has managed to make many sets of players trust in him and his judgement. He has proved to be a successful leader.

Circumstances	What managers do	What leaders do
Key staff are leaving	Recruit new staff with care	Re-think the design and responsibilities within the job
An important customer is threatening to go elsewhere	Get staff to smooth things over as best they can	Take personal responsibility for the customer's disappointment and sort the problem out
A downturn means redundancies are necessary	Hire an HR specialist company to handle the whole process	Call a staff meeting, explain what's happening and deal with the whole thing personally
A very promising new product idea has been proposed	Take control of the development and assemble a large project team	Delegate the project to a bright young manager, providing extra resources when needed

Table 22.1 Response of leaders and managers to different circumstances

22.2 Types of leadership style

The way in which managers deal with their employees is known as their management style. For example, some managers are quite strict with workers. They always expect deadlines to be met and targets to be hit. Others are more relaxed and understanding. If there is a good reason why a particular task has not been completed by the deadline, they will be willing to accept this and give the employee more time. Although the way in which everyone manages will vary slightly from individual to individual, their styles can be categorised under three headings: autocratic, democratic and paternalistic. A further type (laissez-faire) is best understood as a subset of democratic.

Autocratic managers

Autocratic managers are authoritarian: they tell employees what to do and do not listen much to what workers themselves have to say. Autocratic managers know what they want doing and how they want it done. They tend to use one-way, top-down communication. They give orders to workers and do not want feedback.

Democratic managers

Democratic managers, by comparison, like to involve their workers in decisions. They tend to listen to employees' ideas and ensure people contribute to the discussion. Communication by democratic managers tends to be two-way. Managers put forward an idea and employees give their opinion. A democratic manager would regularly delegate decision-making power to junior staff.

The delegation of authority, which is at the heart of democratic leadership, can be approached in one of two main ways: management by objectives and laissez-faire.

Management by objectives

In this situation, the leader agrees clear goals with staff, provides the necessary resources and allows day-to-day decisions to be made by the staff in question; this approach was advocated by management guru Peter Drucker.

Laissez-faire

Meaning 'let it be', this occurs when managers are so busy, or so lazy, that they do not take the time to ensure that junior staff know what to do or how to do it. Some people may respond very well to the freedom to decide how to spend their working lives; others may become frustrated. It is said that Bill Gates, in the early days of Microsoft, hired brilliant students and told them no more than to create brilliant software. Was this a laissez-faire style or management by objectives? Clearly the dividing line can be narrow.

Figure 22.1 Manager and employee

Paternalistic managers

A **paternalistic manager** thinks and acts like a father. He or she tries to do what is best for their staff/children. There may be consultation to find out the views of the employees, but decisions are made by the head of the 'family'. This type of manager believes employees need direction but thinks it is important that they are supported and cared for properly. Paternalistic managers are interested in the security and social needs of staff. They are interested in how workers feel and whether they are happy in their work. Nevertheless, it is quite an autocratic approach.

	Democratic	Paternalistic	Autocratic
Style derived from:	belief in Maslow's higher-order needs or in Herzberg's motivators	Mayo's work on human relations and Maslow's lower- and middle-order needs	a Taylorite view of staff
Approach to staff	Delegation of authority	Consultation with staff	Orders must be obeyed
Approach to staff remuneration	Salary, perhaps plus employee shareholdings	Salary plus extensive fringe benefits	Payment by results, e.g. piece rate
Approach to human resource management	Recruitment and training based on attitudes and teamwork	Emphasis on training and appraisal for personal development	Recruitment and training based on skills; appraisal linked to pay

Table 22.2 Assumptions and approaches of the three types of leader

22.3 McGregor's Theory X and Y

In the 1950s, Douglas McGregor undertook a survey of managers in America and identified two styles of management, which he labelled Theory X and Theory Y (see Table 22.3). Theory X managers tend to distrust their subordinates; they believe employees do not really enjoy their work and that they need to be controlled. In McGregor's own words, many managers believe that 'the average human being has an inherent dislike of work and will avoid it if he can'. Note that McGregor is not putting this forward as a theory about workers, but about managers. In other words, Theory X is about the view managers have of their workforce.

Theory Y managers, by comparison, believe that employees do enjoy work and that they want to contribute ideas and effort. A Theory Y manager is, therefore, more likely to involve employees in decisions and give them greater responsibility. The managerial assumptions identified by McGregor as Theory Y included those set out in the box below.

Evaluation

Managerial assumptions identified by McGregor as Theory Y

'Commitment to objectives is a function of the rewards associated with their achievement.'

'The average human being learns, under proper conditions, not only to accept but to seek responsibility.'

'The capacity to exercise a relatively high degree of imagination, ingenuity and creativity in the solution of organizational problems is widely, not narrowly, distributed in the population.'

Source: D. McGregor (1987) The Human Side of Enterprise, Penguin Books (first published 1960).

It is clear that Theory Y managers would be inclined to adopt a democratic leadership style. Their natural approach would be to delegate authority to meet specific objectives.

The Theory X approach is likely to be self-fulfilling. If you believe people are lazy, they will probably stop trying. Similarly, if you believe workers dislike responsibility, and you fail to give them a chance to develop, they will probably stop showing interest in their work. They will end up focusing purely on their wage packet because of the way you treat them.

In his book *The Human Side of Enterprise,* McGregor drew upon the work of Maslow and Herzberg. It need be no surprise that there are common features to the theories of these three writers. McGregor's unique contribution was to set issues of industrial psychology firmly in the context of the management of organisations. So whereas Herzberg's was a theory of motivation, McGregor's concerned styles of management (and thereby leadership).

So, which is the 'right' approach? Clearly a Theory Y manager would be more pleasant and probably more interesting to work for. A Theory X approach can work, however, and is especially likely to succeed in a business employing many part-time, perhaps student, workers, or in a situation where a business faces a crisis.

Real business

Manchester United's Moyes' mistake

When Alex Ferguson became manager of Manchester United in 1986, he promised that he would 'knock Liverpool right off their [insert expletive] perch!' Ferguson did exactly that, winning trophy after trophy. Ferguson is probably best described as being a paternalistic leader. He established a family atmosphere at the club based on equal status. Tea ladies, cleaners, cooks, all were treated as valued members of the team. Players such as Giggs, Beckham and De Gea have all described Ferguson as

Theory X managers *believe:*	Theory Y managers *believe:*
Employees dislike work and will avoid it if they can.	Putting some effort into work is as natural as play or rest; employees want to work.
Employees prefer to be directed, want to avoid responsibility and have little ambition.	Employees want responsibility, provided there are appropriate rewards.
Employees need to be controlled and coerced.	Employees are generally quite creative.

Table 22.3 Theory X v. Theory Y managers

being 'a father figure'. Sir Alex made all the decisions, but unlike an autocrat he believed that his decisions were based on doing what would be best for his family – the football club.

In 2011, United won the championship for the nineteenth time, overhauling Liverpool's total of 18 league titles: mission accomplished! Two years later, after winning the title yet again, Sir Alex decided to retire. His final act as manager was to appoint David Moyes as his successor. Unfortunately for United, the appointment proved to be a disaster. Moyes was more of an autocrat than a paternalist. For example, without consulting anyone, he sacked all of Ferguson's backroom staff. He inherited a playing squad that had won the league the previous season by 11 points. With virtually the same group of players, United ended up in seventh place and Moyes was promptly sacked.

22.4 Charismatic leadership

Charismatic leaders are people who are able to connect with an audience and who can get others to buy into their ideas. History is littered with charismatic leaders. Some of these leaders have used their communication skills and ability to motivate others to do good things that have benefited the world. There is perhaps no better example of this than Nelson Mandela, who almost single-handedly inspired South Africa into abandoning apartheid. In business, Steve Jobs used his charisma to turn around the fortunes of Apple Computers.

According to research carried out by the University of Lausanne, charismatic leaders create impact with their audience by: setting optimistic goals; and by using analogies, rhetorical questions and by contrasting between 'right' and 'wrong' during their speeches.

Unfortunately, charisma can have a downside. The combination of charisma and early success as a leader can result in too much praise and not enough friendly criticism. On many occasions in business and in history, the result can be **hubris** leading to **nemesis**. Napoleon and Hitler are historical examples; in business, the same has proved true of leaders of Royal Bank of Scotland (RBS/NatWest), of Lloyds Bank and of Tesco.

Figure 22.2 Logic ladder: the risk of hubris

22.5 What is the best style of leadership?

Each style of leadership can work well in different situations. If there is a crisis, for example, people often look for a strong leader to tell them what to do. Imagine that sales have unexpectedly fallen by 50 per cent, causing uncertainty, even panic, within the organisation. The boss needs to take control quickly and put a plan into action. An autocratic style might work well at this moment. In a stable situation, where employees are trained and able to do their work successfully, a more democratic leadership style might be more appropriate. Countries elect very different types of leaders when there is a threat of war or economic instability compared with when the country is doing well. Similarly, think about how people react when they are learning to drive.

The best style depends on an enormous range of factors, such as the personalities and abilities of the leader, of the workers, and the nature of the task. Imagine a confident boss who knows her job well but is faced with an unusually difficult problem. If the staff are well trained and capable, the leader might consult on what to do next. If the staff are largely part-time and temporary (think Sports Direct), an autocratic style of leadership is the only realistic option.

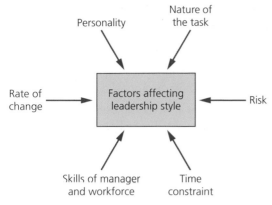

Personality

Nature of the task

Rate of change → **Factors affecting leadership style** ← Risk

Skills of manager and workforce

Time constraint

Figure 22.3 Factors affecting leadership style

Leadership style should therefore change according to the particular situation and the people involved. It will also vary with the time and degree of risk involved. If a decision has to be made urgently and involves a high degree of risk, the leader is likely to be quite autocratic. If there is plenty of time to discuss matters and only a low chance of it going wrong, the style may well be more democratic.

Five whys and a how

Questions	Answers
Why might an uncharismatic leader be successful?	As long as the leader asks the right questions and makes the right calls on the big decisions, charisma is irrelevant.
Why may laissez-faire leadership be a problem in a large organisation such as Unilever or Tesco?	Because it would be impossible to co-ordinate a wide range of wholly different approaches by different parts of the business (management by objectives would work far better).
Why is hubris a problem among leaders?	If they start getting praised to the skies, leaders can become too confident, even arrogant – and nemesis often follows.
Why are so many leaders 'male and pale'?	Although women may be held back from leadership positions by family commitments, there is no reason why those from ethnic minority groups should not be leaders. So probably prejudice is involved in some way.
Why might a leader 'be like a shepherd' (in the words of Nelson Mandela)?	Mandela thought leading from the back was the best approach – that is, letting people show initiative and talent (and only rounding them up if necessary).
How might an autocratic leader learn to be more democratic?	By seeking a training course designed to encourage more consultative and then more democratic behaviours.

22.6 Leadership – evaluation

All firms seek effective managers. Good managers make effective use of the firm's resources and motivate staff; they provide vision and direction, and are therefore a key element of business success. Look at any successful company and you will usually find a strong management team. The problem is knowing what it is that makes a good manager and what is the 'best' management style. Even if we thought we knew the best style, could we train anyone to adopt this approach, or does it depend on personality?

There are, of course, no easy answers to such questions. The 'right' style of management will depend on the particular circumstances and the nature of the task, and while it is possible to help someone to develop a particular style, it will also depend on the individual's personality. However, there are plenty of autocratic managers who also succeed.

Key terms

Autocratic manager: autocratic managers keep most of the authority to themselves; they do not delegate much or share information with employees. Autocratic, or authoritarian, managers tend to tell employees what to do.

Democratic manager: democratic managers take the views of their subordinates into account when making decisions. Managers discuss what needs to be done and employees are involved in the decision.

Hubris: overweening arrogance leading to excessive self-confidence and therefore blindness to the risks being taken ('pride comes before the fall').

Nemesis: divine punishment for wrongdoing or presumption; in other words, the fall that comes after pride.

Paternalistic manager: a paternalistic manager believes he or she knows what is best for employees. Paternalistic managers tend to tell employees what to do, but will often explain their decisions. They are also concerned about the social needs of employees.

22.7 Workbook

Revision questions

(40 marks; 40 minutes)

1 Distinguish between autocratic and paternalistic management. (4)

2 Identify two features of democratic management. (2)

3 Outline one advantage and one disadvantage of an autocratic management approach. (4)

4 Distinguish between McGregor's Theory X and Theory Y. (4)

5 Why is it 'clear that Theory Y managers would be inclined to adopt a democratic leadership style'? (4)

6 Is there one correct leadership style for running a football team or a supermarket chain? (4)

7 Explain why autocratic managers may be of more use in a crisis than democratic ones. (4)

8 Explain a circumstance in which an authoritarian approach to leadership may be desirable. (4)

9 Many managers claim to have a democratic style of leadership. Often, their subordinates disagree. Outline two ways of checking the actual leadership style of a particular manager. (4)

10 Analyse the leadership style adopted by your teacher/tutor. (6)

Data response

Fred 'the Shred' Goodwin

Fred Goodwin was one of Britain's most famous bosses. Before becoming a banker, he trained as an accountant. After a successful stint at Clydesdale Bank, he joined RBS (Royal Bank of Scotland) in 1998. Goodwin rapidly gained promotion by making redundancies to reduce RBS's costs. His ruthlessness earned him the nickname 'Fred the Shred'. At the tender age of 37, he became chief executive.

As praise (and a knighthood) was heaped upon him, Goodwin steadily became more and more dominating within RBS. In his book, published in May 2014, *Shredded: Inside RBS*, Ian Fraser describes how Goodwin took great pleasure in humiliating colleagues in front of their peers in so-called 'morning beatings'. He ruled by fear, keeping a little black book in which he noted down the names of employees who annoyed him. Names written down in pencil were 'on the borderline', while those penned in ink were in serious trouble. A culture of target-setting at the bank indicated that Goodwin believed in the power of performance-related pay as a motivating force. He clearly enjoyed his own corporate luxuries, getting oranges flown in from Paris every morning on expenses.

According to former colleagues, he was a control obsessive who micromanaged RBS. He made all the decisions, even relatively unimportant issues, such as the colour of office carpets and RBS's company cars. Goodwin even stipulated that filing cabinets must have rounded tops because he disliked seeing piles of paper left on top of filing cabinets. Under his leadership, RBS grew rapidly, buying out 26 rivals. He was uncomfortable with discussion, which he usually saw as a challenge to his leadership. Eventually, Goodwin started making mistakes, the biggest of which was paying £49 billion for the ABN AMRO bank, which proved to be riddled with bad debts. As a direct consequence, RBS made a loss of £24.1 billion in 2008 – the biggest in UK corporate history. And RBS had to be bailed out by the British government, i.e. the taxpayer.

Questions (25 marks; 30 minutes)

1 Explain whether Fred the Shred was an autocratic or a paternalistic leader. (5)

2 Explain two weaknesses of Goodwin's style of leadership. (8)

3 Assess whether the democratic approach is always superior to other styles of leadership. (12)

Activity

An investigation into a leader

1 Arrange to interview an employee. Preferably this person should be a full-timer who has worked for at least a year. The employee could be a manager but should not be a director.

2 Your objective is to gain a full understanding of the leadership style prevailing at the employee's workplace, and the style employed by the individual's own manager.

3 Devise your own series of questions in advance, but make sure to include the following themes.

   a) How open are communications within the business?

   b) Are staff encouraged to apply a questioning or critical approach?

   c) Are there any forums for discussion or debate on important policy issues affecting staff?

   d) What does the organisational hierarchy look like? Where is your employee on that diagram? How powerful or powerless does she or he feel?

   e) How exactly does the employee's boss treat him or her? Is there delegation? Is there consultation? How effective is communication between the two of them?

Write at least 600 words summarising your findings and drawing conclusions about how well the experience conforms to the leadership theory dealt with in this unit.

Extended writing

1 Evaluate the view that autocratic leadership has no place in today's business world. (20)

2 'Great leaders are born, not made.' Evaluate this view. (20)

3 Evaluate whether it can ever be right to pay a business leader 1,000 times more than the lowest-paid employee in the organisation. (20)

23 Role of an entrepreneur

Linked to: Entrepreneurial motives and characteristics, Ch 24; Forms of business, Ch 26; Moving from entrepreneur to leader, Ch 28.

▌23.1 Introduction

The personal qualities of entrepreneurs are dealt with in Chapter 24. This chapter looks at the practical issues: what entrepreneurs actually do – and what can hold them back.

Unlike the media image, most entrepreneurs are middle-aged, not young. That is inevitable because starting a business is likely to cost thousands, so young entrepreneurs are likely to come from wealthy backgrounds. The middle-aged entrepreneur comes with huge advantages, but often some drawbacks. Yes, they have money and usually they have a business idea that stems from the business they once worked in. But going from a middle manager in a large business to starting up your own business strips you of some important help: the IT department, the accounting department and so on. Suddenly you have to make decisions about a wide range of different aspects of business: a marketing expert one minute, an accountant the next – and then there's the toilet that needs a clean.

▌23.2 Creating and setting up a business

Generating business ideas

At the heart of successful entrepreneurship is spotting a good business idea. This is usually based on a good understanding of consumer tastes and/or the needs of the retail trade. Both qualities were shown by Martyn Dawes, who spotted the opportunity for machines that could automatically make high-quality coffee. His 'Coffee Nation' machines in motorway service stations and Tesco Express made him a multi-millionaire when Costa decided to buy the business.

The main sources of business ideas are set out below.

- Observation: Martyn Dawes had seen similar machines in New York delis and saw their potential use in Britain.
- Brain-storming: this is where two or more people are encouraged to come up with ideas, without criticising each other's, no matter how bizarre; the appraisal process comes later.
- Thinking ahead: perhaps about the new opportunities that will arise if the weather continues to get warmer (for example, air conditioning, ice cream, and so on).
- Ideas from personal or business experience: for example, 'there are no ice cream parlours for miles around' or 'in my company we need quality sandwiches delivered at lunchtime'.
- **Innovations**: these may come from new science, such as Pilkington's self-cleaning glass (used in skyscrapers worldwide), or from clever re-workings of existing knowledge, such as the Apple iPad

> 'It's really rare for people to have a successful start-up in this industry without a breakthrough product. It has to be something where, when people look at it, at first they say, "I don't get it, I don't understand it. I think it's too weird, I think it's too unusual".'
>
> Marc Andreesen, software engineer and entrepreneur

Spotting an opportunity

It would be easy to become gloomy and to think that all the great business ideas and opportunities have already gone: the hamburger chain, the fizzy cola, and so on. In fact, this is completely wrong. Society changes constantly, with different attitudes or fads marking out the generations. All today's online business opportunities will give way to new ones as computing power gets ever greater. 'Wearable technology' has been around as an idea for nearly ten years, but now computing power has made it a meaningful business opportunity.

In addition to new technology, other ways to spot new business opportunities include the following:

- Think about changes to society: for example, is there now more concern about the body beautiful? If so, what effect will this have on the demand for cosmetic surgery, anti-ageing creams and fashion clothing?
- Think about changes to the economy: will a continuing boom in China give opportunities for British brands such as Burberry, Jaguar and Superdry?
- Think about the local housing market: are people moving into or out of your area? Are prices moving up or down? Many local business opportunities may rise or fall depending on these factors.
- Use the techniques outlined below: small budget research and careful market mapping.

Small budget research

Even before spending money on market research, good entrepreneurs take the time to gain a general understanding of the market. Someone thinking about buying into a Subway **franchise** for Brighton, for example, may do the following:

- Walk around the town, mapping where sandwich bars and other fast food outlets are located (this is called **geographical mapping**). See Figure 23.1 to see how plotting the existing suppliers can help to identify a suitable place to start up.
- While doing so, check on prices, special deals, student discounts, and so on
- Arrange to spend a day with Subway at their franchise in a nearby town, to help understand the customer and the way the service is provided
- Based on the knowledge gained by the above, produce a **market map** (for more on market mapping, see Chapter 4) of fast food in Brighton; this will help to identify whether Subway will have a **market niche** to itself.

Small budget research may also point towards new business opportunities. *The Grocer* magazine provides many useful insights. Each week, it highlights one consumer marketplace. For example, the 4 October 2014

issue highlighted that sales of Christmas novelty chocolate products had risen 53 per cent in the past 12 months. This information could provide the basis for a new small company launching into this market sector – perhaps aiming to establish an upmarket chocolate novelty product.

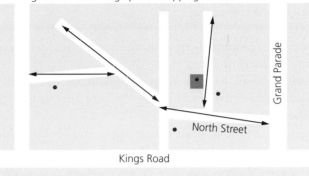

Brighton centre: Geographical mapping of sandwich bars

Key
- Sandwich bars   ←→ Main walkway

Figure 23.1 Geographical mapping of sandwich bars in Brighton centre

23.3 Running and expanding a business

For a first-time entrepreneur, running the business can be as daunting psychologically as starting it. The start-up may be scary, but at least it is bathed in optimism about the future. It's thrilling. But the day-to-day running of the business may be much less so. We have all seen shop proprietors standing in their doorway looking wistfully for customers. They must know that no-one will walk in while they're there, but they can't bear to sit around any longer. Restaurants on Mondays and Tuesdays, snack bars after the lunchtime rush and toy shops in February – all suffer the same punishment of too few customers.

Apart from psychology, there are many practical issues that matter hugely when running a business. For most businesses, success depends upon customer satisfaction – delight, even. This requires a clever combination of flair and warmth in customer service with meticulous organisation. A friendly smile is not enough if a restaurant has forgotten that Table 27 is a birthday celebration – and a cake is sent with the chef's compliments to Table 14 but not 27. This is why it is so hard to be a successful entrepreneur. Start-up is about flair, vision and energy; running the business is about establishing systems that don't fail. Few people are equally strong at these very different qualities.

To run a business successfully:

- you need the ability to obtain and listen to objective measures of its performance; if your business is your baby, it's easy to listen to compliments and shut out criticisms (business TV series such as *Kitchen Nightmares* and *Hotel Inspector* tend always to come back to this problem)
- you need an obsessive eye for detail, whether in the service a customer gets or in the accounting details of the business finances
- you need to be able to step back from day-to-day issues and think strategically – about the long-term plans for the company
- you need to love what you're doing and love making customers happy (see Real Business).

'Make every detail perfect and limit the number of details to perfect.'

Jack Dorsey, Twitter co-founder

Real business

In Wimbledon, South London, Paneteria Italiana has been providing bread, Italian-style, for more than 40 years. Proprietor Salvatore Falcone needs to make a profit, but cares passionately about the bread he bakes. Why is the crust on his granary loaf relatively soft? Well, because he makes the bread so that it stays fresh for 2-3 days. Is that wise, when it would surely be nice to have customers who need to buy bread every day? Well, he answers: 'I like to make bread the *right* way.'

Successful expansion

It may be no surprise that Paneteria Italiana has never expanded beyond the single small bakery. Others need to expand. It may even be that the business model relies on expansion because one outlet will never be able to generate enough profit to keep the shareholders happy.

To expand a business, there are three broad issues that have to be covered: establishing that the extra demand exists, ensuring that the finance is in place and ensuring that the people are in place – especially any new leaders. When Scoop ice cream opened its second outlet, the proprietor tried to be store manager in two places at once. Not good. Later he taught himself the art of delegation. In more detail, then, the three factors are as follows:

- Establishing that extra demand exists. This may seem obvious but can cause problems. An all-business airline called MaxJet started with three staff in America in 2003, flying New York to London. By 2007, it

had expanded to 400 staff and several transatlantic routes – to Paris and London, to Washington, Los Angeles and others. It grew by raising more capital from shareholders, always claiming that it would make profits once it had a big enough network. In 2007, it ran out of money, having never made a profit. Passengers were stranded and staff redundant.

- Ensure the finance is in place. The most perfect form of finance is profit generated within the business; it has no interest charges and doesn't need to be repaid to anyone. So 'reinvested', sometimes called 'ploughed-back', profit is the goal. After all, if you're not making profit now, why do you *want* to expand? Sometimes the answer is that the opportunities are so huge that you want to expand more quickly than your profit level allows. This is often true of start-up digital businesses, from Instagram to ASOS. In this case, the business will have to find some external finance, perhaps borrowed from the bank or invested by shareholders. See Chapter 30 for more details.
- Ensure the people are in place. First-time entrepreneurs tend to think the toughest aspects of business are finding a market and finding the finance. More experienced business leaders say the biggest problems concern people. Rapid expansion quickly stretches the human resources of the business: new layers of hierarchy are needed and new **line managers** must be appointed/promoted, trained and grow into the job.

Figure 23.2 Logic chain: successful expansion

Real business

Richard Branson's tips for expanding a business

1. Know your mission.
2. Get the basic structure right: the back office, relations with suppliers, etc.
3. Get the right team at the top.
4. A strong purpose and a sense of ethics give a solid foundation.
5. No matter how big you are, details count.
6. Listen to your customers and act on what you hear.

Source: www.entrepreneur.com

23.4 Intrapreneurship: innovation within a business

An intrapreneur has the personal characteristics of an entrepreneur, but works within a large organisation. Typically, then, they think creatively ('outside the box'), are willing to take risks and show leadership in making things happen. Some organisations have learnt to recognise and celebrate such people. Others treat them as slightly wayward executives who need to be checked up on. The factors that determine the differences between companies that celebrate and those that mistrust intrapreneurs are:

- high tech v. low tech: high technology companies need bright, even 'disruptive' ideas to keep them one step ahead in a fast-changing environment; famously, Google gives each member of staff 20 per cent free working time to work on their own ideas; this consciously fosters intrapreneurship by building an entrepreneurial workplace culture
- stage in the company's life cycle: companies in an early growth stage want bright new ideas to keep growth going; when companies have become big and rather static (maturity stage), they are more likely to want to avoid mistakes – that is, to keep making lots of money in just the way they are already doing; large companies tend to get bureaucratic, with every decision needing to be signed off by several higher layers of management; that is the opposite of an entrepreneurial culture
- leadership: the personal characteristics of the overall business leader can be very important; some go out of their way to encourage younger staff to have responsibility and some freedom; more autocratic leaders prefer to keep all major decisions at the top – so intrapreneurship is unwelcome.

Real business

The Facebook Hackathon

From early in its life (born: 2004), workers at Facebook organised all-night innovation sessions that came to be called Hackathons. In the early days, founder Mark Zuckerberg was a keen participant. The Hackathons would happen once every six weeks and the only rule was that no-one could work on their day job. In the days leading up to the all-nighter, emails would suggest project ideas and individuals might opt in to someone else's idea, or just experiment with something. The 'Like' button, one of the most important innovations in the company's history, was the product of a Hackathon.

23.5 Barriers to entrepreneurship

Entrepreneurs get praised for their risk-taking, but it is important to remember that some are risking a lot more than others. If, like Richard Branson or Philip Green, you come from a wealthy family, there's a risk that a new business might fail, but probably no risk that failure will hurt you financially. By contrast, some people invest their life savings or borrow on the strength of their family home; this is real risk and real pressure. An obvious barrier to entrepreneurship, then, is lack of personal finance; a good chef can't open a restaurant unless the good chef has great savings. Some get round this by starting on a market stall (famously, Julian Dunkerton, founder of Superdry/Supergroup plc started on Cheltenham market with £40), but this is not a realistic option for many types of business.

A parliamentary report published in 2012 made the following key findings with regards to barriers to entrepreneurship in the UK:

- Since the 2009 financial crisis, banks have become much less willing to lend to small firms; they regard this business as risky and unprofitable; the report says: 'Banks increasingly tend not to lend to businesses without asset backing and this especially impacts upon SMEs [small and medium-sized enterprises] and specifically deters business start-ups.'
- Government research shows that 29 per cent of entrepreneurs are women. The report argues that if women had full 50/50 representation, 150,000 additional start-ups would be created each year. Despite this, other evidence shows that the rate of business start-up is rising faster among women than men, so perhaps this problem will resolve itself over time
- Another key finding was that employees in the public sector struggle to understand or even trust the motives of entrepreneurs. There is a tendency to assume that people running small businesses are motivated by greed and the desire to avoid tax. In fact, says the report, small businesses tend to pay proportionately higher rates of tax than large firms, which not only seems unfair, but may be a barrier to entrepreneurship.

'Most start-up companies fail and it is smart public policy to help entrepreneurs increase their odds of succeeding. But the biggest loss to our economy is not all the start-ups that

didn't make it: it's the ones that might have been created but weren't.'

Eric Ries, business author

23.6 Anticipating risk and uncertainty in the business environment

In August 2014, New Look announced that it was putting on hold its expansion into Russia. In early November, it announced it was pulling out altogether. That was well-timed, as the Russian economy imploded soon after. This is a good example of assessing risk and acting before the overall business is affected by uncertainty.

Entrepreneurs pride themselves on their sensitivity to the market. This is because they are usually in daily, face-to-face contact with customers. So they pick up changing trends or moods among consumers. In autumn 2008, just before the 2009 recession, most firms knew things looked worrying. Yet in Wimbledon an entrepreneur spent over £150,000 opening a French restaurant at just the wrong time. He lasted six months before closing down. He showed no understanding of the risks involved in that specific business environment.

To anticipate risk, it is important to try to quantify it, so that the risks can be compared with the potential rewards. With uncertainty, wise businesspeople see this as the natural state of affairs. They accept that tomorrow's trade may be completely different from yesterday's. So it is vital to keep some capital in hand to cover the day-to-day fluctuations in finances.

23.7 Role of an entrepreneur – evaluation

Within the economy as a whole, entrepreneurs provide two marvellous functions. First, they provide a wide array of competitors to the big companies that would otherwise be able to enjoy safe markets and therefore complacent service and business thinking. Wall's claims a 66 per cent share of the UK market for hand-held ice cream; just think how easy the company's life would be if it wasn't for all the independent ice cream parlours or vans. So the consumer stands to benefit considerably from the work of entrepreneurs.

Their second key function is innovation. This is especially obvious in the IT sector, where established firms want to keep things just as they are (e.g. social media consisting solely of Facebook and Twitter). New entrepreneurs, though, keep coming up with new ideas, such as Instagram and Snapchat. The bright new ideas then force the existing firms to try to catch up with or beat the new competition. Once again, the consumer is the winner.

'**Get big quietly, so you don't tip off potential competitors.**'

Chris Dixon, angel investor

Five whys and a how

Questions	Answers
Why may 'brainstorming' be a useful way to come up with business ideas?	Because it encourages creative, perhaps wacky, ideas that can later be whittled down to what makes sense.
Why might a business do better located near to competitors rather than far away?	Clusters attract customers – for example, someone who wants to buy a bike will go to where there are three bike shops rather than one; the same is true for bars and restaurants.
Why might it be risky to expand a small business rapidly?	Expansion puts pressure on a firm's cash and human resources; rapid expansion may outstrip the entrepreneur's capacity to handle these pressures.
Why might a business want to restrain potential intrapreneurs?	Senior managers may be wary of initiatives that might unsettle stable income streams (such as Heinz Tomato Ketchup).
Why might women be less likely to start a business than men?	The reasons might be practical (more likely to be the primary carer for children) or psychological (women may have less confidence/arrogance/blind optimism than men).
How might a future government help small firms to expand safely?	They might offer a tax window, postponing extra taxes on National Insurance and profits until beyond an agreed 2–3 year expansion period.

23.8 Workbook

Revision questions

(35 marks; 35 minutes)

1 Explain how 'observation' could help a business-minded person to come up with a great new idea for starting a firm. (3)

2 Have you spotted any business opportunities recently? If yes, set out your idea in no more than three sentences. If no, decide now what you believe to be the best opportunity in your local high street or shopping centre. Again, set it out in no more than three sentences. (6)

3 Explain in your own words the purpose of geographical mapping. (3)

4 Which one of Richard Branson's top tips (see page 148) do you think is the most important? Explain your reasoning. (6)

5 Explain why it might be wise for a small firm to turn down a large order from a national supermarket chain. (4)

6 Firms may worry that an intrapreneur wants to leave and become an entrepreneur. Outline two barriers that may prevent the individual from proceeding. (4)

7 You are thinking of starting a new online travel agency focused on extreme sports. Examine three factors that will determine whether or not the business succeeds. (9)

Data response 1

Cara Phelps has worked in Sainsbury's personnel department for eight years and is getting bored. She owns her own flat in Leeds, has managed to save £22,000 and wants to start her own business. Her passion is shoes (she has 70 pairs!) so she wants to start a shoe shop. She has been eyeing a site close to Harvey Nichols, as she wants to target those willing to pay £80–£200 a pair. She has found a super shop for which she must pay £5,000 up front for a five-year lease, and then £24,000 a year as the annual rent.

Figure 23.3 shows a profile of Cara, drawn up by a friend who is a business consultant.

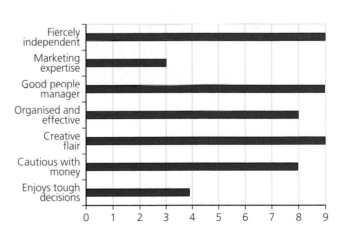

Figure 23.3 A profile of Cara Phelps; '10' = perfect.

Questions (40 marks; 45 minutes)

1 Assess two pieces of small budget research Cara should carry out before taking things any further with her upmarket shoe shop in Leeds. (8)

2 Assess whether an entrepreneur such as Cara should be given financial help by the government in the early stages of her start-up. (12)

3 Use the text and Figure 23.3 to evaluate whether Cara is likely to succeed with her new shoe shop. (20)

Data response 2

Share Radio

Figure 23.4 Gavin Oldham

4 November 2014 was the launch day for a new radio station: 'Share Radio'. This digital-only channel is Britain's first station devoted solely to money – to personal finance. It broadcasts 24/7 and a typical day would see coverage of the economic and business news, discussion about new savings plans or bank accounts, and coverage of the day's events in markets such as shares, exchange rates, oil and gold.

Share Radio is the brainchild of Gavin Oldham, the sole investor in Share Radio. Mr Oldham made his fortune as the founder of the stock-market-listed 'Share plc'. He and his family retain a 76 per cent stake in the business, which the stock market values at around £50 million.

Share Radio will require deep pockets because radio start-ups are notoriously cash-hungry. The costs will have started building up from spring 2014, as the central London offices and studios were acquired and staff began to be hired. The second to arrive was Lexi Diggins, recruited as business development manager, but who now also serves as the station's weather forecaster! By November, there were 25 staff, implying a wage bill of almost £1 million a year.

And where does a new radio station get income from? Eventually audience numbers should rise to the point that advertisers get interested in placing commercials. But at the start it is hard for advertisers to care. Realistically, even if Share Radio does well in building up its listener base, it will take at least three years to break even.

Questions (20 marks; 25 minutes)

1 Assess two possible reasons why staff may enjoy working in a start-up such as Share Radio. (8)

2 Assess Mr Oldham's probable role in the start-up of Share Radio. (12)

Extended writing

1 Outline a new business that you might like to start. Evaluate the benefits and drawbacks to you personally of starting that business. (20)

2 Although he has a personal fortune of around £500 million, Stelios (founder of easyJet) keeps starting up other businesses, including Fastjet – Africa's first low-cost airline. Evaluate the possible motives of a serial entrepreneur such as Stelios. (20)

24 Entrepreneurial motives and characteristics

Linked to: Role of an entrepreneur, Ch 23; Forms of business, Ch 26; Moving from entrepreneur to leader, Ch 28.

24.1. Introduction

Entrepreneurs see the opportunities that others see, but they also have the courage and initiative to act quickly. The past 15 years have seen two clear trends: an increasing desire for travel and more and more thrill-seeking, such as extreme sports. Many people could see that both trends pointed to a gap for a new service: space tourism – that is, individuals going into outer space, just for the fun of it. Richard Branson saw the same opportunity and started Virgin Galactic, which plans to charge £150,000 per trip. Despite a tragic setback in 2014, it still hopes to make its first flight in 2016.

> **'I'm convinced that about half of what separates the successful entrepreneurs from the non-successful ones is pure perseverance.'**

Steve Jobs, founder of Apple Inc

A successful entrepreneur needs the following characteristics:

- understanding of the market – to know what customers want and to see how well or badly current companies are serving them
- determination – to see things through even if there are difficulties
- passion – not just to make money, but to achieve something, such as to design a more efficient solar panel, or to transform rooms from shabby into bright and freshly painted ones
- resilience – that is, the ability to bounce back when things are against you (weaker people retreat into their shell or waste time trying to find others to blame)
- the ability to cope with risk.

Real business

Nancy's Nails

Figure 24.1 Scented top coat 'Got to be Strawberry'

Liberty is London's most unusual, fashion-orientated department store. In summer 2014, it held an open day in which anyone who wanted to supply to Liberty could come and do a three-minute presentation. Arriving at 4.00 in the morning, determined to be first in the queue, was 22-year-old Nancy. Her proposition was 'scented nail polish' in a bottle branded Nancy's Nails. Attracted by in a unique new idea, the store showed great interest and helped Nancy with the final pack and display designs. Even more remarkably, Liberty agreed to pay for their first order in advance because Nancy had used up all her savings on the project so far. In the autumn of 2014, Nancy's Nails were on display in Liberty. Nancy's determination had paid off.

24.2 Risk-taking

Business decisions are always about the future; therefore, they always involve uncertainty. Supermarket giant Tesco's management had a wonderful reputation until it was damaged by a series of corporate failings in 2013 and 2014. 2013 saw embarrassment from the horsemeat scandal and an ignominious withdrawal from China and America. 2014 was even worse, with humiliation in the marketplace at the hands of Lidl and Aldi, and concerns about fraud when Tesco's profits proved to be overstated by more than £250 million.

Good entrepreneurs consider not only what they think will happen, but also what could happen differently. Someone opening a restaurant may expect 60 customers a day, each spending £25. In fact, one month after opening, there may just be 40 customers spending £20 each. Receiving just £800 instead of £1,500 may make it hard for the restaurant to survive financially; there may be a risk of closure. This possibility should have been foreseen so that plans could be made.

An entrepreneur looks at the risks, compares them with the possible rewards and makes a considered decision. If there is a good chance of making £1,000 a week, but also a (small) chance of losing £500 a week, it is worth carrying on. Risk-takers accept that sometimes they will take a loss; that is part of business. See Table 24.1 for details of what makes a good entrepreneur.

> 'A pessimist sees the difficulty in every opportunity; an optimist sees the opportunity in every difficulty.'
>
> Winston Churchill, wartime Prime Minister

24.3 Skills required to be a successful entrepreneur

Whereas characteristics are part of what we are born with, skills can be learned. They range from skills with finance to skills at dealing with people. They include:

- financial skills, including the ability to read and understand key documents, such as a cash flow forecast
- persuasive abilities – entrepreneurs need to persuade others to do things like provide planning permission, supply goods on credit or work harder/faster to get things completed on time; they also may need to persuade staff to take a chance by joining a brand new, risky venture
- problem-solving skills, perhaps based on the ability to investigate possible causes and then to work out the most satisfactory solution
- networking skills: to be able to turn acquaintances into business friends and therefore benefit from network-based **crowdfunding** or social media endorsement.

> '**Every worthwhile accomplishment, big or little, has its stages of drudgery and triumph: a beginning, a struggle and a victory.**'
>
> Mahatma Ghandi, leader, Indian Independence

24.4 Motives for becoming an entrepreneur

Although 20 per cent of entrepreneurs have money as their prime motive, most are looking for more than financial gain. Typically they are looking for 'a challenge' or 'to prove myself'. In other words, people are looking for

People who aren't entrepreneurs	Bad entrepreneurs	Good entrepreneurs
Are very cautious – never want to take any risks	Ignore risks – assume that their own charisma/skill will guarantee success	Take calculated risks, weighing up the potential risks and rewards
Assume that things are the way they have to be	Rush to bring in something new or make huge changes	Launch new ideas in response to changing consumer tastes or attitudes
Like to be sure of next month's pay cheque – and the one after, until retirement	Trust that things will go as planned, spend freely at the start as they are sure the cash will start flowing tomorrow	Accept that the early days of a new business may be very tough, so try to spend as little as possible

Table 24.1 Characteristics of good and bad entrepreneurs

greater satisfaction than they can get from a regular job. A NatWest Bank survey of 1,400 entrepreneurs named the top start-up motive as 'to gain more control and avoid being told what to do'. Just 6 per cent said that they started their venture 'to make money'. Some of the key motivators for entrepreneurs are set out in Figure 24.2.

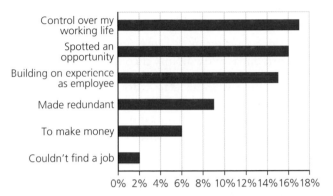

Figure 24.2 Key motivators for entrepreneurs

In some cases, starting a business can be hugely challenging, satisfying, absorbing and profitable. An example is Matteo Pantani, whose passion for ice cream led him to start Scoop ice cream parlour in 2007, opening his second London outlet in 2010 and third in spring 2012 (dreadful weather in the two years to spring 2014 put further expansion on hold). Yet some people deceive themselves about enterprise. They assume it is more satisfying, glamorous and profitable than it often is. Many shopkeepers work very long hours for quite poor rewards. Many small builders speak bitterly about their experiences in dealings with customers, suppliers and employees; they feel it would be easier to just earn a wage. Furthermore, government figures show that 30 per cent of new businesses fail within their first three years.

24.5 Financial motives for becoming an entrepreneur

Profit maximisation

As mentioned above, 20 per cent of those starting a business have profit as their major motivation. It is fair to assume that, of those, most will be thinking of how to maximise that profit. This would make business sense if the market conditions force the entrepreneur to focus on the short term. An example would be someone who has bought a £150,000 flat in a Spanish seaside town and needs to rent it out to pay the mortgage. Realistically, July and August are the only months when meaningful rentals can be charged; therefore, there can be only

one logical approach: short-term profit maximisation. Unfortunately, also coming into this category are all the 'cowboy builders' and other business scams that attempt to extract as much short-term profit as possible from each customer. In such cases the 'business model' is to treat each customer as a one-off opportunity to extract cash – there is no thought for repeat purchase, customer loyalty or long-term branding.

For businesses that are thinking about the long term, the best way to maximise profit may be to satisfice in the short term (see below). In this context, that means accepting a lower profit now in order to make a higher profit in the future. Sony launched its PS4 at a relatively low price, knowing that if it could build up enough loyal customers the real profits would come later, from software purchases.

Profit satisficing

To satisfice means to find the ideal blend between different pressures. In this case it is to find the 'right' profit rather than the biggest. In 1998, after years of profit growth, Marks & Spencer made record profits of £1,155 million. Its net profit margin of 14 per cent was the wonder of the retail world. After that point came an implosion, as shoppers revolted against the company's overpriced products. Nearly 20 years later, it has never regained that level of profit. It had been foolish enough to profit maximise when a business in that position should always satisfice – because it should always be thinking about its long-term future. The story is shown nicely in Figure 24.3, which compares profits at Next plc with those of Marks & Spencer between 1998 and 2014.

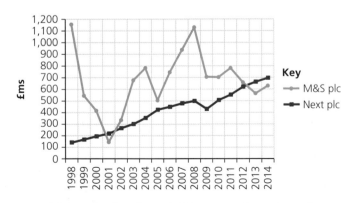

Figure 24.3 Perils of profit maximising – annual pre-tax profits: M&S v. Next

For new, small businesses especially, if they want to build a successful operation for the long term, profit satisficing makes far more sense than short-term maximisation.

24.6 Non-financial motives for becoming an entrepreneur

Independence

Some young people crave independence from the start of their working life, making them desperate to create a business rather than working for others. But vibrant stories about young entrepreneurs risk masking the evidence that the average British entrepreneur sets up in business at the age of 52! In their case, it is likely to be that, after a long career for a large employer, they feel the need (and the confidence; and have the savings/capital) to do something for themselves.

The issue of independence tends to be especially important for immigrants and their families. In Britain, whereas only 10.4 per cent of Britons have ever started a business, 17.2 per cent of non-UK nationals have done so (and they start at a younger age). A March 2014 report found that immigrant entrepreneurs have founded 464,527 businesses that employ 8.3 million people. For immigrants, there is a tendency to mistrust fair career prospects working in large organisations – hence the drive for independence.

So independence can be a psychological need or a practical response to actual or perceived unfairness or discrimination. It is notable that among British entrepreneurs there seems to be a disproportionate number with dyslexia or other issues that dented their self-esteem while at school. Perhaps people like Richard Branson felt something akin to discrimination – and perhaps that led to the same desire for independence felt by many immigrants.

Home-working

Independence can also be a requirement for someone who needs to be at home as a parent or carer. In other words, some need the practical flexibility of home-working because they are unable to physically go to work. Sadly, there are many employers who see this need as an opportunity to get work done at below normal market rates – including below the legal minimum wage. Home-workers often have to accept **piece rate** terms that give no security of income and can work out as a low hourly income.

This is why some who need to work from home try to set up their own business. In an online world, starting a business in a bedroom is quite plausible. Needless to say, such an enterprise will work hugely better if the entrepreneur has some strong IT skills, making website design easier and therefore being able to start up without paying out cash to a third party.

Ethical stance

Some entrepreneurs find it difficult to accept the ethical environment within a large business organisation. Recent mis-selling scandals affecting the banking and insurance sectors are a reminder that modern firms may be good at talking about ethics, but some fail to practise what they preach. As a result, some with strong ethical convictions prefer to start up a business for themselves, in which moral questions are entirely within the individual's control. So, if a repressive government wishes to place an order, the answer can be a straight 'no'. Running their own business gives individuals a remarkable amount of control – as long as they are happy to trade their ethical stance off against profit (and family income).

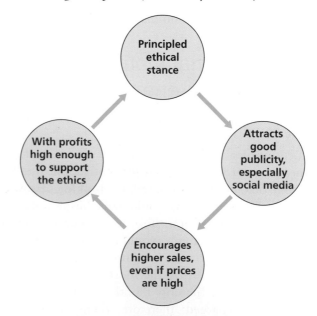

Figure 24.4 Logic chain: ethics can be good business

Social entrepreneurship

Whereas 'ethics' has a clear meaning, social entrepreneurship does not. Many companies claim to be 'doing good' and therefore say they are social enterprises. But it all depends on your point of view. A US company called Hampton Creek launched 'Just Mayo', charging a premium price for a product claiming to have health benefits. In fact, it was an egg-free product pretending (according to a lawsuit from Unilever, owners of Hellman's) to be a mayonnaise. The food category 'free from' has become important in the UK and US. Many companies boast about dairy-free milk (Alpro) or egg-free mayo, making it seem as if there are health benefits. The suppliers often claim to be social enterprises. But far more people buy these foods than need to for health reasons – so they are paying price premiums unnecessarily. The concept of social entrepreneurship is in the eye of the business owner, when it should be in the eye of the beholder.

Five whys and a how

Questions	Answers
Why might determination be more important to a successful start up than talent?	Untalented people with a good idea can make it if they are determined; without determination no amount of talent will provide success.
Why might an entrepreneur 'like' risk?	In the same way that an extreme sportsperson loves the rush of adrenaline.
Why do entrepreneurs seem so keen on control?	Perhaps because they have had little of it previously in their lives.
Why might pessimism be a more useful trait in an entrepreneur than Winston Churchill gave it credit for?	Cautiously low sales forecasts and cautiously high cost estimates should help the business survive the early, financially tricky, months.
Why might profit maximisation be a better target than satisficing?	Because it is more challenging and therefore might be a more effective motivator.
How might 'networking' help a young entrepreneur?	By providing the connections to people with capital or to potential customers.

24.7 Entrepreneurial motives and characteristics – evaluation

Starting a business can mean taking a huge gamble with family savings, perhaps made worse still by racking up personal debt. In such circumstances, the entrepreneur is either foolhardy or is driven by a powerful psychological driving force. Usually this force is to prove that she or he has qualities and skills that no-one has ever acknowledged. Interwoven with this is the need for independence that allows the entrepreneur to take all credit for the success (or failure) of the business. The typical entrepreneur sees the business as an extension of him or herself. It is their baby.

> **'I knew that if I failed I wouldn't regret that, but I knew the one thing I might regret is not trying.'**
>
> Jeff Bezos, founder of Amazon

In these highly personal circumstances, it is understandable that some think they are fulfilling a social enterprise role when, objectively, they are just finding a profitable niche in a complex market. Just because a business says it is socially aware or ethically sound, it doesn't mean that its decisions and actions will bear this out. When an organisation such as the Co-op Bank can claim ethical soundness when it is being fined for mis-selling financial products to its own customers, you know that the modern business world is a complex one.

Key terms

Crowdfunding: obtaining external finance from many individual, small investments, usually through a web-based appeal.

Entrepreneur: someone who makes a business idea happen, either through their own effort or by organising others to do the work.

Piece rate: paying workers per piece they produce (for example, £2 per pair of jeans made).

24.8 Workbook

Revision questions

(25 marks; 25 minutes)

1 Why is 'initiative' an important quality in an entrepreneur? (2)

2 Section 24.1 lists the characteristics needed to be a successful entrepreneur. Which two from this list seem of greatest importance to:

   a) a new firm facing a collapse in demand due to flooding locally

   b) a 19-year-old entrepreneur wanting to start her own airline? (4)

3 Section 24.2 mentions a restaurant that expects to receive 60 customers per day spending £25 each, but actually gets 40 customers spending £20. Calculate the shortfall in revenue that will result from these differences. (3)

4 Explain two actions the government could take to encourage more people to become entrepreneurs. (4)

5 Briefly explain one argument for and one against saying that entrepreneurs are born, not made. (5)

6 Having read this chapter, explain briefly how successful or unsuccessful you think you would be as an entrepreneur. Take care to explain your reasoning. (7)

Data response 1

Travis Sporland is a surfer who believes he has created a revolutionary design for surfboards. His father was made redundant from a Devon boatyard two years ago, so Travis thinks they can start up a small manufacturing business together. The Travis surfboard is designed for children up to the age of 11. He believes the size of the world market may be as high as 1.5 million. Some of his forecasts about the business are set out in Table 24.2.

Questions (20 marks; 20 minutes)

1 If you were to advise Travis, identify four questions you would like to ask him about his business plans. (8)

2 Explain your reasoning behind one of those questions. (4)

3 Assess two main factors you think he should also consider before going ahead. (8)

	UK market only (surfers under 11)	US market only (surfers under 11)	Rest of the world (surfers under 11)
Surfer population	22,000	580,000	460,000
Forecast year 1 sales	2,200	29,000	23,000
Surfboard selling price	£120	$200	$150

Table 24.2 Forecasts for new business

Data response 2

Naked Pizza

In 2006, a pizza takeaway opened in New Orleans. It was called 'The World's Healthiest Pizza'. It attracted attention but, as co-founder Jeff Leach puts it, 'people thought it would taste like the side of a tree'. The business struggled. Then a local advertising specialist advised a name change. He recommended 'Naked Pizza'. Since then, sales have risen dramatically and – in 2009 – two wealthy backers invested in making the business grow. In a country obsessed by food, Naked Pizza's message is 'keep buying the pizza you love, but buy ours because it's better for you'.

The thinking behind the business was to do 'an Activia' in the pizza market. In other words, create probiotic pizza dough that can be friendly towards stomachs. Leach and partner Randy Crochet said they spent $750,000 on research and experimentation to find the perfect dough. It is made from 12 different whole grains and contains probiotic bacteria – just like Activia. Leach says that until Naked Pizza was introduced the usual American pizza was 'nothing more than a doughnut with tomato sauce'. Sceptics have questioned whether these friendly small bacteria can survive a 400° pizza oven, but Leach is sure they can.

Figure 24.5 Naked Pizza

In August 2010, the first all-new Naked Pizza outlet opened in Florida. The company claimed in early 2010 that 'the race is on to open 400 Naked Pizza (franchise) stores between August and December 2010'. In fact, by the end of 2014, there were just nine stores in the US (and six in the Middle East). But founder Jeff Leach remains hugely motivated by the desire to get people eating a healthier pizza.

The Naked Pizza website suggests that an investment of $250,000 is required per franchisee, but it is not clear what fee and royalty Naked Pizza will demand. In its day, many early franchisees in McDonald's became millionaires. The same hopes will be true in this case.

Although there's not yet a Naked Pizza in Britain, there may yet be a rush to become a franchisee. Recent years have seen the rise of Subway. Perhaps it is time for something new on the high street.

Questions (30 marks; 35 minutes)

1 Give two characteristics of successful entrepreneurs shown by the founders of Naked Pizza. (2)

2 Assess two probable motives behind Jeff Leach and Randy Crochet's establishment of their Naked Pizza business. (8)

3 Between August 2010 and 2014, the business was developing quite rapidly. Assess two possible risks that may undermine the success of this expansion. (8)

4 In Britain, Domino's charges £10.49 for a delivered medium pizza such as the Meat Combo and Papa John's charges £12.49. Assess the prices you believe that Naked Pizza should set for delivered pizzas in the UK market. (12)

Extended writing

1 Motor car pioneer Henry Ford once said that 'a business that makes nothing but money is a poor business'. Evaluate that statement. (20)

2 This chapter started by saying that 'The motives of entrepreneurs are often rooted in psychology rather than ambition.' Evaluate whether ambition is likely to create a more successful and profitable business. (20)

25 Business objectives

> **Definition**
>
> Business objectives are the goals set for the business as a whole, also known as **corporate objectives**. They derive from the mission and aims set by the directors.

Linked to: Leadership, Ch 22; Entrepreneurial motives and characteristics, Ch 24; Forms of business, Ch 26; Moving from entrepreneur to leader, Ch 28.

25.1 Introduction to business objectives

Business is best looked at from the boss's point of view. The boss (perhaps the founder or **entrepreneur**) has an idea or **mission**. The chief executive of Sainsbury's may decide that a chain of supermarkets in India represents the next big step forward. This is the mission – Sainsbury's succeeding in India. This can then form the basis for setting targets or **objectives**, such as to open the first ten Sainsbury's supermarkets in India by the end of 2018.

After the chief executive has set that objective, Sainsbury's senior managers must then figure out how to make this happen. What will be needed is a **strategy** that leads to a plan of action – that is, to set out exactly what needs to happen, and by when. That strategy will have to involve the four main business functions: marketing, people, finance and operations (see Table 25.1).

The chief executive will expect the leaders of each of these four functions to come up with their own plan for meeting the overall objective, so there will be a marketing plan, a financial plan and so on. How these things relate to each other can be seen in Figure 25.1

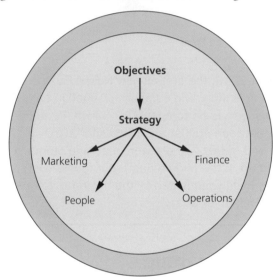

Figure 25.1 How business works

Having established their own plans, the four functional leaders will now need to meet to make sure that everything fits together. It is no good if marketing decides on an image of Sainsbury's Super-value (a kind of Aldi/Lidl idea) while operations chooses to build stores targeting India's rich elite. Each of the functions must talk to each other and trust each other (see Figure 25.2).

Marketing	This department advises the business on consumer trends and the attitudes and purchasing habits of customers – and decides how to advertise and promote new and existing brands.
People (human resources)	Managers of the firm's staff (human resources or HR) plan for and deal with recruitment, training, financial incentives, equal opportunities and also redundancy and dismissals.
Finance	Finance helps to identify what can be afforded and therefore what **budgets** to set for each of the other functions; it also monitors the spending levels to make sure that costs are kept under control.
Operations	Operations manages the supply chain that starts with buying materials and components, then manufactures a finished product and delivers it to the customer. Service businesses also need to plan the flow of work, so operations management is relevant in a bank or a shop as well as in a factory.

Table 25.1 The business functions

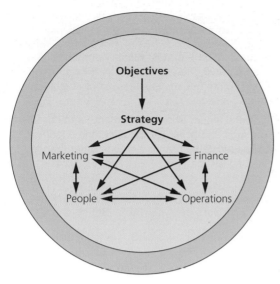

Figure 25.2 How business works (2)

Important though it is to understand the internal workings of a business as shown in Figure 25.2, there are many added complications. Much as a chief executive may wish to set optimistic objectives, a series of outside factors can get in the way of success. Most obviously, competitors may have their own ideas; if Sainsbury's finds that the massive Walmart is fighting for every suitable property site in India, opening ten stores will become a lot harder. Figure 25.3 gives an overview of the process of running a business, taking into account external as well as internal factors.

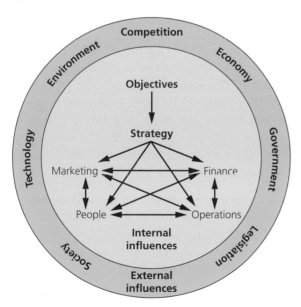

Figure 25.3 How business works (3)

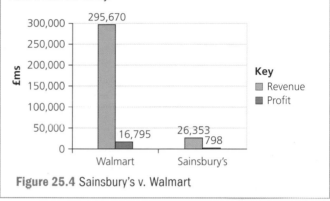
25.2 Mission and objectives

Mission is the aim for the business that is settled upon by the boss (in a small firm) or by the Board of Directors in a large one. An aim is a general statement of where the business is heading; mission usually takes that statement and makes it sound more evangelical or motivational. An aim might be 'to be Number 1 in the market for advanced engines'. When dressed up as a mission, this becomes: 'to provide the finest, most technologically advanced power systems' (Rolls-Royce).

The reason to turn the aim into a motivational statement is to try to excite customers and staff alike – to make them feel part of the project, just as customers once felt that buying Innocent smoothies was helping to 'make the world a little fruitier'. Without doubt, if a business has an exciting aim, it is great to express it as a motivating mission. Often, though, dull aims are jazzed up as '**mission statements**' that mean little or nothing to the staff.

Meaningful mission statement	Meaningless mission statement (would this motivate staff?)
'To become the world's Number 1 online fashion destination for 20-somethings.' ASOS, 2014 (neatly, they call this 'Our Ambition' rather than 'Our Mission')	'We want Tesco to be the most highly valued business by: the customers we serve, the communities in which we operate, our loyal and committed colleagues and of course, our shareholders.' Tesco, 2014
'Maintaining a global viewpoint, we are dedicated to supplying products of the highest quality, yet at a reasonable price for worldwide customer satisfaction. Dreams inspire us to create innovative products that enhance mobility and benefit society.' Honda UK, 2014	'To be the world leader in food ingredients and flavours serving the food and beverage industry, and a leading supplier of added value brands and customer branded foods to the Irish and UK markets.' Kerry Foods, 2014
'Our product mission drives us to make fantastic ice cream – for its own sake.' Ben & Jerry's, 2014	'We create outstanding places which make a positive difference to people's everyday lives.' British Land, 2014

Table 25.2 Good and bad mission statements

From the aims or mission will come the objectives. These will usually be SMART – that is, Specific, Measureable, Achievable, Realistic and Timebound. For ASOS, an example of a SMART objective might be 'to become one of the Top 3 online clothing sellers in China by 1 January 2017'. Ideally this objective would seem challenging but achievable – and should sit neatly as a stepping stone towards the mission of becoming 'the world's Number 1'.

Objectives are set because if you are the boss of 21,300 people running Rolls-Royce, you cannot make every decision. Therefore, you have to give more junior staff the authority to get on and make middle-ranking decisions, perhaps without letting you know. If managers are clear on the overall objectives, they can feel confident in making decisions that contribute towards achieving those goals.

'Objectives are not fate; they are direction. They are not commands; they are commitments. They do not determine the future; they are means to mobilise the resources and energies of the business for the making of the future.'

Peter Drucker, business guru

25.3 Common business objectives

1 Survival. This will be a priority for new, start-up businesses – one third of new businesses fail to survive the first three years. With survival as the objective, managers may avoid actions that look highly profitable yet have a high risk attached to them (such as launching a new product).

Survival is also a priority for businesses that:

- are caught out by a sudden change in the economy: a sudden recession or (for a business such as Iceland or Poundland) an unexpected consumer boom
- have over-expanded, probably using bank finance and therefore are struggling under the weight of interest payments (a rise in interest rates would be a further twist of the knife)
- have been hit by a competitive whirlwind, such as a price war or a new, wealthy, direct competitor.

'Business is like a bicycle. Either you keep moving or you fall down.'

John David Wright

2 Profit maximisation. This is the attempt by a business to make as much profit as possible, probably as fast as possible. Big companies may follow this approach when they suspect a rival is about to try to buy them out. The higher the profit they can show, the higher the price the company will fetch. The same is likely to be the case for companies about to 'float' their shares onto the stock market.

Small firms may also be trying to make as much profit as possible, with no concern for the long-term future. Such businesses may end up on TV programmes such as the BBC's *Watchdog*, which has been uncovering poor business practice for 35 years.

'Growth is a by-product of the pursuit of excellence and is not itself a worthy goal.'

Robert Townsend, Avis chief executive and business author

3 Sales maximisation. The importance of online business has placed growth as one of the most common business objectives. The logic is often to say 'there can only be one giant in this market, so we must make sure it's us'. Therefore decisions are made that focus on rising customer/user numbers instead of rising profits. The assumption is often made that, if you get the growth today, the profits will come tomorrow. This is famously true in the console business, in which selling hardware rarely makes a profit – it is the software and the add-ons that bring profits later.

4 Market share. Gillette has a 70 per cent share of the UK market for razors and blades. That gives it £250 million of sales at comfortably high profit margins. Having a high market share is not only good business today – it puts a company in a marvellous position to feel secure about its future. If Gillette launches a new product, every supermarket and chemist will stock it – and most consumers will try it. And it is very rare for new companies to try to break in to a market so dominated by one business. Everyone knows that Gillette would fight ferociously to stop a newcomer from making serious inroads into its market-leading position.

5 Cost efficiency. This is important for large firms, but critical for small ones, especially business start-ups. If the objective is to minimise costs, it will be vital that everyone in the business is practising the same approach. So even quite junior staff who have been given some decision-making power (through **delegation**) should be aware of the importance of cost minimisation. This is especially the case for businesses that operate in markets where product

differentiation is low. At the time of writing, Tata Steel is planning to sell off its UK steel business because it has struggled to get costs low enough to compete in the world market.

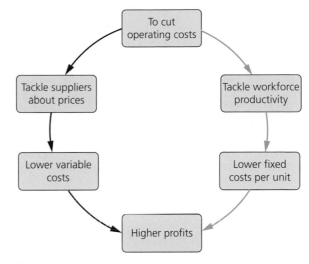

Figure 25.5 Logic chain: cost efficiency and profit

6 Employee welfare. On the face of it, the only business organisation that would place staff as a central business objective would be a workers' co-operative, such as the John Lewis Partnership. Happily there are others who appreciate that good customer service comes from motivated staff. Greggs plc has long been a good example of this. Employee welfare is also important in businesses such as JCB and Jaguar Land Rover, when underlying shortages of skilled engineers force managers to care hugely about **staff retention**. In 2013/2014, staff retention at Jaguar Land Rover was a remarkable 98 per cent – a tribute to its employee welfare. Unfortunately, there are other companies where the cliché 'staff are our most important asset' rings hollow, with managers resorting to wage-cutting devices such as outsourcing and zero-hours contracts.

7 Customer satisfaction. As with employee welfare, customer satisfaction is a goal, but rarely a **corporate objective**. It is necessary but not sufficient for success. In recent years, companies have used the term 'customer delight' to denote the need for something more active than 'satisfaction'. The real essence of customer satisfaction is that it should be at a sufficiently high level to generate customer loyalty, or even commitment (think Apple or the love of a football fan for his club).

8 Social objectives. These are easy to find on company websites; whether they have any significant influence over business decisions is less clear. All through the period that banks were mis-selling service after service to customers, their websites boasted their ethical purity. Ultimately, social and ethical objectives only mean something if the business is willing to sacrifice some profit or some market share. Arguably, Tesco did just this in May 2014 when it volunteered to remove sweets from near its checkouts (though perhaps it was following Lidl's example, as the German firm did the same earlier in the year). It is fair to be sceptical about whether social and ethical objectives are ever much more than image-related add-ons. Financial objectives remain the overwhelming priority for most businesses. Ethical businesses, such as One Water, do exist – but are relatively rare.

Five whys and a how

Questions	Answers
Why must it always be difficult to know if the objective of profit maximisation has been realised?	You'd know if a profit goal of £50,000 had been achieved, but who knows about maximisation? Is £60,000 enough, or £70,000? Staff would rather be measured by a clear target.
Why might a company aim be better expressed as a mission?	If more vibrant, motivating language makes staff care more and work harder, a mission will have paid for itself.
Why do objectives need to be SMART?	Vaguely worded 'objectives' will be too woolly to allow anyone to measure whether they have been achieved or not – so they would have no motivating force.
Why might employee welfare be an unlikely objective for a public limited company?	Because plcs are owned by external shareholders who are looking for shareholder value, either from rising dividends or a rising share price (or both).
Why may social objectives be easy to boast about but hard to carry through?	Boasts about doing good sit well on a website, but may be ignored by bosses intent on high profits and therefore high bonuses.
How should bosses decide on their company objectives?	By talking to their staff, they will find out what's wrong at the moment and what's possible in the future.

25.4 Business objectives – evaluation

Managing a business is a challenge because there are so many variables that can get in the way of success. If the pound rises in value, different executives within a company may come to different judgements about what to do next. In such a situation, the business objectives should help keep everyone pointing in the same direction. If the goal is profit maximisation, the higher pound's impact on import prices can be enjoyed as higher profit levels. If sales maximisation or market share are the goals, lower import prices can feed through to price cuts and therefore higher sales.

A problem can be that, despite staff knowing the official objectives, some believe there are other, unstated but more important, goals. In 2010, at a time when it advertised itself as the 'ethical bank', the Co-op Bank was guilty of mis-selling financial products to its customers. Clearly the sales staff believed that the real goal was profit, not the social objectives claimed by the business.

Key terms

Budgets: an agreed ceiling on the monthly spending by any department or manager.

Corporate objectives: targets for the whole business, such as profits to rise by 20 per cent a year for the next three years.

Delegation: passing authority down the hierarchy, to allow more junior employees some decision-making power.

Entrepreneur: someone who makes a business idea happen, either through their own effort or by organising others to do the work.

Mission: a business aim expressed to make it seem especially purposeful and motivating.

Mission statement: a short, powerfully expressed sentence or two that explains the business aims clearly yet motivationally.

Objectives: targets precise enough to allow praise or blame for the person in charge.

Shareholder value: the mix of shareholder dividends and a rising share price that stem from high and rising profits.

Staff retention: literally retaining (keeping) staff, usually measured as staff still remaining at the end of the year as a percentage of the total workforce.

Strategy: a medium-to-long term plan for meeting your objectives.

25.5 Workbook

Revision questions

(25 marks; 25 minutes)

1 Explain two differences between a mission and objectives. (4)

2 State whether each of the following statements is a mission or an objective:

   a) to become the world's favourite car rental business

   b) to bring healthy eating to Wigan

   c) to achieve a 40 per cent market share by the end of 2018. (3)

3 Outline two possible risks if a business such as Sainsbury's sets itself the objective of sales maximisation. (4)

4 Outline why 'survival' might be the wisest objective for a brand new start-up business. (3)

5 Why might a business suffering bad publicity emphasise a new set of social objectives? (3)

6 Read John David Wright's quotation (see page 162). Explain its meaning in your own words. (4)

7 Outline one strength and one weakness of a business such as Aston Villa FC setting itself objectives for the coming season. (4)

Data response

Snapchat

In late autumn 2013, two 23-year-old Californians were each offered $750 million in cash by Facebook's Mark Zuckerberg. And they turned it down. Evan Spiegel and Bobby Murphy launched Snapchat in July 2011. By 2013 Facebook wanted to buy the business for $3,000 million. The founders had each retained a 25 per cent stake in the business, hence the $750 million figure.

Snapchat began late one night at Stanford University when Reggie Brown stepped into fellow student Spiegel's room groaning about a photo he regretted sending. He then said something like 'I wish there was an app to send disappearing photos'. Spiegel saw the potential, calling Brown's remark 'a million dollar idea'. This conversation is now part of a billion dollar lawsuit, as Brown claims his share of the Snapchat goldmine.

Spiegel developed the app as part of a university project. When he presented it, the feedback was, roughly, who wants a disappearing photo? And when it debuted (under the brand name Picaboo) in the Apple App Store on 13 July 2011, no-one noticed. Luckily, a bust-up over the share split in August 2011 made Spiegel and Murphy cut Brown out – including the Picaboo name that Brown had put forward. The new name was Snapchat. User uptake remained painfully slow until high school students in California started using it at school – as Facebook had been banned. Then the take-off was spectacular, as shown in Table 25.3.

	Snapchat users/ usage	Snapchat funding
August 2011	127	
October 2011	1,000	
December 2011	2,250	
January 2012	20,000	
April 2012	100,000	$485,000
February 2013	60,000,000	$13,500,000
November 2013	400,000,000	$50,000,000
June 2014	1,000,000,000	

Table 25.3 The rise of Snapchat

Having turned $3 billion down in 2013, it was perhaps a relief to the founders that Chinese web giant Alibaba talked in August 2014 about an investment that would value Snapchat at $10 billion. This would be an amazing valuation as Snapchat had, at that time, never generated a dollar of revenue. But Snapchat's huge appeal came from demography. Facebook users were now an average of nearly 40 years old, whereas Snapchat's core target market was 12–24 year olds, with an average age below 18. Facebook might be the present, but Snapchat looked like the future.

The other major issue for Spiegel and Murphy was Brown's huge lawsuit, demanding his fair share of the company. A similar thing happened with Facebook, making it easy to forecast that lawyers will get rich arguing this case – but it will probably be settled out of court for a very large sum.

Questions (40 marks; 45 minutes)

1 Explain the importance of 'funding' to Snapchat. (4)

2 Explain the term 'target market' in the context of Snapchat. (4)

3 Assess whether profit or sales maximisation was the most appropriate business objective for Snapchat in its early years. (12)

4 From your own knowledge of Snapchat, evaluate whether the business could ever generate advertising or other revenue to make it worth billions of dollars. (20)

Extended writing

1 You have been appointed chief executive of Marks & Spencer. Your mission is 'to restore M&S as the clothing store of choice for women over the age of 30'. Evaluate how you will set about this task. (20)

2 Morrisons supermarket chain has decided to reposition itself as 'the ethical grocer'. Evaluate whether they could achieve this while still making a profit. (20)

26 Forms of business

Linked to: Sources of finance, Ch 30; Liability and finance, Ch 31; Business failure, Ch 39.

26.1 Businesses with unlimited liability

Unlimited liability means that the finances of the business are treated as inseparable from the finances of the business owner(s). So if the business loses £1 million, the people owed money (the **creditors**) can get the courts to force the individual owners to pay up. If that means selling their houses, cars, and so on, so be it. If the owner(s) cannot pay, they can be made personally **bankrupt**. Two types of business organisation have unlimited liability: **sole traders** and partnerships.

(For more detail on limited v. unlimited liability, see Chapter 31.)

Sole traders

A sole trader is an individual who owns and operates his or her own business. Although there may be one or two employees, this person makes the final decisions about the running of the business. A sole trader is the only one who benefits financially from success, but must face the burden of any failure. In the eyes of the law, the individual and the business are the same. This means that the owner has unlimited liability for any debts that result from running the firm. If a sole trader cannot pay his or her bills, the courts can allow personal assets to be seized by creditors in order to meet outstanding debts. For example, the family home or car may be sold. If insufficient funds can be raised in this way, the person will be declared bankrupt.

Despite the financial dangers involved, the sole trader is the most common form of legal structure adopted by UK businesses. In some areas of the economy, this kind of business dominates, particularly where little finance is required to set up and run the business and customers demand a personal service. Examples include trades such as builders and plumbers, and many independent shopkeepers.

There are no formal rules to follow when establishing as a sole trader, or administrative costs to pay. Complete confidentiality can be maintained because accounts are not published. As a result, many business start-ups adopt this structure.

The main disadvantages facing a sole trader are the limited sources of finance available, long hours of work involved and the difficulty of running the business during periods of ill health (plus unlimited liability).

Partnerships

Partnerships exist when two or more people start a business without forming a company. Like a sole trader, the individuals have unlimited liability for any debts run up by the business. Because people are working together but are unlimitedly liable for any debts, it is vital that the partners trust each other. As a result, this legal structure is often found in professions such as medicine and law.

The main difference between a sole trader and a partnership is the number of owners.

26.2 Businesses with limited liability

Limited liability means that the legal duty to pay debts run up by a business stays with the business itself, not its owner/shareholders. If a company has £1 million of debts that it lacks the cash to repay, the courts can force the business to sell all its assets (cars, computers, etc.). If there is still not enough money, the company is closed down, but the owner/shareholders have no personal liability for the remaining debts.

To gain the benefits of limited liability, the business must go through a legal process to become a company. The process of **incorporation** creates a separate legal identity for the organisation. In the eyes of the law, the owners of the business and the company itself are now two different things. The business can take legal action against others and have legal action taken against it. In order to gain separate legal status, a company must be registered with the **Registrar of Companies**.

Advantages of forming a limited company

- Shareholders experience the benefits of limited liability, including the confidence to expand.
- A limited company is able to gain access to a wider range of borrowing opportunities than a sole trader or partnership.

Disadvantages of forming a limited company

- Limited companies must make financial information available publicly at Companies House. Small firms are not required to make full disclosure of their company accounts, but they have to reveal more than would be the case for a sole trader or partnership.
- Limited companies have to follow more and more expensive rules than unlimited liability businesses – for example, audited accounts and holding an annual general meeting of shareholders; these things add several thousands of pounds to annual overhead costs.

Real business

One Water

In 2003, Duncan Goose quit his job and founded One Water. He wanted to finance water projects in Africa from profits made selling bottled water in Britain. The particular water project was 'Playpumps': children's roundabouts plumbed into freshly dug water wells. As the children play, each rotation of the roundabout brings up a litre of fresh, clean water.

Duncan thought of forming a charity, but felt that the regulations governing charities might force them to be inefficient. So, for the sum of £125, he founded a limited company, Global Ethics Ltd. This enabled him to set the rules - for instance, that the shareholders receive no dividends and the directors receive no fees. But, of course, it ensured that he and other volunteers who put time into One Water were protected, should something

go wrong and big debts build up. Today, One Water is a major business trading internationally. It has raised more than £10 million, funding more than 900 Playpumps and providing clean water to more than two million people, permanently.

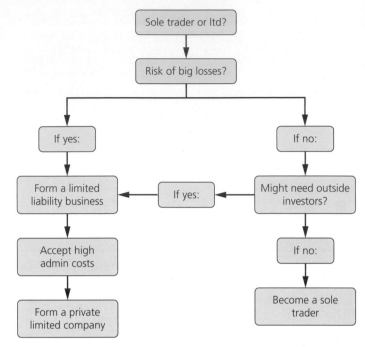

Figure 26.1 Logic chain: sole trader or limited company?

26.3 Private limited companies

For a private limited company, the start-up capital will often be £100, which can be wholly owned by the entrepreneur, or other people can be brought in as investors. The shares of a private limited company cannot be bought and sold without the agreement of the other directors. This means the company cannot be listed on the stock market. As a result, it is possible to maintain close control over the way the business is run. This form of business is often run by a family or small group of friends. It may be very profit focused or, like Global Ethics Ltd, have wholly different objectives than maximising profit.

> **'I couldn't be more thrilled to have control over my own destiny in a way that is not possible as a public company.'**

Michael Dell, after paying $25 billion to take Dell Computers private in 2013

A legal requirement for private companies is that they must state 'Ltd' after the company name. This warns those dealing with the business that the firm is relatively small and has limited liability. Remember, limited liability protects shareholders from business debts, so there is a risk that 'cowboy' businesspeople might start a company, run it into the ground and then walk away from its debts. Therefore, the cheques of a limited company are not as secure as ones from an unlimited liability business. This is why many petrol stations have notices saying 'No company cheques allowed'.

Some of the factors that may determine when a business should start up as a sole trader and when as a private limited company are outlined in Table 26.1.

Sole trader	Private limited company
When the entrepreneur has no intention of expanding, e.g. just wants to run one local restaurant	When the entrepreneur has ambitions to expand quickly, therefore needs it to be easier to raise extra finance
When there is no need for substantial bank borrowing, i.e. start-up costs are low	When large borrowings mean significant chances of large losses if things go wrong
When the business will be small enough to mean that one person can make all the big decisions	When the business may require others to make decisions, e.g. when the entrepreneur is on holiday or unwell

Table 26.1 Factors influencing choice between starting a new business as a sole trader or private limited company

26.4 Growth to plc and stock market flotation

When a private limited company expands to the point of having share capital of more than £50,000, it can convert to a public limited company (plc). Then it can be floated on the stock market, which allows any member of the general public to buy shares. This increases the company's access to share capital, which enables it to expand considerably. The term 'plc' will appear after the company name – for example, Marks & Spencer plc or Tesco plc.

The principal differences between private and public limited companies are as follows:

- A public company can raise capital from the general public, while a private limited company is prohibited from doing so.
- The minimum capital requirement of a public company is £50,000. There is no minimum for a private limited company.

- Public companies must publish far more detailed accounts than private limited companies.

Most large businesses are plcs. Yet the process of converting from a private to a public company can be difficult. Usually, successful small firms grow steadily, perhaps at a rate of 10 or 15 per cent a year. Even that pace of growth causes problems, but good managers can cope. The problem of floating on the stock market is that it provides a sudden, huge injection of cash. This sounds great, but it forces the firm to try to grow more quickly (otherwise the new shareholders will say: 'what are you doing with our cash?'). Note that the media increasingly uses the US term IPO (initial public offering) instead of the British term 'flotation'.

'When the operations of capitalism come to resemble the casino, ill fortune will be the lot of many.'

John Maynard Keynes, economist

26.5 Other forms of business

Franchising

Starting a new business with a new idea requires a huge amount of planning, skill and perhaps luck on the part of the businessperson. Many of these problems can be avoided if entrepreneurs go for a situation that is a 'half-way house' towards running their own business: a franchise. NatWest Bank suggests that 93 per cent of franchises survive their first three years, compared with slightly under 70 per cent for businesses generally.

For example, if you start up an independent optician, you have to:

- design and decorate a store that will create the right customer image
- create systems for staff training, stock control and accounting
- do your own advertising to bring in customers and create a brand strong enough to justify the high prices charged by high street opticians.

Alternatively, you could start up your own, independent limited company, and sign up for a Specsavers franchise. This would mean, for example, access to the specially written Specsavers store management software. From a scan of a sold pair of glasses, the software ensures that all the necessary stock ordering and accounting actions are taken. The franchise owner (Specsavers) also provides full training for the **franchisee** (the entrepreneur), plus advice and supplier contacts for store decoration and display and, of course, the huge marketing support from a multi-million pound TV advertising campaign. If you start up J. Bloggs Opticians, how many people will come through the doors? If you open up Specsavers, customers will trust the business from day one.

Pitfalls of running a franchise

It is important to be clear that really independent-minded people may hate being franchisees; after all, they may want to 'be their own boss'. A franchisee is the boss of the business, but without the normal freedoms of decision making. This could be very frustrating. It will also be important to choose the right franchise. On the fringes of franchising are some dubious businesses that sell the promises of training and advertising support, but supply very little after they have pocketed the franchise fee. As with anything in business, careful research is essential; better franchise operators are members of the British Franchise Association, the BFA. It should also be borne in mind that the franchise owner's slice of your income may make it difficult to make good profits from 'your' business.

Benefits of running a franchise

A young businessperson could treat being a franchisee as wonderful training towards becoming a full entrepreneur. 'Today I'll open a Subway; in five years I'll sell it and open my own restaurant.' Very few people have the range of skills required of the independent business owner. Who is expert at: marketing, buying, store design, window display, staff management, sales, stock control and accounting? This is why the failure rate for new independent businesses is higher than for franchise businesses.

Due to the different failure rates, the attitude of bankers is very different when you seek finance for a franchise start-up. Ask NatWest for £100,000 to start J. Bloggs sandwich shop, and the door will quickly be closed; ask for the same amount to help finance a Subway franchise and the response will be far more positive. Franchisees find finance easier and cheaper to get. The interest rate charged by a bank for a potential Subway franchisee will be lower than the rate they would charge to the founder of an independent business start-up.

Social enterprise

Whereas 'private limited company' is a legal term with specific rules, 'social enterprise' sounds great but promises little. It actually means nothing more than 'we claim to do good' – but good for whom is not stated. Duncan Goose, founder of the genuine social enterprise One Water, says that a rival water business claims to give all profits to African clean-water charities, but the directors pay themselves so generously that there is little profit left at the end of the year. Note that One Water is legally a private limited company (not a charity), yet the business uses all profit for charitable purposes. Duncan says that registering as a charity would mean that lots of potential donations would be sucked up in bureaucracy (to meet Charity Commission rules).

A specific type of potentially social enterprise is the co-operative. Co-operatives can be worker-owned, such as John Lewis/Waitrose, or customer-owned, such as the retail Co-op. Co-operatives have the potential to offer a more united cause for the workforce than the profit of shareholders. Workers at John Lewis can enjoy annual bonuses of 20 per cent of their salary, as their share of the company's profits. The Co-op has been less successful, though its focus on ethical trading has helped it become relevant to today's shoppers.

Lifestyle businesses

Some entrepreneurs start a business based on their own or their family's needs. A young couple might start a surf school by the sea as a way to earn while enjoying their passion for the surf. Less glamorously, a family-run bed-and-breakfast may be a great way to keep a small farm going – and to keep the family together. With a lifestyle business, usual rules about objectives and strategies might not apply. For example, the surfer-entrepreneurs might target plenty of customers above plenty of revenue, therefore setting lower prices than would any profit-seeking business.

Online businesses

Online businesses are so common today that they hardly need a separate category. They have to decide on a limited or unlimited liability structure like any other. All that marks online businesses out is the different balance between risk and reward. With ordinary 'bricks' businesses, such as a restaurant, there has to be a heavy financial outlay before the business begins trading. With online, the heavy investment is usually in time, not money. So a university student can programme an app and test it online – and therefore be pretty certain of success before risking much capital at all. Better still, the 'scalability' of online businesses is usually quite limitless. In June 2014, the taxi service 'Uber' was valued at $18 billion by financiers, less than five years after it started. Such upsides are far more likely with 'click' than 'brick' businesses. So the financial risks are lower and potential rewards are higher. Go figure.

Five whys and a how

Questions	Answers
Why might an entrepreneur choose to be a sole trader instead of forming a private limited company?	To minimise administration costs – and presumably on the assumption of very few risks involved in the business.
Why would anyone sell goods on credit to a limited liability business?	Because they trust that the proprietors will not close the business down and shelter behind limited personal liability (some have regretted that trust).
Why might a growing business turn itself into a plc and then float its shares on the stock market?	To raise extra capital for expansion – and/or to allow the early-stage investors to sell part of their own holding (perhaps making them millionaires).
Why might 'the divorce of ownership and control' matter to an investor?	It may mean that senior management are more interested in money/power for themselves than building up the business in the long term.
Why may a 'social enterprise' prove no more ethically sound than a profit-seeking company?	Ethics are partly a consequence of personal morality; it may be wrong to assume that those working for social enterprises such as the Co-op are any different from those working for companies.
How do you form a company?	To achieve incorporation you need to complete the memorandum and the articles of association and send them, plus fee, to the Registrar of Companies.

26.6 Forms of business – evaluation

Business organisation is a dry, technical subject. It does contain some important business themes, however, two of which are particularly valuable sources of evaluative comment.

1 The existence of limited liability has had huge effects on business. Some have been unarguably beneficial. How could firms become really big if the owners felt threatened by equally big debts? Limited liability helps firms to take reasonable business risks. It also, however, gives scope for dubious business practices. For example, it is possible to start a firm, live a great lifestyle, then go into liquidation, leaving the customers/creditors out of

pocket, and then start again. All too often this is the story told by programmes such as the BBC's *Watchdog*. Companies Acts lay down legislation that tries to make this harder to do, but it still happens. Such unethical behaviour is why government intervention to protect the consumer can always be justified.

2 Short-termism is a curse for effective business decision making. There is no proof that a stock exchange listing leads to short-termism, only the suspicion that in many cases it does. Massive companies such as Unilever, Nestlé and Shell may be above the pressures for short-term performance. In many other cases, though, it seems that British company directors focus too much on the short-term share price. Could this be because their huge bonuses depend on how high the share price is? Worries about shareholder pressures or takeover bids may distract managers from building a long-term business in the way that companies such as BMW and Toyota have done.

'Too many companies, especially large ones, are driven more and more narrowly by the need to ensure that investors get good returns and to justify executives' high salaries. Too often, this means they view employees as costs.'

Hillary Clinton, US politician

26.7 Workbook

Revision questions

(30 marks; 30 minutes)

1 Explain two differences between a sole trader and a partnership. (4)

2 In your own words, try to explain the importance of establishing a separate legal entity to separate the business from the individual owner. (4)

3 You can start a business today. All you have to do is tell HM Revenue & Customs (the taxman). Outline two risks of starting in this way. (4)

4 Briefly discuss whether each of the following businesses should start as a sole trader, a partnership or a private limited company.

   a) A clothes shop started by Claire Wells with £40,000 of her own money plus £10,000 from the bank. It is located close to her home in Wrexham. (3)

   b) A builder's started by Jim Barton and Lee Clark, who plan to become the number one for loft extensions in Sheffield. They have each invested £15,000 and are borrowing £30,000 from the bank. (3)

5 Explain the possible risks to a growing business of making the jump from a private limited company to 'going public', then floating its shares on the stock market. (5)

6 Why are good franchise owners keen to inspect their franchisees regularly, even though they have no ownership stake in the franchise businesses? (3)

7 Why should a potential franchisee be very careful to research fully the background of the franchise owner? (4)

Data response 1

UK business categories

In 2013, the Federation of Small Businesses estimated that there were five million businesses in the UK. Use this information plus Figure 26.2 to answer the questions below.

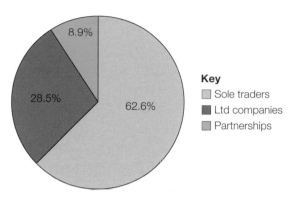

Key
- Sole traders
- Ltd companies
- Partnerships

8.9%
28.5%
62.6%

Figure 26.2 UK business organisations (source: Office of National Statistics, October 2013)

Questions (30 marks; 30 minutes)

1 **a)** Calculate the number of sole traders in the UK; then calculate the number of limited companies. (3)

   b) Assess two possible reasons why there are so many more sole traders than companies. (8)

2 Calculate how many British businesses operate with unlimited liability. (3)

3 Research conducted at Warwick Business School shows that one in five businesses is principally owned by a woman, 93 per cent of business owners are white and 7 per cent are from ethnic minorities.

   a) Assess two possible reasons why women are so much less likely to own a business than men. (8)

   b) The percentage figures for ethnic minorities show business ownership to be below representation in the population (around 13 per cent). Assess two reasons that may explain this. (8)

Data response 2

Starting a new business

Forming a limited company can be time-consuming. According to the World Bank, the number of actions required to get started varies from one in New Zealand to 13 in Brazil and China. As a result of the different processes, the number of days it takes to start up varies from one day in New Zealand (the world's quickest) to 144 days in Venezuela (the world's slowest).

Figure 26.3 provides data selected from the World Bank's 2013–2014 'Global Competitiveness Report'.

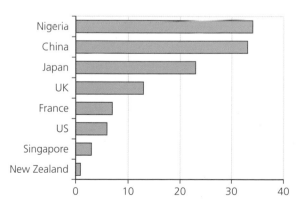

Figure 26.3 Time required to start a business (days) (source: Global Competitiveness Report 2013–2014)

Questions (20 marks; 20 minutes)

1 Explain the implications for starting a business in Nigeria of the following two factors in business start-up:

   a) cash flow – that is, the daily flows of cash into and out of the business

   b) hiring and training new staff. (8)

2 A sole trader can start a business straight away, whereas forming a limited company takes the time shown in Figure 26.3. Assess whether an entrepreneur should be influenced by this data when deciding whether to form a company or act as a sole trader. (12)

Extended writing

1 Social enterprises such as charities and co-operatives run businesses including shops and banks. Evaluate whether you should expect better value for money from a social enterprise than from an ordinary limited company. (20)

2 Sunil Mittal, an Indian software entrepreneur, once said: 'We want to manage and grow our companies ourselves. If we give up 51 per cent we might as well get out of the business.' Evaluate whether he is right to feel that way. (20)

27 Business choices

Definition

Business choices must be made bearing in mind opportunity cost. This is the cost of missing out on the next best alternative when making a decision. For example, the opportunity cost of not going to university may be to risk missing out of an (200,000 of extra lifetime earnings (according to government data). Similarly, trade-offs look at what you have to give up in order to get what you want most.

Linked to: Business objectives, Ch 25; Stock control, Ch 43.

27.1 Introduction to opportunity cost

This concept will be useful throughout the A level Business course. It is at the heart of every business decision, from small to multinational companies. Every business faces the same issue: limited resources mean that hiring a marketing manager leaves less money to spend on a marketing campaign. For a start-up business, spending lots of money on a flash opening party means there is less money to pay for staff training.

For a new business, the two most important resources are money and time. Both have an **opportunity cost**. Time spent by an entrepreneur in creating a pretty website could mean too little time is left for recruiting and training staff, or too little time to sit back to reflect on priorities. The same issue arises with money: it can only be spent once.

It follows that every business decision has an opportunity cost, measured in time, money, and often both. The same is true in other walks of life. A prime minister focused on foreign adventures may lose sight of the key issues affecting people at home. A chancellor who spends an extra £10 billion on education may have to cut back on healthcare.

For a new business start-up, the most important opportunity cost issues are as follows.

- Do not tie up too much capital in stock (inventory), as this cash could be used more productively elsewhere in the business.
- Do not overstretch yourself: good decisions take time, so make sure you are not doing too much yourself.
- Take care with every decision that uses up cash; at the start of a business, it is hard to get more of it, but more is always needed.

27.2 Opportunity costs in developing a business idea

Personal opportunity costs

Starting your first business is likely to be tough. Long hours and highly pressured decisions may cause stress, but the biggest problems are beyond psychology. A difficult cash flow position is quite normal, yet places a huge strain on the business and its owner(s).

The owner of a first business will probably have come from a background as a salary earner, possibly a very well-paid one. So the first opportunity cost is missing out on the opportunity to earn a regular income. As it could take six months or more to get a business going, this is a long period of financial hardship.

Then comes the investment spending itself, such as the outlay on a lease, on building work, on fixtures and fittings, on machinery and then on the human resources (staff) to make everything work with a human face. All this is using money that could otherwise be used on the proprietor's house, holidays, and so on. The personal opportunity costs add up massively.

The wear and tear on the family must also be considered. Starting a business is a hugely time-consuming and wholly absorbing activity. The restaurant owner might easily spend 80 hours a week on site in the early days, then take further paperwork home. An American business psychologist has said: 'Even when you are home, you're still thinking about the business – it's easy for a spouse to feel neglected, even jealous.'

> **'Perpetual devotion to what a man calls his business is only to be sustained by perpetual neglect of many other things.'**
>
> Robert Louis Stevenson, writer

Despite this, research by a US investment business has shown that, although 32 per cent of new entrepreneurs said that the experience had caused marriage difficulties, 42 per cent of chief executives in fast-growing new firms said that the pressures and exhilarations made their marriages stronger.

The opportunity costs of developing one business idea as opposed to another

When 30-year-old Mike Clare opened his first Sofabed Centre in 1985, he could raise only £16,000 of capital, even though his estimates showed that £20,000 to £25,000 was needed. Fortunately, hard work plus a great first month's sales brought in the cash he needed to get the business going properly. At that time, none of the banks would lend him any money. In the lead-up to Mike Clare's first store opening, he spent time organising public relations events (to get coverage in the local newspaper), helping with the building work, wrangling with suppliers over credit terms and making decisions about pricing and display. When the store opened, he spent 18 hours a day 'doing everything'. When the first store took £30,000 in month 1, he started looking for a second location, which was open within six months. Quite clearly, there was no possibility of starting more than one business at a time.

Later he built up a bedding business called Dreams, which he sold in 2008 for £170 million. Sadly, Dreams collapsed in 2013, in the aftermath of the great recession. Mike Clare, though, had turned £16,000 into £170 million. Given how short of money he was at the start, it would have been impossible for him to have chosen to launch two different businesses at the same time. He had to choose one. Fortunately, he chose wisely.

Given the need for focus, the main opportunity cost arises when an entrepreneur has two ideas. One should be chosen and one rejected. This is possible if the entrepreneur is ruthless. After evaluating the two options carefully, the weaker of the two should be stopped completely. The reason is simple: opening one business is tough enough; two would be impossible.

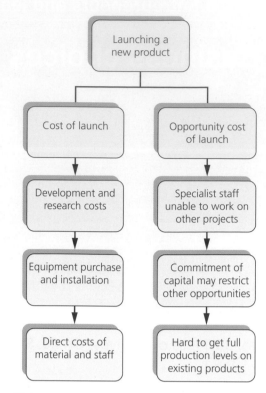

Figure 27.1 Logic chain: opportunity costs of new product launch

27.3 Deciding between opportunities

Successful businesspeople are those who can make successful decisions. The three founders of Innocent Drinks wanted to start a business together, but had no idea what type of business to start. As friends at university, they had already run nightclub events together, and two ran an annual music festival in west London. They could have developed a successful festival business, but stumbled upon the idea of a business that made all-fruit smoothies. On finding an investor, in 1999, who could help turn their dream into a reality, they left their salaried jobs, gave up their other business opportunities and concentrated on building the Innocent brand. The 2010 sale of a majority of the Innocent shares to Coca-Cola for £75 million showed the success of this start-up.

> **'Alice came to a fork in the road. "Which road do I take?" she asked.**
>
> **"Where do you want to go?" responded the Cheshire cat.**
>
> **"I don't know", Alice answered.**
>
> **"Then," said the cat "it doesn't matter."**
>
> Lewis Caroll, *Alice in Wonderland*

When deciding between business start-up opportunities, certain factors are crucial.

Estimating the potential sales that could be achieved by each idea

This is hugely difficult, both in the short term and – even more – in the longer term. Innocent's first-year sales were £0.4 million. Who could have guessed that, eight years later, its sales would be more than 300 times greater? Yet estimates must be made, either by the use of market research or by using the expertise of the entrepreneur. Mike Clare of Dreams had previously worked as an area manager for a furniture retailer, so he had a reasonable idea about what the sales might be. Inside knowledge is, of course, hard to beat.

Considering carefully the cash requirements of each idea

The Innocent trio were very lucky to find an American investor who put £250,000 into the start of the business in return for a 20 per cent stake. Some new businesses are very hungry for cash (such as setting up a new restaurant in London, which costs over £1 million); other new business ideas (such as a new website) can be started from a back bedroom, keeping initial costs very low.

Deciding whether the time is right

Innocent's launch fitted wonderfully with a time of luxury spending plus growing concern about diet. In the same year, a small business started in west London, focusing on customising cars: 'souping up' the engines to make the cars go faster and give the engines a 'throaty roar'. As rising fuel prices became a greater concern, the business was squeezed out. Five years earlier, it might have made a lot of money, but it no longer did so.

Deciding whether the skills needed fit your own set of skills

Running a restaurant requires a mix of organisational skills, discipline and meticulous attention to detail. Does that describe you? Or are you better suited to running an online business that can be handled in a relaxed way behind the scenes?

27.4 Choices and trade-offs

In business, there are many occasions when one factor has to be traded off against another. An entrepreneur might get huge help at the start from friends, yet realise that these same friends lack the professionalism to help the business grow. The needs of the business may have to be traded off against the friendships. Can a softie be a real business success? Probably not: some inner toughness is clearly important.

Other **trade-offs** may include:

- when starting in the first place, trading off the start-up against a year's international travel (perhaps with friends); or trading the start-up against going to university
- trading off the aspects of the business you most enjoy doing against those that prove most profitable for the business; the chef/owner may love cooking, yet find the business works far better when she or he has the time to mix with the customers, motivate the waiting staff and negotiate hard with suppliers
- trading off time today and time tomorrow; the entrepreneur's ambition may be to 'retire by the time I'm 40'; that may sound great in the long term but, in the short term, her or his spouse and children may see little of them.

Overall, the key to success will be to be clear about what you and your family want from the business. It may be to become outrageously rich, no matter what, or – more likely – to find a balance between the freedom and independence of running your own business and the need to find time for the family. Books on business success assume that success can be measured only in money. Many people running their own small businesses would tell a different story; the independence alone may be the key to their personal satisfaction.

> 'Strategy is about making choices, trade-offs; it's about deliberately choosing to be different.'
>
> Michael Porter, business author/guru

Five whys and a how

Questions	Answers
Why is opportunity cost involved in every business decision?	Because every decision commits resources that can then not be used for other things.
Why might an increase in interest rates be relevant to opportunity cost?	Because spending on assets such as inventories or machinery requires taking cash out of the bank so it won't be earning interest – and the higher the interest rate the higher the opportunity cost of that withdrawal.
Why might opportunity cost be especially important for a new start-up business?	Because it will almost certainly have little spare capital and even less spare management time – so every wrong decision and every overspend has especially damaging knock-on effects.
Why is the projected £42.6 billion price of HS2 high-speed railway criticised both for the cost and for the opportunity cost?	The cost is a problem at a time when Britain's fiscal deficit remains huge; the opportunity cost can be measured in potential cutbacks in NHS, education or welfare spending.
Why is time the ultimate opportunity cost?	Because although it is easy to buy the time of lots of staff, there are usually only a few people in a business who make the important decisions – so their time is very limited and very valuable.
How might a firm value the opportunity cost of *not* launching a new product?	Make careful estimates of all the revenues and costs involved in this project, then calculate the potential profit over its lifetime. That is the potential cost of what you're missing out on.

27.5 Business choices – evaluation

A level Business exam papers are laced with big questions about decision making, strategy and problem solving. Ultimately, all of these questions boil down to one thing – what is our best option given the objectives we have and the circumstances we are in? In every case, a crucial line of analysis is to consider the alternatives and therefore the opportunity cost of the decision. The risk is that the significance of the opportunity cost will not be emphasised sufficiently because it will be underestimated. If Topshop has traded-off America against China in its (slow) move to open stores in the US in 2013 and 2014, that is surely a mistake. Senior management often seem to focus on pursuing a strategy without real consideration of the opportunity cost.

Key terms

Opportunity cost: the cost of missing out on the next best alternative when making a decision (or when committing resources).

Trade-off: accepting less of one thing to achieve more of another (for example, slightly lower quality in exchange for cheapness).

27.6 Workbook

Revision questions

(20 marks; 20 minutes)

1 Explain in your own words why time is an important aspect of opportunity cost. (3)

2 Give two ways of measuring the opportunity cost to you of doing this homework. (2)

3 Examine one opportunity cost to a restaurant chef/owner of opening a second restaurant. (5)

4 Explain the trade-offs that may exist in the following business situations. Choose the two contexts you feel most comfortable with.

a) Levi's pushes its workers to produce more pairs of jeans per hour.

b) A chocolate producer, short of cash, must decide whether to cut its advertising spending or cut back on its research and development into new product ideas.

c) A football manager decides to double the number of training sessions per week.

d) A celebrity magazine must decide whether or not to run photos that will generate huge publicity, but probably make the celebrity unwilling to co-operate with the magazine in future. (6)

5 According to the Robert Louis Stevenson quote on page 175, what is the opportunity cost of devotion to business? (4)

Data response

In 2002, a co-operative agreement between coffee farmers in 250 Ugandan villages broke down. It had taken years to put together, but disagreements made it collapse. The prize for a successful co-operative was to produce organic coffee beans grown to Fairtrade standards for partners such as Cafédirect. This would ensure getting significantly higher prices for the raw coffee beans and also much better credit terms (being paid quickly to help with cash flow).

Over the next two years, countless hours of work were put into forming a new co-operative. In early 2004, the new Gumutindo coffee co-operative was Fairtrade certified. By 2014, 7,000 farmers had joined the Gumutindo co-operative. They receive a guaranteed price of $1.26 per pound of coffee beans, whereas the world price has been as low as $0.80 over the last eight years. The extra (and stable) income helps the farmers, of whom only 25 per cent have running water and 79 per cent live in mud huts with iron sheet roofing. The Fairtrade organisation has supported the co-operative in starting up its own production plant, converting the raw coffee into packs of coffee ready for sale. Ongoing investments include motorised pulpers and a major investment in solar panels to create electricity in the home as well as the production plant.

Sources: www.fairtrade.org.uk and www.gumutindocoffee.coop

Questions (30 marks; 35 minutes)

1 Explain the opportunity cost of the farmers who put 'countless hours of work' into forming a new co-operative. (4)

2 Assess one risk for the farmers and one risk for the Fairtrade organisation in forming a new co-operative with high guaranteed prices for coffee beans. (8)

3 Some commentators have suggested that Waitrose should make all its coffee 'Fairtrade', therefore getting rid of brands such as Nescafé Gold Blend. Assess two trade-offs Waitrose management would have to consider before making any such decision. (8)

4 Assess whether producing coffee ready for sale would definitely increase the income levels of the 7,000 members of the co-operative. (10)

Extended writing

1 Examine the different opportunity costs involved in the decisions made by a business leader such as Dave Lewis, chief executive of Tesco plc. Evaluate which might be the most important for the business. (20)

2 In the 1990s, the chairman of Samsung started to send the company's best and brightest young staff to live abroad for a year, to learn about American and European lifestyles. Some directors complained that this was a waste of their time and talent. Evaluate whether the chairman was right to trade off management time against consumer knowledge. (20)

28 Moving from entrepreneur to leader

Linked to: Forms of business Ch 26; Sources of finance, Ch 30; Planning and cash flow, Ch 32; Business failure, Ch 39.

28.1 Small business growth

Although start-up is the hardest time for an entrepreneur, many small firms find themselves struggling during periods of rapid growth. It is hard to keep on top of the financial and the organisational pressures of expansion. For example, in the first stage in the rapid growth of Instagram (the social photo site that launched in 2010 and was bought for $1 billion 18 months later), the founders frequently found themselves working through the night when the site crashed through overuse. On the first day, there were 25,000 users and within three months it hit one million. This stunning growth took the business from small to major in no time at all. Luckily for the founders, the enthusiasm at the time for all things digital ensured that it was easy to raise extra external finance when needed.

'Growth stresses systems.'

Larry McFadin, businessman

28.2 Business effects of forecast rapid growth

In certain circumstances, managers can anticipate a period of rapid growth. This may be temporary (such as the effect of a change in the law) or may seem likely to be permanent (such as the rise of a new social network).

The most successful firms will be those that devise a plan that is detailed enough to help in a practical way, but flexible enough to allow for the differences between forecasts and reality.

When rapid growth has been forecast, firms can:

- compare the sales estimate with the available production capacity
- budget for any necessary increases in capacity and staffing
- produce a cash flow forecast to anticipate any short-term financing shortfall
- discuss how to raise any extra capital needed.

Timescales remain important, though. The forecast may cover the next three months; but increasing capacity may involve building a factory extension, which will take eight months, in which case there may be five months of excess demand to cope with (perhaps by subcontracting). In 2014, Center Parcs opened a new site near London. It opened exactly ten years after management made the decision to open it, and at a cost of £250 million!

However accurate the forecast, there remains a lot of scope for error. The starting point is the increased workload on staff. Extra sales may put pressure on the accounting system, the warehouse manager and the delivery drivers. With everyone being kept busy, things can start to go wrong. Invoices are sent out a little later, unpaid bills are not chased as quickly and stock deliveries are not checked as carefully. Suddenly the cash flow position worsens and costs start to rise. A strong, effective manager could retrieve this but, to paraphrase the Peter Principle (see below), many have been promoted to 'their level of incompetence'. Once they start to go wrong, plans are hard to sort out.

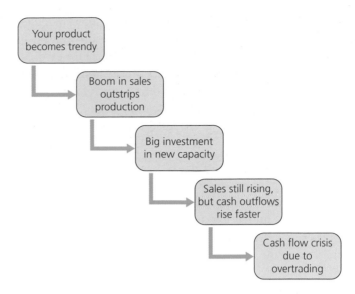

Figure 28.1 Logic chain: how overtrading happens

28.3 The risks of overtrading

Overtrading refers to the situation where a business expands at a rate that cannot be sustained by its capital base. A sudden surge in orders may tempt firms to buy additional stock on credit. However, if customers are slow to pay, the business may run into **liquidity** problems. Inadequate funding is one of the most common reasons why apparently successful businesses end up failing.

Adequate finance means having access to sufficient levels of funding to meet the firm's needs, as and when they occur. Established firms will need to pay workers, suppliers and other expenses on time, regardless of whether enough cash has been generated from sales to cover such expenses. They will also need to replace equipment and machinery when it wears out or becomes obsolete. Few businesses are faced with totally predictable demand. Therefore, adequate resources (including finance) need to be available to respond to an unexpected upsurge in orders, as well as coping with an unwanted fall in sales.

Ensuring access to adequate funding is especially important for firms looking to expand. Such firms will require capital not only for the purchase of new assets, but also to cover additional day-to-day capital requirements in the form of increased materials, wages and fuel. Overtrading is the business equivalent of the cliché: 'Don't run before you can walk'.

28.4 Problem of adjustment from entrepreneur to leader/manager

The typical creator of a successful new business is lively, energetic, creative, often impatient and always a risk-taker. Such a person will have a strong personality, and quite possibly an autocratic and charismatic leadership style. When the business started, their own speed of decision making, attention to detail and hard work were fundamental to the firm's success.

With success comes a problem. How to cope with the additional workload? At first, the entrepreneur works ever harder; then she or he takes on more junior staff. Then comes the crunch. Is she or he willing to appoint a senior manager with real decision-making power? Or will a weak manager be appointed who always has to check decisions with the boss?

> **'Owner-run companies are often run in an arbitrary, dictatorial way. Often, that is what limits their growth.'**
>
> Andy Grove, chief executive, Intel

Staff will always find it hard to accept a new manager because everyone will know that it is really the boss's business. It is said that, ten years after Walt Disney died, managers were still rejecting ideas on the basis that 'Walt wouldn't have done it that way.' How much harder if the founder is still there: James Dyson at Dyson and Larry Page and Sergey Brin at Google.

The boss must make the break, however. No longer should she or he attend every key meeting or demand regular reports on day-to-day matters. **Delegation** is necessary. In other words, authority should be passed down the hierarchy to middle managers without interference from above. And instead of looking for the next great opportunity, the boss may have to focus on getting the right management structure to ensure a smooth-running business.

Even if the founder of the company *is* able to adjust to managing a large organisation, there remains the problem of motivation. Will the new staff be as 'hungry' as the small team that built the business? Usually the answer is no.

'He who stands on tiptoe does not stand firm.'

Lao-Tzu, ancient Chinese philosopher

Change in management structure or hierarchy

As a business grows, the management structure has not only to grow too, but also to change. New layers of management may be needed and completely new departments may be founded, such as personnel or public relations. And all the time, as the business grows, new staff are being recruited, inducted and trained. So there is constant change in personnel and their responsibilities. This can be disconcerting for customers and suppliers. Strong relationships are hard to build, making customer loyalty tough to achieve.

Even more important, though, is the internal effect of these personnel changes. With new staff appearing frequently, and managerial changes occurring regularly, team spirit may be hard to achieve. Junior and middle managers may spend too much of their time looking upwards to the promotion prospects instead of concentrating on their own departments.

The potential for inefficiency, or even chaos, is clear. Too many new staff may mean too many mistakes. If customer relations are relatively weak, the result could easily be loss of business.

These unpleasant possibilities can largely be set aside if a good example is set from the top. If the founder of the business continues to be involved – especially on customer service – all may still be well. The leader needs to make sure staff keep sight of the qualities that brought the business its success in the first place. If new management structures threaten to create communication barriers, the leader should set an example by visiting staff, chatting to them and acting on their advice. The leader must fight against being cut off from the grassroots: the staff and the customers.

Risk of loss of direction and control

Each year, Templeton College Oxford produces data on what it calls the Fast Track 100. These are the fastest-growing 100 small companies in Britain. The December 2014 survey showed that the top ten of these firms enjoyed three-year growth rates of:

- sales turnover +200 per cent per year
- employees +120 per cent per year.

The typical Fast Track 100 firm had gone from 15 to 80 staff in the past three years. No wonder, then, that the key challenges faced by these companies were managing the growth in staff and infrastructure (source: www.fasttrack.co.uk).

The entrepreneurs who get swamped by the success of the business are those whose firms will fail to sustain their growth. They may become side-tracked by the attractions of expense account living; or – the other extreme – become so excited by their own success that they start opening up several different businesses. They assume that their golden touch will ensure success in whatever they do. Instead, just as their core business becomes harder to handle, they are looking at a different venture altogether. Problems may then hit from several directions at once.

The key message is, therefore: focus on what you are good at.

Five whys and a how

Questions	Answers
Why does growth put a strain on a firm's cash position?	To grow, you first expand production, and that uses up a lot of cash.
Why might rapid growth cause problems with management control?	Rapid growth implies many more staff, and therefore more management layers, causing confusion over roles and responsibilities.
Why may rapid growth turn into 'overtrading'?	Because the capital base of the business is too narrow to support the extra capital needed (e.g. borrowing too much).
Why may some great entrepreneurs make poor leaders?	They have the confidence and initiative for successful start-up, but can't 'let go', so they fail to delegate at the time they need to.
Why did Stelios, founder of easyJet, decide to resign as chairman quite shortly after the airline started up?	He told the press he was an entrepreneur, not someone who gets involved in the day-to-day running of a big business.
How might a growing company check that it is not overtrading?	Regularly check the company's cash balances, liquidity and debt levels.

28.5 Moving from entrepreneur to leader – evaluation

One of Britain's best-known businesspeople, Alan (Lord) Sugar now runs little more than a property business. Once he was the head of Amstrad, a company he founded. But Amstrad grew so rapidly that it became increasingly hard for Sugar to make all the decisions. Being Alan Sugar, he was incapable of delegating so the business hit the buffers with a series of poor new product launches and quality problems. Sugar later admitted that he was one of nature's entrepreneurs, not bosses.

> 'No person will make a great business who wants to do it all himself or get all the credit.'

Andrew Carnegie, businessman (1835–1919)

Often, then, the founder of a business will hand over to others – or be forced to by outside shareholders.

Famously, some bosses who were forced out came back later – older, wiser and more capable of delegating. Steve Jobs at Apple and Howard Schulz at Starbucks are good examples. Most business founders find that 'letting go of their baby' is a huge challenge. That's why it is so impressive that people like Facebook's Mark Zuckerberg have made the transition so effectively.

Key terms

Delegation: passing authority down the hierarchy, to allow more junior employees some decision-making power.

Liquidity: the ability of a business to pay its bills on time, which all depends upon having enough cash in the bank.

Overtrading: when a business expands at a rate that cannot be sustained by its capital base.

28.6 Workbook

Revision questions

(30 marks; 30 minutes)

1 Explain one factor that could cause rapid growth at a new food manufacturing business. (4)

2 Explain why rapid growth can cause problems for a company's:
   a) cash flow
   b) management control. (6)

3 Explain why there may be a problem in adjusting from 'entrepreneur' to 'leader/manager'. (4)

4 Identify three problems for a fast-growing firm caused by changes in the management structure. (3)

5 Explain how a growing company might make sure that it doesn't suffer from overtrading. (4)

6 Give two reasons why it may be hard to grow from 15 staff to 80 in one year. (2)

ASFC
LEARNING RESOURCE CENTRE

7 Explain why it may be hard for young, inexperienced managers of a successful business start-up to cope effectively with an unexpected, dramatic change. (4)

8 Explain the meaning of the quote from Andrew Carnegie on page 182. (3)

Data response

Lush profits

In 2012, the cosmetics producer and retailer Lush was able to declare dividends of £5.8 million from its annual profits of £26.2 million. This was a wonderful reward for founders Mark and Mo Constantine, who still own 60 per cent of the shares. Founded in 1994, the business has 830 stores in 51 countries. Growth has been dramatic and the business now supports over 4,000 jobs.

When it was founded, in 1990, Body Shop was the store to beat. Now, Lush's indulgent, attractive cosmetics are starting to overshadow Body Shop. Lush also benefits from the enthusiasm of its staff for the company's backing for ethical causes such as banning foxhunting, or demanding legal representation for the Guantanamo Bay detainees. Body Shop, bought by multinational L'Oréal in 2006, no longer stands out as the ethical retailer.

Growing sales from £0 to £360 million (2014) in 20 years inevitably involves problems. When Lush had grown to £50 million of sales, the manufacturing staff noticed that products made from essential oils (that can cost £3,000 per kg) were 'behaving' wrongly. After some weeks of panic, Lush decided to get a chemist to analyse the oils. It emerged that suppliers had been adulterating the oils with as much as 70 per cent synthetic chemicals. This problem led to the establishment of a professional buying team, together with a quality control manager.

Questions (40 marks; 35 minutes)

1 a) Assess why Lush is likely to have had a significant increase in the number of layers of hierarchy within its business over recent years. (12)

   b) Assess two ways in which an increase in the layers of hierarchy might harm operational performance at Lush. (8)

2 If Lush appointed a new chief executive, evaluate the advantages and disadvantages of the business now being run by a successor to the Constantines – the founders. (20)

Extended writing

1 Choose one of these three business contexts: extreme sportswear, travel agency or a private school. Evaluate the likely reasons why a small company specialising in that market might be able to expand successfully. (20)

2 ASOS plc has grown at a rate of 30–50 per cent per year for nearly a decade. Outline the problems this may cause. Evaluate the most effective way for management to tackle them. (20)

Theme 2

Managing business activities

29 Introduction to finance

> **Definition**
>
> Finance has two main aspects: it can provide the numbers that help managers to make better decisions, and it can count what is happening and what has happened. Here the focus is on finance for decision making.

Linked to: Role of an entrepreneur, Ch 23; Moving from entrepreneur to leader, Ch 28; Sources of finance, Ch 30; Planning and cash flow, Ch 32; Sales forecasting, Ch 33; Sales, revenue and costs, Ch 34; Budgets, Ch 36.

29.1 Finance and start-up

Of the 60 per cent of new restaurants that close within three years, almost all die because the business has run out of cash. As the crisis point starts to draw near, the staff will notice irate suppliers 'dropping by' to demand payment. Key supplies may not arrive, as the suppliers get increasingly tough about payment. So it is crucial to keep cash spending under tight control.

The main underlying problem is that people get starry-eyed about the process of business start-up. They start to believe their own publicity, and assume that their restaurant is going to be 'hot' from day one, or their nightclub is going to be 'cool'. The consequence of this is that too much of the start-up capital is tied up in fixed assets, such as interior design and equipment. Far too little is left for the day-to-day running of the business: the **working capital**.

> 'Entrepreneurship is "risky" mainly because so few of the so-called entrepreneurs know what they are doing.'
>
> Peter Drucker, global management guru

The problem is an obvious one. To be an entrepreneur, you have to be an optimist; but optimists do not look for the downside. They expect business to be fantastic from week one, ignoring the evidence that most businesses find it hard to establish a loyal base of customers at the start. For most new businesses, it is wise to set aside half the start-up capital as working capital. That will be the money used in the early weeks of operation, to pay the wages, pay the rent and pay upfront when suspicious suppliers demand to be paid with cash, not credit. Once the weekly takings are high enough, the money coming in will pay for all the costs that have to be paid out, but that may take time.

Look at Table 29.1; among small business start-ups in south London, this shows how long it took until weekly cash in started to exceed weekly cash outflows.

Type of business	Location	Weeks until cash drain ceased
Barber	Near tube station	26 (i.e. six months)
Pizza restaurant	Residential area	10
Sports trophy shop	Local shopping street	156 (i.e. three years) (that was 20 years ago, so it was worth it)
Sweet shop	High street	6

Table 29.1 Small business start-ups in south London: weeks until cash drain ceased

29.2 Working capital

The key is to keep on top of the working capital. The top priority is to keep an everyday check on costs, credit transactions and cash payments. This can be hard if you have several people working for you. Each could expect to be given the authority to make a decision, such as to buy a pizza oven from supplier X rather than supplier Y. But if lots of people are spending your money, it will be virtually impossible to keep track of everything.

New entrepreneurs often choose one person to be the 'moneybags', the person with sole control over spending. Clever entrepreneurs make sure to give the job to someone else. Then even the business owner has to work at justifying why exactly he wants brand new kitchen equipment instead of second-hand.

In addition to keeping a check on a firm's day-to-day finance – its working capital – managers need to:

- identify the costs involved in making a product; this can be the first step in deciding the selling price
- work out how many products they need to sell to make a profit
- find out how much capital they will need in the coming months, and then decide on the best way to obtain this extra finance
- keep tight control over the way in which the firm's money is spent.

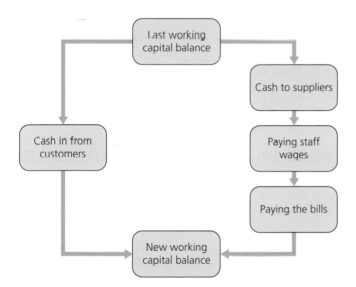

Figure 29.1 Logic chain: working capital in practice

29.3 Key financial concerns for new business start-ups

The starting point is to work out the following three things.

1 How much it will cost to get from a business idea to opening the doors on the first day (the start-up costs). For a new clothes shop, this will include a huge range of items and could reach a figure such as £40,000.

2 How much the running costs will be (the costs week by week when the business is operating fully). These will come in two parts: the costs that will be fixed, no matter whether the business is going well or badly, such as the rent, heating and lighting and staff salaries; in addition, there will be costs that vary in line with sales, such as the cost of purchasing the items you are selling (the dress sold for £80 may cost you £40 to buy from the dress designer). Every entrepreneur needs a solid understanding of the firm's **fixed costs** and **variable costs**. (Broader coverage of this topic is provided in Chapter 34.)

3 How much revenue can you expect from the customers you serve? Broadly, this is a simple calculation of customers served multiplied by the amount they spend. Although the calculation is simple, it is very hard to anticipate what the figures will be. In August 2010, there were rumours that Microsoft was starting to research the Xbox One, to be launched in 2014/2015. So many years in advance, who could know the likely selling price or how many would be sold? Market research could help in making a sales forecast, but as only one in seven new products proves a success, six out of every seven new products must come with an incorrect sales forecast (no one would launch a new product that was forecast to flop, so presumably there was a faulty forecast). For new small businesses, the problem is always the same: how can we forecast the number of loyal customers we can expect? (This issue is tackled in Chapter 33.)

> 'Accountants focus on the past rather than the future, because that alone can be accurately measured... Their training regards risk, uncertainty and the unknown as undesirable.'
>
> Charles Handy, Britain's only management guru

29.4 Raising finance

When a business is operating fully and successfully, cash coming in from customers will provide all the finance necessary for effective operation. Until then, raising finance is an important issue, especially for young entrepreneurs with little personal capital. Table 29.2 lists the sources of finance available to firms.

Short term (under one year)		
Bank overdraft	• Allowing the firm's bank account to go into the red up to an agreed limit. • Flexible and easy to arrange but interest charges are high.	
Trade credit	• Suppliers agree to accept cash payment at a given date in the future. • Failure to pay on time can present problems for future orders.	
Medium term (2–4 years)		
Bank term loan	• Banks lend sums of capital, often at a fixed rate of interest, to be repaid over a fixed period. • Makes financial planning easy but interest rates can be high, particularly for small firms.	
Leasing	• Firms sign a contract to pay a rental fee to the owner of an asset in return for the use of that asset over a period of two to four years (usually). • Expensive, but avoids large cash outflows when buying new assets.	
Long term (5+ years)		
Owners' savings	• Most small businesses are set up with the owners' savings. • They are 'interest free' but will be lost if the business fails. • Banks will not provide a loan or overdraft unless the owners are sharing the financial risk.	
Sale of shares	• Private and public limited companies can sell shares in the ownership of the company. • In return, shareholders gain a say in how the firm is run and are entitled to a share of profits.	
Reinvested profits	• Profits are the most important source of long-term finance. • This form of finance is good because there are no interest payments to be made.	
Venture capital loans	• These specialist providers of risk capital can provide large sums. • The finance is usually partly loan capital and partly share capital.	

Table 29.2 Sources of business finance

Real business

Financing Facebook

Facebook was started in February 2004 by college student Mark Zuckerberg. That summer he was introduced to a wealthy co-founder of PayPal, who invested $500,000 in establishing Facebook as a limited company. Within a month, Zuckerberg was offered $10 million for the business, but turned it down. Two years later, in 2006, Yahoo offered $1,000 million, but was also rejected!

In Facebook's early years, there was no doubting the growth in users, but lots of doubt about how to turn users into cash. Fortunately for Zuckerberg, people kept investing. A big break came in 2007 when Microsoft handed over $240 million for just 1.6 per cent of the share capital. This valued Facebook at a then-amazing $15 billion ($15,000 million).

In 2012, Facebook decided to float as a public company on the US stock market. Its valuation of $65 billion set the value of Zuckerberg's shares at $12 billion. The shares performed poorly at first, but by late November 2014 Facebook's market capitalisation (the value of all its shares) was £204 billion.

29.5 Financial management for an established business

Companies that stay small tend to keep focused on cash. Bigger businesses find a developing disconnect between the revenue and the cost aspects of the business. Marketing people boast about rising sales while factory managers fret about 'costs being out of control'. Often, the solution is to bring in a budgetary control system. This used to be a bit of a nightmare, but modern software makes it relatively easy to set and monitor spending. A system of budgeting can make sure that the marketing department's efforts at boosting sales are kept related to the costs being incurred to manufacture and distribute the products – therefore making sure that profits are made. Chapter 36 covers budgets and budgeting in detail.

The other big consideration for an established business is how to respond if sales start to boom, perhaps because a strong trend is moving in the firm's direction. Booms sound great, but are actually extremely difficult to handle. Rapid expansion requires a lot of cash to finance extra staff, more or bigger premises and perhaps a bigger advertising campaign. Budgeting is helpful, but cash flow forecasting is even more important. (See Chapter 32.)

Five whys and a how

Questions	Answers
Why is optimism a problem when managing finance?	It is better if estimates are pessimistic, so that there are good surprises, not bad ones.
Why are new restaurants particularly prone to financial disaster?	It is very hard to forecast demand for a new restaurant, and many first-timers struggle to work out the likely profit margins; so uncertainty levels are exceptionally high.
Why may an overdraft be a helpful form of finance for a brand new business?	At the start, no-one's sure how much cash will be needed, and for how long; that makes an overdraft perfect, as it is a very flexible form of borrowing.
Why may some firms reach cash break-even in 6 weeks and others in 156 weeks (see Table 29.1)?	A sweet shop costs relatively little to set up, and will find plenty of customers from day one; a sports trophy shop takes a long time to build a loyal customer base – costs start high while revenues stay low for years.
Why may a sales boom lead to bust?	A sales boom requires heavy investment in extra output and capacity; this can overstretch the finances of the business.
How does a venture capital company make its money?	By investing in many businesses with great potential; some may flop but as long as the successes have a big upside, they can be sold off for profits big enough to cover the flops.

29.6 Introduction to finance – evaluation

Reliability is a key issue when looking at any financial statement. Management accounts, such as cash flow forecasts, are predictions. In other words, they are not statements of fact but educated guesses. This means that they should be used only as a guideline. Questions need to be asked, such as who drew up the figures and do they have an interest in making the accounts point in a particular direction? For example, have forecasts been produced to try to persuade outsiders to invest, or are they produced by managers for their own use? In the first case, it may be that the desire to squeeze finance out of a bank or venture capital firm encourages an excessively optimistic set of forecasts.

A second key point to remember is how finance fits into the big picture of business. Feel the weight of this book. There are several units dedicated to finance, but many more covering other areas of business activity. Accounts are good at dealing with quantitative information, but qualitative factors may be more important, such as whether the business is building strong customer loyalty. Today's high sales may collapse tomorrow if they are based only on special offers, not on repeat purchase.

'Business is not financial science, it's about trading… buying and selling. It's about creating a product or service so good that people will pay for it.'

Anita Roddick, founder of Body Shop

29.7 Workbook

Revision questions

(30 marks; 30 minutes)

1 Outline two possible reasons why a new restaurant could run out of cash. (4)

2 Explain what is meant by working capital. (3)

3 Give two examples of situations in which a small bakery business could use each of the following sources of finance:

   a) short-term   b) medium-term   c) long-term. (6)

4 Reread 'Real business: Scoop' on page 189.

   a) Outline two possible sources of finance for Scoop's £100,000 expansion. (4)

   b) Pick the one you think would be most suitable. Explain why. (4)

5 Explain one advantage and one disadvantage to a firm of having large sums of cash for a long period of time. (6)

6 Explain how a seaside hotel business might benefit from budgeting. (3)

Data response

Starting up Moneysupermarket.com

Moneysupermarket.com was started in 1999 by 32-year-old Simon Nixon. The site was designed to provide people with easy-to-compare information on, for example, the interest charges on different credit cards. The start-up costs were 'around £100,000', all of which came from the sale of an earlier online business. Nixon's earlier experience made sure that he pursued a 'no frills' policy to his start-up, focusing most of the start-up capital on public relations (PR). He employed a City of London PR firm to contact financial journalists regularly. The journalists came to use the site as an easy source of data, referencing all their articles to 'Source: Moneysupermarket.com'. Spreading the name in this way encouraged increasing usage by ordinary customers, providing a hit rate of 50,000 customers a month by the end of its first year.

Nixon built the business up steadily and by 2006 he could afford his first TV advertising campaign. In the first half of 2007, visitors to the group's websites rose by 58 per cent, helping sales revenue to rise from £48 million to £78 million. So although the advertising spending rose from £2.7 million to £9.8 million between 2006 and 2007, overall operating profits went up by £14 million.

Although Nixon managed to build the business largely through internal finance (reinvested profit), by 2007 he decided to sell up by floating the shares on the London stock market. On 31 July 2007, shares in Moneysupermarket.com were floated at 170p. This netted Nixon over £100 million in cash, but also gave the company over £50 million for expansion. Not long after, the shares plunged to 38p during the 2009 recession, but by December 2014 had recovered to over 200p. In a world of competition with Comparethemarket.com and many others, Moneysupermarket.com has done remarkably well.

Questions (25 marks; 30 minutes)

1 Explain why Simon Nixon was able to limit the start-up costs of Moneysupermarket.com to £100,000. (4)

2 a) Calculate the percentage increase in sales revenue between the first half of 2006 and the first half of 2007. (3)

   b) Assess two factors that may have led to this sales increase. (8)

3 Simon Nixon is a fabulously wealthy man today, apparently 'worth' £400 million. Assess whether the entrepreneurial skills he showed are a justification for becoming that rich. (10)

Extended writing

1 Billionaire inventor James Dyson says that business is not about finance, it is about designing and producing great products. Evaluate whether Dyson is right in relation to all businesses. (20)

2 'Companies succeed because of great marketing management; they fail because of bad financial management.' Evaluate whether this old business saying is still true today. (20)

30 Sources of finance: internal and external

> **Definition**
>
> All businesses need money. Where the money comes from is known as 'sources of finance'.

Linked to: Forms of business, Ch 26; Liability and finance, Ch 31; Planning and cash flow, Ch 32; Liquidity, Ch 38.

30.1 The need for finance

Starting up

New businesses starting up need money to invest in long-term assets such as buildings and equipment. They also need cash to purchase materials, pay wages and pay the day-to-day bills, such as water and electricity. Inexperienced entrepreneurs often underestimate the capital needed for the day-to-day running of the business. Generally, for every £1,000 required to establish the business, another £1,000 is needed for the day-to-day needs.

Growing

Once the business is established, there will be income from sales. If this is greater than the operating costs, the business will be making a profit. This should be kept in the business and used to help finance growth. Later on, the owners can draw money out, but at this stage as much as possible should be left in. Even so, there may not be enough to allow the business to grow as fast as it would like to. It may need to find additional finance and this will probably be from external sources such as bank loans.

Other situations

Businesses may also need finance in other circumstances, such as a cash flow problem. A major customer may refuse to pay for the goods, causing a huge gap in cash inflows. Or there may be a large order, requiring the purchase of additional raw materials. In all these cases, businesses will need to find additional funding.

Finance for business comes from two main sources:

1 inside the business: known as internal finance

2 outside the business: known as external finance.

30.2 Internal finance

Capital can be generated from within the business in three ways:

1 Retained profit. Nothing soothes a difficult cash situation better than profit. It is also the best (and most common) way to finance investment into a firm's future. Research shows that over 60 per cent of business investment comes from reinvested profit. Logically, then, the higher a firm's profit the more likely it is that it can finance its expansion from within.

2 Sale of assets. In autumn 2014, Tesco was in need of more capital. It could have raised some from external shareholders, or it could sell assets. Some were non-core businesses such as Dobbies Garden Centre and Giraffe restaurants. Others were property assets now considered surplus to requirements as there was suddenly no appetite for opening new hypermarkets. By selling these assets, Tesco would easily be able to raise the £2 billion widely seen as necessary to give new boss Dave Lewis an effective financial fighting fund.

3 Improved management of working capital. Existing capital can be made to stretch further. The business may be able to negotiate to pay its bills later or work at getting cash in earlier from customers; the average small firm waits 75 days to be paid; if that period of time could be halved, it would provide a huge boost to cash flow. Working capital is dealt with in greater detail in Chapter 38.

One other form of finance can be regarded as internal: the personal savings of the owner; these can be invested in the form of **share capital** or lent to the business, perhaps as a director's loan.

30.3 External sources of finance

If the business is unable to generate sufficient funds from internal sources then it may need to look to external sources. There are two sources of external capital: loan capital (debt) and share capital (equity). Loan capital carries specific annual interest charges and must be repaid to an agreed time schedule. Share capital is usually rewarded by annual dividend payments, but the directors have the flexibility to cut or scrap those payments in a difficult year. There is also no agreed timescale for repaying share capital, so it can be kept within the business indefinitely.

Sources of finance include the following.

Family and friends

Family and friends can provide share capital (taking an equity stake in the business and its profits) or can lend money. Despite the rise of crowdfunding, the overwhelming majority of businesses start with a combination of owner's capital and family and friends'. Banks, in particular, provide start-up capital to far fewer businesses than their TV advertisements claim.

Banks

Two recent research reports give very different figures for the percentage of businesses that were able to get a bank loan to help start the business. A company called Amigo Loans said that 20 per cent of its 200 sample achieved a start-up loan, while PeoplePerHour found a figure of just 3 per cent. Either way, it is clear that a start-up loan is a rarity.

If you can get a loan, the bank will insist on rock-solid **collateral**. If the loan is to buy a five-year lease on a shop, that lease will be the collateral. If the business is starting up without property assets, the collateral will be personal, such as the deeds to the owner's house or flat. Banks are not interested in sharing the risks involved when starting a business. They want to provide finance, not become a partner.

> 'The old saying holds. Owe your banker £1,000 and you are at his mercy; owe him £1 million and the position is reversed.'
>
> John Maynard Keynes, British economist and author

Peer-to-peer funding

The reluctance of banks to lend following the 2009 recession created an opportunity for online matching platforms to match individuals who want to lend (at a relatively high rate of interest) to individual business borrowers. These websites cut out the bank middleman and therefore allow lenders and borrowers to get a better deal – as long as the loan doesn't go sour.

Peer-to-peer funding seems to work well if there is an attractive-sounding business, such as a new restaurant; for duller businesses, investors seem less inclined to bother.

Business angels

The term 'angels' has long been used for individuals who invest in West End plays and musicals. Most lose their money, but the 500 who each put £10,000 into 'Cats' received £20,000 a year for more than 25 years. That's a £500,000 return on a £10,000 investment.

The BBC series *Dragons' Den* has always presented itself as a matter of **venture capital** investment. In fact, it would be truer to call most of the proposals 'angel' rather than dragon investments because they are at a very early stage. **Angel investors** take huge risks in the hope of the occasional blockbuster success. In reality, in the UK, the only businesspeople likely to find an angel investor are those whose families move in wealthy circles. For ordinary people, an angel investment is even more unlikely than a bank loan.

Real business

3D finance

The 18-year-old entrepreneur Josh Valman started MiProto in 2012 while still doing his A levels. He began with £2,500 of start-up funding from the **seedcorn capital** business run by former Dragon James Caan. Then, in June 2013 four 'angel' investors put in £40,000, topped up by a further £160,000 of venture capital finance in summer 2013. In all cases, the investors loved the business concept: a one-stop shop for turning ideas into physical prototypes using 3D printing technology. MiProto can turn an idea into a design and then a design into a printed product that can then be tested on retail buyers or on a sample of consumers. It is a marvellous example of new technology being brought alive by a bright young businessperson.

Sources: MiProto website and James Caan's article in *The Guardian*, 18 December 2013

Crowdfunding

Crowdfunding is a way of getting small investors to put money into a new business – often with an incentive such as to get a sample product or service in return for their investment. It works via the internet and works most effectively when the sponsors use social media to promote their business. In the UK, Seedrs and Kickstarter are two of the best-known sponsors of crowdfunding.

Other businesses

Some companies allocate a chunk of their capital to 'seedcorn', early-stage investments. The companies hope to get the occasional winner from among a number of duds. In Silicon Valley, USA, this type of investment is commonplace, but not in the UK.

30.4 External methods of finance

Loans

The most usual way is through borrowing from a bank. This may be in the form of a bank loan or an overdraft. A loan is usually for a set period of time. It may be short term – one or two years; medium term – three to five years; or long term – more than five years. The loan can be repaid either in instalments over time or at the end of the loan period. The bank will charge interest on the loan. This can be fixed or variable. The bank will demand collateral to provide security in case the loan cannot be repaid.

An overdraft is a very short-term loan. It is a facility that allows the business to be 'overdrawn'. This means that the account is allowed to go 'into the red'. The length of time that this runs for will have to be negotiated. The interest charges on overdrafts are usually much higher than on loans. Fortunately, the interest charges only apply to actual debts instead of the facility itself. For firms that use the overdraft as a way of smoothing short-term cash variations, the interest payments can be quite small.

Share capital

As an alternative to debt, if the business is a limited company, it may look for additional share capital. This could come from private investors or venture capital funds. Venture capital providers are interested in investing in businesses with dynamic growth prospects. They are willing to take a risk on a business that may fail, or may do spectacularly well. They believe that if they make ten investments, five can flop and four do 'OK' as long as one does fantastically. Peter Theil, the original investor in Facebook, turned his $0.5 million investment into just over $1,000 million, making a profit of 199,900 per cent between 2004 and 2012!

Once it has become a **public limited company (plc)**, the firm may consider floating on the stock exchange. For smaller UK businesses, this will usually be on the Alternative Investment Market (AIM).

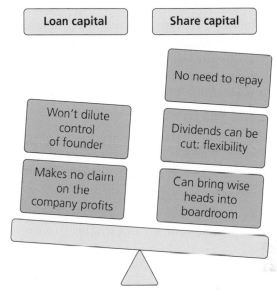

Figure 30.1 The value of share capital

Venture capital

This is a way of getting outside investment for businesses that are unable to raise finance through the **stock market** or from banks. Venture capitalists invest in smaller, riskier companies. To compensate for the risks, venture capital providers usually require a substantial part of the ownership of the company. They are also likely to want to contribute to the running of the business. This dilutes the owner's control but brings in new experience and knowledge. Typically, venture capital houses put money into businesses that have survived the early stages and are looking to grow. In 2013, the venture capital association announced that its members' average investment amounted to £800,000. This emphasises that venture capital investment is rarely about start-up.

> 'One thing I'm so grateful for is sidestepping the usual venture capital, private equity route. My friends who have gone that way are many times beholden to their boards of directors, to "sell" ideas to a team.'
>
> Blake Mycoskie, founder of Toms Shoes

Overdrafts

An overdraft is a facility that allows a company to spend up to an agreed negative balance on its current account – for example, minus £3,000. When the bank balance is negative, the company is overdrawn and must pay interest calculated on a daily basis – for example, 1/365th of 12 per cent (if 12 per cent is the bank's overdraft interest rate). Because the business can dip in and out of 'the red', its interest bill at the end of the year will usually be quite a lot lower than with a bank loan. As shown in Table 30.1, overdrafts are the main form of external finance for small firms.

Although overdrafts are flexible and well matched to the ups and downs of small company cash flows, their risk-level should not be underestimated. All overdrafts are on 24-hour recall. In other words, the bank can cancel them at any time, often leaving the business unable to repay the negative balance – and forcing the business into administration. This was one of the features of the early stages of the recent recession. As mentioned in the *Daily Mail* on 29 October 2009: 'Thousands of small businesses were suddenly refused credit by banks.' A sudden drama such as this cannot happen with a bank loan, which is a legal agreement for a fixed period of time (e.g. three years).

Overdraft	19%
Credit cards	17%
Bank loan/commercial mortgage	8%
Leasing	6%
Loans/equity from family and friends	5%
Loans/equity from directors	4%
Grants	1%
Any form of external finance	41%

Table 30.1 Principal sources of external finance for small and medium-sized enterprises (SMEs) (source: BDRC Continental, SME Finance Monitor, August 2013)

Leasing

For small or fast-growing businesses, keeping cash flow positive is a huge challenge. A constant problem is having to spend chunks of cash buying new assets, such as delivery vans, computer networks or machinery. A solution is to lease instead of buying the assets. Leasing the asset means agreeing to pay a fixed monthly rental for a fixed period, such as three years. Instead of buying an asset for £5,000, you may pay £200 a month. £200 a month means paying £200 × 36 months = £7,200 over the three years. Pricey, perhaps, but at least you are keeping cash in your own bank account at the start of the period.

In Figure 30.2, you can see that buying an asset hits short-term cash flow hard. In the longer term, it is better to buy than lease, but for many firms short-term needs outweigh long-term wishes. In the graph, the assumption has been made that the £5,000 asset yields a contribution of £250 a month over the three-year period.

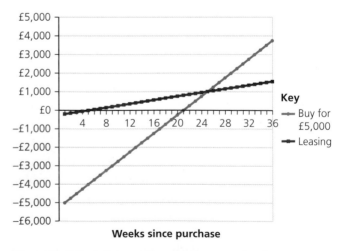

Figure 30.2 Cash flow position: buying versus leasing an asset

Trade credit

This is the simplest form of external financing. The business obtains goods or services from another business but does not pay for these immediately. The average credit period is two months. It is a good way of boosting day-to-day finance. A disadvantage could be that other businesses may be reluctant to trade with the business if they do not get paid in good time.

Grants

Grants are, in effect, hand-outs to small firms, perhaps from a local authority or central government. A grant may be given to encourage a start-up or a relocation that is considered valuable – probably because banks have refused to lend. However, a recent report (SME Finance Monitor, August 2013) showed that just 1 per cent of small and medium-sized enterprises (SMEs) obtained finance from grants. Governments love to boast about how much help they give small firms, but it rarely amounts to much. Within that 1 per cent would also be any grants received from the Prince's Trust, which, again, makes relatively small sums of money go a long way in terms of publicity. Table 30.1 provides more data on external finance. Note that only 41 per cent of firms use any external finance. Small firms would prefer to finance their start-up and growth from within.

30.5 Sources of finance – evaluation

Raising finance is a perfect example of the different skills required by businesspeople. When starting out, the personality of the entrepreneur is likely to be of critical importance, as angel investors must decide in part on whether they want to work with this person. Later on, when the start-up has progressed to the point of needing more capital for expansion, the need is for an organised person with thorough records of cash flow and profit. At first, charisma counts; now it is competence that matters. Not many people have both qualities, so it is important to hire wisely, and to delegate to someone who has skills you lack.

Whatever the situation, debt should still be taken as a threat to any business. Advisors tell firms to borrow more when times are good, but good turns to bad amazingly quickly, which can leave over-stretched companies floundering. Debt always means risk; but of course some risks may be worth taking.

Five whys and a how

Questions	Answers
Why might a business finance expansion using debt rather than equity?	Issuing more equity dilutes the value of shares, putting the founders' control of the business at risk.
Why should companies be wary of over-using their overdraft facility?	Because of the risk that their bank might withdraw the facility with no more than 24 hours' notice – making it almost impossible to repay.
Why might a bank refuse to lend to a business?	It may doubt the firm's ability to repay, i.e. see it as too risky; or the bank may think it can make more profit elsewhere, e.g. property speculation.
Why might a business collapse from overtrading (growing too fast)?	If sales increases outstrip the firm's capital base, it can run out of cash and slide into administration.
Why do venture capital companies invest in some businesses but not others?	Venture capitalists seek huge potential gains. Therefore, they love 'scalability': a high potential for the business to grow massively.
How might crowdfunding prove harmful to a new small business?	Getting a bank loan for £250,000 is simple to administer; 50,000 crowdfunders investing £5 each could become an administrative nightmare.

30.6 Workbook

Revision questions

(30 marks; 30 minutes)

1 Describe the problem caused to a company if a major customer refuses to pay a big bill. (3)

2 Why do banks demand collateral before they agree to provide a bank loan? (2)

3 Outline two ways in which businesses can raise money from internal sources. (4)

4 What information may a bank manager want when considering a loan to a business? (4)

5 Read 'Real business: 3D finance' on page 192. Explain why it may have been difficult for a business such as this to get a bank loan. (4)

6 Outline two sources of finance that can be used for long-term business development. (4)

7 Explain why a new business could find it difficult to get external funding for its development. (5)

8 Outline one advantage and one disadvantage of using an overdraft. (4)

Data response 1

Indian in China?

'Hi everyone, I am from India and wish to open a quick takeaway and a small restaurant or café but with Indian snacks and food in Nanjing, near the International University. I would like to know about:

1 the rules and regulations

2 the approximate budget

3 the minimum area requirement

4 the real estate prices in an area like Shanghai Lu, Nanjing.

Please contact me by leaving a comment here.

Thank you, Karishma'

'Hi Karishma,

You have to know that the life expectancy of a new foreign restaurant on Nanjing Road is between three and six months, in 50 per cent of cases. Many foreigners open restaurants without complying with all the rules… Be ready to have enough funds to survive for one year minimum without any revenues. If you want I could give you contacts with very good companies that could help you for all legal aspects. Good luck, and I will come to your restaurant!

Paul Martin'

Source: posting to www.chinasuccessstories.com

Questions

(30 marks; 35 minutes)

1 Explain to Karishma two implications of Paul Martin's reply for her plans for start-up finance. (8)

2 Assess the circumstances in which Karishma should proceed with her idea, if she were able to obtain the start-up finance. (10)

3 Assuming this information is widely known, assess the probable attitude of any Chinese banks that Karishma approaches. (12)

Data response 2

Kickstarter

In recent years, 'crowdfunding' has become an alternative to traditional market research and also a different way to finance a start-up. The Kickstarter website helps a creative business idea to be put to the public, asking for start-up capital in exchange for a free 'taste' of the product.

One successful 2014 start-up was Chivote, a producer of leather bags and accessories. It raised £20,000 through Kickstarter by offering products in exchange for investment. A £7 investment received a leather nametag in return, while £240 yielded a 'Boombox' bag.

Figure 30.3 The Boombox bag

Crowdfunding uses online technology and social media to replace the traditional role of banks.

Chivote has another unusual aspect to its business. It sources its leather goods from a small partnership of craftsmen who work as partners instead of suppliers to Chivote. This is another way to help minimise the capital needed to start up the business. Usually a new business would have to pay cash up front for supplies; the partnership ensures that normal credit terms can smooth the cash flow requirements.

Questions

(30 marks; 35 minutes)

1 A weakness of crowdfunding might be that it is effective only with consumer-friendly, attractive products or services. Examine whether that is really a problem. (6)

2 Explain the benefit to your cash flow of having a supplier who offers credit terms instead of cash only. (4)

3 Evaluate the benefits of crowdfunding compared with traditional venture capital funding when starting a business such as Chivote. (20)

Extended writing

1 While at university, you develop a game for mobiles based on tractors, farms, rabbits and foxes – and everyone loves it. Your parents lend you £4,000 and you have £2,000 but you estimate that it will cost about £20,000 simply to get the game ready for use and to give it some publicity. Evaluate the best way to finance the start-up of your business. (20)

2 For the founder of a rapidly growing small business, evaluate whether it is better to keep at least 51 per cent of the share capital or to finance growth in the safest way for the long-term health of the company. (20)

31 Liability and finance

> **Definition**
>
> Every potential entrepreneur needs to know the financial risks being run when starting up. Debts are liabilities that can overwhelm a business owner's personal as well as business finances.

Linked to: Business objectives, Ch 25; Forms of business, Ch 26; Sources of finance, Ch 30.

31.1 Implications of unlimited liability

Unlimited liability means that the finances of the business are treated as inseparable from the finances of the business owner(s). So if the business loses £1 million, the people owed money (the **creditors**) can get the courts to force the individual owners to pay up. If that means selling their houses, cars, and so on, so be it. If the owner(s) cannot pay, they can be made personally **bankrupt**. Two types of business organisation have unlimited liability: **sole traders** and partnerships. They were covered in Chapter 26.

In Britain, the great majority of businesses have unlimited liability. Even though that means avoiding certain accounting costs, it still seems extraordinary that people are willing to take even a slight chance of bankruptcy.

> 'There are few experiences in life as painful and brutal as the failure of a small business. For a small business conceived and nurtured by its owner is like a living, breathing child. Its loss is no less traumatic than losing a loved one.'
>
> William Manchee, business author

> **Real business**
>
> In 2012, Creative Learning Software closed down. It had enjoyed ten years as a profitable business, designing and selling software to schools. Because its finances had always been cash flow positive, the proprietor never worried about limited liability. He had often said: 'I wouldn't give the accountants the satisfaction' (of auditing the published ltd accounts).
>
> Unfortunately, the proprietor had not thought about *all* the potential liabilities. In 2011, a school sued the business because it claimed that Creative Learning Software had damaged the entire school computer network. The school demanded £100,000 compensation. But the small supplier couldn't afford that and therefore the proprietor became personally liable for the huge debts.

31.2 Implications of limited liability

Limited liability means that the legal duty to pay debts run up by a business stays with the business itself, not its owner/shareholders. If a company has £1 million of debts that it lacks the cash to repay, the courts can force the business to sell all its assets (cars, computers, etc.). If there is still not enough money, the company is closed down, but the owner/shareholders have no personal liability for the remaining debts.

The key implication is that limited liability can give owners the confidence to push their business forward to the next level. Expansion can be financed by bank loans without threatening the well-being of the owners' families. Without the legal protections of limited liability, economies would struggle to grow.

Despite this strength, limited liability has a downside. It gives huge scope for fraud. Proprietors can start a business, take customers' money, enjoy a fantastic lifestyle, then put the company into liquidation before customers receive the service they paid for. If such actions could be proved to be deliberate, they would constitute fraud. But there is little doubt that many scams go unpunished because it is hard to distinguish between fraud (illegal) and business incompetence (legal). This factor explains why most petrol stations display a sign saying 'company cheques not accepted'.

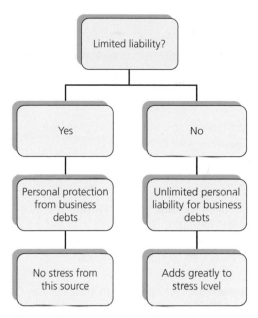

Figure 31.1 Logic chain: liability and stress

31.3 Finance appropriate for unlimited liability businesses

Unlimited liability businesses are, by definition, *not* companies. Therefore, they have no access to share capital (equity). So a sole trader or a partnership must be financed in one of the following ways:

- Owners' capital: in the case of a partnership, an agreement might be drawn up basing the proportionate ownership of the business on the amount of capital invested by each partner.
- Bank finance, either loan or overdraft: it is often easier for an unlimited liability business to obtain bank finance because even if the business fails, the bank can recoup its cash from the personal assets of the individual owners.
- Leasing: signing an agreement to rent a specific asset for a specific period (perhaps three years), therefore avoiding the cash drain caused by purchase.

- Trade credit: as with bank finance, supplier companies would often prefer to deal with a sole trader or partnership, as they know they can recoup any debts from the individual owners if the business fails.

It should never be forgotten, though, that the most important form of capital comes from within the business: from trading profit.

31.4 Finance appropriate for limited liability businesses

Companies have access to more types of finance than unlimited liability businesses. Both private and public limited companies have access to the following forms of finance:

- Share capital, part of which may be under the control of the founder and part sold on to family and friends (ltd) or more widely to the general public (plc).
- Bank finance: bank loans would typically need to be backed by specific collateral, especially for small companies (banks are wary of limited liability). Overdrafts will also need to be backed by security; for new small companies, it is highly likely that a bank would demand a personal guarantee by the founder shareholder.
- Angel or venture capital investment, both of which tend to be a combination of share and loan capital: so the founder suffers dilution of control over the business and the company will probably find that the loan capital is at a much higher interest rate than an ordinary bank loan.
- Peer-to-peer or crowdfunding: both these sources tend to keep control more effectively in the hands of the founder.
- Leasing and trade credit are both open to limited liability companies.

For limited companies, even giant plcs, the biggest source of capital for expansion comes from within the business: from trading profit.

Five whys and a how

Questions	Answers
Why would anybody start a business with unlimited personal liability?	Beats me too! But the majority of UK business have unlimited liability, as proprietors believe there are tax advantages and dislike the extra fiddle and admin costs of running a company.
Why might it be easier for a partnership to raise finance for expansion than a sole trader?	Simply because the partnership has more than one owner, i.e. there are more pockets to dip in to.
Why might suppliers refuse to give credit to a new small company?	A company, by definition, has limited liability. So suppliers are wary of giving credit when, if the company fails, there is no way to recoup the cash from the business owners.
Why don't companies buy assets outright? Surely it is cheaper in the long run than leasing?	It is, it is. But many firms are so strapped for cash that they take a long-term hit from leasing to gain improved short-term cash flow.
Why do companies pay dividends when the profit they make is so important for financing growth and avoiding debt?	Shareholders expect an income from their investment; only early-stage, fast-growers such as Snapchat can get away with paying no dividends.
How expensive is it to run a company instead of a sole trader?	Not *that* costly. You can form a company for little more than £100, and the ongoing accounting costs are around £1,200 a year.

31.5 Liability – evaluation

There is a case for placing limited liability among the key factors that have led to the wealth of the western world. Without that legal protection, the industrial revolution of the nineteenth century could not have happened. Therefore, it is usually the case that unlimited liability businesses are small and plan to stay small, whereas those that are formed into companies have greater ambitions. Ultimately, the businesses that in recent times have gone from start–up to billion–dollar sale in a year or two have all been limited liability companies.

'Capitalism without bankruptcy is like Christianity without hell.'

Frank Borman, airline chief executive

For those dealing with businesses, either as a supplier or as a banker/lender, the advantages of a company structure are offset by a huge downside: the risk of the company putting itself into voluntary liquidation – leaving the creditors with nothing. As elsewhere in business, morality matters. Some businesspeople lack the moral compass needed to ensure that they are being fair to everyone they deal with.

Key terms

Bankrupt: when an individual is unable to meet personal liabilities, some or all of which can be as a consequence of business activities.

Creditors: those owed money by a business – for example, suppliers and bankers.

Limited liability: owners are not liable for the debts of the business; they can lose no more than the sum they invested.

Sole trader: a one-person business with unlimited liability.

Unlimited liability: owners are liable for any debts incurred by the business, even if it requires them to sell all their assets and possessions and become personally bankrupt.

31.6 Workbook

Revision questions

(25 marks; 25 minutes)

1 Explain in your own words the risks involved in starting a business that has unlimited liability. (4)

2 Outline why the liabilities involved as a business partner might be even more of a worry than for a sole trader. (4)

3 Outline two circumstances in which a supplier might give credit to a newly formed limited company. (4)

4 Explain why a sole trader cannot raise share capital. (4)

5 From your general knowledge, give three examples of public limited companies. (3)

6 An aunt is about to start a business and asks you to advise on whether to start as a sole trader or a private limited company. Please do so. (6)

Data response

A recent report to parliament shows the remarkable growth in business start-ups in recent years. Figure 31.2 shows the net growth in start-ups (births *minus* deaths) per year, plus the percentage of small businesses that employ other people. In 2001, 33 per cent of small businesses were employers; by 2014, this figure had fallen to 24 per cent. In 2014, then, 76 per cent of small businesses were sole proprietors (in effect, self-employed). The data for businesses employing other people is measured using the graph's right-hand scale (rhs).

The report did not provide information on how many of the new business were sole traders, partnerships or private limited companies.

Questions

(20 marks; 25 minutes)

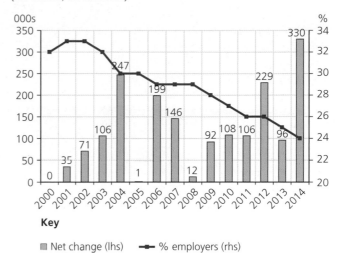

Key

■ Net change (lhs) —■— % employers (rhs)

Figure 31.2 Net growth in UK business start-ups (source: Parliamentary report, November 2014)

1 Assess two possible reasons why the rate of net new business start-ups jumped in 2014. (8)

2 Assess the importance to the UK of the decline in the percentage of small firms that employ any staff. (12)

Extended writing

1 As part of your plan to open a new restaurant, you establish Prime Ribz Ltd as a private limited company. Examine the financial issues that may arise in your first year and evaluate which issue might prove the most difficult. (20)

2 Your parents have decided to open a greengrocer selling only organic produce. They plan on making it a 50/50 partnership. Evaluate whether this business idea is wise. (20)

32 Planning and cash flow

> **Definition**
>
> Planning a firm's financial requirements is helped by a clear, detailed business plan. Cash flow is the flow of money into and out of a business in a given time period.

Linked to: Sources of finance, Ch 30; Profit, Ch 37.

32.1 The relevance of a business plan in obtaining finance

A good plan should be persuasive to an outside investor and useful to the entrepreneur. It should explain what makes the business special and help the entrepreneur to focus on what she or he is trying to achieve. The plan will also help the outsider understand the risks and rewards involved in the proposal. The outsider might be a bank or a 'Dragon' type of investor interested in an ownership stake in the business. A bank's main concern is that the start-up will be a safe investment, whereas a 'Dragon' is mainly interested in the upside potential – that is, the chance of making a huge profit. Either type of financier will want to see a carefully prepared plan with a well-considered proposal for the sums of money needed.

The heart of the **business plan** should be based around competitive advantage; this means identifying the features of your own product or service that will make it succeed against competitors. This may be based on a unique idea, a better product or service or the protection provided by a patent or copyright. On the other hand, a business may decide to strip a product or service down, to make it possible to be the cheapest in the market.

Business plans usually contain the following sections:

1 Executive summary: this should be short, but compelling enough to persuade the busy banker to want to read on. It should say who you are, what the customer's 'pain' is and how you will 'relieve' it, why your team is ideal for the task, how much capital you need for the start-up, and how much you are putting in yourself.

2 The product/service: explain it from the customer's point of view; for example, when describing smoothies, do not say 'we'll crush fruit and put it in bottles', but 'it'll provide busy people with two portions of fruit in an enjoyable, unmessy way'. If others already offer the service, you must explain what is different about your idea.

3 The market: focus on market trends rather than market size, such as whether the market is growing and, if so, how rapidly. Also there is a need to provide a brief analysis of key competitors.

4 Marketing plan: who are you targeting and how do you plan to communicate to them? How expensive will this be? Within this section, there should be an explanation and justification for the prices you plan to set plus a forecast of likely sales per month for the first two years.

5 Operational plan: how will the product or service be produced and delivered? This could involve production in China, in which case you will need to have already made contacts with willing suppliers.

6 Financial plan: the heart of this will be a **cash flow forecast** – that is, a prediction of monthly cash out and cash in from the start of the business until at least two years after the firm has started trading. This will give an idea of the bank balances over the start-up period, and therefore the financing needs.

7 Conclusion: this will include some idea of the longer-term plans for the business, including any 'exit strategy' – for example, a plan to sell the business within five years.

Estimating financial needs

Tom Doyle worked as a motor auctioneer for ten years before, at the age of 28, he decided to set up his own car dealership. He would specialise in German cars, especially BMWs, Audis and Volkswagen. He knew all the local garages and felt confident that he could get cars serviced, painted and valeted in order to maximise the value added. The business model was simple: buy slightly run-down German cars at the auction, make them look good to potential purchasers and then sell them at a higher price. He thought that he could make £300–£500 net profit per car.

Tom wrote up his plans with care, using a blank business plan from NatWest Bank. He made his sales forecasts, his cash flow projections and committed himself to putting in half of the £100,000 to start up the business. When he went to see the regional business bank manager, the conversation went well until it came to the financial needs. The bank manager thought Tom had underestimated the finance needed to run the business day by day. Tom was turned down because he had asked for £20,000 too little!

32.2 Interpreting a cash flow forecast

A cash flow forecast is carried out by estimating all the money coming into and out of the business, month by month. These flows of money are then set onto a grid showing the cash movements in each month – and how those movements affect the overall cash holdings (the closing balance).

Table 32.1 shows a new business starting up in March with £30,000 of capital. The key headings to be aware of are as follows.

Cash inflow

These are the sums expected to arrive each month, either from financial sources or from customers. In Table 32.1, sales start to generate cash from May onwards, and then start to grow impressively each month.

Cash outflow

These are the planned payments per month, such as wages, paying suppliers and paying the landlord. Here, a big outlay of £27,000 is needed in March to pay the start-up costs of the business, such as decoration and equipment.

The cash flow forecast is completed by calculating the following.

Monthly balance

This is cash inflow for the month minus cash outflow. It shows each month if there is a positive or a negative movement of cash. When outflow is greater than inflow, the monthly balance will be negative. This is shown in brackets to indicate that it is a minus figure.

Opening and closing balance

This is like a bank statement. It shows what cash the business has at the beginning of the month (opening balance) and what the cash position is at the end of the month (closing balance). The closing balance is the opening balance plus the monthly balance. For example, the business starts with £3,000 in the bank in April; a net £8,500 flows out during the month, so the closing bank balance is (£5,500).

The closing balance shows the overall state of the bank account at the end of the month. Table 32.1 shows a negative cash balance from April onwards, though the

Month £s	March	April	May	June	July	August
Opening balance	0	3,000	(5,500)	(8,500)	(10,000)	(9,500)
Capital invested	30,000					
Cash received from sales			7,000	10,000	13,000	15,000
Cash inflow	**30,000**	**0**	**7,000**	**10,000**	**13,000**	**15,000**
Cash outflow	**27,000**	**8,500**	**10,000**	**11,500**	**12,500**	**12,500**
Monthly balance	3,000	(8,500)	(3,000)	(1,500)	500	2,500
Closing balance	**3,000**	**(5,500)**	**(8,500)**	**(10,000)**	**(9,500)**	**(7,000)**

Table 32.1 Example of a cash flow forecast

accumulated position (the closing balance) is improving from the end of June.

As there is no such thing as negative money, the cash flow forecast shows that action is needed to avoid problems in the early months. The easiest remedy would be to negotiate a bank overdraft.

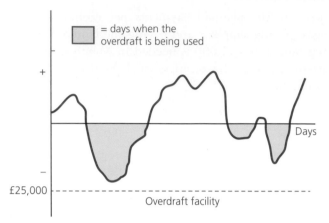

Figure 32.1 Daily cash balances for a firm with a £25,000 overdraft

32.3 Calculations based on changes in cash flow forecasts

In Table 32.2, you can see a cash flow forecast for a small firm. It looks very comfortable and stable, with no negative balances.

All figs in £s	January	February	March	April
Opening balance	2,000	2,800	3,700	4,700
Cash inflow from sales	4,000	4,500	5,000	5,500
Cash outflow	3,200	3,600	4,000	4,400
Net monthly cash flow	800	900	1,000	1,100
Closing balance	2,800	3,700	4,700	5,800

Table 32.2 Cash flow forecast

But what if the cash inflow expected for March is from a single buyer – let's say Tesco? And what if Tesco decide to hold up the March payment because they say they are unhappy with three deliveries that arrived late at Tesco stores? The result would be to throw the cash flow position of the business into the red (and remember, a negative cash balance is only possible if you have an overdraft agreement with your bank; otherwise your payments will bounce). See Table 32.3.

All figs in £s	January	February	March	April
Opening balance	2,000	2,800	3,700	(300)
Cash inflow from sales	4,000	4,500	0	5,500
Cash outflow	3,200	3,600	4,000	4,400
Net monthly cash flow	800	900	(4,000)	1,100
Closing balance	2,800	3,700	(300)	800

Table 32.3 Cash flow forecast (2)

If the dispute with Tesco can be resolved and the payment made in April, the final cash flow position will look like this (Table 32.4)

All figs in £s	January	February	March	April
Opening balance	2,000	2,800	3,700	4,700
Cash inflow from sales	4,000	4,500	0	10,500
Cash outflow	3,200	3,600	4,000	4,400
Net monthly cash flow	800	900	(4,000)	6,100
Closing balance	2,800	3,700	(300)	5,800

Table 32.4 Cash flow forecast (3)

Other calculations that may come up in exams:

- An unexpected payment is needed, such as a big fine for health and safety failings: this increases the cash outflow, which worsens the monthly balance, which then worsens the closing balance for that month – and all the following opening and closing balances.

- A customer decides they'll take an extra month's credit period – for example, paying you 60 days after the invoice date instead of 30 days. That delay by one month would actually have the effect shown in Table 32.3 – that is, you would lose a month's cash inflow (you'll get the money later on, but that doesn't help you now).

32.4 Analysis of cash flow forecasts

There are three main ways to analyse a cash flow forecast:

1 Calculate the difference between the closing balance at the end of the period and the opening balance at the start. This gives a sense of what is happening over time. If the overall cash balances are building up, then cash inflows are greater than cash outflows and the situation is comfortable. If the balance is declining, urgent action may be necessary.

2 Use the monthly closing balance to assess trends in the data. If the closing balance from Table 32.1 is turned into a graph, it helps highlight that the short-term plunge into the red seems, by July, to be stabilising into a steady recovery in the cash position of the business (see Figure 32.1).

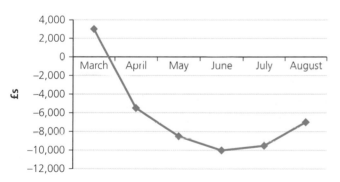

Figure 32.2 Closing balance from Table 32.1

3 Analyse the timings of cash inflows and outflows. Although some firms sell goods for cash, most provide customers with interest-free credit (e.g. Cadbury selling to Tesco). The longer the customers take to pay, the longer the seller is without their cash. So any method of speeding up customer payments can boost a firm's cash flow. The sum of money outstanding from customers is known as 'receivables'. Logically, firms should want this figure to be as low as possible.

Firms not only have customers, they also have suppliers. When buying goods on credit, the longer the credit period you can negotiate from suppliers, the longer your cash will be sitting in your bank account. As it sits in your bank account, this money owed is known as 'payables'.

> 'An important thing in business is to look after your suppliers. They must look after you, but you need them, so I always pay my bills on time.'
>
> Duncan Bannatyne, Dragon investor

If a company has customers who pay in 30 days and suppliers who are paid in 30 days, businesses call this a 'cash-to-cash' figure of zero (which is fantastic). If customers take 60 days to pay but suppliers have to be paid in cash, that is a cash-to-cash figure of 60 – which would put a strain on any business's cash flow position.

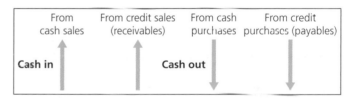

Figure 32.3 Cash flow

32.5 Uses and limitations of a cash flow forecast

If a business forecasts a period of negative cash flow, it can work to improve its positions in several ways.

- Getting goods to the market in the shortest possible time: the sooner goods reach the customer, the sooner payment is received. Production and distribution should be as efficient as possible.
- Getting paid as quickly as possible: the ideal arrangement is to get paid cash on delivery. Most business, though, works on credit. Even worse, it is interest-free credit, so the customer has little incentive to pay up quickly. Early payment should be encouraged by offering incentives, such as discounts for early payment.
- Keeping stocks of raw materials to a minimum. Good stock management such as a **just-in-time** system means that the business is not paying for stocks before it needs them for production.

> 'A wise business owner once said: "Happiness is positive cash flow".'
>
> Quoted at www.freetaxquotes.com

Cash flow can also be improved by keeping cash in the business. Minimising short-term spending on new equipment keeps cash in the business. Things that the business can do include:

- leasing rather than buying equipment; this increases expenses but conserves capital
- renting rather than buying buildings; this also allows capital to remain in the business
- postponing expenditure – for example, on new company cars.

Cash flow forecasts have their limitations, however:

- They are only as good as the raw data put in. Entrepreneurs *have* to be optimistic by nature, so they may overestimate sales and underestimate operational difficulties (and therefore cash outflows).
- They risk giving the impression of certainty where none exists; especially at start-up, who knows how long business customers will take to pay? Tesco may say they will pay in 60 days, but if it proves to be 90, what can a small firm do? Threaten to walk away from 30 per cent of the market?
- Because of these things it is vital to allow for contingencies – that is, things that can wrong. So a clever cash flow forecast includes a planned overstatement of costs, to allow for unexpected problems.

32.6 Planning and cash flow – evaluation

At the heart of any attempt to raise start-up capital is a business plan. And at *its* heart is a cash flow forecast. For a new business, cash flow forecasting helps to answer key questions:

- Is the venture viable?
- How much capital is needed?
- Which are the most dangerous months?

For an existing business, the cash flow forecast identifies the amount and timing of any cash flow problems in the future. It is also useful for evaluating new orders or ventures.

Nevertheless, completing a cash flow forecast does not ensure survival. And whereas 'estimates' sounds impressive, businesspeople admit that many are 'guesstimates': not just the amounts but also the timings. When preparing cash flow forecasts, managers need to ask themselves 'what if?' A huge mistake is to only look at one forecast. It is far better to look at **best case** and **worst case** possibilities. In addition, every firm needs to be continually aware of the economic and market climate and its current cash position.

> 'There's nothing more important than cash flow. I lost my computer business when I was 29 because I gave credit to firms I didn't investigate (credit check).'
>
> Peter Jones, Dragon investor (worth £475 million, Sunday Times Rich List 2014)

Five whys and a how

Questions	Answers
Why is it important to ask who constructed the cash flow forecast?	Because unconscious bias may have slipped in, e.g. an entrepreneur's optimism may make the cash inflow projections unrealistic.
Why may it be a concern if a company's sales are dominated by one large customer?	Because any disagreements about the invoice may lead to payment delays – which may be crippling if the bulk of cash inflow is due from that one customer.
Why is cash flow often referred to as 'the lifeblood' of the business?	Partly because it's *that* important to business survival and partly because, like blood, you only think about it when something's gone wrong.
Why is it important to distinguish between slow payment and slow sales as causes of cash flow problems?	Slow payment is a purely cash-related issue that could be sorted out between accounts departments; slow sales may be a far more long-term problem – and will involve the marketing department.
Why should a business analyse the causes of a cash problem before opting to increase its overdraft limits?	Because overdrafts are expensive and all they do is cover over the cash flow problems; they don't solve them.
How should a business make its estimates for future cash inflows and outflows?	By being pessimistic with the cash inflows (keep them low) and also with the cash outflows (be pessimistic; suspect they will be quite high).

32.7 Workbook

Revision questions

(40 marks; 40 minutes)

1 Identify two circumstances in which a new business might decide not to write a business plan. (2)

2 What is meant by 'cash flow'? (2)

3 Why is it important to manage cash flow? (4)

4 What is a cash flow forecast? (3)

5 Explain two limitations of cash flow forecasts. (4)

6 Give two reasons why a bank manager may want to see a cash flow forecast before giving a loan to a new business. (2)

7 How could a firm benefit from delaying its cash outflows? (3)

8 What problems could a firm face if its cash flow forecast proved unreliable? (3)

9 How could a firm benefit from constructing its cash flow forecasts on a computer spreadsheet? (4)

10 Explain why 'good management of cash flow starts with good forecasting'. (3)

11 Outline two problems that may arise if a firm is operating with very poor cash flow. (4)

12 Outline three ways in which a business can improve its cash flow situation. (6)

Data response 1

Cash flow

(18 marks; 20 minutes)

A business is to be started up on 1 January next year with £40,000 of share capital. It will be opening a designer clothes shop. During January, it plans to spend £45,000 on start-up costs (buying a lease, buying equipment, decorating, and so on). On 1 February, it will open its doors and gain sales over the next five months of: £12,000, £16,000, £20,000, £25,000 and £24,000, respectively. Each month it must pay £10,000 in fixed overheads (salaries, heat, light, telephone, and so on) and its variable costs will amount to half the revenue.

Draw up a cash flow table as per Table 32.5 to find out:

1 the company's forecast cash position at the end of June

2 the maximum level of overdraft the owners will need to negotiate with the bank before starting up.

	Jan	Feb	Mar	Apr	May	June
Cash at start						
Cash in						
Cash out						
Net cash flow						
Opening balance						
Closing balance						

Table 32.5 Cash flow (all figures in £000s)

Data response 2

Cash problems at a pound store

PoundLandline was quickly a media success after opening day publicity due to a row between the online start-up and the long-established Poundland retail chain. As the row spread over social media, opening day sales through PoundLandline were eight times higher than the budget. At 3.00pm, the site crashed – incapable of dealing with all the hits to its website. Founders Sonia and Colin had set the site up with an expectation of selling 8,000 items a day at £1 each, leading to annual revenue of £2.8 million but with slim gross margins and therefore gross profit of £420,000. With fixed overheads of £200,000 (covering the warehouse rental and other costs), they anticipated a very satisfactory net profit.

The problem now was the cost of fixing the website crash. They needed extra bandwidth and a more robust site. Although Colin was a very good programmer, he needed to hire extra expertise. Their budget had 'been too tight for contingency allowances', according to Sonia, so this was a strain on cash flow. A second issue was that high sales would mean speedy purchasing of extra stock – and paying for it. There was much to be done.

An underlying problem faced by the two entrepreneurs had been the unhelpful attitude of the banks. Despite TV advertisements boasting how much banks help small firms, Sonia and Colin had found them unwilling to commit to the slightest risk. Therefore, they refused to give bank loans and would only provide an overdraft when guaranteed by the security of Sonia's flat. If things went wrong, even though the business was PoundLandline Ltd, Sonia could end up homeless. As shown in the cash flow forecast, the pair had needed to invest £54,000 to get the business up and running. That was the limit of their financial resources.

So now, with customers desperate to shop at the first online pound store, the entrepreneurs had a cash flow problem – on day one of month one! The carefully constructed cash flow forecast was already being disrupted.

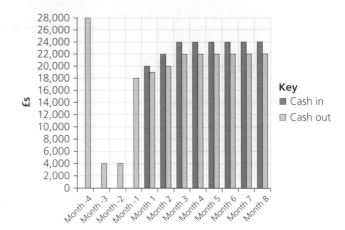

Figure 32.4 Cash flow forecast for PoundLandline Ltd

Questions

(35 marks; 40 minutes)

1 a) Explain the day one cash flow problems at PoundLandline Ltd. (5)

  b) Assess whether Sonia and Colin could be blamed for these causes of the cash flow difficulties. (10)

2 Given the situation the business was in by the end of day one, evaluate the actions the entrepreneurs might take to overcome their cash flow problems. (20)

Extended writing

1 Evaluate the importance of cash flow forecasting for a new retail business. (20)

2 'Cash flow management is important for small companies but not for large companies.' Evaluate this statement. (20)

33 Sales forecasting

> **Definition**
>
> Forecasting is the art and science of estimating future sales or costs with accuracy.

Linked to: Market research, Ch 3; Demand, Ch 5; Income elasticity of demand, Ch 9; Planning and cash flow, Ch 32; Business failure, Ch 39.

33.1 Purpose of sales forecasts

It is very important for managers to look ahead. They need to think about what is likely to happen in their industry and prepare accordingly in all areas of the business. One of the most important forecasts that needs to be made is the **sales forecast**. This forms the basis of most of the other plans within the organisation. For example:

- the human resource plan will need to be based on the expected level of sales; a growth in sales may require more staff
- the cash flow forecast will depend on projected sales
- profit forecasts will depend on the level of revenue predicted
- production scheduling will depend on the level of output required.

The sales forecast therefore drives many of the other plans within the business and is an essential element of effective management planning.

When a business starts up, it is extremely difficult to interpret its sales data. An ice cream parlour that starts up in April may find that sales double in May, again in June and again in July. Excited by the business success, the entrepreneurs may rush to open a second outlet. Yet a wet August may see sales knocked back followed by a sales slump in the autumn. The business may be overstretched and in liquidation by February.

As long as a business can survive the first year or two, managers can start to interpret the sales data. Managers need to understand the **trend** in product sales and compare it to the market as a whole.

> 'Entrepreneurs can't forecast accurately because they are trying something fundamentally new. So they will often be laughably behind plan – yet on the brink of success.'
>
> Eric Ries, business author

> **Real business**
>
> Booths has reduced the amount of fresh stock wastage by 20 per cent since adopting new forecasting software. This saved 'a six-figure sum' in the ten months since it was introduced. The 30-strong supermarket chain has faced the same competitiveness pressures as every other grocer in 2014, so the cost saving is a great help. The forecasting system analyses historic sales and weather data to identify demand patterns for individual products, stores and events (such as the FA Cup Final). The greater accuracy of the sales forecasts has not only allowed Booths to hold lower stock levels but has also boosted product availability. Both these factors will help profitability.

33.2 Factors affecting sales forecasts

Consumer trends

Consumer tastes and habits change over time. The changes can be quite dramatic. Sales of fruit juice were growing steadily until worries about the (natural) sugar in fruit made sales fall away in the last few years. And the desire for greater personal convenience and freedom has boosted sales of a wide range of products, from crisps to mobile phones.

A natural way for a forecaster to deal with this is to plot the past (historic) trends and then consider what the likely future pattern will look like. An interesting case is that of Beechams Powders, a long–established remedy for colds. As shown in Figure 33.1, sales were rising until 2009 but have been sliding ever since. This is in line with the general market for 'winter remedies'. The actual data is from 2006 to 2014, but an Excel sales forecast based on the polynomial trend (don't worry about this technicality) suggests that sales will have fallen from £27.7 million in 2014 to £21 million in 2016.

Of course, data such as this is affected by more than consumer trends. Although people are no more likely to catch a cold or flu in a cold winter, consumers buy more remedies when it is cold. So a particularly bad winter in 2015/2016 could help sales to buck the trend.

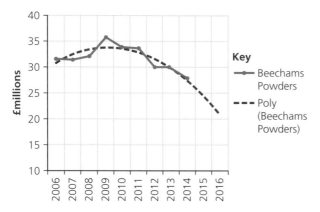

Figure 33.1 Sales of Beechams cold products (source: *The Grocer* magazine)

Factors that affect medium-to-long term consumer trends:

- changing tastes and habits, such as concern for body shape and image, or the trend for time-saving devices, eating and lifestyle
- demographics, such as the ageing of the population; the over-80s category is expected to double in Britain by 2025; this creates huge new business opportunities
- globalisation, both as a force in business and due to more adventurous holidaymaking; not long ago Mexican food was niche; now it's mass market
- affluence; the idea of buying water was unthinkable in the past; now it is a £750 million market – and still growing.

Economic variables

Many products, such as Marmite, chocolate, toothpaste, umbrellas and paint, have sales that are largely proof against changes in the economy. Others are highly sensitive because their income elasticity is high. In other words, their sales are heavily dependent on changes in consumers' **real incomes**. In the first half of 2014, with the UK's growth rate at 3 per cent, sales of Rolls-Royce cars rose by 33 per cent, implying an income elasticity of +11.

Other economic variables that could affect a sales forecast include:

- a sharp fall in the pound, making imports to the UK more expensive, which might help boost the sales of UK produced products (as imported ones price themselves out of the market); so the sales forecast for a UK manufacturer might prove overly cautious
- a sharp rise in taxation, such as the 2010 coalition government's VAT increase from 17.5 to 20 per cent; this hit sales of many items, especially 'big ticket' ones such as cars and carpets
- inflation; this can be a factor if price rises are not being matched by rises in household incomes – consumers will suffer a fall in the spending power as their real incomes decline.

Actions of competitors

In the period 2010–2013, Samsung could do no wrong in the market for mobile phones. Its Galaxy models outsold Apple's iPhone. At the beginning of 2014, Samsung looked forward to a successful year boosted by the launch of its Galaxy 5 phone. In fact, Chinese manufacturers such as Huawei (which saw sales jump from 10.4 million to 20.3 million units) took the Samsung market share from the bottom of the market, while the iPhone 6 saw Apple retake market share at the top end. Samsung's share of the global smartphone market fell from 32.3 per cent in 2013 to 25.2 per cent in 2014, causing actual sales volumes to decline. The actions of its competitors undermined Samsung's sales forecast.

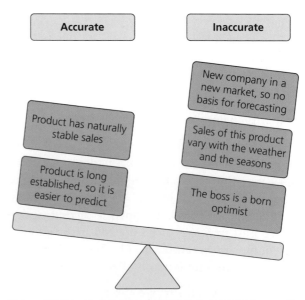

Figure 33.2 Logic balance: factors in successful forecasting

33.3 Difficulties of sales forecasting

The simplest way of predicting the future is to assume that it will be just like the past. For the immediate future, this may be realistic. It is unlikely (though not impossible) that the economy or demand will change dramatically tomorrow. Therefore, it is reasonable to assume that the pattern of near-term future sales will continue to follow recent trends.

Forecasting based on the continuation of past trends is known as extrapolation. It is overwhelmingly the most common form of forecasting and is the basis of almost all economic forecasts. Unfortunately, by definition, it will only be correct if the future does continue to be like the past. Sometimes that will work; at other times it will be disastrously wrong.

> 'It's tough to make predictions, especially about the future.'
>
> Yogi Berra, legendary baseball coach

When Branston launched tomato ketchup, sales grew rapidly between 2006 and 2010. It would have been fair, on the basis of the data, to forecast a great future for the brand – see Figure 33.3.

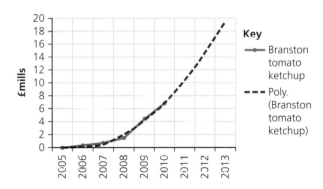

Figure 33.3 Branston Ketchup sales, 2005-2010, with extrapolated future sales

In fact, what happened after 2010 was that sales of the brand collapsed. Retailers had been stocking it as a rival to Heinz, but consumer sales were too weak to support it. So it started to lose distribution. The extrapolated forecast suggested sales of £15 million by 2012. As Figure 33.4 shows, the actual sales were no more than £3.5 million in 2012. 2010 proved to be the sales peak rather than a stepping stone towards a higher peak. This illustrates the difficulties of making a sales forecast.

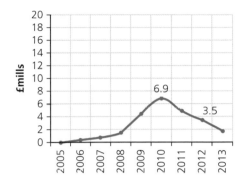

Figure 33.4 Actual Branston Ketchup sales, 2005-2013

> 'There are known knowns. These are things we know that we know. There are known unknowns. That is to say, there are things that we know we don't know. But there are also unknown unknowns. There are things we don't know we don't know.'
>
> Donald Rumsfeld, US politician

Real business

When a young couple decided to open a brand new fish and chip shop in Nottingham, they made a sales forecast based on the average sales turnover of established outlets across the country. On the 'Federation of Fish Fryers' website, they found that the British eat £1.2 billion worth of fish and chips a year, and there are 10,500 chip shops. Therefore, the average chippie has sales of £1.2 billion / 10,500 = £114,286 a year (£2,200 a week). They then assumed that it would take a while to get established, so they used the following sales forecast:

Week 1: £1,600

Week 2: £1,800

Week 3: £2,000

Week 4 and thereafter: £2,200

At the time of writing, their finance is in place but they haven't opened yet. So the accuracy of the forecast is unknown.

Five whys and a how

Questions	Answers
Why do firms need sales forecasts?	Because they are the starting point for all planning, e.g. financial, HR or marketing plans.
Why forecast, if the forecast is unlikely to be correct?	If you have worked out the impact of X,000 sales on your finances and staffing, it becomes easier to understand what to do if actual sales turn out to be 10 per cent below X,000.
Why is extrapolation a widely used, but clearly flawed, method of forecasting?	Extrapolation can only be correct if the future works out exactly the same as the past; when customer tastes/habits change, extrapolation can be hopelessly wrong.
Why should firms be aware of the possibility of 'unknown unknowns' (see Donald Rumsfeld quote, page 211)?	Because the completely unexpected is always possible, firms need **contingency plans** – especially a financial cushion.
Why may it be quite easy for Heinz to forecast UK sales of its ketchup?	It is a long established product, with a dominant market share (no real competition) and is probably unaffected by economic ups and downs; to the Brits, it is a daily essential.
How can a brand new business hope to make an accurate sales forecast?	It is often near-impossible, but a valid approach is to calculate average sales within the market, and assume those will be true (see 'Real business' on page 211).

33.4 Sales forecasting – evaluation

Sales forecasts are important to every business because so many other plans rely on them. They determine how many people to employ, how much to produce and decisions on future production capacity. They may not always be accurate, but they can provide important guidelines for planning.

A badly run business will find itself in a crisis because its forecast proves inaccurate. An intelligent manager tries hard to predict with precision, but thinks about the effect of sales being unexpectedly high or low. Nothing demoralises staff more than a sudden lurch by management (hiring one minute, firing the next). So the future needs to be thought through carefully, with contingency plans in case things turn out rather differently from forecast.

'You don't want to influence the same system you are trying to forecast.'

Nate Silver, US forecasting guru

Key terms

Contingency plans: plans held in reserve in case things go wrong – for example, a cash flow forecast based on sales being 10 per cent lower than expected.

Real incomes: changes in household incomes after allowing for changes in prices, i.e. percentage change in household income minus inflation = real income.

Sales forecast: a method of predicting future sales using statistical methods.

Trend: the general path that a series of values (for example, sales) follows over time, disregarding variations or random fluctuations.

33.5 Workbook

Revision questions

(30 marks; 30 minutes)

1 What is a sales forecast? (2)

2 Explain how you can show the trend in a series of data. (4)

3 Explain how *two* of the following Heinz managers could be helped by two weeks' warning that sales are forecast to rise by 15 per cent:
   a) the operations manager
   b) the marketing manager, Heinz Beans
   c) the human resource manager
   d) the chief accountant. (8)

4 Trends are important in sales forecasting, and can be affected by fashion. Outline two factors that might lead to a product falling out of fashion. (4)

5 Marks & Spencer is forecasting a sales increase of 2 per cent in the coming year. Explain how two possible actions by rivals Next and John Lewis might cause actual sales to perform less well than this. (6)

6 What is meant by an 'economic variable'? (2)

7 Explain briefly how Superdry's brand owner, Supergroup plc, might make use of contingency planning. (4)

Data response

Bikes from India

In the 1960s, the British motorcycle industry was wiped out by competition from Japan: Honda, Yamaha Suzuki and Kawasaki. An important part of Britain's motorcycle heritage was Royal Enfield, which went bust, though the brand ended up in the hands of an Indian company: the Eicher Group. This group built a substantial business in India based on the brand Royal Enfield. In 2013, around 175,000 Royal Enfield bikes were produced (more than double the entire UK motorbike market).

Figure 33.5 Royal Enfield motorbike

With plans to expand output to 250,000 in 2014, the Eicher Group was eyeing the UK market. It wanted to export 5,000 bikes to Britain, which would mean taking a 6 per cent market share. It believes that its market potential is rooted in the fastest growing UK biker demographic: oldie bikers – that is, those aged 55+. Today younger people are more likely to ride a bike than a motorbike. Fears of accidents have made motorbikes a tough sell to younger people. Eicher Motor's chief executive, Siddhartha Lal, says that, following secondary research, his group is targeting 'a nostalgic population of older and wealthier leisure riders'. With a price tag set at £5,200 for the October 2013 launch of the Royal Enfield Continental GT, the pitch certainly was at the wealthier end of the market.

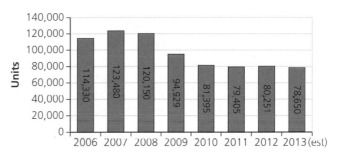

Figure 33.6 Annual UK motorbike sales, 2006–2013 (source: www.mcia.co.uk)

In the UK, the most obvious direct competitor to the Enfield bike is the rival heritage brand Triumph, the UK's top-selling bike. Although these bikes are made in Thailand, the brand owner has successfully recreated a British image to the Triumph brand, which adds value. The Royal Enfield is priced at £1,000 below the equivalent Triumph, but it has yet to be seen whether British bikers will trust in the quality standards of bikes from India.

There is another demographic that is not yet being targeted by Eicher. According to a 24-year-old British biker who rented a Royal Enfield during a year-long stay in India, the bikes: 'occupy cult status in India. Countless heroes of Bollywood films have been shown riding them... The look and feel of the thing, the rawness of the engine, the noise: everyone is obsessed by that.' So perhaps there are also prospects among wealthier Indians living in Britain. Fortunately for Eicher, 56 per cent growth in revenues in 2012 to £120 million gave the group a degree of financial solidity, which makes success in the UK launch desirable but not essential.

One other factor that Eicher will need to face in Britain is the highly seasonal nature of bike sales. In January, people think of warm coats, not bikes, so the sales season is limited to the summer months.

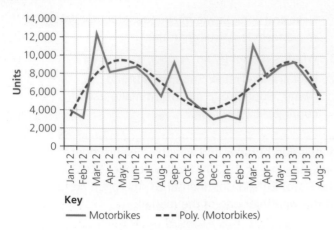

Key

―― Motorbikes   ▪▪▪ Poly. (Motorbikes)

Figure 33.7 Monthly sales of motorbikes in the UK, January 2012–August 2013 (source: www.mcia.co.uk)

All in all, the future of this UK launch seems uncertain. An early review of the Continental GT raises doubts about the 'build compromises', even though it praises the road

handling and general modernity of the bike. Siddhartha Lal is hoping that UK success will kickstart a global push by Royal Enfield into export markets. It remains to be seen.

Questions (40 marks; 45 minutes)

1 Use Figure 33.6 to assess one reason in favour and one reason against launching into the UK market for motorbikes in 2013. (8)

2 Assess how a British motorcycle producer might use the sales trend information provided in Figures 33.6 and 33.7. (10)

3 Use Figure 33.7 to assess the possible difficulties created for a motorbike manufacturer from the strongly seasonal sales pattern in the UK market. (10)

4 Assess whether Eicher is right to price the Royal Enfield CT at £1,000 below the equivalent Triumph bike. (12)

Extended writing

1 Evaluate this statement: 'Since we can never know the future, it is pointless trying to forecast it.' (20)

2 'Quantitative sales forecasting techniques have only limited use. Qualitative judgements are needed in a constantly changing world.' Evaluate this statement. (20)

34 Sales, revenue and costs

> **Definition**
>
> Revenue is the value of total sales made by a business within a period, usually one year. Costs are the expenses incurred by a firm in producing and selling its products, such as wages and raw materials.

Linked to: Sales forecasting, Ch 33; Break-even, Ch 35; Profit, Ch 37.

34.1 Sales

There are two ways to measure sales: by volume and by value. **Sales volume** is simply the number of units sold – for example, Toyota's global sales of ten million cars in 2014 (the world's number one producer). **Sales revenue** is what those units were sold for – in other words, volume × price. If the average Toyota sold for £15,000, that would put the value of its 2014 sales at the stunning figure of £150 billion.

Sales volume × Price = Sales revenue

Toyota: 10 million cars × £15,000 = £150,000 million

Jaguar Land Rover: 430,000 cars × £45,000
= £19,350 million (2013/2014)

For companies, calculating volume sales is easy. But sales revenue can be more difficult. Many products are sold on credit, so although the sale has been made, until the payment arrives there is scope for uncertainty. When La Senza went into liquidation in 2014, millions of pounds owed to suppliers went unpaid. Those supplier companies had to 'write-off' the sales revenue they thought they had achieved. Infuriating.

34.2 Business revenues

The revenue received by a firm as a result of trading activities is a critical factor in its success. Entrepreneurs start their financial planning by assessing the revenue that they are likely to receive during the coming financial year. A firm seeking to increase its revenue can plan to sell more or aim to sell at a higher price. Some firms may maintain high prices even though this policy depresses sales. Such companies, perhaps selling fashion and high-technology products, believe that in the long run this approach will lead to higher revenue and higher profits.

> **Real business**
>
> ### Blackberry's falling revenue
>
> In the three months ending 30 November, Blackberry saw its revenue plunge from £1,660 million in 2012 to £730 million in 2013. The reason for the 56 per cent fall in revenue was a collapse in phone sales from 3.7 million to 1.9 million, plus a fall in the average price charged per Blackberry. The company had pinned everything on a new range of phones based on a new operating system – but it proved unable to dent sales of the iPhone and the Samsung Galaxy. As a consequence of the revenue decline, Blackberry made losses of £2.7 billion in its third quarter of 2013.

The other way to boost revenue is to charge a low price in an attempt to sell as many units as possible. The high sales volumes may lead to high revenues and profits. Firms following this approach are likely to be operating in markets in which the goods are fairly similar and consumers do not exhibit strong preferences for any brand. This is true of the market for young holidaymakers going to Spain or Thailand. Price competition is fierce as businesses seek to maximise their revenue.

Traditionally, companies printed price lists that might run for 12 months. These days online purchasing makes variable pricing more common – that is, allowing prices to rise and fall depending on demand and supply conditions. This is a way to maximise revenue, by charging high prices when demand is at its highest, but much more modestly during periods of low demand. Football teams such as West Ham do something similar, offering 'Kids for a Quid' when their home game is against an unfashionable opponent, such as Stoke City.

Price manipulation for maximised revenue

In a world increasingly dominated by online purchasing, businesses have the ability to vary prices to maximise revenue. This is quite open with airline prices – for example, the easyJet Sunday 11.40am flight to Barcelona was priced at £108.99 for 28 December 2014, £44.99 for 25 January 2015 and £149.99 for 15 February 2015 (prices as at 20 December 2014). But it is less clear-cut with online purchasing of insurance, where the same car might cost £475 to insure in the morning and £650 in the afternoon, as the sellers try to reward those who can be bothered to spend time shopping around. As the saying goes: let the buyer beware!

'Today, recorded music is more a marketing tool than a revenue source.'

Irving Azoff, manager to Christine Aguilera and The Eagles

34.3 The costs of production

Costs are a critical element of the information necessary to manage a business successfully. Managers need to be aware of the costs of all aspects of their business for a number of reasons:

- They need to know the cost of production to assess whether it is profitable to supply the market at the current price.
- They need to know actual costs to allow comparisons with their forecasted (or budgeted) figures. This will allow them to make judgements concerning the cost efficiency of different parts of the business.

'Watch the costs and the profits will look after themselves.'

Andrew Carnegie, US steel magnate (at one time, the world's second richest man)

Fixed and variable costs

This is an important classification of the costs encountered by businesses. This classification has a number of uses. For example, it is the basis of calculating break–even, which is covered in Chapter 35.

Fixed costs

Fixed costs are any costs that do not vary directly with the level of output. These costs are linked to time rather than to level of business activity. Fixed costs exist even if a business is not producing any goods or services. An example of a fixed cost is rent, which is usually calculated monthly, but will remain the same whether business is great or awful that month. The landlord doesn't care; s/he just wants to be paid!

If a manufacturer can double output from within the same factory, the amount of rent will not alter, thus it is a fixed cost. In the same way, a seaside hotel has mortgage and salary costs during the winter, even though there may be very few guests. Given that fixed costs are inevitable, it is vital that managers work hard at bringing in customers to keep the fixed costs covered.

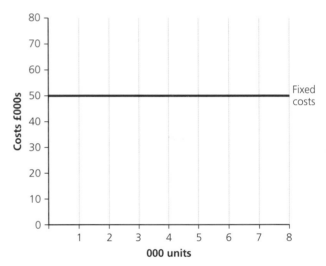

Figure 34.1 Fixed costs of £50,000 per year

In Figure 34.1, you can see that the firm faces fixed costs of £50,000 irrespective of the level of output.

Other examples of fixed costs include the uniform business rate (local taxes), management salaries, interest charges and depreciation.

In the long term, fixed costs can alter. The manufacturer referred to earlier may decide to increase output significantly. This may require renting additional factory space and negotiating loans for additional capital equipment. Thus rent will rise, as may interest payments. We can see that in the long term fixed costs may alter, but that in the short term they are – as their name suggests – fixed.

Variable costs

Variable costs are those costs which vary directly with the level of output. They represent payments made for the use of inputs such as labour, fuel and raw materials. If a manufacturer doubled output, then these costs would double. A doubling of the sales of Innocent Strawberry Smoothies would require twice the purchasing of strawberries and bananas. There would also be extra costs for the packaging, the wage bill and the energy required to fuel the production line.

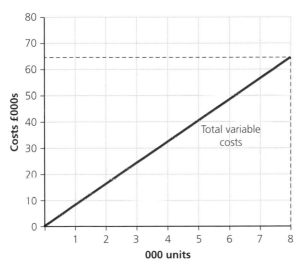

Figure 34.2 Variable costs of £8 per unit

The graph in Figure 34.2 shows a firm with variable costs of £8 per unit of production. This means that variable costs rise steadily with, and proportionately to, the level of output. Thus a 10 per cent rise in output will increase **total variable costs** by the same percentage.

However, it is not always the case that variable costs rise in proportion to output. Many small businesses discover that, as they expand, variable costs do not rise as quickly as output. A key reason for this is that, as the business becomes larger, it is able to negotiate better prices with suppliers. Its suppliers are likely to agree to sell at lower unit prices when the business places larger orders.

Examples of some variable, fixed and hard-to-classify costs are given in Table 34.1.

Variable costs	Fixed costs	Hard to classify
• Raw materials • Packaging • Piece-rate labour • Commission (percentage on sales)	• Rent • Heating and lighting • Salaries • Interest charges	• Delivery costs • Electricity • Machine maintenance costs • Energy

Table 34.1 Some costs are easy to classify; some are hard

Total costs

When added together, fixed and variable costs give the **total costs** for a business. This is, of course, a very important element in the calculation of the profits earned by a business.

The relationship between fixed, variable and total costs is straightforward to calculate but has some important implications for a business. If a business has relatively high fixed costs as a proportion of total costs, then it is likely to seek to maximise its sales to ensure that the fixed costs are spread across as many units of output as possible. In this way, the impact of high fixed costs is lessened.

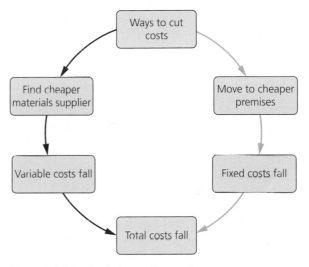

Figure 34.3 Logic chain: cutting costs

'On the internet, companies are scale businesses, characterised by high fixed costs and relatively low variable costs.'

Jeff Bezos, founder of Amazon

Real business

Paying the costs

In 2012, Scoop opened its third London ice cream parlour. The company intended to continue making all the ice cream at the original Covent Garden store, but deliver ice cream daily to the new branch at Gloucester Road (two miles away). This meant that all the fixed production costs would remain unchanged (rent on the floor space, the machinery and the professional ice cream maker's salary). Variable costs would increase by around 50 per cent, as long as the new parlour's sales matched the first two. These costs would be the ingredients, especially milk, cream and sugar; plus the cost of the electricity to run the ice cream-making machines. There would also be some brand new fixed costs: an extra refrigerated van, plus the rent and the staff at the new premises. Overall, owner Matteo Pantani knew that he could increase his revenue by 50 per cent, while total costs should increase by no more than 30 per cent. This should boost profit considerably.

Five whys and a how

Questions	Answers
Why do firms care more about sales revenue than sales volume?	Ultimately, costs are covered by revenue (i.e. money) not by the number of units you sell.
Why might a business want to separate its variable from its fixed costs?	Because it helps analyse the impact on profit of a change in demand or change in price.
Why would a firm be worried if its revenue had slipped below its total costs?	Because it would be making operating losses; in the short-term that might be OK, but continual operating losses would force the company to close.
Why might a business choose to lower its prices?	Because it feels that the increase in sales volume would outweigh the price cut, pushing revenue up.
Why might there be an increase in a firm's variable costs per unit?	Raw material costs might rise or the firm's production quality might slip, forcing it to redo the shoddy work.
How might a company cut its fixed costs?	Move to a cheaper location or cut salaried staff.

34.4 Sales, revenue and costs – evaluation

One important issue for evaluation in relation to revenues and costs for a new enterprise is to judge the likely accuracy of the forecast figures and the degree of reliance that can be placed upon them. This is an important judgement for a number of people who may have an interest in the new business. Investors will look closely at any forecast figures before committing money to the enterprise, and suppliers will want to be assured of payment before agreeing to supply any raw materials.

Ultimately, the test of management is whether it can keep revenues rising faster than costs. This might be quite easy when the economy is on the up, but extremely hard when a recession is underway. So it is always wise to reflect on the circumstances of the business.

Key terms

Fixed costs: those that do not change as the number of sales change (for example, rent or salaries).

Piece-rate labour: paying workers per item they make – that is, without regular pay.

Sales revenue: the number of units sold in a time period multiplied by the average selling price of those units.

Sales volume: the number of units sold in a time period, e.g. a year.

Total costs: all the costs of producing a specific output level, i.e. fixed costs plus total variable costs.

Total variable costs: all the variable costs of producing a specific output level – that is, variable costs per unit multiplied by the number of units sold.

Variable costs: those that change in line with the amount of business (for example, the cost of buying raw materials).

34.5 Workbook

Revision questions

(25 marks; 25 minutes)

1 Why may a business initially receive relatively low revenues from a product newly introduced to the market? (3)

2 State two circumstances in which a company may be able to charge high prices for a new product. (2)

3 For what reasons may a firm seek to maximise its sales revenue? (3)

4 If a business sells 4,000 units of Brand X at £4 each and 2,000 units of Brand Y at £3 each, what is its total revenue? (4)

5 State two reasons why firms have to know the costs they incur in production. (2)

6 Distinguish, with the aid of examples, between fixed and variable costs. (4)

7 Explain why fixed costs can only alter in the long term. (3)

8 Examine the view that 'cost-cutting is a short-sighted approach to business'. (4)

Calculation practice questions

(25 marks; 25 minutes)

1 During the summer weeks, Devon Ice Cream has average sales of 4,000 units a week. Each ice cream sells for £1 and has variable costs of 25p. Fixed costs are £800.

   a) Calculate the total weekly costs for the business in the summer weeks. (3)

   b) Calculate Devon Ice Cream's weekly revenue in the summer. (2)

2 a) If a firm sells 200 Widgets at £3.20 and 40 Squidgets at £4, calculate its total revenue. (3)

   b) Each Widget costs £1.20 to make, while each Squidget costs £1.50. Calculate the firm's total variable costs. (3)

3 'Last week our sales revenue was £12,000, which was great. Our price is £2 a unit, which I think is a bit too cheap.'

   a) Calculate how many unit sales were made last week. (2)

   b) If a price rise to £2.25 cuts sales to 5,600 units, calculate the change in the firm's revenue. (4)

   c) Express that change in revenue as a percentage. (3)

4 At full capacity output of 24,000 units, a firm's costs are as follows:
   - managers' salaries: £48,000
   - materials: £12,000
   - rent and rates: £24,000
   - piece-rate labour: £36,000.

   Calculate the firm's total costs at 20,000 units. (5)

Data response

Chalfont Computer Services Ltd

Robert has decided to give up his job with BT and to work for himself offering computer services to local people. He has paid off his mortgage and owns his house outright, so feels this is the time to take a risk. Robert has no experience of running a business, but is skilled in repairing computers and solving software problems. In the past, Robert has repaired computers belonging to friends and family and is aware of the costs involved in providing this service. He believes that with the increase in internet usage there will be plenty of demand for his services. Robert has spoken to a few people in his local pub and this has confirmed his opinion. Robert needs to raise £10,000 to purchase equipment for his business and to pay for a new vehicle and intends to ask his bank for a loan.

The work Robert has already done allows him to forecast that the average revenue from each customer will be £40, while the variable costs will be £15. His monthly fixed costs will be £1,000. Table 34.2 gives Robert's estimates of the number of customers he expects to have.

Month	Number of customers
January	40
February	50
March	60
April	82

Table 34.2 Estimates of number of customers

Questions (25 marks; 30 minutes)

1 What is meant by the term 'variable costs'? Give an example. (2)

2 Robert estimates that if he cut his prices by 10 per cent, he would have 20 per cent more customers each month.

   a) Calculate the outcome of these changes. (3)

   b) Assess whether this change would benefit Robert. (10)

3 Assess the case for and against a bank lending Robert £10,000 on the basis of his forecast profits. (10)

Extended writing

1 In 2014, Tesco plc suffered a slide in its sales, with weekly data showing a 4 per cent decline compared with 2013. Evaluate how a supermarket chain such as Tesco could set about rebuilding its sales revenue. (20)

2 When a rival surfing school opened next door, 'Jo's Surf School' saw a sharp fall in sales. Evaluate the most important actions it should take to rebuild its sales revenue. (20)

35 Break-even

Definition

Break-even compares a firm's revenue with its fixed and variable costs to identify the minimum level of sales needed to cover costs. So break-even is the point at which total fixed costs + total variable costs = total revenue.

Linked to: Sales, revenue and costs, Ch 34; Profit, Ch 37.

35.1 Introduction

Businesses need to know how many products they have to produce and sell in order to cover all of their costs. This is particularly important for new businesses with limited experience of their markets.

Look at Table 35.1, which shows forecast revenue and cost figures for a new business.

Output of ties (per week)	Sales income (£ per week)	Total costs (£ per week)
0	0	10,000
100	4,000	11,500
200	8,000	13,000
300	12,000	14,500
400	**16,000**	**16,000**
500	20,000	17,500
600	24,000	19,000

Table 35.1 Forecast revenue and cost figures for a new business ltd

You can easily identify that 400 is the number of sales that must be achieved each week to break even. If sales are only 200 units, the business will be making losses of a punishing £5,000 a week, so the break-even analysis is providing vital data.

To calculate the break-even point, we need information on both costs and prices. Break-even can be shown on a graph or, more quickly, calculated as in the following section.

35.2 Calculating the break-even point

Calculating the break-even point for a product requires knowledge of:

- the selling price of the product
- its **fixed costs**
- its **variable costs** per unit.

Fixed costs are expenses which do not change in response to changing demand or output, such as rent and salaries. Variable costs will alter in relation to changes in demand and therefore output. A doubling of demand will double variable costs, but leave fixed costs the same.

The break-even output level can be calculated by the following formula:

$$\text{Break-even output} = \frac{\text{Fixed costs}}{(\text{selling price per unit} - \text{variable cost per unit})}$$

Worked example:

Igloo ice cream costs 50p per unit to make and is sold for £2.50. The fixed costs of running the production process and the shop amount to £2,000 per week. Therefore, the break-even output level is:

$$\frac{\text{Fixed costs}}{(\text{selling price per unit} - \text{variable cost per unit})}$$
$$= \frac{£2,000}{£2.50 - 50p}$$
$$= 1,000 \text{ ice creams per week}$$

So although a £2 surplus per ice cream seems a lot of profit, it is only the 1001st that really makes £2. Before getting to the break-even point, each ice cream sold is simply reducing the losses.

'[HMV] is now in danger of failing to break even in the full-year.'

Nick Bubb, retail analyst (in December 2011, not long before the company collapsed into administration)

35.3 Contribution

In the above formula for break-even, price *minus* variable costs is known as **contribution**. It is the surplus of £2 between the £2.50 selling price and the variable costs of 50p per unit.

Contribution per unit = selling price *minus* variable costs per unit

Total contribution = contribution per unit × quantity sold

So, in the above example, if 1,200 ice creams were sold, the total contribution would be:

£2 × 1,200 ice creams = £2,400

Total contribution is a useful short-cut way to calculate profit, as:

Total contribution − Fixed costs = Profit

So:

£2,400 − £2,000 = £400 profit

35.4 Break-even charts

A **break-even chart** is a graph showing the revenue and costs for a business at all possible levels of demand or output. The break-even chart uses the horizontal axis to represent the output per time period for the business – for example, between 0 and 1,000 units a month. The vertical axis represents costs and sales in pounds.

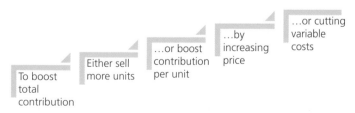

Figure 35.1 Logic chain: boosting total contribution

Example: Berry & Hall Ltd

Berry & Hall Ltd manufactures confectionery. The company is planning to launch a new sweet called Aromatics at a price of £5 per kg. The variable cost of production per kg is forecast at £3 and the fixed costs associated with this product are estimated to be £50,000 a year. The company's maximum output of Aromatics will be 50,000kg per year.

First, put scales on the axes. The horizontal output scale has a range from zero to the company's maximum output of 50,000kg. The vertical axis records values of costs and revenues. For the maximum vertical value, multiply the maximum output by the selling price and then place values on the axis up to this figure. In this case, it will have a maximum value on the axis of £250,000 (£5 per kg × 50,000kg).

Having drawn the axes and placed scales upon them, the first line we enter is fixed costs. Since this value does not change with output, it is simply a horizontal line drawn at £50,000.

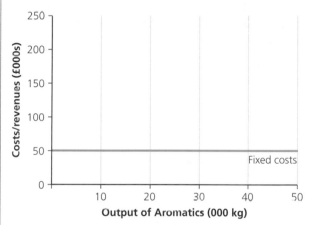

Figure 35.2 Fixed costs for Aromatics

Next, add variable costs to the fixed costs to arrive at total costs. Total costs start from the left hand of the fixed costs line and rise diagonally. To see where they rise to, calculate the total cost at the maximum output level. In the case of Aromatics, this is 50,000kg per year. The total cost is fixed costs (£50,000) plus variable costs of producing 50,000kg (£3 × 50,000 = £150,000). The total cost at this level of output is £50,000 + £150,000 = £200,000.

This point can now be marked on the chart; that is, £200,000 at an output level of 50,000kg. This can be joined by a straight line to total costs at zero output: £50,000. This is illustrated in Figure 35.3.

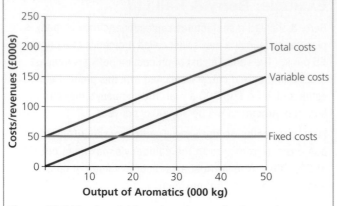

Figure 35.3 Fixed, variable and total costs for Aromatics

Finally, sales revenue must be added. For the maximum level of output, calculate the sales revenue and mark this on the chart. In the case of Aromatics, the maximum output per year is 50,000kg; multiplied by the selling price, this gives £250,000 each year. If Berry & Hall does not produce and sell any Aromatics, it will not have any sales revenue. Thus zero output results in zero income. A straight diagonal line from zero to £250,000 represents the sales revenue (see Figure 35.4).

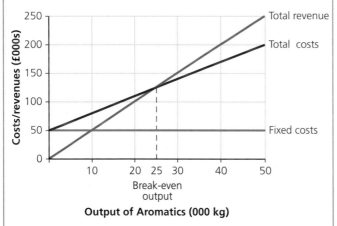

Figure 35.4 Break-even output for Aromatics

This brings together costs and revenues for Aromatics. A line drawn down from the point at which total costs and sales revenue cross shows the break-even output. For Aromatics, it is 25,000kg per year. This can be checked using the formula method explained earlier.

35.5 Using break-even charts

Various pieces of information can be taken from break-even charts such as that shown in Figure 35.4. As well as the level of break-even output, it also shows the level of profits or losses at every possible level of output. Many conclusions can be reached, such as:

- Any level of output lower than 25,000kg per year will mean the product is making a loss. The amount of the loss is indicated by the vertical distance between the total cost and the total revenue line.
- Sales in excess of 25,000kg of Aromatics per year will earn the company a profit. If the company produces and sells 30,000kg of Aromatics annually, it will earn a profit of £10,000.
- The **margin of safety**: this is the amount by which demand can fall before the firm starts making losses. It is the difference between current sales and the break-even point. If annual sales of Aromatics were 40,000kg, with a break-even output of 25,000kg, then the margin of safety would be 15,000kg.

margin of safety = sales *minus* break-even point

margin of safety = 40,000 − 25,000 = 15,000 kg

The higher the margin of safety, the less likely it is that a loss-making situation will develop. The margin of safety is illustrated in Figure 35.5.

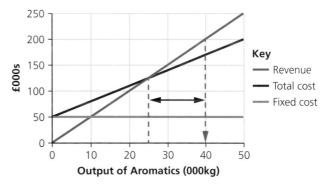

Figure 35.5 Margin of safety

Table 35.2 shows how changes in business circumstances affect the break-even chart.

	Cause	Effect
Internal factors	• Extra launch advertising	• Fixed costs rise, so total costs rise and the break-even point rises
	• Planned price increase	• Revenue rises more steeply; break-even point falls
	• Using more machinery (and less labour) in production	• Fixed costs rise while variable costs fall; uncertain effect on break-even point
External factors	• Fall in demand	• Break-even point is not affected, though margin of safety is reduced
	• Competitors' actions force price cut	• Revenue rises less steeply; break-even point rises
	• Fuel costs rise	• Variable and total cost lines rise more steeply; break-even point rises

Table 35.2 How changes in business circumstances affect the break-even chart

35.6 The effects of changes in price, output and cost

On its own, a limitation of the break-even chart is that it is a static model. It does not show sales trends over time. Fortunately, it can be a useful method for showing when changes are planned – for example, when the business is considering a price increase.

The main changes to consider are:

1 the impact on revenue, profits and break-even of a change in price

2 the impact on revenue and profits of change in demand, perhaps because the product has become more or less fashionable

3 the effect of a rise or fall in variable costs, such as raw materials

4 the effect of a rise or fall in fixed costs, perhaps when a business chooses to 'downsize' to smaller, cheaper head office premises.

Price rise

If a company increases its prices, its revenue line will rise more steeply than before. The line will start at the same point as before (0 sales = 0 revenue) but will rise

to a higher revenue point at maximum output. This steepening of the revenue line will increase the profit potential at each level of output and lower the break-even point. So if you charge more, you don't need to sell as many to break even. This is shown in Figure 35.6.

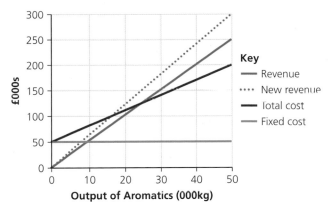

Figure 35.6 A rise in price

A rise or fall in demand

A change in demand has no effect on the lines of the break-even chart. It is simply that you have to read the change off the chart by drawing a line vertically up from the new sales quantity.

Rise in variable costs

Between March and November 2013, the price of cocoa beans rose from $2,150 per tonne to $2,700. This 25 per cent increase would make the variable costs line rise more steeply, though it will start from the same point (zero). Naturally, if the variable costs rise, the total costs must also be affected. So if an exam question asks you to show the effect on a break-even chart of a rise in variable costs, you must also adjust the total cost line. This is shown in Figure 35.7 – though in relation to Aromatics, not cocoa beans.

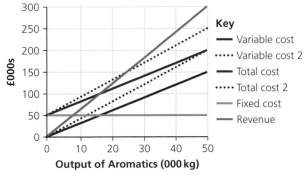

Figure 35.7 A rise in variable costs

Fall in fixed costs

If a company's sales are falling, it may be necessary to cut fixed costs in order to lower the break-even point. The fall in fixed costs will cut the total costs. All these things are indicated in Figure 35.8.

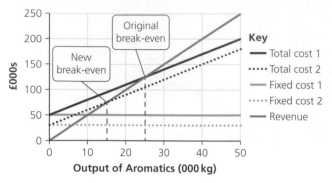

Figure 35.8 A fall in fixed costs

Evaluation

Summary of possible changes to the break-even chart to look out for in an exam:

1 Prices can go up or down. If a price is increased, the revenue line starts in the same place but rises more steeply.

2 Fixed costs can rise or fall, so you may have to draw a new horizontal line. But remember that a change to fixed costs will also affect the total cost line.

3 Variable costs can rise or fall. An increase will make the variable cost line rise more steeply, though it will still start at the same point – at the fixed cost line. A change in variable costs will change the total costs line as well.

Note that each of these three changes will alter the break-even point.

'Because break-even points shift as conditions change, break-even analyses should be performed regularly, preferably on a quarterly basis.'

35.7 Interpretation of break-even charts

Break-even analysis is simple to understand; it is particularly useful for small and newly established businesses, where the managers may not be able to employ more sophisticated techniques. Businesses can use break-even to:

● estimate the future level of output they will need to produce and sell in order to meet given profit objectives
● assess the impact of planned price changes upon profit and the level of output needed to break even
● take decisions on whether to produce their own products or components or whether to purchase from external sources.

Key factors in interpreting break-even charts include:

● understanding that profit can be estimated as the vertical difference between the revenue line and the total costs line at any single level of output
● acknowledging that no company really has static sales – that is, the same sales level per month or per year – yet this is what the break-even chart assumes; it is important to remember that the chart is just a snapshot of a point in time, when sales happen to be at a particular level.

35.8 Limitations of break-even analysis

The limitations of break-even analysis are set out below.

● The model is a simplification. It assumes that variable costs increase constantly, which ignores the benefits of bulk buying. If a firm negotiates lower prices for purchasing larger quantities of raw materials, then its total cost line will no longer be straight.
● Similarly, break-even analysis assumes the firm sells all its output at a single price. In reality, firms frequently offer discounts for bulk purchases.
● A major flaw in the technique is that it assumes that all output is sold. In times of low demand, a firm may have difficulty in selling all that it produces.
● The most important practical limitation, though, is that it is a static model. It does not take sales trends into account, so it is only true at a point in time. If the horizontal axis represented time instead of quantity, one could show sales trends and therefore have an idea about possible future profits or losses.

Five whys and a how

Questions	Answers
Why might a business want to calculate its margin of safety?	To know how much of a cushion it has between current (profitable) sales and the break-even point.
Why might a sales revenue line pivot more steeply (to the left), even though it will start at £0 = 0 units?	Because there has been a price increase.
Why might a cut in variable costs affect the total costs line?	Total costs consists of fixed costs plus variable costs, so of course a change in variable costs will change the total costs line.
Why might it be useful to calculate profit using contribution instead of revenue minus total costs?	It is significantly quicker, and time has a substantial opportunity cost in exam conditions.
Why might it be hard for a brand new business to use break-even analysis effectively?	Because the entrepreneurs cannot yet be sure of running costs or revenues – making the exercise a bit of a guess.
How is the margin of safety calculated?	Sales volume *minus* break-even output.

35.9 Break-even – evaluation

There is a risk in exams of assuming that break-even charts tell you 'facts'. Break-even analysis seems simple to conduct and understand. That assumes the business knows all its costs and can break them down into variable and fixed. Coca-Cola certainly can, but not every business is as well managed. Football clubs such as Sheffield Wednesday, Portsmouth and Darlington have hit financial problems partly because of ignorance of their financial circumstances. Similarly, few NHS hospitals could say with confidence how much it costs to provide a heart transplant.

Break-even analysis is of particular value when a business is first established. Having to work out the fixed and variable costs will help the managers to make better decisions, for example, on pricing. As long as the figures are accurate, break-even becomes especially useful when changes occur, such as rising raw material costs. The technique can allow for changing revenues and costs and gives a valuable guide to potential profitability.

Key formulae

Break-even output: $\dfrac{\text{Fixed costs}}{\text{Contribution per unit}}$

Contribution per unit: Selling price – Variable costs per unit

Margin of safety: Sales volume – Break-even output

Total contribution: Contribution per unit × unit sales

Key terms

Break-even chart: a line graph showing total revenues and total costs at all possible levels of output or demand from zero to maximum capacity.

Contribution: this is total revenue less variable costs. The calculation of contribution is useful for businesses that are responsible for a range of products.

Fixed costs: those that do not change as the number of sales change (for example, rent or salaries).

Margin of safety: the amount by which current output exceeds the level of output necessary to break-even.

Variable costs: those that change in line with the amount of business (for example, the cost of buying raw materials).

35.10 Workbook

Revision questions

(25 marks; 25 minutes)

1 What is meant by the term 'break-even point'? (2)

2 State three reasons why a business may conduct a break-even analysis. (3)

3 List the information necessary to construct a break-even chart. (4)

4 How would you calculate the contribution made by each unit of production that is sold? (2)

5 A business sells its products for £10 each and the variable cost of producing a single unit is £6. If its monthly fixed costs are £18,000, how many units must it sell to break even each month? (3)

6 Explain why the variable cost and total revenue lines commence at the origin of a break-even chart. (3)

7 What point on a break-even chart actually illustrates break-even output? (2)

8 Explain how, using a break-even chart, you would illustrate the amount of profit or loss made at any given level of output. (2)

9 Why might a business wish to calculate its margin of safety? (2)

10 A business is currently producing 200,000 units of output annually, and its break-even output is 120,000 units. What is its margin of safety? (2)

Data response 1

An entrepreneur's first hotel

Paul Jarvis is an entrepreneur and about to open his first hotel. He has forecast the following costs and revenues:

- Maximum number of customers per month: 800
- Monthly fixed costs: £10,000
- Average revenue per customer: £110
- Typical variable costs per customer: £90

Some secondary market research has suggested that Paul's prices may be too low. He is considering charging higher prices, though he is nervous about the impact this might have on his forecast sales. Paul has found his break-even chart useful during the planning of his new business, but is concerned that it might be misleading too.

Questions (45 marks, 45 minutes)

1 a) Construct the break-even chart for Paul's planned business. (9)

b) State, and show on the graph, the profit or loss made at a monthly sales level of 600 customers. (4)

c) State, and show on the graph, the margin of safety at that level of output (4)

2 Paul's market research shows that in his first month of trading he can expect 450 customers at his hotel.

a) If Paul's research is correct, calculate the level of profit or loss he will make. (5)

b) Illustrate this level of output on your graph and show the profit or loss. (3)

3 Paul has decided to increase his prices to give an average revenue per customer of £120.

a) Draw the new total revenue line on your break-even chart to show the effect of this change. (3)

b) Mark on your diagram the new break-even point. (1)

c) Calculate Paul's new break-even number of customers to confirm the result shown on your chart. (6)

4 Paul is worried that his break-even chart may be 'misleading'. Do you agree with him? Justify your view. (10)

Data response 2

The Successful T-Shirt Company

Shelley has recently launched the Successful T-Shirt Company. It sells a small range of fashion t-shirts. The shirts are available in a range of colours and contain the company's logo, which is becoming increasingly desirable for young fashion-conscious people.

The shirts are sold to retailers for £35 each. They cost £16.50 to manufacture and the salesperson receives £2.50 commission for each item sold to retailers. The distribution cost for each shirt is £1.00 and current sales are 1,000 per month. The fixed costs of production are £11,250 per month.

The company is considering expanding its range of t-shirts and has approached its bank for a loan. The bank has requested that the company draw up a business plan including a cash flow forecast and break-even chart.

Questions (30 marks, 30 minutes)

1 What is meant by the term 'break-even chart'? (2)

2 Calculate the following:

a) the variable cost of producing 1,000 t-shirts

b) the contribution earned through the sale of one t-shirt. (6)

3 Shelley has decided to manufacture the shirts in Poland. As a result, the variable cost per t-shirt (including commission and distribution costs) will fall to £15 per t-shirt. However, fixed costs will rise to £12,000.

　　a) Calculate the new level of break-even for Shelley's t-shirts.

b) Calculate the margin of safety if sales are 1,000 t-shirts per month. (10)

4 Assess whether Shelley should rely on break-even analysis when taking business decisions. Justify your view. (12)

Data response 3

Start-up break-even analysis

On 27 September 2013, Mary's Garden opened in Raynes Park, south London. Mary's Garden is a Japanese restaurant. It opened without any fanfare; without even putting a menu outside for passers-by. This was because, as at 1.30 that afternoon, 'we haven't decided on the prices yet'. Amazingly, at 7.30 that evening, every table was taken.

The premises had been unused for more than a year, since an Indian restaurant closed down. Accordingly, Mary's had been able to negotiate a stunningly low rent: £1,000 per month; business rates of £500 a month must be added, however. By Monday 30 September, Mary had been able to estimate a probable average spend of £40 per customer, of which £15 goes on food costs and another £5 on other variable costs. With staffing costs of £5,000 a month and other monthly fixed costs amounting to £1,500, Mary's Garden has most of the information required for a break-even chart.

There remains one difficult issue, though: what is the maximum capacity level of the restaurant? Amazingly, the current opening times are from 9.00am to 11.00pm; it surely is the only Japanese restaurant in suburbia offering a breakfast menu. The restaurant itself is small, with just 25 seats. Theoretically, it could fill them lots of times in 14 hours, but it seems wise to bet on a maximum of just 50 customers per day, six days a week, so 1,200 a month.

For break-even analysis, the above is sufficient, but for real business insight there is one more critical variable: the actual level of customer demand. In conversation with Mary's son, it emerged that no research has been done into this. My own local knowledge suggests that it should be full on Friday and Saturday evenings, a third full on Monday–Thursday and gain a smattering of breakfast and lunchtime customers (until this loss-making approach is stopped). Overall, my estimate is for 500 customers a month.

Questions (20 marks; 25 minutes)

1 Calculate the total:

　　a) monthly fixed costs

　　b) variable costs per customer

　　c) contribution per customer. (3)

2 Calculate the monthly:

　　a) break-even number of customers

　　b) margin of safety based on estimated customer numbers. (5)

3 Outline three ways in which Mary's Garden's margin of safety could be expanded. (6)

4 a) Calculate the monthly profit based on the estimated number of customers. (3)

　　b) Calculate the monthly profit if customer numbers prove to be 50 per cent higher. (3)

Extended writing

1 Evaluate the different ways in which break-even analysis might benefit a new small business offering Thai food for takeaway and delivery. (20)

2 Evaluate the extent to which break-even analysis might be of value when running a business such as Primark, or any other business you have researched. (20)

36 Budgets

> **Definition**
>
> A budget is a target for costs or revenue that a firm or department must aim to reach over a given period of time. An **income budget** sets a floor, i.e. a minimum target, while an **expenditure budget** sets a ceiling, e.g. a maximum target for costs.

Linked to: Planning and cash flow, Ch 32; Sales forecasting, Ch 33.

36.1 The purpose of budgets

Budgeting is used:

- to ensure that no department or individual spends more than the company expects, thereby preventing unpleasant surprises
- to provide a yardstick against which a manager's success or failure can be measured (and rewarded)

  For example, a store manager may have to meet a monthly sales budget of £25,000 at a maximum operating cost of £18,000. As long as the budget holder believes this target is possible, the attempt to achieve it will be motivating. The company can then provide bonuses for achieving or beating the profit target.

- to enable spending power to be delegated to local managers, who are in a better position to know how best to use the firm's money; this should improve and speed up the decision-making process and help to motivate the local budget holders

  Management expert Peter Drucker refers to 'management by self-control'. He regards this as the ideal approach. Managers should have clear targets, clear budgets and the power to decide how to achieve them. Then they will try their hardest to succeed.

- to motivate the staff in a department – budget figures can be used as a clear basis for assessing staff performance; then staff know what they must achieve in order to be considered successful.

'The budget is our guide. It tells us what we're supposed to do for the year. We couldn't get along without it.'

Jim Bell, US factory manager

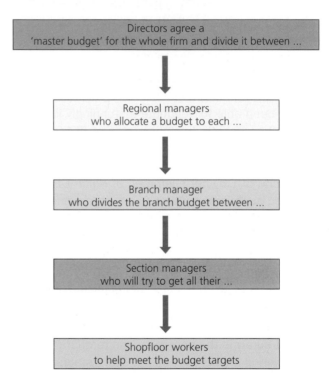

Figure 36.1 Budget holders

> **Real business**
>
> ### The BP disaster
>
> On 23 March 2005, a huge explosion at BP's Texas oil refinery killed 15 people and injured more than 180. Most were the company's own staff. After an inquiry, the chairwoman of the US Chemical Safety Board reported that 'BP implemented a 25 per cent cut on fixed costs from 1998 to 2000 that adversely impacted maintenance expenditures at the refinery'.

36.2 How to construct a budget

Budgeting is the process of setting targets, covering all aspects of costs and revenues. It is a method for turning a firm's strategy into reality. Nothing can be done in business without money; budgets tell individual managers how much they can spend to achieve their objectives. For instance, a football manager may be given a transfer expenditure budget of £20 million to buy players. With the budget in place, the transfer dealing can get under way.

A budgeting system shows how much can be spent per time period and gives managers a way to check whether they are on track. Most firms use a system of budgetary control as a means of supervision. The process is as follows:

1 Make a judgement of the likely sales revenues for the coming year.

2 Set a cost ceiling that allows for an acceptable level of profit.

3 The budget for the whole company's costs is then broken down by division, department or by cost centre.

4 The budget may then be broken down further so that each manager has a budget and therefore some spending power.

In a business start-up, the budget should provide enough spending power to finance vital needs such as building work, decoration, recruiting and paying staff, and marketing. If a manager overspends in one area, she or he knows that it is essential to cut back elsewhere. A good manager gets the best possible value from the budgeted sum.

36.3 Types of budget

Historical budget

Setting budgets is not an easy job. How do you decide exactly what level of sales are likely next year, especially for new businesses with no previous trading to rely on? Furthermore, how can you plan for costs if the cost of your raw materials tends to fluctuate? Most firms treat last year's budget figures as the main determinant of this year's budget. Minor adjustments will be made for inflation and other foreseeable changes.

As a new school year approaches, a Head of Business will be told the department's budget for the coming year. Usually it will just be last year's plus a percentage or two for inflation, but if a new syllabus is coming in (as in 2015) there should be a budget increase to allow for new textbooks and other resources to be purchased.

Zero-based budget

An alternative approach is zero-based budgeting. This sets each department's budget at zero and demands that budget holders, in setting their budget, justify every pound they ask for. This helps to avoid the common phenomenon of budgets creeping upwards each year.

The only serious drawback to **zero budgeting** is that it takes a long time to find good reasons to justify why you need a budget of £150,000 instead of £110,000. As it is so time-consuming for managers, it is sensible to use zero budgeting every few years, rather than every year. Figure 36.2 shows the benefits of this approach.

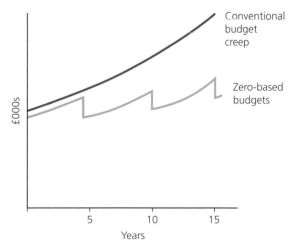

Figure 36.2 The benefits of zero budgeting

The best **criteria** for setting budgets are:

- to relate the budget directly to the business objective; if a company wants to increase sales and market share, the best method may be to increase the advertising budget and thereby boost demand
- to involve as many people as possible in the process; people will be more committed to reaching the targets if they have had a say in how the budget was set.

Simple budget statements

A simple example of a budget statement is shown in Table 36.1.

	January	February	March
Income	25,000	28,000	30,000
Variable costs	10,000	12,000	13,000
Fixed costs	10,000	10,000	11,000
Total expenditure	20,000	22,000	24,000
Profit	5,000	6,000	6,000

Table 36.1 Example of a budget statement

This information is only of value if it proves possible for a manager to believe that these figures are achievable. Only then will she or he be motivated to try to turn the budgets into reality.

> 'Any jackass can draw up a balanced budget on paper.'
>
> Lane Kirkland, US trade union president

36.4 Variance analysis

Variance is the amount by which the actual result differs from the budgeted figure. It is usually measured each month, by comparing the actual outcome with the budgeted one. It is important to note that variances are referred to as adverse or favourable – not positive or negative. A **favourable variance** is one that leads to higher than expected profit (revenue up or costs down). An **adverse variance** is one that reduces profit, such as costs being higher than the budgeted level. Table 36.2 shows when variances are adverse or favourable.

Variable	Budget	Actual	Variance	
Sales of X	150	160	10	Favourable
Sales of Y	150	145	(5)	Adverse
Material costs	100	90	10	Favourable
Labour costs	100	105	(5)	Adverse

Table 36.2 Adverse or favourable variance?

The value of regular variance statements is that they provide an early warning. If a product's sales are slipping below budget, managers can respond by increasing marketing support or by cutting back on production plans. In an ideal world, slippage could be noted in March, a new strategy put into place by May and a recovery in sales achieved by September. Clearly, no firm wishes to wait until the end-of-year to find out that things went badly. An early warning can lead to an early solution.

36.5 Analysing budgets and variances

When significant variances occur, management should first consider whether the fault was in the budget or in the actual achievement. In January 2014, Nintendo apologised to shareholders that it was cutting the sales budget for its Wii U from 9 million units to 2.8 million in the period to the end of March 2014. That is a cut of about 70 per cent! Nintendo's management decided that its budget was at fault and it would not therefore blame its marketing managers. The launch of the PS4 had been known about, but Nintendo never expected it to be so successful.

When adverse variances occur, senior managers are likely to want to hear an explanation from the responsible 'line manager'. He or she will need to have a clear explanation about what has gone wrong. Clearly, if recession has hit sales throughout a market, it will be easy to explain adverse income variances. Far tougher is when the blame lies with falling market share rather than market size.

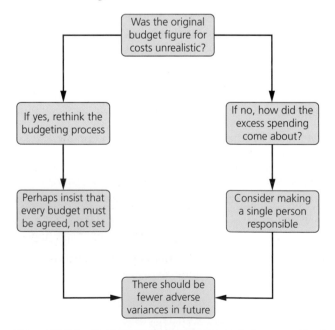

Figure 36.3 Logic chain: making variance analysis more effective

36.6 Difficulties of budgeting

Budgeting is used very widely in organisations – corporate and in the public sector. But it isn't always appropriate. Chessington World of Adventures uses budgeting for its catering outlets and its shops. But the overwhelming factor determining sales is outside the control of the managers: the weather. So a manager given a target of boosting sales in June by 5 per cent may quickly find that rain has made that impossible, in which case, the budget becomes either an irritation or a source of stress.

> '[Budgets] must not be prepared on high and caste as pearls before swine. They must be prepared by the operating divisions.'
>
> Robert Townsend, the original business guru

Businesses need to decide whether designing and implementing a budgeting system will cost more in terms of time and money than it could save, in other words assess the opportunity costs. In the often chaotic world of a small business start-up, it is easy to see how time spent talking to customers and suppliers would be more valuable than working on a spreadsheet.

Five whys and a how

Questions	Answers
Why are budgets used in most organisations?	To keep costs under control while allowing some degree of **delegation** of power.
Why may over-optimistic revenue budgets be demoralising?	Because managers feel they are being set up to fail.
Why might an adverse cost variance be forgivable?	If it is a new product or a new technique, there is a learning curve for staff to climb.
Why might it be wise to re-set budgets during the middle of a financial year?	If variances have been high, perhaps the original budgets were wrongly set – so now is the time to try to get them right.
Why should positive variances be investigated?	Because you need to understand why things have gone well in order to achieve the same again.
How are variances calculated?	By comparing the actual data to the forecast data.

36.7 Budgets – evaluation

The sophistication of budgeting systems is usually directly linked to the size of a business. Huge multinationals have incredibly complex budgeting systems. For a small business start-up, any budgeting system will be quite simple. Most will rely on a rough breakdown of how the start-up budget is to be divided between the competing demands. There is, however, no doubt that budgeting provides a more effective system of controlling a business's finances than no system at all.

Budgets are a management tool. The way in which they are used can tell you a lot about a firm's culture. Firms with a culture of bossy management will tend to use a tightly controlled budgetary system. Managers will have budgets imposed upon them and variances will be watched closely by supervisors. Organisations with a more open culture will use budgeting as an aid to discussion and empowerment. Whatever the culture, if a manager is to be held accountable for meeting a budget, she or he should be given influence over setting it, and control over reaching it.

Key terms

Adverse variance: a difference between budgeted and actual figures that is damaging to the firm's profit (for example, costs up or revenue down).

Criteria: yardsticks against which success (or the lack of it) can be measured.

Delegation: passing authority down the hierarchy, to allow more junior employees some decision-making power.

Expenditure budget: setting a maximum figure on what a department or manager can spend over a period of time; this is to control costs.

Favourable variance: a difference between budgeted and actual figures that boosts a firm's profit (for example, revenue up or costs down).

Income budget: setting a minimum figure for the revenue to be generated by a product, a department or a manager.

Zero budgeting: setting all future budgets at £0, to force managers to have to justify the spending levels they say they need in future.

36.8 Workbook

Revision questions

(45 marks; 45 minutes)

1 Explain the meaning of the term 'budgeting'. (3)

2 List three advantages that a budgeting system brings to a company. (3)

3 Why is it valuable to have a yardstick against which performance can be measured? (3)

4 What are the advantages of a zero-based budgeting system? (4)

5 Briefly explain how most companies actually set next year's budgets. (3)

6 Why should budget holders have a say in the setting of their budgets? (4)

	January	February	March	April
Income	4,200	4,500	4,000	
Variable costs	1,800		2,000	1,800
Fixed costs	1,200	1,600		1,600
Total costs		3,600	4,100	
Profit				600

Table 36.3 A budget statement

7 Copy and complete the budget statement shown in Table 36.3 by filling in the gaps. (8)

8 How could a firm respond to an increasingly adverse variance in labour costs? (4)

9 Explain what is meant by a 'favourable cost variance'. (3)

10 Look at Table 36.4, then answer the following questions.

	May		June	
	Budgeted	Actual	Budgeted	Actual
Revenue	3,500	3,200	4,000	4,200
Variable costs	1,000	900	1,200	1,500
Fixed costs	1,200	1,200	1,300	1,100
Total costs	2,200	2,100	2,500	2,600
Profit				

Table 36.4 Budgeted and actual figures for May and June

a) Calculate the budgeted and actual profit figures for both months. (2)

b) Identify a month with:

  i) a favourable revenue variance

  ii) an adverse variable cost variance

  iii) a favourable fixed cost variance

  iv) an adverse total cost variance

  v) an adverse revenue variance

  vi) a favourable total cost variance

  vii) an adverse profit variance

  viii) a favourable profit variance. (8)

Data response 1

	January			February		
	B	A	V	B	A	V
Sales revenue	140	150	10	180	175	?
Materials	70	80	(10)	90	95	?
Other direct costs	30	35	(5)	40	40	0
Overheads	20	20	0	25	22	?
Profit	20	15	(5)	?	18	?

Table 36.5 Variance analysis (all figures in £000s)
B budgeted,
A actual,
V variance.

Questions (25 marks; 25 minutes)

1 Give the five numbers missing from the variance analysis shown in Table 36.5. (5)

2 Assess one financial strength and two weaknesses in these data, from the company's viewpoint. (12)

3 Assess two ways in which a manager might set about improving the accuracy of a sales budget. (8)

Data response 2

	January		February		March		April	
	B	A	B	A	B	A	B	A
Sales revenue	160	144	180	156	208	168	240	188
Materials	40	38	48	44	52	48	58	54
Labour	52	48	60	54	66	62	72	68
Overheads	76	76	76	78	76	80	76	80
Profit	(8)	(18)	(4)	(20)	14	(22)	34	(14)

Table 36.6 Budget data for Clinton & Collins Ltd (£000s)

Questions (25 marks; 25 minutes)

1 Use the data given in Table 36.6 to explain why February's profits were worse than expected. (5)

2 Explain why Clinton & Collins Ltd may have chosen to set monthly budgets. (4)

3 Explain how the firm could have set these budgets. (4)

4 The directors of Clinton & Collins Ltd knew that the recession was causing problems for the firm but were unsure as to whether things were improving or worsening. Assess the extent to which the data suggests an improvement. (12)

Data response 3

Chessington World of Adventures

In April 2014, Chessington World of Adventures opened up for its summer season. The newly appointed merchandise manager (in charge of all non-food sales) was given his sales budget for the year. It had been set 4 per cent higher than for 2013. He thought the budget was quite ambitious, especially when a wet April and May meant that there were fewer visitors in the early part of the season. Then the period July to August saw hot, dry weather and the turnstiles were 'buzzing' again. As a hot day at Chessington can boost crowds by 50 per cent, the merchandise manager did not need to make any effort to meet his budget.

Questions (20 marks; 25 minutes)

1 Explain two other ways in which management might have constructed the sales budget for 2014. (4)

2 On a particularly hot week in August, the actual sales figures were 41 per cent higher than the budget. Did the merchandise manager deserve a bonus? (4)

3 Assess whether budgets have a purpose in a business such as Chessington. (12)

Extended writing

1 'Budgeting systems can often be demotivating for middle managers.' Evaluate the extent to which this might be true. (20)

2 Evaluate whether it is true to suggest that budgets are the most important financial documents for most managers. (20)

37 Profit

> **Definition**
>
> Profit is the difference between revenue and all the costs involved in generating that revenue. It is the food that enables the business to grow.

Linked to: Sources of finance, Ch 30; Sales, revenue and costs, Ch 34; Break-even, Ch 35; Liquidity, Ch 38.

37.1 Calculating gross profit, operating profit and profit for the year

Profit can be calculated in many different ways. For most business purposes, though, it is enough to know gross profit, operating profit and net profit (the after-tax profit for the year).

Each type of profit is calculated after allowing for different types of cost. This is useful to the business because it

can help identify where things are going wrong (or right). For example, coffee bars charge £s for coffee that costs pence to make. So their gross profit level is huge. Unfortunately, spacious seating in expensive high street locations means big rents and therefore more modest operating profits. Table 37.1 sets out the calculations and implications, based on the annual accounts of a small, independent bakery.

37.2 Statement of comprehensive income (profit and loss account)

Large businesses established as public limited companies (plcs) are required to state their annual profits in a document called a 'statement of comprehensive income'. Most businesspeople call this the 'profit and loss account' or 'P&L'. The document sets out the revenues generated in the year together with many lines of detail about the

Item	Figure (£S)	Method of calculation	Comment
Revenue	220,000		The value of all the sales to customers
Cost of sales	(70,000)*		The cost of the flour, sugar, yeast and other raw materials
Gross profit	**150,000**	Revenue – cost of sales	
Fixed overheads	(100,000)		Cost of rent, salaries and bills, such as electricity and advertising
Operating profit	**50,000**	Gross profit – **fixed overheads**	
Net financing cost	(5,000)		Interest paid on a bank loan
Corporation tax	(9,000)		Small firms pay 20 per cent corporation (profit) tax
Profit for the year (net profit)	**36,000**	Operating profit – financing and tax	

*Accountants use brackets () to show when a number needs to be deducted

Table 37.1 Annual accounts of an independent bakery

costs incurred. From this can be read a series of different types of profit. The most important are the gross profit, the operating profit and the after-tax net profit. The last shows how much the directors can pay out in shareholder **dividends** and how much will be left to reinvest in the growth of the business.

> 'Market leadership can translate directly to higher revenue, higher profitability, greater capital velocity, and correspondingly stronger returns on invested capital.'
>
> Jeff Bezos, founder of Amazon

Table 37.2 shows a simplified version of Ted Baker plc's 2014 statement of comprehensive income, to help show how these three levels of profit are calculated.

Accounting item	Figure (£ms)	Method of calculation	Comment
Revenue	322.0		The value of all the sales made in the financial year
Cost of sales	(123.5)		The cost of the clothes Ted buys in
Gross profit	**198.5**	Revenue – cost of sales	
Fixed overheads	(159.0)		Cost of running the stores and head office
Operating profit	**39.5**	Gross profit – fixed overheads	
Net financing cost	(0.6)		
Corporation tax	(10.0)		Unlike some, Ted pays his taxes
Profit for the year (net profit)	**28.9**	Operating profit – financing and tax	

Table 37.2 Ted Baker plc's 2014 statement of comprehensive income

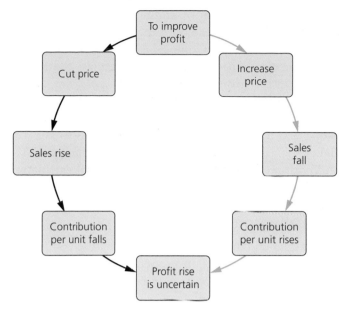

Figure 37.1 Logic chain: difficult to increase profit

▌37.3 Measuring profitability

The gross profit of a business is an absolute number (e.g. £10,000). The number is calculated by deducting direct costs from sales revenue. Is £10,000 a good level of profit or not? To find out, it is helpful to measure the profit in relation to the sales revenue. This gives a relative measure of profit known as profitability. Marks & Spencer makes far more profit than Ted Baker, but so it should – it has far, far more shops and staff. When you calculate their profits as a percentage of sales, Ted Baker makes about twice as much per £ of sales as M&S. So Marks & Spencer makes more profit, but Ted Baker is more profitable.

Profitability can be measured for each of the three types of profit identified earlier in the chapter: gross, operating and net.

This is the gross profit margin:

$$\text{Gross profit margin} = \frac{\text{gross profit}}{\text{sales revenue}} \times 100$$

For example, if the gross profit is £10,000 and the sales are £40,000, the gross profit margin is:

$$\frac{£10,000}{£40,000} \times 100 = 25\%$$

Having turned the profit figure into a percentage, a comparison can be made with the profitability achieved by other companies. Comparing fashion retailers Ted Baker plc and Supergroup plc, for example: the former made a 2014 gross margin of 61.5 per cent, while Supergroup's margins were 59.7 per cent. Both figures are remarkably high, confirming the strength of the Ted Baker and SuperDry brand names. Needless to say, Ted Baker's is a little more impressive than Supergroup's – and both are hugely better than the original calculation of 25 per cent.

Operating profit margin

When City and media analysts are evaluating companies, the number they focus on is operating profit. And then they take that as a percentage of revenue to calculate the operating profit margin:

$$\text{Operating profit margin} = \frac{\text{operating profit}}{\text{sales revenue}} \times 100$$

For example, if the operating profit is £3,000 and the sales are £40,000 the operating margin is:

$$\frac{£3,000}{£40,000} \times 100 = 7.5\%$$

Having turned the profit figure into a percentage, a comparison can be made with the profitability achieved by other companies, or looking at one company over time. In 2014, Ted Baker plc had an operating margin of 12.3 per cent. Sainsbury's, by contrast, had a 2014 operating margin of just 3.3 per cent. As the businesses operate in different types of retailing, it would be unfair to conclude that Ted Baker is better run than Sainsbury's. Nevertheless, the management of Sainsbury's would be interested in such findings (for example, it may make Sainsbury's determined to boost their sales of clothing).

Real business

If a business cannot make a reasonable operating profit, it has no chance of long-term survival. A good example is Blockbuster UK. In its 2010 financial year, it made an operating profit that was less than 1 per cent of its sales. Since then, with sales falling as the DVD market declined, operating profits of £1.7 million slipped to losses of £8.5 million in 2011 and £11.2 million in 2012 before collapse in 2013. The final Blockbuster stores closed by early 2014.

Net profit margin

$$\text{Net profit margin} = \frac{\text{profit for the year}}{\text{sales revenue}} \times 100$$

For example, if the profit after tax is £2,000 and the sales are £40,000, the net profit margin is:

$$\frac{£2,000}{£40,000} \times 100 = 5\%$$

Although this percentage figure can be compared with the profitability achieved by other companies, it is hard to interpret the findings. A company might have a relatively high net margin because it has been aggressive in tax avoidance. If, the following year, the tax authorities closed the loophole being used by the company, their tax bill would rise and net profits fall – perhaps sharply. This is why media analysis of company profits focuses on profit before tax – this is operating profit margins.

37.4 The value of measuring profit margins

The calculation of profit margins allows questions to be asked, and sometimes answered. Table 37.3 provides data on Tesco plc over time, and then shows Tesco versus Sainsbury's and Morrisons. Over time, it is clear that Tesco's profitability has fallen steadily. Nevertheless, in 2014, despite Sainsbury's steady improvement in its operating profit margin, Tesco remained significantly more profitable. As for Morrisons, in 2014 it made operating losses rather than profits. So, up until 2014, there were positives in Tesco's profitability as well as (well publicised) negatives.

	Tesco (UK only)	Sainsbury's	Morrisons
2009	6.65%	3.0%	4.6%
2010	6.2%	3.1%	5.3%
2011	6.15%	3.2%	5.5%
2012	5.8%	3.2%	5.5%
2013	5.2%	3.25%	5.2%
2014	5.0%	3.3%	(0.55%)

Table 37.3 Trading profit margins in the UK grocery market

'I generally disagree with most of the very high margin opportunities. Why? Because it's a business strategy tradeoff: the lower the margin you take, the faster you grow.'

Vinod Khosla, Indian billionaire entrepreneur

37.5 Ways to improve profits

To increase profits a business must:

1 increase revenue

2 decrease costs

3 do a combination of 1 and 2.

To increase revenue, a business may want to consider its marketing mix. Changes to the product may mean that it becomes more appealing to customers. Better distribution may make it more available. Changes to promotion may make customers more aware of its benefits. However, the business needs to be careful that rising costs do not swallow up the rise in sales revenues.

To reduce costs, a business may examine many of the functional areas (such as marketing, operations, people and finance):

- Could the firm continue with fewer staff?
- Could money be saved by switching suppliers?
- Do the firm's sales really benefit from sponsoring the opera?
- Are there ways of reducing wastage?

Essentially, a business should look for ways of making the product more efficiently (for example, with better technology) by using fewer inputs or paying less for the inputs being used. However, a business must be careful that, when it reduces costs, the quality of service is not reduced. After all, this might lead to a fall in sales and revenue. Cutting staff in your coffee shop may cut costs, but if long queues form it may also reduce the number of customers and your income. Managers must weigh up the consequences of any decision to reduce costs.

Real business

Vietnam as a production base

Average wages in Vietnam are lower than those of two of its neighbours: Thailand and China. Vietnamese factory workers earn just two-thirds of what their colleagues in China take home (about 65p an hour compared with £1 in China).

Companies such as Foxconn, which assembles consumer electronics and phones for big-brand companies like Apple and Sony, operate on very low profit margins and so try to find the lowest cost location they can. This makes Vietnam very attractive as a production base. Even high profit-margin businesses such as Nike are shifting production to Vietnam, simply to keep costs down and therefore margins up.

37.6 Ways to improve profitability

Profitability (as opposed to 'profits') is a relative term. It is mainly measured using the operating profit margin. To increase operating profits in relation to sales, a business could do the following.

Increase the price

Increasing the price would boost the profit per sale, but the danger is that the sales overall may fall so much that the overall profits of the business are reduced. (Notice the important difference again between the operating profit margin and the overall level of profits; you could make a high level of profit on one can of beans relative to its price, but if you only sell one can your total profits are not that impressive!) The impact of any price increase will depend on the price elasticity of demand; the more price elastic demand is, the greater the fall in demand will be, and the less likely it is that a firm will want to put up its prices.

Cut costs

If cutting costs can be done without damaging the quality in any significant way, then this clearly makes sense. Better bargaining to get the supply prices down or better ways of producing may lead to higher profits per sale. However, as we saw above, the business needs to be careful to ensure that reducing costs does not lead to a deterioration of the service or quality of the product.

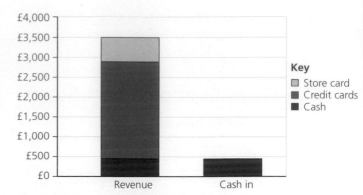

Figure 37.2 Saturday takings at a clothing outlet

37.7 Distinction between profit and cash

A year ago, a busy bar in Wimbledon closed down. Regulars were surprised, shocked even, that such a successful business had failed. The business was operating profitably, but the owners had become too excited by their success. Their investment into two new bars elsewhere in London had drained too much cash from the business, and the bank had panicked over the mounting debts. It forced the business to close. A profitable business had run out of cash.

> 'Revenue is vanity... profit is sanity... cash is King.'
>
> Anon

To understand how cash differs from profit, the key is to master profit. On the face of it, profit is easy: total revenue *minus* total costs. Common sense tells you that revenue = money in, and costs = money out. Unfortunately, that is far too much of a simplification.

To understand the difference, it is helpful to look separately at the two components.

Distinguishing revenue from cash inflow

Revenue is *not* the same as money in. Revenue is the value of sales made over a specified period: a day, a month or a year. For example, the takings at a Topshop outlet last Saturday: £450 of cash sales, £2,450 on credit cards and £600 on the Topshop store card (£3,500 in total). Note that the cash inflow for the day is just £450, so revenue is not the same as 'cash in'. See Figure 37.2.

Whereas revenue comes from just one source (customers), cash inflow can come from many sources. It is not limited to trading. Selling an old warehouse for £600,000 does not generate revenue, but it does bring in cash. Similarly, taking out a bank loan could not be classed as revenue, but it does put cash into your bank current account.

So cash inflows *can* be part of the revenue, but they do not have to be. Therefore, cash and revenue are not the same. Examples of differences between cash inflows and revenue are given in Table 37.4.

Financial item	Cash inflow	Revenue
Cash sales made to customers	✓	✓
Credit sales made to customers	✗	✓
Capital raised from share sales	✓	✗
Charge rent on flat upstairs	✓	✓
Take out a £20,000 bank loan	✓	✗
Carry out a sale and leaseback	✓	✗

Table 37.4 Differences between cash inflows and revenue

Distinguishing costs from cash outflow

The same distinction applies to costs and cash outflows. There are many reasons why a firm might pay out cash. Paying for the business costs is only one of them. For example, the firm may pay out dividends to its shareholders, or it may repay a bank loan, or it may buy a piece of land as an investment.

In the case of the Wimbledon bar, the £200,000 annual profit gave the owners the confidence to buy leases on two new premises. They put together a business plan for expansion and received a £90,000 bank loan plus an £80,000 overdraft facility from a high street bank. They then hired architects and builders to turn the premises into attractive bars. Unfortunately, building hitches added to costs while delaying the opening times. The first of the new bars opened without any marketing support (there was no spare cash) and with the second of the bars still draining the business of cash, the bank demanded to have its overdraft repaid. As there was no way to repay the overdraft, the business went into liquidation.

> 'Every calculation of net profit reflects choices from competing theories of accounting... Profit is an opinion, cash is a fact.'
>
> Alex Pollock, American Enterprise Institute

37.8 Profit – evaluation

A difficulty with questions about poor profits is that many suggestions made in exams are too obvious. Sainsbury's has a significantly lower profit margin than Tesco. But is it worth pointing out to Sainsbury's that it could look for bulk-buying discounts on its supplies? Surely it will be doing that already. A good exam answer needs to look beyond the obvious to consider, perhaps, that Sainsbury's may have to address its head office (fixed overhead) costs in order to boost its margins to match those of Tesco.

Key terms

Corporation tax: a levy on the incomes of companies, i.e. you pay a percentage of your pre-tax profit.

Dividends: annual payments made to shareholders.

Fixed overheads: the indirect costs that have to be paid however the business is performing, e.g. rent and salaries.

Five whys and a how

Questions	Answers
Why might Sainsbury's want to compare its gross profit margin with Tesco?	To see which is creating a wider gap between costs paid to suppliers and prices charged to customers.
What's the difference between gross profit and operating profit?	Fixed overheads.
Why is 'profitability' looked at separately from 'profit'?	Because profit is an absolute (number), whereas profitability is a relative figure (e.g. as a percentage of revenue).
Why is 'profit for the year' so important to companies?	Because it pays for dividends and reinvestment; both are crucial for financing long-term growth.
Why is it important to fair, long-term competition that every company should pay the same percentage rate of corporation tax?	If Ted Baker pays up but rivals find ways to avoid tax, in the long run the competitors will keep more profit for the year, be able to invest more and therefore have an unfair advantage.
How might a struggling firm attempt to increase its operating profitability?	By squeezing supply costs a bit more or by acting on fixed overhead costs, e.g. moving head office to somewhere smaller and cheaper.

37.9 Workbook

Revision questions

(40 marks; 40 minutes)

1 What is meant by 'revenue'? (2)

2 What is meant by 'operating profit'? (2)

3 Does an increase in price necessarily increase revenue? Explain your answer. (5)

4 How could a company jeopardise its future by paying out generous dividends to shareholders? (4)

5 Is profitability measured in pounds or percentages? (1)

6 What is the formula for the operating profit margin? (2)

7 Explain two ways of increasing profits. (6)

8 Explain why cutting costs might end up reducing profits. (5)

9 Explain one way in which operating profit might be affected by a decision within:

   a) the marketing function

   b) the operations function. (8)

10 Give two reasons why a profitable business could run out of cash when it expands too rapidly. (2)

11 Identify whether each of the following business start-ups would be cash-rich or cash-poor in the early years of the business:

   a) a pension fund, in which people save money in return for later pay-outs

   b) building a hotel

   c) starting a vineyard (grapes only pickable after 3–5 years). (3)

Data response

SOFA-SOGOOD Ltd is a retailer of sofas. It had been experiencing a 'very slow' summer. Revenues had been falling but costs had been pushed up by pay increases, higher rent costs and higher interest payments on debts. As a result, net profits had fallen by 20 per cent on last year. Renis, the managing director, was very disappointed that revenue had fallen because he had cut prices by 5 per cent and had expected customer numbers to increase sharply. Once it became clear that this discounting policy was not working, he imposed a pay freeze on everyone in the company and a policy of non-recruitment. If any staff member left, she or he would not be replaced.

Questions (30 marks; 30 minutes)

1 What is meant by:

   a) revenue

   b) costs

   c) net profit? (6)

2 Explain why a fall in price might not have led to an increase in revenue. (4)

3 Apart from the methods mentioned in the text, assess two other actions SOFA-SOGOOD could take to improve its profitability. (8)

4 Assess the advantages and disadvantages to the business of the staff cost-saving actions taken by Renis. (12)

Extended writing

1 When recession hits, wise financial managers focus more on cash flow and less on profit. Evaluate why that might be the case. (20)

2 In 2014, Snapchat boosted user numbers to more than 200 million people, but had not found a way to generate revenue, let alone profit. Evaluate the difficulties for a new app in turning usage into profit. (20)

38 Liquidity

> **Definition**
>
> **Liquidity** measures the ability of a firm to find the cash to pay its bills. The cash needs to be available in a current bank account or close to being available, such as a payment promised for next week.

Linked to: Sources of finance, Ch 30; Profit, Ch 37; Business failure, Ch 39.

38.1 Statement of financial position

Each year, every limited company must send a statement of its financial position to Companies House. That statement is widely known as a balance sheet. This is an accounting statement that shows an organisation's assets and liabilities on the last day of the financial year.

In effect, the balance sheet answers the question: 'How rich are you?' To find out how rich someone is, you would need to find out what they own and what they owe. The balance sheet does this for a business, adding up the totals on the last day of the financial year. Balance sheets show the wealth, or the indebtedness, of the business – vital information for shareholders, managers, financiers and suppliers.

> 'Our liquidity is fine. As a matter of fact, it's better than fine. It's strong.'
>
> Kenneth Lay, boss of Enron (shortly before Enron collapsed)

38.2 Measuring liquidity

A balance sheet contains a great deal of financial and therefore numerical information. Liquidity concerns just one issue: can the company pay the bills it will receive in the next 12 months? If the answer is no, further, serious questions must be asked about how the company is going to survive.

To measure a firm's liquidity, the first thing is to identify the bills – that is, liabilities – that will need to be paid in the next 12 months; these are called current liabilities. In the case of Mulberry plc, Table 38.1 shows their position on 31 March 2014, the final day of their 2013/2014 financial year.

	£000s
Trade and other payables	29,500
Current tax liabilities	500
Total current liabilities	**30,000**

Table 38.1 Current liabilities of Mulberry plc, 2013/2014

So Mulberry owed £30 million to their suppliers and to the government, and the fact that they were current liabilities shows that the bills needed to be paid within 12 months.

So what finance did Mulberry have available to pay these bills? The answer is found in the current assets section of their balance sheet, as shown in Table 38.2.

	£000s
Inventories (stocks)	33,600
Trade and other receivables	13,400
Cash at bank	23,500
Total current assets	**70,500**

Table 38.2 Current assets of Mulberry plc, 2013/2014

So although they had £30 million of short-term liabilities, they held more than £70 million of current (short-term) assets. They couldn't quite pay the bills from cash alone, but within the next 12 months they could expect to sell stocks to customers, thereby turning assets into cash.

As long as a company has enough current assets to cover their current liabilities, their liquidity is sound. But how much is enough? That question is tackled through the use of accounting ratios.

38.3 Calculating liquidity ratios

A ratio relates one number to another, to show the relative position, e.g. 2:1. The value of this is to give a warning about when the current liabilities are getting too high in relation to the current assets. There are two liquidity ratios used commonly: the current ratio and the acid test.

Current ratio

This ratio looks at the relationship between current assets and current liabilities. It examines the liquidity position of the firm. It is given by the formula:

$$\text{current ratio} = \frac{\text{current assets}}{\text{current liabilities}}$$

This is expressed as a ratio, such as, for example, 2:1 or 3:1.

Example

Mulberry plc has current assets of £70.5 million and current liabilities of £30 million:

$$
\begin{aligned}
\text{current ratio} &= \text{current assets} \quad : \quad \text{current liabilities} \\
&= £70.5 \text{ million} \quad : \quad £30 \text{ million} \\
&= \quad 2.35 \quad\quad : \quad 1 \\
\text{current ratio} &= \quad 2.35
\end{aligned}
$$

Interpretation

The above worked example shows that Mulberry has more than twice as many current assets as current liabilities. This means that, for every £1 of short-term debts owed, it has £2.35 of assets to pay them. This is a comfortable position.

Accountants suggest the 'ideal' current ratio should be approximately 1.5:1 (that is, £1.50 of assets for every £1 of debt). Any higher than this and the organisation can be criticised for having too many resources tied up in unproductive assets; these could be invested more profitably (or the cash could be handed back to shareholders). A low current ratio means a business may not be able to pay its debts. It is possible that the result may well be something like 0.8:1. This shows the firm has only 80p of current assets to pay every £1 it owes.

The current ratios of a selection of public companies in 2014 are shown in Table 38.3. As this table shows, it would be wrong to panic about a liquidity ratio of less than 1. Huge firms such as Tesco have often had spells when their liquidity levels were less than 1.

Acid test ratio

This ratio also examines the business's liquidity position by comparing current assets and liabilities, but it omits stock from the total of current assets. The reason for this is that stock is the most illiquid current asset (the hardest to turn into cash without a loss in its value). It can take a long time to convert stock into cash. Furthermore, stock may be old or obsolete and thus unsellable.

By omitting stock, the ratio provides a tougher measure of a firm's liquidity. It is given by the formula:

$$\text{acid test ratio} = \frac{(\text{current assets} - \text{inventories})}{\text{current liabilities}}$$

Again, it is expressed in the form of a ratio, such as 2:1.

Example

Mulberry plc has highly liquid assets of £36.9 million and current liabilities of £30 million:

$$
\begin{aligned}
\text{acid test ratio} &= \text{current assets} : \text{current liabilities} \\
&= £36.9 \text{ million} : £30 \text{ million} \\
&= \quad 1.23 \quad\quad : \quad 1 \\
\text{Acid test ratio} &= \quad 1.23
\end{aligned}
$$

Interpretation

Accountants recommend that an 'ideal' result for this ratio should be approximately 1:1, thus showing that the organisation has £1 of highly liquid assets for every £1 of short-term debt. A result below this (for example, 0.5:1) indicates that the firm may have difficulties meeting short-term payments. Clearly, Mulberry is in a very comfortable position, with strong liquidity.

The acid test ratios of a selection of public companies in 2014 are shown in Table 38.4. It can be seen that the 2014 liquidity position of Morrisons looks very uncomfortable.

Company	Balance sheet date	Current assets	Current liabilities	Current ratio
French Connection plc	31/01/2014	£89,400,000	£45,200,000	1.98
Ted Baker plc	25/01/2014	£144,400,000	£89,500,000	1.61
Tesco plc	22/02/2014	£13,085,000,000	£20,206,000,000	0.65
Morrisons plc	02/02/2014	£1,430,000,000	£2,873,000,000	0.50
JD Wetherspoon	26/01/2014	£79,400,000	£241,300,000	0.33

Table 38.3 The current ratios of a selection of public companies in 2014

Company	Balance sheet date	Current assets – stock (inventories)	Current liabilities	Current ratio
French Connection plc	31/01/2014	£50,800,000	£45,200,000	1.12
Ted Baker plc	25/01/2014	£64,000,000	£89,500,000	0.71
Tesco plc	22/02/2014	£9,509,000,000	£20,206,000,000	0.47
JD Wetherspoon	26/01/2014	£58,300,000	£241,300,000	0.24
Morrisons plc	02/02/2014	£578,000,000	£2,873,000,000	0.20

Table 38.4 The acid test ratios of a selection of public companies in 2014

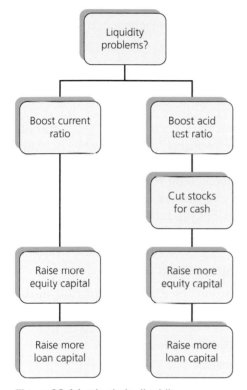

Figure 38.1 Logic chain: liquidity

38.4 Ways to improve liquidity

If the ratio is so low that it is becoming hard to pay the bills, the company will have to try to bring more cash into the balance sheet. This could be done by:

- selling under-used fixed assets
- raising more share capital
- increasing long-term borrowings
- postponing planned investments.

One further way to improve liquidity is to work hard at improving the management of working capital.

38.5 Working capital and its management

Working capital is the finance available for the day-to-day running of the business. All businesses need money; it is required for the purchase of machinery and equipment. This expenditure on fixed assets is known as capital expenditure. The business also needs money to buy materials or stock and to pay wages and the day-to-day bills, such as electricity and telephone bills. This money is known as working capital.

Managing working capital is about ensuring that the cash available is sufficient to meet the cash requirements at any one time. If the bills cannot be paid on time, there are serious consequences. In the worst situation, the business may fail. Insufficient working capital is the commonest cause of business failure. Managing working capital is therefore a vital business activity.

The working capital cycle

Managing working capital is a continuous process. When a business starts up, it takes time to generate income. Money to pay for stock and the running costs will need to be found from the initial capital invested in the business. As the business cycle gets going, income from customers will be available to pay for expenditure.

The firm needs to ensure that there is always sufficient cash to meet daily requirements. If the business is expanding or takes on a special order, extra care needs to be taken. Sufficient funds are needed to pay for the additional expenditure until the revenue arrives. This continuous process is shown in Figure 38.2.

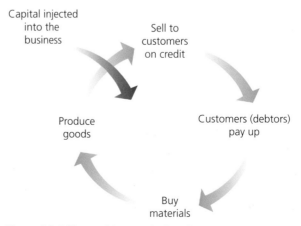

Figure 38.2 The working capital cycle

As can be seen from Figure 38.2, managing working capital is about two things:

1 ensuring the business has enough finance to meet its needs
2 keeping cash moving rapidly through the cycle, so there is enough to meet future orders.

Each business will have its own distinct cycle. Businesses will also be subject to unexpected events and need to be able to cope with these. Therefore, it is helpful to have a generous overdraft limit, which can be drawn upon when needed.

Examples of unexpected events include the following:

- A major customer gets into financial difficulties and is therefore unable to pay its bills on time.
- The cost of materials rises quickly, as with the 50 per cent increase in the price of beef in the year to October 2014.

Uncertainty and working capital

A business needs to take into account both the timing and the amounts involved when working out its working capital requirements. It also needs to include an allowance for uncertainty. An extra 10 per cent on top of the expected cash requirement would be the very minimum required. For a new, small firm such as a new restaurant, though, a bigger safety net can be wise. It can take months for word to spread sufficiently to push a business above its break-even point.

Figure 38.3 shows the need for **contingency finance**; in other words, the financial back-up to allow for the unexpected. In recent years, Somerset has been hit several times by flooding, with thousands of home evacuated. Think of the hit that would have been inflicted on small businesses in the flooded areas. They could have faced sales revenue down by, perhaps, 30 per cent as residents moved away to temporary accommodation. For a new business with little cash in the bank, the position would have threatened its survival. Figure 38.3 shows the role of contingency finance, such as an agreed overdraft facility.

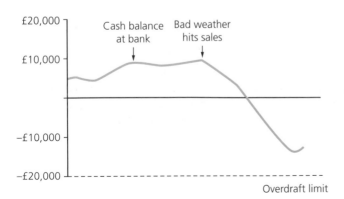

Figure 38.3 The need for contingency finance

'Many financial measurements which are useful and valid in static situations are strategic traps in growth situations.'

Bruce Henderson, chief executive, Boston Consulting Group

How should a business manage its working capital?

Intelligent working capital management is centred on the following aspects.

Control cash used

Businesses can control the amount of cash used by:

- minimising stock levels
- keeping customer credit as low as possible (without pushing customers away)
- trying to get as much credit from suppliers as you can
- getting goods to the market in the shortest possible time; the sooner goods reach the customer, the sooner payment is received.

Minimise spending on fixed assets

Minimising spending on fixed assets keeps cash in the business. The business must balance its need for cash and its need for fixed assets. A compromise is to lease rather than buy equipment. This increases expenses but conserves working capital.

Plan ahead by estimating cash needed

Planning ahead by estimating the amount of cash needed next month and beyond means that cash shortfalls can be anticipated and planned for. If the next two months look problematic, perhaps that purchase of the boss's new BMW should be delayed for a while.

'A small loan makes a debtor; a great one, an enemy.'

Pubilius Syrus, 42BC

38.6 The importance of cash

Working capital is a technical term used widely in business, but ultimately it is a posh way of looking at cash. Businesses fail when bills cannot be paid – that is, the cash runs out. In addition to the downside risks of being short of cash, it is important to be aware of missed opportunities that may arise. If working capital is too tight and cash is short, the business may not be able to buy supplies in bulk. This may result in variable costs per unit being higher than competitors'. Perhaps even more importantly, a company may have to refuse a large order because it cannot finance the extra working capital requirement.

In the longer term, shortage of cash means that no funds are available for development. The business will not be able to grow. In a world where technological and other developments are so rapid, 'not being able to grow' may be a step towards the long-term demise of the business.

> 'The only thing that matters is cash flow... where it's coming from and where it's going and how much is left over.'
>
> William McGowan, company chairman

Five whys and a how

Questions	Answers
Why does liquidity matter?	If you don't pay your bills, suppliers may refuse to supply, or may take you to court – perhaps forcing the business into liquidation.
Why are there two liquidity ratios?	The current ratio is a useful quick check on liquidity, but the acid test ratio is the real test; if there is only time for one in an exam: go for acid test.
Why do business analysts like to see tight liquidity positions with relatively little cash available?	Because they worry that too much cash makes companies lazy; they think that 'a tight ship' will generate better profits and growth.
Why might an OK liquidity ratio prove a 'strategic trap' in a growth situation (see quote from Bruce Henderson, page 244)?	Growth is good, but puts pressure on cash flow, e.g. building a new factory, building a new distribution network overseas, and so on; so today's OK liquidity ratio might be under huge strain in a year's time.
Why do some companies (especially retailers) have negative working capital?	Hugely powerful, monopolistic retailers like Boots can force suppliers to give long credit periods; this makes Boots' working capital negative, yet implies no serious risks for the company (as the suppliers wouldn't dare to force Boots to pay on time).
How does working capital affect liquidity?	Over-used working capital will mean poor liquidity – for example, too much capital tied up in stock or in payables (over-generous customer credit).

38.7 Liquidity – evaluation

Managing liquidity is very important for every business. As in many other areas of business, it is about getting the balance right. Too much working capital may be wasteful; too little can be disastrous. Businesses need to consider working capital requirements right from the outset. Most new businesses underestimate these needs, allowing only £20 of working capital for every £100 of fixed capital. Accountants advise a 50:50 ratio. Shortage of working capital will mean a shortage of liquidity.

Managing liquidity is not just about managing cash flow. The timing and amounts of cash flow are important, but liquidity management goes beyond that. It is about managing the whole business. In this respect, it is an integrated activity. It involves each aspect of the company. Efficient production keeps costs to a minimum and turns raw inputs into finished goods in the shortest possible time. Effective management of stock can have considerable impact on liquidity. Effective marketing ensures that the goods are sold and that demand is correctly estimated. This avoids wasted production. Cash then flows in from sales. Efficient distribution gets the goods to the customer quickly. The accounting department can help to control costs. Effective credit control improves cash flow. Each of these can reduce the need for cash and therefore ensure that cash is available to keep liquidity stable.

Key terms

Contingency finance: planning for the unexpected by either keeping a cash cushion in the firm's current account or keeping an overdraft facility little-used.

Credit period: the length of time a supplier allows a buyer to wait before paying, e.g. 60 days after the bill has been sent.

Liquidation: closing the business down by selling off all the assets, paying debts and returning what is left to the shareholders.

Liquidity: the ability of a business to pay its bills on time, which all depends upon having enough cash in the bank.

Working capital cycle: how long it takes for a complete cycle from cash out (buying stock) to cash back in from a customer payment. It could vary from one day (for example, for a fruit and veg stall) to one year (for example, a house builder).

38.8 Workbook

Revision questions

(30 marks; 30 minutes)

1 What is working capital? (2)

2 What is capital expenditure? (2)

3 What is working capital used for? Give two examples. (4)

4 What problems could arise if a firm is operating with very low working capital? (4)

5 Why may a business be unable to get a loan or overdraft if it has working capital difficulties? (4)

6 On 1 February, JG Co received an order for £20,000 worth of office furniture. Between 15 February and 20 March, the company spent £11,000 on materials and labour. Between 20 March and 31 March, a further £4,000 was contributed to fixed costs such as quality control. The finished order was delivered on 1 April, together with an invoice requiring payment in 60 days. On 1 June, the payment of £20,000 was received. How long is JG Co's working capital cycle? (4)

7 Outline three ways in which a business can improve its working capital situation. (6)

8 How does better stock management help a firm to control its working capital requirements? (4)

Data response

Life and death

Managing cash flow effectively is really a matter of life and death for a new business. Government figures show that small businesses are owed as much as £17 billion from customers at any one time, and that 10,000 UK businesses fail each year because of late payment from customers.

Ironically, one of the reasons for cash flow problems is that small, growing businesses can find themselves 'overtrading' (i.e. sales may be strong, but the company lacks the cash to buy more stock or pay its bills).

A previous client of mine was worth over £1 million, yet was at the end of its bank overdraft limit simply because one customer was too large for its business. It used all its working capital supplying this one customer! In addition, though the client was paying its own bills immediately, it wasn't being firm about collecting money from its own customers.

To put the situation right, the firm first had to walk away from its large customer and focus on smaller ones, and then actively chase late payments. Chasing invoices is perfectly acceptable, and in fact some businesses will never pay until chased. Finally, the company also negotiated better terms with its own suppliers.

I recommend a number of important cash flow rules.

- Make payment terms a central part of the contract and enforce them.
- Invoice as soon as possible.
- Chase invoices the moment they become due.
- Walk away from bad payers.
- Do a cash flow forecast and reforecast regularly – at least every month.
- Cash cheques as soon as you receive them.

  Source: adapted from an article by Jeff Maplin at http://startups.co.uk

Questions

(25 marks; 30 minutes)

1 Explain why late payment from customers can be such a serious matter. (4)

2 Explain the difficulties that may arise for a business that uses all its working capital supplying one customer. (4)

3 Outline one advantage and one disadvantage involved in chasing late payers. (7)

4 Assess what you see as the three main themes that come through from the 'important cash flow rules'. (10)

Extended writing

1 Evaluate the extent to which working capital management is vital for the future of any business. (20)

2 Evaluate the following statement: 'Managing working capital is not just the business of the finance department; it is the responsibility of everyone in the business.' (20)

39 Business failure

> **Definition**
>
> Business failure can be defined as the inability to keep the business going, either because of inability to keep up with the bills/liabilities or because the profits being made are too meagre to be worth continuing.

Linked to: Liability and finance, Ch 31; Planning and cash flow, Ch 32; Profit, Ch 37; Liquidity, Ch 38.

39.1 Introduction to business failure

The failure of any business has a tinge of tragedy. When La Senza collapsed (again) in 2014, hundreds of people lost their jobs. Most were low-paid, therefore having few savings, and most received no financial compensation at all. Even harsher can be a failure by an entrepreneur, who might have invested personal or family savings into a business flop. This situation can put pressure on family relationships as well as on the self-confidence of the failed entrepreneur. In America, a failed start-up can be seen as a badge of honour (especially if a subsequent enterprise succeeds), but in Britain it is more likely to be seen as a mistake.

'We can afford almost any mistake *once*.'

Lewis Lehr, chairman of the vast 3M company

Recently, *Forbes* magazine published an article by a US entrepreneur setting out the five reasons new businesses fail. They are interesting, partly because some are not obvious:

1 Not really in touch with customers through deep dialogue. Tweets won't do; the entrepreneur needs to 'walk 1,000 miles in the shoes of customers'.

2 No real differentiation (lacking a unique value proposition): too little that is unique and different from others in the marketplace.

3 Failure to communicate your unique proposition in a concise and compelling way – that is, you have the right business idea, but fail to communicate it to the right target market.

4 Leadership breakdown at the top: a dysfunctional leader who is perhaps too aggressive or too weak to lead the business towards success.

5 Inability to nail a profitable **business model** with sufficient revenue streams.

Source: Eric T. Wagner, *Forbes* magazine

It is striking that the five factors have little to do with finance. They are more about the business/marketing strategy behind the business (plus the character of the entrepreneur/leader). This seems right. In 2014, Tesco was publicly humiliated by a £260 million overstatement of its profits. But far more important was its underlying marketing failure: shoppers were leaving Tesco to go to Aldi, Lidl and Waitrose.

39.2 Internal causes of business failure

In the 2014/2015 football season, suffering from inconsistent performances and results, the managers of Arsenal and Manchester City both gave the same quote to reporters: 'We have to look to ourselves.' In other words, don't blame others; look for internal causes of failure. This seems right. When retailers blame the weather for poor trading, stock market analysts groan. They want to see the management take responsibility for their actions and their disappointments.

When businesses fall into **administration**, the same key internal reasons are usually to blame:

1 A marketing failure. In September 2014, Phones4U suddenly announced it was going into administration because it had lost its supply contracts with EE and

Vodafone. Although the cause was external, such a big company (more than 5,000 staff) should have foreseen the threat to its business and found a marketing solution – that is. finding new products or services to meet the needs of today's customers.

2 A financial failure. In April 2014, food manufacturer Fabulous Bakin' Boys collapsed, owing more than £3.5 million to its suppliers and the taxman. It had over-expanded by investing too much in new machinery at a time when declining sales suggested the brand's strength was weakening. Sales had fallen from £17.7 million in 2012 to £14.6 million in 2013. In May, the administrators announced that suppliers would receive between 5 and 17 per cent of what they were owed – that is, have to withstand huge losses. The business collapsed due to bad management.

3 A systems failure. Ultimately, businesses run on information, on data. If a new IT system causes confusion rather than certainty, the result can be disastrous. Stock ordering may go wrong, leaving some shelves empty while others overflow. This seems to have been the problem behind the 2014 collapse of Bloom.fm, a UK music streaming business with 1.2 million users.

39.3 External causes of business failure

In November 2014, the wave power firm Pelamis called in the administrators, with the potential loss of 56 jobs. Pelamis was a world leader in renewable energy, but energy companies such as E.ON had stopped funding the business. As it had not yet reached break-even in its commercial operations, it simply ran out of cash and had to close.

Among the main external causes of business failure are:

1 A fundamental change in technology which gives a rival (or a new entrant) a competitive advantage that is too great to be matched. Effectively this is what happened to Nokia when the Apple iPhone arrived. Nokia's share of the global smartphone market collapsed from 40 per cent to 4 per cent within two years.

2 The arrival of a competitor who is so effective at acquiring and keeping customers that others fall by the wayside. Amazon had (and has) this effect on the world's bookshops. In Britain, there were 1,535 independent bookshops in the country; by the end of 2013, the number had fallen to 987. So around 550 businesses were wiped out in this way.

3 Economic change. In 2009, production of cars in Britain fell 35 per cent in response to the world recession. For manufacturers of car parts, such as spark plugs, this collapse in demand threatened to wipe out several longstanding companies. The US company Visteon closed its factories in Enfield and Basildon with the loss of 565 jobs. Although one could urge companies to have a balanced product portfolio, including some products that will sell well in hard times, economic shocks such as 2009 caught out many well-run businesses.

4 The behaviour of banks. Banks such as Lloyds and NatWest love running TV commercials showing their warm, friendly backing of small firms. But RBS (owner of NatWest) has been accused of running a division that was set up to make a profit out of client companies in financial difficulties. More than 1,000 companies were dealt with in ways that included forced closure so that RBS could sell off company assets at a profit. In August 2014, RBS closed the unit down, following huge pressure from the government and the Bank of England. In November 2014, Vince Cable, government Secretary of State, told the BBC *Panorama* programme: 'Good companies appear to have been put at risk or in some cases destroyed by banks.'

'The old saying holds. Owe your banker £1,000 and you are at his mercy; owe him £1 million and the position is reversed.'

John Maynard Keynes, British economist and author

39.4 Financial causes of business failure

There are two triggers to financial failure: one is the inability to pay the bills – i.e. run out of cash – which is a liquidity crisis; the other is a matter of insolvency, meaning that liabilities outweigh assets, leaving the business with no legal alternative to closure. The latter could happen as a result of a big investment going spectacularly wrong. So there may be a profitable business still operating, yet the bad investment could have wiped out the value of the firm's assets. This is largely what happened to RBS in the 2009 financial crisis; because it spent over £50 billion on a bank that proved worthless, the bank's capital was wiped out, forcing the government to rescue this private sector business.

Most financial collapses, though, are due to running out of cash. This can come about because:

1 The business may have been running below break-even for some period of time. The lossmaking drains the business of its cash, as cash outflows regularly exceed cash inflows. If the business cannot be returned to profit, cash will run out at some point. This is the regular life of most of Britain's professional football clubs – always needing a new investor to inject more cash than sense.

2 A cash flow crisis may occur, perhaps quite unexpectedly. Tesco has 28 per cent of the UK grocery market, so there are many small food companies who have managed to get distribution through Tesco but are now horribly dependent on this one supermarket chain. If Tesco is unhappy and argues about a large bill, the clock could be ticking on the small supplier running out of the cash to pay its own bills; if the small firm turns to its bank for help, the bank may choose to protect itself by insisting that an overdraft facility is repaid within 24 hours; this makes things worse, with too little cash to cope, and the bank may call in the administrators.

3 Overtrading. As mentioned in Chapter 28, if a rise in demand encourages a business to pursue rapid sales growth, the strain on cash flow can prove too great, causing the company to collapse. Overtrading is one of the most common causes of business collapse.

39.5 Non-financial causes of business failure

Apart from finance, the two things most likely to cause a business to fail are a sudden lurch in sales towards competitors or a steady drip-drip of sales decline as the business loses its long-term competitiveness. A fusion between these two was seen at HMV, where the steady loss of competitiveness compared with online music distribution was compounded by the highly aggressive stance taken by Amazon, in DVDs as well as CDs. HMV's market was pulled from under its feet.

Although both these points sound like marketing problems, it is important to remember that the underlying difficulty could have stemmed from people management or resource management. Unhappy staff may have stopped giving customers an enjoyable experience, so sales steadily slide towards a rival. Or repeated IT failures make the customer experience so frustrating that they turn elsewhere. Ultimately, business failure can be caused by poor management of people or operations, not just marketing and finance.

'In Britain the quickest way to riches is to fail at the top. Sign a three-year contract and then fail in the first six months, walk away with a million pounds for six months' work.'

Charles Handy, management thinker

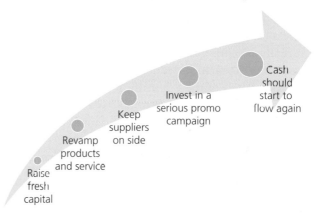

Figure 39.1 Logic ladder: overcoming financial crisis

Five whys and a how

Questions	Answers
Why might a profitable business fail?	Despite making apparent profit, if a business runs out of cash, suppliers and staff lose faith and walk away; then the bank comes in and finishes things off.
Why don't firms use their past profits to keep them going?	They have probably either paid them out to shareholders, in the form of dividends, or reinvested the profits within the business – and the same money can't be used twice.
Why might it be financially risky to have sales dominated by one large customer?	If the customer refuses to pay (or cancels the order and walks away), the impact on cash flow would be devastating.
Why may a bank overdraft be a small firm's Achilles heel?	Banks can insist on the overdraft being repaid within 24 hours; few businesses could cope with such a tough demand.
Why are brand new businesses the most vulnerable of all?	Because a new firm has not yet built up the regular cash inflows that come from loyal customers, yet has the heavy cash outflows coming from paying suppliers cash on delivery.
How could a firm pull itself out of a financial crisis?	As long as it has a profitable business, investors are likely to gather round, want to keep the business going and therefore invest more capital.

39.6 Business failure – evaluation

When, in 2014, Tesco admitted overstating its profit by over £260 million, it became clear that even the biggest companies can struggle to keep on top of their costs. For small firms, this can be even more the case. A business may believe itself to be more profitable than it really is. This year, a publisher sells one million textbooks at £20 each; it deducts £17 million of costs and pays out much of the £3 million profit to the taxman and its shareholders. But next year WHSmith sends a lorry with 100,000 books and demands £2 million back; it shows a small clause in the contract saying, in effect, 'If they don't sell, we will return them and *will* get our money back.'

Business is interesting precisely because it is so hard to be sure that everything is going well; Samsung's glorious 2013 turned into an awful 2014, as did Snickers', which had enjoyed a 10 per cent sales boost in 2013 ('Get some nuts!') followed by a 30 per cent sales collapse in 2014. All that is certain about business finance is that clever firms keep healthy cash balances just in case things go wrong. One day, they will.

Key terms

Administration: when the directors of a business feel forced by the threat of insolvency to hand over management control to an administrator (usually an accountant), who may try to sell the business, or perhaps close it down and sell off the assets.

Business model: the underlying plan of how the business is going to make a profit in the long term.

39.7 Workbook

Revision questions

(35 marks; 35 minutes)

1 Briefly look again at *Forbes* magazine's 'five reasons new businesses fail' on page 247. Which do you think is the single most important reason and why? (5)

2 Explain how a change in technology might harm the position of a small driving school in a rural area. (4)

3 Explain what Lewis Lehr meant by his quote on page 247. (4)

4 Explain in detail the effect a sudden loss of a big customer might have on the cash flow of a small company. (4)

5 In your own words, explain the meaning of the term 'overtrading'. (3)

6 Explain how each of the following might damage the financial position of a new small firm:

   a) a rise in interest rates

   b) fewer customers arriving than had been forecast. (6)

7 Must a business failure always have a personal failure at its heart? Explain your thinking. (6)

8 Explain what John Maynard Keynes meant by his quote on page 248. (3)

Data response 1

Bad banking

The following is an extract from the Tomlinson Report into banks' 'Treatment of Businesses in Distress' (published on behalf of HM Government in 2013).

'The cases and experiences of businesses we received can be categorised as part of an overall process as follows:

1 The bank artificially distresses an otherwise viable business and through their actions puts them on a journey towards administration, receivership and liquidation.

2 Once transferred into the business support division of the bank the business is not supported in a manner consistent with good turnaround practice and this has a catalytic effect on the business' journey to insolvency.

3 The insolvency process lacks fairness and accountability leading to financial implications and biased outcomes to the detriment of the business owner.

This report considers each part of this "process" separately and the mechanisms adopted by the bank. From the evidence that we received, it was apparent that, while each case is different and has its own characteristics, when taken as a whole the pattern soon clearly emerges. Many of the businesses who submitted evidence have done so in confidence.

Not all of the cases that we heard about go through the full process from stage 1–3 and some relate to specific parts of the process outlined above. However, it became very clear, very quickly that this process is systematic and institutional. Conversations with whistle blowers, experts and lawyers have also confirmed that it is often, in fact, the better businesses that enter such a path as there is more to be gained by the bank from this than from a less asset-rich business. This suggests an element of intent in the bank's decision to distress these businesses.'

Later, in evidence to a parliamentary committee, senior RBS executives denied that they treated their 'business support division' as a profit centre. Within a month, they retracted that evidence, admitting that RBS did seek to make a profit out of businesses that were struggling to survive.

Questions

(30 marks; 35 minutes)

1 **a)** Explain what might be meant by the phrase 'artificially distresses an otherwise viable business'. (4)

   b) Explain one action a bank could take that would distress a business customer. (4)

2 Assess the possible impact on the business owner of being put on a 'journey towards administration, receivership and liquidation' (10)

3 Assess whether the short extract from the report proves its case that there was 'an element of intent in the bank's decision to distress these businesses'. (12)

Data response 2

Ninety jobs lost as Tinsley Special Products enters administration

Trailer engineers Tinsley Special Products have gone into administration with the loss of 90 jobs, just months after securing £3.5 million in Regional Growth Fund money.

Just this year the County Durham-based manufacturer of trailer vehicles acquired Marshall Aerospace and Defence Group's Mildenhall operations in Suffolk, and in January they bought Tanfield Engineering Systems Ltd out of administration.

Administrators Ian Kings and Allan Kelly from Baker Tilly were appointed to Tinsley early this month and confirmed 90 redundancies across the firm's Peterlee and Suffolk operations.

Allan Kelly, joint administrator and partner in Baker Tilly's North East region said:

'Tinsley Special Products Limited has suffered from a downturn in trade which has impacted on profit and cash flow. Unfortunately the contract position and financial requirements of the Company left us with little option but to cease trading shortly after appointment.

We are in the process of realising the assets and quantifying the liabilities of the company to ascertain if a distribution can be made to creditors. Additionally, our specialist employment team are assisting the employees in making the relevant claims for any outstanding wage arrears, holiday pay and other claims from the Redundancy Payments Service.'

Source: *The Journal*, 24 November 2014

Questions

(30 marks; 35 minutes)

1 Assess what might cause a 'downturn in trade' for a small manufacturer such as Tinsley Special Products. (10)

2 Assess two factors that may have 'impacted' on cash flow so negatively as to cause the collapse of the business. (8)

3 Tinsley Special Products was based mainly in the North East of England, where income levels are among the lowest in the country. Assess whether the business should therefore have been propped up with central government funding. (12)

Extended writing

1 A pizza company's sales go through the roof when it advertises a 'low-carb pizza'. Evaluate the possible reasons why this business might still face financial failure within the next few years. (20)

2 A fashion clothing retailer has made losses for the past two years and its bank is discussing whether the business should close down. Evaluate the ways in which the retailer might be turned back into a profitable business. (20)

40 Introduction to resource management

Linked to: Supply, Ch 6; Introduction to managing people, Ch 16; Production, productivity and efficiency, Ch 41; Capacity utilisation, Ch 42; Stock control, Ch 43; Quality management, Ch 44.

40.1 Introduction

Resource management is the central business function of creating the product or service and delivering it to the customer (that is, meeting the customer requirement). At Jaguar Land Rover, it means designing the cars and the machinery for making them, ordering the supplies, manufacturing the products, delivering them to the car showrooms and handling customer service issues such as warranty claims. Marketing creates the demand; resource management creates the supply to meet the demand. To achieve this, it requires human and financial resources.

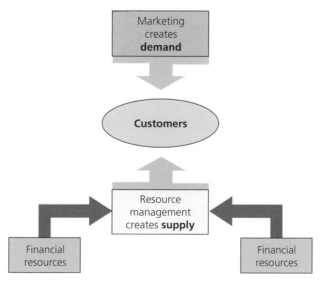

Figure 40.1 The central role of resource management

The importance of resource management is especially clear in the car industry. Rover Cars once commanded more than a 50 per cent share of the British car market. Its cars were well designed but poorly made. In 2005, the business ceased to exist as a British producer. In the years of Rover's decline, Toyota moved from being outside the top 20 world car producers to its current position as number one, selling ten million cars in 2014. Toyota has never been famous for producing stylish cars, but their quality and reliability have built its reputation worldwide. Toyota's business success has been built not on marketing but on resource management. By 2014, this success brought it annual profits of over £10 billion and a balance sheet cash cushion of £30 billion. Even though Toyota has had some quality problems in recent years, the fundamental strength of the business (and its customer loyalty) keeps it motoring.

Figure 40.2 A car factory

40.2 What is resource management?

Step 1: design

The process starts by designing a product or service to meet the needs or desires of a particular type of customer (see Table 40.1 for examples). The key at this, and every

Market	Type of customer	Customer needs or wants	Outline operational design
Hotels	Busy traveller and busy worker	Low-cost but comfortable hotel room in city centre	Well-located building with small but very well-equipped rooms; all food and drink from vending machines
Car market	Family with young children	A car to make family journeys more pleasant	Spacious car with good entertainment (seat-back monitors etc.) and a small refrigerated drinks unit
Mortgages	University students	Students wanting to buy a flat on a joint mortgage – to stop relying on landlords	Flexible, low-cost mortgage, which is easy to get into and out of; available online to students with limited financial histories

Table 40.1 Examples of designs that aim to meet customer requirements

other, stage is to be clear about the customer and his/her requirements. If a tablet computer manufacturer's target customer is a student, the design of the tablet must be simple, economical and effective in order to help keep costs low enough to provide the low prices the student wants.

> 'Almost all quality improvement comes via simplification of design, manufacturing, layout, processes and procedures.'
>
> Tom Peters, author of *In Search of Excellence*

Step 2: establishing the supply chain

In a manufacturing process, the heart of the operation will be the factory. This is where a collection of materials and parts will be turned into a finished product. In the case of a car, literally thousands of parts are involved in making each vehicle. Components that may cost little to produce, such as metal fixings for seat belts, all combine to turn £4,000 worth of parts into a car worth £10,000.

This does not mean, though, that the car maker receives £6,000 of profit for every car sold; £6,000 of value has been added to the components, but at what cost? The most obvious cost is labour (that is, the staff needed to organise and run the factory). This will typically cost about 20 to 25 per cent of the value of the output. There are other factors that are a clear waste of money for the business, such as those listed below.

● Production line errors leading to 'wastage': if a car reaches the end of the production line and, when tested, fails to start, labour time is wasted finding the fault, and more time and components involved in correcting the problem. Modern companies try to eliminate all activities that waste time, but failing to take care over quality can never make sense for any company that wants to build a long-term future.

● Breakdowns, perhaps due to faulty maintenance, or just due to wear and tear: a well-run business uses preventative maintenance – checking machinery and replacing worn parts before a breakdown occurs.

Having established a well-run factory, the business can establish the other key parts of the **supply chain**, as indicated in Figure 40.3.

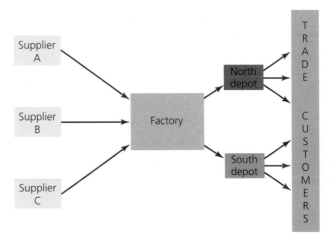

Figure 40.3 The supply chain

Step 3: working with suppliers

Very few businesses produce 100 per cent of a product or service. Almost all use suppliers. In some cases, suppliers may do most of the operational work. Companies that 'bottle' Coca-Cola buy in: the aluminium cans, already printed with the can design; the water; the carbon dioxide used to create the fizz; and the secret Coke syrup (sent from the Coca-Cola factory in America). They may also get a distribution company such as Exel to make all the deliveries to wholesale and retail customers. So what does the Coca-Cola bottler actually do? Well, not a huge amount, clearly. But it must still be responsible for the co-ordination of all the suppliers and the quality of their work. If Waitrose ordered a container load of Coke Zero to reach its Bracknell depot at 10.00am on a Tuesday morning, did it turn up on time? If not, why not?

For many companies, working with suppliers is a key to success. A homemade ice cream parlour may do all the production operations on-site, but still relies on suppliers of: fresh fruit, fresh milk and cream, grocery items such as sugar, wafer biscuits and cones, paper cups and plastic spoons, and so on. To run the parlour successfully, all the operations have to be carried out successfully. If you have run out of cones, the best ice creams will remain unsold.

A company must therefore select suppliers that can deliver the right goods reliably and must negotiate low enough prices for the supplies to make it possible to run the business economically.

Step 4: managing quality

Quality is not easy to define. It is a combination of real factors plus psychological ones. A haircut may be carried out very expertly, yet the customer may go away and cry! A less expert hairdresser may produce a technically worse cut, yet the effect may be just what the customer wants. In this case, providing quality means providing what the customer wants (that is, delivering customer satisfaction).

Effective resource management requires certain quality objectives:

- The product/service must do what the customer has been promised.
- It must arrive on time, in good condition.
- It must last at least as long as the customer expects.
- Customer service should be effective (for example, phones answered quickly).
- After-sales service should also be effective (for example, speedy repair if something goes wrong).

These are the basics; on top of these should come the psychological factors that can mean a huge amount, such as service with a warm smile. Modern business theory suggests that, to stand out, a company needs to achieve 'customer delight' not just customer satisfaction. The easiest way to delight a customer is to be genuinely welcoming.

'I consider a bad bottle of Heineken to be a personal insult to me.'

Freddy Heineken, founder of Heineken

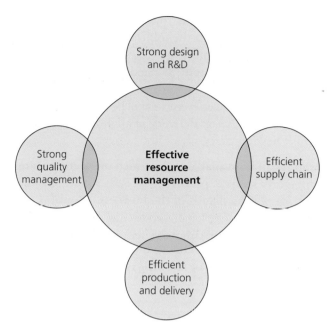

Figure 40.4 Logic circle: effective resource management

Step 5: achieving high levels of efficiency

Chapter 41 shows the importance of efficiency in business. This comes partly from using resources fully, such as a school hiring out five-a-side all-weather pitches at the weekends. It also comes from high-productivity processes, probably backed by regularly updated equipment and technology. According to Moore's law, computing power doubles every two years. Technological advances in IT can speed up existing production processes hugely. In some cases, technology can substitute for labour, reducing costs. However, the most successful firms tend to encourage staff to help re-think their processes regularly – but especially during periods of rapid technological change.

'Engineering is treated with disdain, on the whole. It's considered to be rather boring and irrelevant, yet neither of those is true.'

James Dyson, billionaire engineer and entrepreneur

Within the resource management function, a key requirement is software that will satisfactorily manage the day-to-day process, from supplies through to delivery. For example, if fashion retailer Zara of Spain suddenly orders 4,000 'Glastonbury' jackets from your clothing factory, you need instantly to know:

- how many metres of cloth to order from your suppliers, and how many metres of lining
- how many buttons and zips to order

- when is the earliest date that all the above can be received, and therefore the job can begin
- how many hours of machine time will be needed
- how much overtime will be needed from staff, if the factory is already busy
- how many extra delivery vehicles will be needed and when
- when Zara can expect delivery of all 4,000 items to its Spanish headquarters.

This should all be available at the touch of a button using **enterprise resource planning** (ERP) software. This software has all the details of the business operation and provides the planning plus day-to-day monitoring of whether things are working to schedule.

Five whys and a how

Questions	Answers
Why does resource management matter?	Because business is not about ideas, it is about putting ideas into action; and that is what resource management does.
Why might a business struggle when 'improvements' are made to its supply chain?	Improvements mean change, and change creates scope for mistakes, perhaps by the contractors carrying the change out; that does not mean that improvements should be ignored.
Why would any business choose to buy on a one-off auction basis instead of setting up a long-term relationship with suppliers?	Perhaps because of too few staff working on purchasing; building relationships takes time, so staff shortages encourage a short-term, one-off approach.
Why might simplification be so important (see Tom Peters' quote on page 254)?	Because it makes it easy for hard-pressed staff to get things right first time, avoiding mistakes.
Why might the customer experience of quality be different from the quality checked by inspectors in the factory?	If it is chocolate, it can melt in transit or in the shop; if it is a car, a slight scratch may be the fault of the delivery driver.
How might the quality of a chocolate bar be measured?	By the level of repeat purchase or by an online rating system, perhaps advertised on the pack.

40.3 Introduction to resource management – evaluation

Every business is different, especially in the status given to resource management staff. In Toyota or BMW, top engineers are the stars of the business and resource management will be at the heart of all major decisions. In a business such as Innocent Drinks, the marketing people lead the business, with resources changing to suit the market. Usually the importance and power of resource staff reflect the needs and history of the business. Regrettably there are also national characteristics to consider. The title 'engineer' is prestigious in Germany, Japan and India. In Britain, it is a struggle to find many A level students who desperately want to be engineers. Bankers, management consultants and media careers are much preferred. So some UK companies that should be based on strong resource management are actually dominated by marketing and finance executives. Therefore, decisions about the future may be too focused on the short term. The hugely successful engineer billionaire James Dyson once said: 'Advertising is the British answer to everything. But that is the way to a fast buck, not real money.'

Key terms

Enterprise resource planning (ERP): planning that logs all of a firm's costs, working methods and resources (machinery, labour, stocks of materials) within a piece of software; this provides a model of the business that can be used to answer questions such as 'When do we need to start working to get stocks made in time for delivery before Christmas?'

Supply chain: the whole path from suppliers of raw materials through production and storage on to customer delivery.

40.4 Workbook

Revision questions

(25 marks; 25 minutes)

1 Why may the quality of product design be less important for some businesses than others? (3)

2 Explain two key elements of resource management for:

   a) a children's shoe shop

   b) a new, all-business-class airline. (8)

3 Choose one of the examples in Table 40.1 and outline one strength and one weakness of that business idea. (4)

4 Identify three ways in which staff might be at fault in production line errors that cause wastage. (3)

5 Examine the possible effects on a firm such as Coca-Cola of being unreliable in delivering to a big customer like Waitrose. (5)

6 Outline one possible benefit to a business from 'delighting' rather than 'satisfying' its customers. (2)

Data response

IKEA resource management

The furniture retailer IKEA was established in 1943 by a 17-year-old Swede called Ingvar Kamprad. His aim was very similar to Henry Ford's: sell high-quality products at prices low enough to make them affordable to a mass market. The business thrived because IKEA successfully delivered products that met customer requirements. People liked IKEA's designs and were happy to buy into the company's vision that beautiful, high-quality furniture should be affordable for all. The company grew rapidly. By 2014, IKEA was a global giant, operating worldwide in 43 countries. Last year, its annual turnover ($38 billion) was greater than the GDP of Serbia.

IKEA's highly effective resource management is crucial to its success. This is because low prices will only be profitable if operating costs are kept under control. One of IKEA's most significant innovations was to sell its furniture in flat packs. These take up less room than furniture that is displayed conventionally, which means that IKEA is able to generate high revenues per cubic metre of floor space. Staffing costs at IKEA stores are kept low in two ways. First, customers are asked to collect their purchases themselves from the in-store warehouse. Second, IKEA does not have to pay staff to assemble its products; the consumers assemble the furniture that they have bought themselves by following instruction leaflets included inside the flat packs. Families that buy IKEA flat packs are therefore *prosumers* – half consumer and half producer.

Source: www.ikea.com/gb/en/

Questions

(40 marks; 45 minutes)

1 Outline one aspect of IKEA'S resource management that helps the company to minimise its costs. (2)

2 Assess whether IKEA's highly effective resource management is the most important factor in determining the company's success. (10)

3 Assess two possible weaknesses of IKEA'S resource management. (8)

4 IKEA sources its raw materials from suppliers all over the world. Evaluate the challenges that this might pose for IKEA's supply chain management. (20)

Extended writing

1 In 2014, UK food producer Pasta Reale collapsed into administration, costing 169 jobs. Even though its sales revenue was £39 million in the 18 months to March 2013, the business lost money. Evaluate how likely it is that poor resource management was the key factor in its operating losses. (20)

2 For a business such as Tesco, evaluate whether marketing or resource management is more likely to be the key to improving operational performance. (20)

41 Production, productivity and efficiency

> **Definition**
>
> Production measures the quantity of output. Productivity is a measure of efficiency, calculated by dividing output by the inputs per time period, e.g. labour productivity at Nissan UK: 100 cars per worker per year.

Linked to: Supply, Ch 6; Approaches to staffing, Ch 17; Introduction to resource management, Ch 40; Capacity utilisation, Ch 42. .

41.1 Methods of production

Job production

This means producing a one-off item for a one-off customer. Prince Charles gets his shoes hand-made at John Lobb Bootmaker in central London. So does Calvin Klein. It takes five years of training to become a John Lobb shoemaker. And the price of a pair starts at £3,500. That's job production: tailor-made to suit an individual's needs. It is how everything used to be made, long ago when labour was cheap.

Batch production

This means producing a set number of identical items – for example, 500 pairs of size 11 army boots for the British armed forces. When producing batches of this size, the producer would find it worthwhile to invest in some machinery to speed up the production process. Instead of hand-stitching, up-to-date machinery will do the job far better; there will also be a machine purchased to stick the sole of the shoe to the upper. And whereas at John Lobb one person performs every task required to complete the pair of shoes, batch production usually involves division of labour – that is, dividing up the tasks between different employees, each of whom can specialise and therefore become more efficient. Batch production is more efficient than job production, which keeps costs down, thereby allowing prices to fall. The 500 army boots might cost the army £60 each.

Flow production

This is continuous production of a single item, such as cans of Heinz Baked Beans. With 250 million cans produced each year in the UK Heinz factory, a production line can be set up to churn out five million cans a week. It will be highly automated, with the only human labour being to feed in materials, to check on quality and to maintain the machines. Whereas the labour cost of John Lobb shoes might amount to more than £1,000 per pair; the labour cost per can of beans might be little more than 1p. Flow production is the most efficient way to produce an item with predictable, high-volume sales.

Cell production

This means setting up a small production line or group-working process so that items can be produced quite flexibly. A good example would be Brompton Bikes (the UK's biggest producer – 45,000 a year), which has the flexibility to produce every bike to order. They can produce a bike for a customer who is 6ft 6in tall, or one with a titanium frame, or one with special gearing for going up mountains. Brompton used to produce on a job basis, but moved to cell production in 2010 when business started to boom. Group working allows the company to produce to higher productivity and higher output levels.

Job	Batch	Flow	Cell
When every customer wants something unique, e.g. a wedding dress	When production has to be split into chunks, e.g. shoes in different sizes and colours	When there is consistent, high demand for a single product, e.g. *The Sun* newspaper	When there is a need for flexibility but also high production volumes, i.e. **lean production**
When labour costs are low, e.g. suits tailor-made in Bangkok	When labour costs are high enough to mean job production is too costly	When labour costs are high, e.g. in France or Sweden	When labour has a lot to contribute to ideas and improved efficiency
When tailor-making something adds real value, e.g. shoes for a marathon runner	When a firm wants to limit the availability of an item, e.g. Hermès with their 'Birkin' bag	When efficiency allows prices low enough to boost sales on everyday items, e.g. baked beans	When a degree of uniqueness adds value for the customer

Table 41.1 Circumstances when each production method is at its most effective

41.2 Productivity: what is it?

Labour productivity measures the amount a worker produces over a given time. For example, an employee might make ten pairs of jeans in an hour. Measuring productivity is relatively easy in manufacturing where the number of goods can be counted. In the service sector, it is not always possible to be sure what to measure. Productivity in services can be measured in some cases: the number of customers served, number of patients seen and the sales per employee. But how can the productivity of a receptionist be measured?

It is important to distinguish between productivity and total output. By hiring more employees, a firm may increase the total output, but this does not mean that the output per employee has gone up. Similarly it is possible to have lower production with higher productivity because of a fall in the number of employees. Imagine, for example, 20 employees producing 40 tables a week at a furniture company. Their productivity on average is two tables per week per worker. If new machinery enables 10 employees to make 30 tables, the overall output has fallen, but the output per worker has risen to three. This rise in productivity would lower the labour cost per table. In the formula below, 'inputs' primarily means labour, but could also be land or capital.

$$\text{Productivity formula: } \frac{\text{Outputs}}{\text{Inputs per time period}}$$

41.3 The importance of productivity

The output per employee is a very important measure of a firm's performance. It has a direct impact on the cost of producing a unit. If productivity increases then, assuming wages are unchanged, the labour cost per unit will fall. Imagine that in one factory employees make five pairs of shoes per day, but in another they make ten pairs per day; assuming the wage rate is the same, this means the labour cost of a pair of shoes will be halved in the second factory (see Table 41.2). With lower labour costs, this firm is likely to be in a better competitive position.

	Daily wage rate (£)	Productivity rate (per day)	Wage cost per pair (£)
Factory 1	50	5	10
Factory 2	50	10	5

Table 41.2 Shoe factory productivity and wage costs

By increasing productivity, a firm can improve its competitiveness (ability to equal or beat its rivals). It can either sell its products at a lower price or keep the price as it was and enjoy a higher profit margin. This is why firms continually monitor their productivity relative to their competitors and, where possible, try to increase it. However, they need to make sure that quality does not suffer in the rush to produce more. It may be necessary to set both productivity and quality targets.

41.4 Factors influencing productivity

The level of investment in modern equipment

By investing in modern, sophisticated machines and better production processes, it shouldn't be hard to improve output per worker. That, in turn, would improve individual companies' competitiveness and help to boost the country's economic growth. Yet Figure 41.1 is a reminder that Britain consistently invests less than other countries as a share of **GDP** – despite repeated cuts to corporation tax that are said to encourage greater business investment.

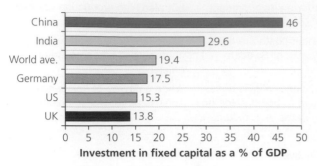

Figure 41.1 Investment spending: too low in UK (source: CIA Factbook, 2014)

'Engineering is the ability to do for $1 what any damn fool can do for $5.'

Arthur Wellington, nineteenth-century US engineer

The ability level of those at work

To increase productivity, a firm may need to introduce more or better training for its employees. A skilled and well-trained workforce is likely to produce more and make fewer mistakes. Employees should be able to complete tasks more quickly and will not need as much supervision or advice. They will be able to solve their own work-related problems and may be in a better position to contribute ideas on how to increase productivity further.

However, firms are often reluctant to invest in training because employees may leave and work for another firm once they have gained more skills. There is a danger that the training will not provide sufficient gains to justify the initial investment and so any spending in this area needs to be properly costed and evaluated. In general, UK firms do not have a particularly good record in training; more investment here could help the UK's productivity levels.

Improve employee motivation

Professor Herzberg once said that most people's idea of a fair day's work is less than half what they can give. The key to success, he felt, was to design jobs that contained motivators to help employees give much, much more. His suggestions on how to provide **job enrichment** are detailed in Chapter 20.

There is no doubt that motivation matters. A motivated sales force may achieve twice the sales level of an

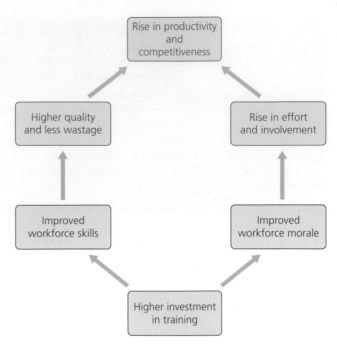

Figure 41.2 Logic chain: boosting productivity through training

unmotivated one. A motivated computer technician may correct twice the computer faults of an unmotivated one. And, in both cases, overall business performance will be boosted.

'Looking for differences between the more productive and less productive organisations, we found that the most striking difference is the number of people who are involved and feel responsibility for solving problems.'

Michael McTague, management consultant

Real business

Motivation on the pitch

When Fulham Football Club appointed a new groundsman, few people even noticed. The fans had always been proud of the pitch, but newly appointed Frank Boahene was not impressed. He thought it needed a dramatic improvement before the start of the new season in August. With no time to reseed the pitch, he decided the best way to strengthen the grass was to cut it three times a day. Doing so, first thing in the morning and last thing in the afternoon, was not a problem. But he also chose to 'pop back' from his home in Reading (an hour's drive) to do the third cut at 11.00 at night. Every day! That's motivation.

Figure 41.3 Motivation and the football pitch

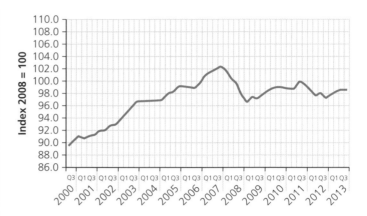

Figure 41.4 UK productivity index, output per worker (source: ONS, June 2014)

41.5 Difficulties increasing productivity

The role of management

A serious problem for UK management is that productivity has never been a central focus for directors. In the UK, directors focus on profits; elsewhere they look for efficiency first, trusting that profits will follow.

Perhaps the key management role is to identify increasing productivity as a permanent objective. The Japanese bulldozer company Komatsu set a target of a 10 per cent productivity increase every year, until they caught up with the world-leading American producer Caterpillar. Today Komatsu is the world number two producer, with annual sales of £11.5 billion.

In many firms, productivity is not a direct target. The focus, day by day, is on production, not productivity. After all, it is production which ensures customer orders are fulfilled. An operations manager, faced with a 10 per cent increase in orders, may simply ask the workforce to do overtime. The work gets done; the workforce is happy to earn extra money; and it is all rather easy to do. It is harder by far to re-organise the workplace to make production more effective. Managers whose main focus is on the short term, therefore, think of production not productivity.

As shown in Figure 41.4, productivity growth has been very weak in Britain since 2007. If this continues, the economic recovery will stall.

41.6 Link between productivity and competitiveness

Figure 41.5 shows changes in productivity among selected EU countries. In 2004, UK productivity was 16.3 per cent higher than the EU average – not too far off the figures for Germany and France. Since then, UK productivity has fallen significantly, to below the EU average and about 30 per cent below that of France and Germany. Ultimately, as lower productivity inevitably causes higher labour costs per unit, this makes UK producers less competitive with our rivals. It makes it more likely that, in future, UK producers will have to hold wage levels down to stay in business.

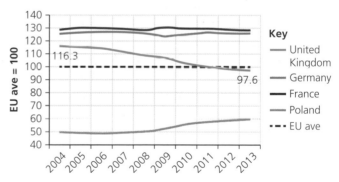

Figure 41.5 Labour productivity per hour in Europe (source: Eurostat, September 2014)

Fortunately, competitiveness is not just about costs. Jaguar Land Rover is enjoying a sales boom that is nothing to do with the prices of its cars. It is simply that people want the cars – and are willing to pay top prices if necessary. In other words, the price elasticity of JLR cars is low, and therefore neither prices nor costs matter too much. The same is true of some other important UK manufactures, such as Brompton bikes, JCB construction vehicles and GKN composite materials for making fuel-efficient passenger planes.

> 'Not everything that can be counted counts, and not everything that counts can be counted.'
>
> Albert Einstein, the ultimate boffin

41.7 Are efficiency and productivity the same thing?

Directly, the answer is no. Productivity is output per worker per time period (hour, month or year). That ignores some other key features of efficiency, notably waste. One super-fast worker may produce a lot of output, but in a wasteful manner. A decorator may paint speedily but messily, wasting 20 per cent of the paint. So productivity may be high but overall efficiency no better than average. And a company may produce chemicals with high productivity, but create pollution locally (waste products leaking out of the chimney, perhaps). Again this would not be efficient. Despite this, labour productivity is regarded by business as one of the most important tests of management efficiency.

41.8 Production at minimum average cost

By definition, the most efficient production level is the one at which total unit costs are as low as possible. Figure 41.6 shows this point, with its implication that average unit costs don't simply fall for ever – they fall at first but then rise as cost inefficiencies kick in. Note that this diagram shows the short-term position for a company; 'minimum average costs' are at the point marked as 'minimum level of unit costs'.

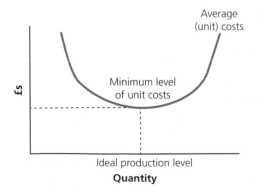

Figure 41.6 Production at minimum average cost

Factors influencing efficiency include:

- level of wastage in the production process (as explained in Section 41.7)
- whether the right technology is being used – for example, is the production process utilising the very latest methods?

  When Nestlé started packing four-finger KitKats into a 'flow' plastic wrapper (instead of the old-style silver foil with a paper cover) they claimed that the efficiency gains would be 'substantial' as it would speed up the production line.

- whether managers have achieved the right balance between the variable factors that affect efficiency. For example a supermarket may have all the latest equipment to make it efficient, yet recruit too few staff at the peak shopping hours to cope with the customer volumes; this might lead to long queues and, ultimately, fewer returning customers.

41.9 Capital and labour intensity

A further factor affecting production efficiency concerns the balance struck between capital- and labour-intensive production. Measuring up a bride-to-be and then making a wedding dress by hand is the ultimate in labour-intensive production. However hard the dressmaker works, his/her productivity will be very low. This is because so little can be mechanised or automated. By contrast, a dress designer for Topshop may be able to order 10,000 identical size 10 dresses to be distributed across the Topshop stores. This batch of 10,000 can be produced largely by machine (that is, through capital- rather than labour-intensive production).

The importance of this topic is that it points to a huge opportunity for small firms. In almost every industry, there is scope for some labour-intensive production. This is because there are always some people who want – and can afford – an entirely individual product. In addition, there are businesses where labour-intensive production is inevitable, such as plumbing, advertising (creating and producing commercials), legal advice and running a school. Starting a new car manufacturing firm will be massively expensive and make you compete head-on with huge firms. Starting a new advertising agency has neither problem.

Labour-intensive production

Labour-intensive production:

- means that labour costs form a high percentage of total costs
- has low financial **barriers to entry** because it is cheap to start up production

- makes it necessary for management to focus on the cost of labour (making it especially attractive to switch production to a low-cost country such as Cambodia)
- has the advantage of being highly flexible, making it possible for a small firm to operate successfully without direct competition from a large one.

> 'When a man tells you that he got rich through hard work, ask him whose.'
>
> Don Marquis, author and playwright

Capital-intensive production

Capital-intensive production:

- has a large percentage of its total costs tied up in the fixed costs of purchasing and operating machinery
- has high financial barriers to entry
- may be able to keep producing in a high-cost country because labour costs are such a small proportion of the total costs (for example, mass production of Coca-Cola or Heinz Beans)
- can be inflexible, both in terms of switching from one product to another and in the ability to tailor a product to an individual customer.

> 'Capital intensive production is great on the way up, but trouble on the way down.'
>
> Anon

Figure 41.7 Labour- versus capital-intensive production

Five whys and a how

41.10 Production, productivity and efficiency – evaluation

Greater labour productivity can lead to greater efficiency and higher profitability. This is because, other things being equal, it lowers the labour cost per unit. However, productivity is only one factor that contributes to a firm's success. A firm must also ensure it produces a good-quality product, that it is marketed effectively and that costs are controlled. There is little point increasing productivity by 20 per cent if at the same time you pay your staff 30 per cent more. Similarly, there is no point producing more if there is no actual demand. Higher productivity, therefore, contributes to better performance but needs to be accompanied by effective decision making throughout the firm.

The importance of productivity to a firm depends primarily on the level of value added. Top-price perfumes such as Chanel have huge profit margins. Production costs are a tiny proportion of the selling price. Therefore, a 10 per cent productivity increase might have only a marginal effect on profit and virtually none on the competitiveness of the brand. For mass market products in competitive markets, high productivity is likely to be essential for survival. A 5 per cent cost advantage might make all the difference. Therefore, when judging an appropriate recommendation for solving a business problem, a judgement is required as to whether boosting productivity is a top priority for the business concerned.

Questions	Answers
Why might employees be concerned about moves to increase productivity?	Because if the business operates in a static market, higher productivity probably means fewer jobs.
Why might it be hard to measure the productivity of a doctor?	Although you could measure patients seen per month, you couldn't measure the quality of diagnosis and care.
Why might it be useful for a manufacturing company to set targets for annual productivity improvement?	Because this would help the business gain competitiveness in relation to UK and overseas rivals.
Why may it matter that capital spending in the UK is relatively low (see Figure 41.1)?	As capital spending is an important way to boost productivity, low spending is a concern for long-term UK competitiveness.
Why is it a concern that UK productivity growth flattened out between 2007 and 2013 (see Figure 41.4)?	Because rising efficiency is what creates economic growth; if productivity stays flat, Britain's economic growth will be flat as well.
How might a service business try to increase productivity?	By getting staff to care more, work smarter and contribute ideas on how the business could work more effectively.

41.11 Workbook

Revision questions

(40 marks; 40 minutes)

1 What is meant by the term 'productivity'? (3)

2 Why may it be hard to measure the productivity of staff who work in service industries? (4)

3 How does productivity relate to labour costs per unit? (4)

4 Explain how a firm may be able to increase its employees' productivity. (4)

5 How can increased investment in machinery help to boost productivity? (3)

6 Identify two factors which help and two factors which limit your productivity as a student. (4)

7 Outline the likely effect of increased motivation on the productivity of a teacher. (5)

8 Calculate the change in productivity at BDQ Co (see Table 41.3) since last year. (4)

	Output	Number of staff
Last year	32,000	50
This year	30,000	40

Table 41.3 Productivity at BDQ Co

9 Explain how motivation and productivity may be linked. (4)

10 Explain how productivity can be linked to unit labour costs. (5)

Data response 1

In developing countries, labour is often wasted by employers because it is relatively cheap. The result is workers being profitably employed in low productivity activities such as shoe-cleaning, street vending and sandwich boards (a human, walking advertising poster).

Real wages in the UK have fallen sharply over the last decade. This has encouraged some British firms to adopt some of the same methods used by employers in developing countries. Cheap British labour is now being employed in activities that are profitable, but where productivity is very low.

A good example is Domino's pizza.

Figure 41.8 A Domino's 'wobble boarder'

In recent years, the take-away chain has used some of its employees to act as human advertisements. Workers are asked to wave and dance at passing motorists on busy street corners while wearing giant pizza boxes featuring the company's brand and details of special promotional prices. The company has defended their use of 'wobble boarding' by claiming that 'it is a key part of our marketing activity'. The use of wobble boards to boost sales of pizza has attracted criticism. In Cambridge, local residents wrote letters of complaint arguing that it was demeaning and degrading for young people, including graduates, to be paid minimum wages to act as little more than walking advertisements. Others criticised the adverts on the grounds that they could distract motorists, causing accidents. Presumably, Domino's uses wobble boards because the extra revenue generated from this form of advertising exceeds the wages paid to wobble boarders.

Questions

(30 marks; 35 minutes)

1 Explain how the manager of a Domino's pizza outlet might measure the productivity of their wobble boarders. (4)

2 The manager of a Pizza Express estimates that a team of five wobble boarders working for eight hours daily will boost the restaurant's gross profit by £500 per day. According to the local job centre, there will be plenty of people willing to undertake this work at the national minimum wage of £6.50 per hour. On the basis of these figures, calculate whether it would be profitable for Pizza Express to employ the wobble boarders. (4)

3 Assess the view that low productivity always leads to low profitability. (10)

4 Assess whether it is ethical to employ graduates to act as human advertisements. (12)

Data response 2

Going potty

Farah Stewart was trying to explain the need to boost productivity to the employees at her ceramics factory, FS Ltd. Relations between Farah and her staff had not been good in recent years. The company was not doing well and she blamed the workers.

'On average you work eight hours a day at £8 an hour and produce around 160 pots each. Meanwhile at Frandon, I am told, they produce 280 pots a day. Can't you see that this makes it cheaper for them and if things go on like this we'll be out of business? You need to work much harder to get our unit costs down! I know you are expecting to get a pay rise this year, but I cannot afford it until you produce more; then we'll think about it.'

Jeff Battersby, the spokesperson for the employees, was clearly annoyed by Farah's tone.

'Firstly, Ms Stewart, have you ever considered that if you paid us more we might produce more for you? I'm not surprised productivity is higher at Frandon – they get about £80 a day. There's no point demanding more work from us if you are not willing to pay for it – we're not slaves you know. If you paid us £10 an hour, like Frandon, I reckon we could increase productivity by 50 per

cent. However, that's not the only issue: they've got better equipment. It's not our fault if the kilns don't work half the time and take an age to heat up. Sort out the equipment and our pay and you'll soon see productivity improve. Why not ask us next time instead of jumping to conclusions?'

Questions

(60 marks; 75 minutes)

1 a) FS Ltd employs 50 pot makers while Frandon Ltd employs 30 people in production. Calculate the total output for each of the two companies. (4)

   b) With reference to FS Ltd and Frandon Ltd, explain the difference between 'total output' and 'productivity'. (4)

2 a) Calculate the average labour cost per pot at FS Ltd if employees are paid £8 an hour and their daily output is 160 pots each. (4)

   b) Calculate the wage cost per pot at Frandon (assume an eight-hour day). (4)

   c) Assess the short- and long-term benefits to Frandon of its lower labour costs per unit. (10)

   d) Jeff Battersby claims that if the employees at FS Ltd were paid £10 an hour their productivity would increase by 50 per cent. Calculate what the unit wage cost would be then. (4)

3 Assess whether Farah should increase the pay of her employees to £10 an hour. (10)

4 Evaluate the possible gains from involving employees in discussions about how to improve productivity. (20)

Extended writing

1 Faced with falling sales and sharply falling market share, the boss at Morrisons supermarkets decides to implement a 12-month Productivity Improvement Programme (PIP). Evaluate how the boss should set about this task. (20)

2 New competition from Chinese-made cars is undercutting the prices of British-made cars by 35 per cent. Evaluate the possible impact of a sustained programme by management to boost labour productivity at a British car factory. (20)

42 Capacity utilisation

Linked to: Approaches to staffing, Ch 17; Introduction to resource management, Ch 40; Production, productivity and efficiency, Ch 41.

42.1 The importance of capacity

Few products have completely predictable sales (perhaps baked beans or Marmite?) and therefore these is a fine balance to be struck between using your factory capacity fully and therefore efficiently – yet having the wiggle room to meet unexpectedly high orders. So it is vital to have sufficient spare capacity to cope with higher demand, while keeping capacity low enough to keep costs down. A fine balance.

42.2 Why and how to change capacity

In growth markets, capacity may need to be increased regularly. If an individual firm decides against increasing its own capacity, it will lose market share if it cannot meet demand. Yet capacity increases can take years to put into practice. The risk, then, is that the decision to increase capacity looks foolish when – a year or two later – the bigger factory or huge new office block opens at a time when boom has turned to bust. Clever businesses make sure that they anticipate changes in demand, so that capacity increases are managed. A little at a time is greatly preferable to a great leap forward.

Real business

India's railways are crumbling, due to a lack of investment over many years. At the same time, the demand for passenger and freight transport in India has been increasing. This is mostly due to economic growth, which has pushed up commuter numbers and the amount of raw materials and goods that have to be moved around the country. The combination of rising demand and static capacity has caused overcrowding on many routes – bottlenecks on routes cause delays, which slow journeys. A shortage of space on trains means that passengers frequently have to stand in very crowded conditions, indicating that capacity utilisation is well above 100 per cent.

Figure 42.1 India's overcrowded railways

In January 2014, the Indian government announced a $10 billion plan to reduce overcrowding by investing in new trains and by building new rail lines and stations. This will not go far within such a vast country.

42.3 How is capacity utilisation measured?

Capacity utilisation is measured using the formula:

$$\frac{\text{current output}}{\text{maximum possible output}} \times 100$$

What does capacity depend upon? A firm's maximum output level is determined by the quantity of buildings, machinery and labour it has available. Maximum capacity is achieved when the firm is making full use of all the buildings, machinery and labour available – that is, 100 per cent capacity utilisation.

For a service business, the same logic applies, though it is much harder to identify a precise figure. This is because it may take a different time to serve each customer. Many service businesses cope with fluctuating demand by employing temporary or part-time staff. These employees provide a far greater degree of flexibility to employers. Part-time hours can be increased, or extra temporary staff can be employed to increase capacity easily. If demand falls, temporary staff can be laid off without redundancy payments, or part-time staff can have their hours reduced, thus reducing capacity easily and cheaply.

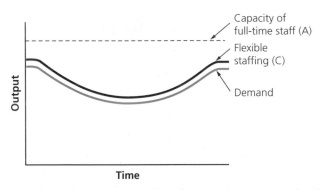

Figure 42.2 How flexible staffing (C) can reduce wastage implied by having under-used full-time staff (A)

42.4 Implications of under-utilisation of capacity

Fixed costs are fixed in relation to output. This means that whether capacity utilisation is 50 per cent or 100 per cent, fixed costs will not change. So if a football club invests in an expensive playing staff (whose salaries are a fixed cost) but matches are played to a half-empty stadium, the fixed costs will become a huge burden. This is because the very fact that fixed costs do not change *in total* as output changes means that they do change *per unit* of output/demand.

A half-empty stadium means that the fixed costs per unit are double the level at maximum capacity (see Table 42.1).

	Full stadium	Half-empty stadium
	50,000 fans	25,000 fans
Weekly salary bill (fixed costs)	£750,000	£750,000
Salary fixed cost per fan	£15 (£750,000/ 50,000)	£30 (£750,000/ 25,000)

Table 42.1 Fixed costs and capacity

When the stadium capacity utilisation is at 50 per cent, £30 of the ticket price is needed for the players' wages alone. The many other fixed and variable costs of running a football club would be on top of this, of course.

The reason why capacity utilisation is so important is that it has an inverse (opposite) effect upon fixed costs per unit. In other words, when utilisation is high, fixed costs are spread over many units. This cuts the cost per unit, which enables the producer either to cut prices to boost demand further or to enjoy large profit margins. If utilisation is low, fixed costs per unit become punishingly high. In June 2014, a newspaper in Zimbabwe reported that manufacturing capacity utilisation had fallen in the last year by 10 per cent to 30 per cent. According to the report, firms had reduced output in response to falling demand. This would make fixed costs per unit three times higher than necessary, which is an almost impossible situation.

42.5 Implications of over-utilisation of capacity

There are two key concerns about operating at maximum capacity for long, however. These are the risks that:

- if demand rises further, you will have to turn it away, enabling your competitors to benefit
- you will struggle to service the machinery and train/ retrain staff; this may prove costly in the long term, and will increase the chances of production breakdowns in the short term.

And is it possible to have a capacity utilisation rate of 105 or 110 per cent? Yes, in the service sector. If the business was a hotel or airline, then 'overbooking' will mean disappointed customers, 'bumped' off the flight they had chosen. For a shop, though, it might mean an uncomfortably overcrowded store, or queues having to form outside (as was true of Ugg Boots outlets when they were hugely trendy).

The ideal, therefore, is a capacity utilisation of around 90 per cent.

42.6 Ways of improving capacity utilisation

If a firm's capacity utilisation is an unsatisfactory 45 per cent, how could it be increased to a more acceptable level of around 90 per cent? There are two possible approaches, as discussed below.

Increase demand (in this case, double it!)

Demand for existing products could be boosted by extra promotional spending, price cutting or – more fundamentally – devising a new strategy to reposition the products into growth sectors. If supermarket own-label products are flourishing, perhaps offer to produce under the Tesco or Sainsbury's banner. If doubling of sales is needed, it is unlikely that existing products will provide the whole answer. The other approach is to launch new products. This could be highly effective, but implies long-term planning and investment.

Cut capacity

If your current factory and labour force is capable of producing 10,000 units a week, but there is demand for only 4,500, there will be a great temptation to cut capacity to 5,000. This may be done by cutting out the night shift (that is, making those workers redundant). This would avoid the disruption and inflexibility caused by the alternative, which is to move to smaller premises. Moving will enable all fixed costs to be cut (rent, rates, salaries, and so on), but may look silly if, six months later, demand has recovered to 6,000 units when your new factory capacity is only 5,000.

How to select the best option

A key factor in deciding whether to cut capacity or boost demand is the underlying cause of the low utilisation. It may be the result of a known temporary demand shortfall, such as a seasonal low point in the toy business. Or it may be due to an economic recession, which (on past experience) may hit demand for around 18–24 months. Either way, it could prove to be a mistake in the long run to cut capacity. Nevertheless, if a firm faces huge short-term losses from its excess fixed costs, it may have to forget the future and concentrate on short-term survival.

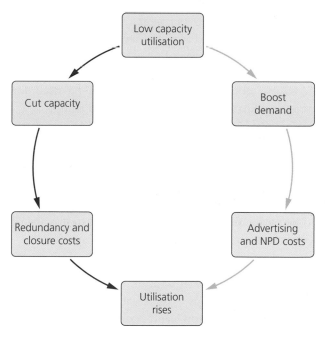

Figure 42.3 Logic chain: improving capacity utilisation

Five whys and a how

Questions	Answers
Why is a company's capacity utilisation an important non-accounting ratio?	Because it gives insight into: unit costs, the effectiveness of its marketing strategy and the job security of its staff.
Why might a company's capacity utilisation vary during the year?	For a seasonal business such as hotels, it will be much harder to sell rooms in the winter than in the summer.
Why might a struggling business choose not to cut its maximum capacity level during a recession?	It may be confident that the end of the recession will see a recovery in sales, i.e. it would be short-sighted to cut capacity today, then run out of capacity tomorrow.
Why may over-utilisation of capacity be a potential problem in a music festival?	Because of the potential hazards of having overcrowded facilities. At the least, it would be uncomfortable; at worst, dangerous.
Why does capacity utilisation affect a firm's profit margins?	The lower the utilisation, the higher the fixed costs per unit, pushing total unit costs up and profit margins down.
How might a business boost its capacity utilisation?	Either find a way to increase demand/usage or cut the maximum capacity at the existing premises.

42.7 Capacity utilisation – evaluation

Most firms will aim to operate close to full capacity, but probably not at 100 per cent. A small amount of spare capacity is accepted as necessary, bringing a certain degree of flexibility in case of need. In this way, sudden surges of demand can be coped with in the short run by increasing output, or **downtime** can be used for maintenance. Spare capacity can be a good thing.

Firms operating close to full capacity are those that may be considering investing in new premises or machinery. Building new factories takes time, as well as huge quantities of money. Can the firm afford to wait 18 months for its capacity to be expanded? Perhaps the firm would be better served **subcontracting** certain areas of its work to other companies, thus freeing capacity.

Capacity utilisation also raises the difficult issue of cutting capacity by **rationalisation** and, often, redundancy. This incorporates many issues of human resource management, motivation and social responsibility. There are fewer more important tests of the skills and far-sightedness of senior managers.

'You cannot endow even the best machine with initiative.'

Walter Lippmann, journalist and writer

When tackling this type of case study, it is important that you take a step back, to consider the cause and the effect. Is **excess capacity** the problem or an indicator of another problem, such as declining market share? By showing the broader picture in this way, you can also show the skill of evaluation.

Key terms

Downtime: any period when machinery is not being used in production; some downtime is necessary for maintenance, but too much may suggest incompetence.

Excess capacity: when there is more capacity than justified by current demand (that is, utilisation is low).

Rationalisation: reorganising in order to increase efficiency. This often implies cutting capacity to increase the percentage utilisation.

Subcontracting: where another business is used to perform or supply certain aspects of a firm's operations.

42.8 Workbook

Revision questions

(30 marks; 30 minutes)

1 What is meant by the phrase '100 per cent capacity utilisation'? (3)

2 At what level of capacity utilisation will fixed costs per unit be lowest for any firm? Briefly explain your answer. (4)

3 What formula is used to calculate the capacity utilisation of a firm? (2)

4 How can a firm increase its capacity utilisation without increasing output? (3)

5 If a firm is currently selling 11,000 units per month and this represents a capacity utilisation of 55 per cent, what is its maximum capacity? (4)

6 Use the information given in Table 42.2 to calculate profit per week at 50 per cent, 75 per cent and 100 per cent capacity utilisation. (7)

Maximum capacity	800 units per week
Variable cost per unit	£1,800
Total fixed cost per week	£1.5 million
Selling price	£4,300

Table 42.2 A firm's data

7 Briefly explain the risks of operating at 100 per cent capacity utilisation for any extended period of time. (3)

8 Outline two ways you might be able to tell that a supermarket was over-utilising its capacity. (4)

Data response 1

R. Sivyer & Co was founded 50 years ago. It has a successful history of manufacturing high-quality bicycle chains, which are supplied direct to retailers. In recent years, orders from retail customers have fallen, meaning that the firm is now manufacturing and selling only 12,000 chains per month.

The cost information given in Table 42.3 has been made available.

Materials cost per unit	80p
Shop-floor worker's salary	£10,000 p.a.
Salary paid to other staff	£12,000 p.a.
Manager's salary	£32,000 p.a.
Maximum capacity	20,000 units per month
General overheads	£40,000 per month
Current selling price	£5.80
Number of managers currently employed	3
Number of shop-floor staff currently employed	10
Number of other staff currently employed	4

Table 42.3 Cost information for R. Sivyer & Co

The finance manager has called the other two managers to a meeting to discuss the firm's future. She puts forward two alternative courses of action:

1 Make four shop-floor and two other staff redundant, thus cutting the firm's fixed costs, and reducing maximum capacity to 12,000 units per month.

2 Sign a contract to supply a large bicycle manufacturer with a fixed quantity of 8,000 chains per month at £5.80 each for the next four years; breaking the contract will lead to heavy financial penalties.

Questions (30 marks; 35 minutes)

1 Calculate the firm's current monthly profit. (4)

2 Calculate the monthly profit that would result from each of the two options. (8)

3 Assess the advantages and disadvantages of each option. (10)

4 State which of the two options you would choose, and explain any other information you would need before making the final decision. (8)

Data response 2

Ryanair load factors

The Irish low-cost airline Ryanair carried over 81 million passengers in 2013, making it the world's most popular airline. The company's success is based on highly efficient operations management. The low fares charged by Ryanair will only generate profit if the company can minimise its costs. To that end, the airline operates with only one type of plane, the Boeing 737. This decision enables the company to benefit from a range of economies of scale. Some airlines operate with leased planes; others, like Ryanair, buy outright. In July 2014, a Boeing 737 could be leased for $463,000 per month or bought outright for $81 million; either way, the fixed costs are significant. In these circumstances, load factors (the phrase used in the aviation business for capacity utilisation) must be kept very high in order to dilute the punishing fixed costs. The tactics used by Ryanair to achieve high load factors include:

- charging low prices
- reducing seat pitch – by removing some leg room, extra rows of seats can be crammed into each plane
- fast turnarounds in-between flights, ensuring that each plane spends as much time in the air as possible earning revenue.

According to the Centre for Aviation in March 2014, the number of passengers carried by Ryanair grew by over 7 per cent compared with the previous year and their load factor averaged 78 per cent.

Questions (35 marks; 40 minutes)

1 a) A Boeing 737 can accommodate 213 passengers when full. Calculate the load factor of a flight carrying 150 passengers. (4)

   b) The operating cost of flying a 737 is approximately £7,000 per hour. Calculate the average cost per passenger of a two-hour flight to Ibiza, assuming a load factor of 70 per cent. (5)

   c) Calculate the new average cost per passenger for the same flight if the load factor can be increased to 95 per cent? (4)

2 Other than price, assess the tactics Ryanair could employ in order to increase its load factors. (10)

3 In recent years, Ryanair has been on the receiving end of bad publicity regarding the quality of its customer service. Assess whether this could be due to the airline's high load factors/capacity utilisation. (12)

Extended writing

1 Evaluate the implications of a decision by Arsenal FC to increase its stadium capacity from 60,000 to 80,000. (By all means substitute Arsenal for any other sports club with which you are familiar.) (20)

2 Owing to a significant change in shopping habits, Tesco finds that its huge Tesco Extra shops are 40 per cent under-utilised. Evaluate what might be the right strategy for dealing with this. (20)

43 Stock control

Linked to: Markets and equilibrium, Ch 7; Sales forecasting, Ch 33; Liquidity, Ch 38; Production, productivity and efficiency, Ch 41.

43.1 Types of stock

Manufacturing firms hold three types of stock. These are:

- *raw materials and components*: these are the stocks the business has purchased from outside suppliers; they will be held by the firm until it is ready to process them into its finished output
- *work in progress*: at any given moment, a manufacturing firm will have some items it has started to process, but that are incomplete; this may be because they are presently moving through the production process; it may be because the firm stores unfinished goods to give it some flexibility to meet consumer demand
- *finished goods*: once a product is complete, the firm may keep possession of it for some time; this could be because it sells goods in large batches or no buyer has yet come in for the product; for producers of seasonal goods, such as toys, most of the year's production may be building stock in preparation for the pre-Christmas sales rush, a process known as producing for stock, or stockpiling.

The firm's costs increase if it holds more stock. However, this needs to be set against the **opportunity cost** of keeping too little stock, such as not being able to meet customer demand. One theory is that a firm should try to keep as little stock as possible at all times. This system, known as just-in-time, is covered later in this chapter.

43.2 Stock control charts

One way in which a firm analyses its stock situation is by using a control chart. This line graph looks at the level of stock in the firm over time. Managers can see how stock levels are changing and act quickly if slow sales have led to excessive stock levels.

A typical stock control chart looks like Figure 43.1. The chart shows four lines which represent the levels described below.

- *Stock levels*: this line shows how stock levels have changed over this time period. As the stock is used up, the level of stock gradually falls from left to right. When a delivery is made, however, the stock level leaps upwards in a vertical line. The greater the rise in the vertical line, the more stock has been delivered.
- *Maximum stock level*: this shows the largest amount that the firm is either willing or able to hold in stock.
- *Re-order level*: this is a 'trigger' quantity. When stocks fall to this level, a new order will be sent in to the supplier. The re-order level is reached some time before the delivery (shown by the vertical part of the stock level line). This is because the supplier will need some 'lead time' to process the order and make the delivery.
- *Minimum stock level*: this is also known as the **buffer stock**. The firm will want to keep a certain minimum level of stock so that it will have something to fall back on if supplies fail to arrive on time or if there is a sudden increase in demand.

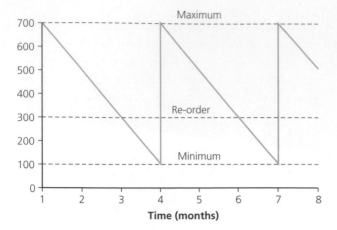

Figure 43.1 Stock control chart

Diagrams such as this, showing a neat and regular pattern to stockholding, will not happen in reality. Orders may arrive late and may not always be of the correct quantity. The rate of usage is unlikely to be constant. The slope of the stock level line may be steeper, showing more stock being used than normal, or shallower, showing a slower use of stock.

However, stock control charts such as these give managers a clear picture of how things have changed, and show them what questions need to be asked. For example, perhaps suppliers are regularly delivering late. Managers would then know to ask if suppliers were taking longer than the agreed lead time, or if orders were being placed too late.

Figure 43.2 shows a more realistic stock control graph. It is based on actual sales of Nestlé Lion Bars at a newsagent in south-west London.

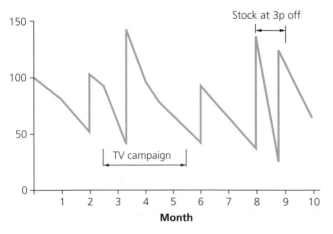

Figure 43.2 Monthly sales of Lion Bars at one newsagent

43.3 Implications of poor stock control

A firm can hold too much or too little stock. Both cases will add to the costs of the firm. Too much stock can lead to:

- *opportunity cost*: holding the firm's wealth in the form of stock prevents it using its capital in other ways, such as investing in new machinery or research and development on a new product; this may dent its **competitiveness**
- *cash flow problems*: holding the firm's wealth as stock may cause problems if it proves slow moving; there may be insufficient cash to pay suppliers
- *increased storage costs*: as well as the rental cost of the space needed to hold the stocks, the higher the stock value, the higher the cost of insurance against fire and theft
- *increased finance costs*: if the capital for the extra stock needs to be borrowed, the cost of that capital (the interest rate) will be a significant added annual overhead
- *increased stock wastage*: the more stock that is held, the greater the risk of it going out of date.

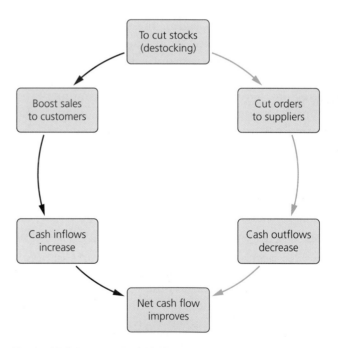

Figure 43.3 Logic chain: how destocking boosts cash

This does not, however, mean that the business is free to carry very low stocks. There are potential costs from holding too few stocks, including:

- lost orders, if urgent customer orders cannot be met because there is too little finished goods stock
- worker downtime, if essential components have been delayed in arriving from suppliers (and the very low buffer has been used up already)
- the loss of the firm's reputation and any goodwill it has been able to build up with its customers.

The total **stockholding cost** will therefore be a combination of these factors. As stock levels rise, the costs of holding the stock increases, but the costs of being out of stock decrease. The cost of holding stock will therefore look like Figure 43.4.

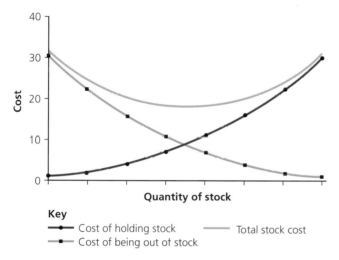

Key
— Cost of holding stock   — Total stock cost
—■— Cost of being out of stock

Figure 43.4 The cost of stockholding

For a firm, the optimum level of stock is where the total costs of holding stock are the lowest.

43.4 Just-in-time

Just-in-time (JIT) is a Japanese system of stock control that has been popular with UK firms over recent decades. JIT is the attempt to operate with a zero buffer stock. At the same time, a system must be developed so that the costs and risks of running out of stock are avoided by the firm.

Establishing a JIT system is not something that can or should be achieved overnight. The risks of running out of stock are too great. Figure 43.5 shows how a firm might set out to achieve a JIT system in a carefully planned way. The diagram shows five phases, after which the firm would intend to continue with phases six, seven and thereafter, until it could get as close as possible to zero buffer stock. The five phases are as follows:

1 The firm orders 20,000 units of stock to arrive every third week.

2 Suppliers are asked to move to weekly deliveries; therefore only one-third of the quantity is ordered.

3 As phase two has proved successful, there is no longer any need for such a high buffer stock. Stock levels are allowed to fall to a new, lower level.

4 With phase three complete, the firm now moves to receiving deliveries twice a week. Therefore, the order level is halved.

5 The suppliers have proved reliable enough to allow the buffer to be cut again…

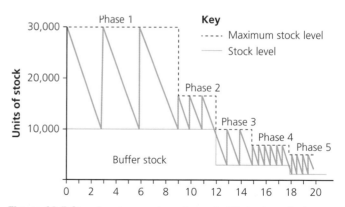

Figure 43.5 Step-by-step progress towards JIT stock control

'Stock in work-in-progress hides inefficiencies. It's better to expose them by removing buffer stock.'

J.K. Liker, business author

43.5 Waste minimisation

When the idea of just-in-time spread from Japan, most western companies looked to the benefits from lower working capital and potentially greater profitability. When companies tried the new approach, they suddenly found inefficiencies they hadn't known before. A late delivery from a supplier might leave workers idle on the shop floor, if there was no longer any buffer stock. And a faulty component could also cause the factory to shut down.

JIT puts pressure on managers to demand much higher quality standards and more efficiency from everyone involved in the business. Years ago, a supermarket's stockroom held huge stocks – including some forgotten stockpiles that might go out of date before they had made it to the shop floor. JIT reduced such levels of wastage and has helped grocers to become among the greenest of modern businesses – as measured by the reduction in their greenhouse gas emissions.

43.6 Competitive advantage from lean production

Lean production aims to produce more using less, by eliminating all forms of waste ('waste' being defined as anything that does not add value to the final product). The rise of the Japanese approach to lean production has been unstoppable. It is based upon a combined focus by management and workers on minimising the use of the key business resources: materials, manpower, capital, floor space and time. Largely originated by Toyota, lean production works by a process of continuous refinement that:

- maximises the input from staff
- focuses attention upon the quality of supplies and production
- minimises wasted resources in stock through just-in-time
- focuses upon the **competitive advantage** represented by speed.

For Toyota, a focus in new product development was to shorten the time between product conception and product launch. With its ability to be 'first-to-market' and its terrific reputation for quality, in 2013 Toyota became the world's number one car producer.

Lean production:

- creates higher levels of labour productivity; therefore, it uses less labour
- requires less stock, less factory space and less capital equipment than a mass producer of comparable size; the lean producer therefore has substantial cost advantages over the mass producer
- creates substantial marketing advantages: first, it results in far fewer defects, improving quality and reliability for the customer; second, lean production requires fewer engineering hours to develop a new product; this means that the lean producer can speedily develop a wide range of new products.

'To be competitive, we have to look for every opportunity to improve efficiencies and productivity while increasing quality. Lean manufacturing principles have improved every aspect of our processes.'

Cynthia Fanning, general manager, General Electric

Real business

Lean production ideas are starting to influence modern biotech companies. Innovative R&D is no longer enough; business success requires manufacturing efficiency. So biotech companies are implementing lean principles on the equipment and labour aspects of their business.

A US producer of proteins, Aldevron, has hired researchers from the University of Wisconsin to study the company's manufacturing processes and outline a strategy for improving efficiency. The company hopes to shrink the facility's product delivery timeline by at least 25 per cent – shaving a week or two off a typical four-to-five-week process. 'Because our labour force is more expensive, we've got to figure out how to do things faster', said Aldevron's vice president. The productivity gains from lean manufacturing could help Aldevron fend off overseas manufacturers that provide the same services at cheaper rates.

Five whys and a how

Questions	Answers
Why is stock control especially important for some firms, such as greengrocers?	Too much stock would mean tired displays and high wastage levels; too little would mean frustrated customers.
Why might an umbrella seller want relatively high buffer stocks?	Because rain arrives erratically and high customer demand arrives instantly.
Why is there a high opportunity cost to holding a large buffer stock?	Because all the money tied up in the stock could be used – profitably – elsewhere in the business.
Why may JIT be the wrong approach for managing stock at a hospital?	Because running out of stock may be a life-and-death matter – so buffer stocks are essential.
Why should companies wanting to minimise stock levels look for suppliers with short lead times?	The faster the supplier can deliver, the less stock you need to hold as a buffer.
How might the rise of online shopping affect decisions by retailers about stock levels?	It gives suppliers a slight buffer between the customer order and the delivery time, making it easier to operate with minimal buffer stock.

43.7 Stock control – evaluation

Stock control is at the heart of many business operations. For retailers such as Zara, Topshop and Primark, the desire for a constant flow of new, fashion-orientated stock means huge pressure to clear away old stock. Therefore, a JIT approach is ideal, with little or no buffer stock. In some cases, it is quite helpful commercially to run out of stock, if it means that, next Saturday, shoppers come earlier to make sure they can get the must-have item. The only thing that will not work is when customers go to a clothes shop and see tired, over-fingered stock that is outdated.

Making a just-in-time approach work requires close collaboration between purchasers and suppliers. The purchasing firm needs to bring the supplier into discussions on product development. Advice may be needed on components and materials as well as gaining the supplier's commitment to the new project. This Japanese way of doing business has taken off in Britain, making it much easier to provide customers with what they need.

Yet there are still firms that believe mass production plus high inventories is the only way to be efficient. If that is what Cadbury says about making chocolate – even the highly seasonal Creme Egg – it would be arrogant to argue. So it is always important to keep an open mind about what is right for a specific company.

Key terms

Buffer stock: the desired minimum stock level held by a firm just in case something goes wrong.

Competitive advantage: a feature that gives one business an edge over its rivals.

Competitiveness: the extent to which a firm can stand up to – or beat – its rivals.

Opportunity cost: the cost of missing out on the next best alternative when making a decision (or when committing resources).

Stockholding cost: the overheads resulting from the stock levels held by a firm.

43.8 Workbook

Revision questions

(35 marks; 35 minutes)

1 Why may it be important to maintain good relationships with suppliers? (3)

2 State the three main categories of stock. (3)

3 Outline two factors that might lead to a fall in stockholding costs. (4)

4 Explain the difference between lead time and re-order level. (4)

5   Sketch a typical stock control chart.   (6)

6   State three costs associated with holding too much stock.   (3)

7   Give three costs associated with running out of stock.   (3)

8   What is meant by just-in-time stock control?   (3)

9   Explain the meaning of the sentence: 'The purchaser's reputation is placed in the hands of the external supplier.'   (3)

10 Why is stock control of particular importance to an ice cream seller?   (3)

Activities

(35 marks; 40 minutes)

1   A firm sells 40,000 units a month. It receives monthly deliveries. Its maximum stock level is 50,000 and minimum (buffer) stock is 10,000. After two months (eight weeks), it decides to switch to weekly deliveries.

a) Sketch a 12-week stock control graph to illustrate this situation. Assume the firm starts the first week with 50,000 units of stock.   (10)

b) What short-term problems may the firm face in switching to weekly deliveries?   (6)

c) Consider the long-term benefits that may result from the change.   (9)

2   Sketch a graph to show the impact upon stock levels of a downturn in demand for a product for which a company has a non-cancellable fixed order from its suppliers. Fully label the graph to explain *what* happens *when*.   (10)

Data response 1

Ann Brennan established a bakery in Wigan 20 years ago. Although the firm is profitable, Ann is considering the introduction of modern techniques to help the company develop. In particular, she wishes to introduce information technology to improve communications between her five shops and the central bakery, and to help her manage her stock of raw materials more effectively.

Stocks of raw materials at the business are currently purchased in response to usage. For example, the bakery uses on average 500kg of flour per week. The most Ann wishes to hold at any time is 2,000kg. She would be worried if the stock fell below 500kg. An order takes one week to arrive, so Ann always re-orders when her stock falls to 1,000kg.

Questions (30 marks; 35 minutes)

1   What is meant by the following terms:

a) re-order level

b) buffer stock

c) lead time?   (6)

2   a) Draw a stock control graph for flour at Brennan's Bakery over a six-week period.   (6)

b) Draw a second graph showing the situation if twice the normal amount of flour were used in the fourth week.   (6)

3   Explain how information technology might be used to improve communication between Ann's shops and between the bakery and its suppliers.   (4)

4   Assess two possible effects of a 'stock-out' on Brennan's Bakery.   (8)

Data response 2

Is JIT always the best option?

In March 2011, a devastating earthquake and tsunami hit Japan. The effects of this natural disaster were arguably amplified by the widespread use of just-in-time production in Japan, whereby firms operate with very little, if any, buffer stock. This means that a whole production line will grind to a halt if just one component or raw material fails to be delivered by a supplier. The globalised nature of modern supply chains also meant that firms as far away as Britain and America suffered from the natural disaster in Japan. For example, Honda's factory in Britain quickly ran out of imported components from Japan causing car production to halt in Swindon.

Fujitsu is one of the leading suppliers of semi-conductors in Japan. One of its Japanese factories was badly damaged by the 2011 earthquake, which reduced output. Despite this, Fujitsu was able to bounce back quickly. In less than three months, production was back up to the pre-earthquake level. The key to Fujitsu's success was planning. Three years earlier, in response to another earthquake, the company developed an emergency response strategy. The strategy was based on creating additional capacity in other Fujitsu factories located in areas less susceptible to earthquakes. In 2011, Fujitsu wasted no time in implementing its plan, which worked.

Aside from acts of nature and war, manufacturers who want to be successful with JIT need to prepare for demand spikes. (A demand spike is a sudden, unexpected upsurge in demand.) Both Nintendo and Sony Corp. have had out-of-stock issues with their console systems, notably the PS4 in 2014. 'Just-in-time is OK, but if all of a sudden there is a surge in demand, you may not have the flexibility available to meet the demand', says one noted business analyst.

Questions (26 marks; 30 minutes)

1 Explain the weakness of JIT that was revealed by the 2011 earthquake and tsunami in Japan. (4)

2 A noted business analyst has said that 'JIT is about meticulous planning'. How well did Fujitsu stand up to that test? Explain your answer. (5)

3 a) Explain why manufacturing businesses hold stock. (3)

   b) Explain one benefit to a business from operating JIT with a zero buffer stock level. (4)

4 Assess whether a JIT approach to stock management is appropriate to a business with demand 'spikes', such as Sony. (10)

Extended writing

1 In November 2014, a mystery shopper went to five different stores and found the following level of products out of stock: Asda, 10 per cent; Morrisons, 15.6 per cent; Sainsbury's, 6.2 per cent; Tesco, 9.1 per cent; and Waitrose, 3.1 per cent. Evaluate the implications of this for two of the businesses concerned. (20)

2 Primark has decided to launch its first five shops in China. Up until now, it has had no presence in the country. Evaluate the challenges it will face in establishing an efficient system of stock management. (20)

44 Quality management

Linked to: Product and service design, Ch 10; Marketing strategy, Ch 15; Introduction to resource management, Ch 40..

44.1 The importance of quality

W. Edwards Deming, the American quality guru, said that 'quality is defined by the customer'. The customer may insist on certain specifications, or demand exceptional levels of customer comfort. Another definition of quality is 'fit for use'. Although hard to define, there is no doubt that customers are very aware of quality. Their perception of quality is an important part of the buying decision.

Customers will accept some **trade-off** between price and quality. There is, however, a minimum level of quality that is acceptable. The customer wants the product to work (be fit for use), regardless of the price. If the customers think that the quality is below a minimum level, they will not buy. Above the minimum level of acceptable quality, customers will expect to get more as they pay more.

The importance of quality is related to the level of **competitiveness** in the market. When competition is fierce, the quality of the product can tip the balance in the customer's decision making. For all customers, quality is about satisfying their expectations. The customer will take into account the total buying experience. Customer service and after-sales service may be as important as the product itself. The way the product is sold, even *where* it is sold, all contribute to the customer's feelings about the quality of the product.

Real business

Ryanair

Between 1991 and 2013, Ryanair boss Michael O'Leary built up the airline from almost nothing to become Europe's largest carrier. In all that time, O'Leary focused on three things: low costs to make low prices possible, plus two aspects of quality – on-time arrivals and fewest bags lost. By 2005, Ryanair was the best in Europe on both these measures of customer quality. Yet in 2013 O'Leary announced that, in future, Ryanair would be more sensitive to other aspects of customer quality – above all else, being friendlier, smilier and keener to give customers a more pleasant flying experience. Customers' quality needs had changed, and quality had become more important in customers' purchasing decisions.

Quality quotes

'Reducing the cost of quality is in fact an opportunity to increase profits without raising sales, buying new equipment, or hiring new people.'

Philip Crosby, American quality guru

'Quality is remembered long after the price is forgotten.'

Gucci slogan

'Quality has to be caused, not controlled.'

Philip Crosby

'Quality is our best assurance of customer allegiance, our strongest defence against foreign competition, and the only path to sustained growth and earnings.'

Jack Welch, General Electric chief

Source: Stuart Crainer (1997) *The Ultimate Book of Business Quotations*, Capstone Publishing

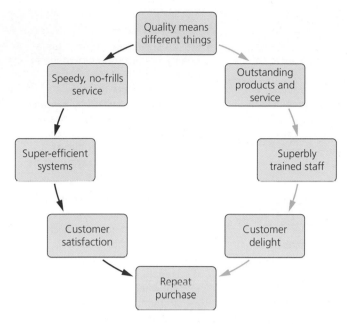

Figure 44.1 Logic chain: quality is different things to different people

44.2 Methods of improving quality

Quality control

Quality control (QC) is the traditional way to manage quality, and is based on inspection. Workers get on with producing as many units as possible, and quality control inspectors check that the output meets minimum acceptable standards. This might be done by checking every product; for example, starting up every newly built car and driving it from the factory to a storage area. Or it might be done by checking every 200th KitKat coming off the end of the factory's production line. If one KitKat is faulty, inspectors will check others from the same batch and – if concerned – may scrap the whole batch. The problem with this system is that faulty products can slip through, and it stops staff from producing the best quality: they just focus on products 'good enough' to pass the checks. Total quality management (below) is therefore a superior approach.

Quality assurance

Quality assurance (QA) is a system that assures customers that detailed systems are in place to govern quality at every stage in production. It would start with the quality-checking process for newly arrived raw materials and components. Companies have to put in place a documented quality assurance system. This should operate throughout the company, involving suppliers and subcontractors. The main criticism of QA is that it is a paper-based system and therefore encourages staff to tick boxes rather than care about the customer experience.

Total quality management

Total quality management (TQM) was introduced by W. Edwards Deming. He worked with Japanese firms, and his techniques are said to be one of the reasons for the success of businesses such as Honda and Toyota. TQM is not a management tool: it is a philosophy. It is a way of looking at quality issues. It requires commitment from the whole organisation, not just the quality control department. The business considers quality in every part of the business process – from design right through to sales. TQM is about building-in rather than inspecting-out. For it to be successful, it should be woven in to the organisational culture.

44.3 Other quality initiatives

Quality circles

A quality circle is a group of employees who meet together regularly for the purpose of identifying problems and recommending adjustments to the working processes. This is done to improve the product or process. It is used to address known quality issues such as defective products. It can also be useful for identifying better practices that may improve quality. In addition, it has the advantage of improving staff morale through employee involvement. It takes advantage of the knowledge of operators.

Zero defects

The aim is to produce goods and services with no faults or problems. This is vital in industries such as passenger aircraft production or the manufacture of surgical equipment. For many firms, **zero defects** is a target to move towards without any realistic expectation of getting there. For others, it is a deadly serious goal because a fault can be a life-and-death matter.

To achieve zero defects, in addition to a perfectionist approach to quality from all staff, there is likely to be a two-stage system for quality control – perhaps inspection by machine and then again by a quality inspector.

	TQM	QC	QA
Pros	• Should become deeply rooted into the company culture (e.g. product safety at a producer of baby car seats) • Once all staff think about quality, it should show through from design to manufacture and after-sales service (e.g. at Lexus or BMW)	• Can be used to guarantee that no defective item will leave the factory • Requires little staff training; therefore suits a business with unskilled or temporary staff (as ordinary workers don't need to worry about quality)	• Makes sure the company has a quality system for every stage in the production process • Some customers like the reassurance provided by keeping records about quality checks at every stage in production; they believe they will get a higher-quality service and may therefore be willing to pay more
Cons	• Especially at first, staff sceptical of management initiatives may treat TQM as 'hot air'; it lacks the clear, concrete programme of QC or QA • To get TQM into the culture of a business may be expensive, as it would require extensive training among all staff (e.g. all British Airways staff flying economy from Heathrow to New York)	• Leaving quality for the inspectors to sort out may mean poor quality is built in to the product (e.g. clothes with seams that soon unpick) • QC can be trusted when 100 per cent of output is tested, but not when it is based on sampling; Ford used to test just one in seven of its new cars; that led to quality problems	• QA does not promise a high-quality product, only a high-quality, reliable process; this process may churn out 'OK' products reliably • QA may encourage complacency; it suggests quality has been sorted, whereas rising customer requirements mean quality should keep moving ahead

Table 44.1 Pros and cons of TQM, QC and QA

Real business

Boeing 'Dreamliner'

In January 2013, all of Boeing's new 787 'Dreamliner' aircraft were grounded. With each plane having a list price of over $200 million, this was a huge and costly embarrassment for the American plane maker and its global airline customers.

The specific problem was a battery on the plane that overheated and sometimes caught fire. In fact, though, the Dreamliner had already suffered far more teething problems than would usually be expected from Boeing.

The reason proved to be the way Boeing had organised the huge operation of developing and engineering the production process. Due to lack of production capacity, 60 per cent of the design and production of key components had been outsourced to suppliers from around the world. Because Boeing's own quality standards had not been applied uniformly, the company's quality assurance and quality control systems struggled to cope.

44.4 Continuous improvement (kaizen)

Kaizen is a Japanese term meaning continuous improvement. Staff at firms like Toyota generate thousands of new ideas every year, each aimed at improving productivity or quality. Over time, these small steps forward add up to significant improvements in competitiveness.

There are two key elements to kaizen:

1 Most kaizen improvements are based around people and their ideas rather than investment in new technology.

2 Each change on its own may be of little importance. However, if hundreds of small changes are made, the cumulative effects can be substantial.

According to the Kaizen Institute, the goal of any kaizen programme should be to convince all employees that they have two jobs to do: doing the job and then looking for ways of improving it. The kaizen culture is based on the belief that the production line worker is the real expert. The worker on the assembly line does the job day in, day out. This means knowing more about the causes of problems and their solutions than the highly qualified engineer who sits in an office.

To operate kaizen successfully, employees cannot be allowed to work as isolated individuals. Team working is vital to the process of continuous improvement. These teams are composed of employees who work on the same section of the production line as a self-contained unit. Each team is often referred to as a 'cell'. The members of a cell are responsible for the quality of the work in their section. Over time, the cell becomes expert about the processes within its section of the production line.

Once the necessary kaizen apparatus is in place, good ideas and the resulting improvements should continue. The number of suggestions made each month should improve over time once employees see the effects of their own solutions.

> 'Continuous improvement is better than delayed perfection.'
>
> Mark Twain, famous American writer
>
> 'If there's a way to do it better... find it.'
>
> Thomas Edison, inventor

44.5 Competitive advantage from quality management

The traditional belief was that high quality was costly: in terms of materials, labour, training and checking systems. Therefore, managements should beware of building too much quality into a product (the term given to this was 'over-engineered'). The alternative approach, put forward by the American writer Philip Crosby, is that 'quality is free'. The latter view suggests that getting things **right first time** can save a huge amount of time and money.

In addition to cost advantages from high-quality production, there are potential benefits from adding value to the customer experience and therefore price tag. High-quality standards have disproportionate impacts upon reputation and therefore potential price levels. At the time of writing, Waitrose has champagne at prices from £20 to £255 for a bottle. At the upper end, brand image matters greatly, but is heavily underpinned by a reputation for high quality.

Where the consumer has choice, quality is vital. A reputation for good quality brings competitive advantages. A good-quality product will:

- generate a high level of repeat purchase, and therefore a longer product life cycle
- allow brand building and marketing benefits that can spread from one brand to others, e.g. Cadbury Twirl benefiting from the reputation of Cadbury Dairy Milk

- allow a price premium (this is often greater than any added costs of quality improvements; in other words, quality adds value and additional profit)
- make products easier to place (retailers are more likely to stock products with a good reputation).

Five whys and a how

Questions	Answers
Why are some companies able to get away with the appalling quality revealed on TV programmes such as *Cowboy Builders* or *Watchdog*?	Some companies can make high, long-term profits without needing customer loyalty. They rely on finding a steady stream of naïve customers; consumer protection laws try – but often fail – to stop these things happening.
Why may companies find it hard to correct a poor-quality image?	Images tend to build up over time, so they can be hard to shift. Change may require consistent quality programmes over several years.
Why is quality assurance more popular these days than quality control?	Quality assurance can be used to check the whole supply chain, rather than just the final product; that fits with the needs of Tesco or Waitrose, who want to be sure of provenance.
Why does quality matter if you are buying a £10 skirt from Primark?	It still matters, even if the customer may not mind about queues or scruffy displays. The skirt must be cut well enough and made of fabrics that look good.
Why do new firms sometimes struggle with quality?	They may have a very positive culture, but not yet have the processes in place to make sure of quality.
How would you set about improving quality at a struggling handbag maker?	First, give each worker a complete unit of work, i.e. producing the whole bag without division of labour; that would be hugely motivating; and drop any piecework payments.

44.6 Quality management – evaluation

In recent years, there has been a change in the emphasis on quality. The quality business has itself grown. The management section of any book shop will reveal several titles dedicated to quality management. The growth of initiatives such as TQM and continuous improvement goes on. With an increase in the international awareness of quality, British businesses will have to ensure that they continue to be competitive.

This growth in emphasis on quality has undoubtedly brought benefits to business. Increased quality brings rewards in the marketplace. Companies have also found that the initiatives, especially where they are people-based, have brought other advantages: changes in working practices have improved motivation and efficiency, and have reduced waste and costs.

Key terms

Competitiveness: the extent to which a firm can stand up to – or beat – its rivals.

Right first time: avoiding mistakes and therefore achieving high quality with no wastage of time or materials.

Trade-off: accepting less of one thing to achieve more of another (for example, slightly lower quality in exchange for cheapness).

Zero defects: eliminating quality defects by getting things right first time.

44.7 Workbook

Revision questions

(35 marks; 35 minutes)

1 State two reasons why quality management is important. (2)

2 How important is quality to the consumer? (3)

3 Suggest two criteria customers may use to judge quality at:

   a) a budget-priced hotel chain

   b) a Tesco supermarket

   c) a McDonald's. (6)

4 Why has there been an increase in awareness of the importance of improving the quality of products? (3)

5 Give two marketing advantages that come from a quality reputation. (2)

6 What costs are involved if the firm has quality problems? (3)

7 What are the four stages of quality management? (4)

8 What is total quality management? (4)

9 Outline two benefits of adopting quality circles to a clothing chain such as Topshop. (4)

10 Outline two additional costs that may be incurred in order to improve quality. (4)

Data response 1

Horsemeat and food quality in 2013

In January 2013, supermarkets were hit by an extraordinary scandal as it emerged that foods made of processed 'beef' actually contained horsemeat. Tesco was quickly forced to admit that one of its products contained 30 per cent horsemeat. Discounter Aldi also had to endure some tough headlines. Broadly, higher-priced retailers such as Waitrose, Sainsbury's and Marks & Spencer came out of the saga pretty well; Tesco, Asda and Morrisons fared worse. In the 12 weeks to 17 February, Tesco's market share slipped below 30 per cent for the first time in several years.

So how could it happen?

Amazingly, most supermarkets do not check the meat when it arrives at their depots. This task is outsourced ('farmed out') to companies approved by the British Retail Consortium. The inspectors go once to the source of supply, acting on behalf of all retailers. But according to Paul Smith, a recently retired food inspector:

> 'The suppliers can select which "approved inspection body" they use. They also pay for the audit. Yes, they can pick which audit company, the alleged policeman, they wish. In practice they also pick the individual auditor by heaping praise and requesting the same individual for the next visit.'

Source: evidence to a government committee, February 2013

'Throughout the world, our customers want safe, affordable products. Many also want to know that what they buy is sourced to robust ethical and environmental standards.

'We believe it is possible to provide for all our customers, whatever their needs, whilst upholding strong standards across our business and in our supply chains.'

Source: Tesco Social Responsibility Report

So despite the claims it makes in its Social Responsibility Report, Tesco does nothing to check on its food supplies. Other companies such as Waitrose may well do so, as they had no problem with horsemeat contamination.

The consequence of this slack approach to quality was clear in the impact of the scandal on food sales. In the four weeks after the scandal first hit, sales of frozen burgers were down (nationally) by over 40 per cent and sales of all ready meals were down by 12 per cent.

So what should Tesco be doing? First, it should switch its focus from public relations to quality management. Tesco shoppers probably believed that tough Tesco buyers went to suppliers, checked the quality standards, then negotiated toughly on price. Clearly the checking part may be a bit of a myth. To clear the air, the company should bring in a new policy of checking

at the producer, then checking as products arrive at Tesco. In effect this would be a full quality assurance regime. Having set the new policy up, it is then time to tell the consumer.

Tesco knows perfectly well that government inspection of food has been run down in recent years (see below), so it should have been making greater efforts to protect its customers (and its own reputation). It seems to have been very short-sighted in its approach to quality. It is likely to keep feeling the impact on its market share.

'The meat inspection workforce managed by the Food Standards agency has shrunk from a high point of 1700 – during the BSE and e-Coli crises in the 1990s – to around 800 today. This has been a direct consequence of the deregulatory policies of both the European Commission and UK government to hand over more and more meat inspection duties to the meat industry and dispense with proper independent inspection.'

Source: Unison (trade union)

Questions (20 marks; 25 minutes)

1 Assess Tesco's performance at choosing effective suppliers. (10)

2 Assess the importance of quality to a business such as Tesco. (10)

Data response 2

Manufacturing defects – producer comparisons: PcNow

PcNow is a small computer manufacturer based in the East Midlands. It tailor-makes computers and accessories based on customers' own specifications. Although business grew steadily initially, it is now worried about falling sales. It believes it is losing sales to Japanese and American companies that have set up manufacturing facilities in Europe, as well as to other European and UK-based firms. An industry survey has produced data on industry levels of production defects. It has added its own figures and produced the chart shown in Figure 44.2.

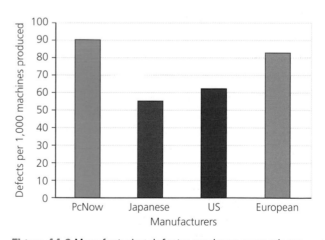

Figure 44.2 Manufacturing defects: producer comparisons

The firm realises that survival depends upon addressing the quality problems. It has decided to employ a quality manager, Cara Davenport, to address the issues. Her first suggestion is to get together workers from each department to discuss the problems and issues. Following a survey of the factory, she has also suggested that the layout of the production facilities should be changed. This will be an expensive exercise, and management is reluctant to make the changes as they will require production to stop for a week and there will need to be investment in new equipment. The firm's weak cash flow position makes it hard for the owners to accept new capital spending. The other area that Cara has identified is a problem with one particular component. She has suggested that a new supplier should be found, or that she should work with the existing supplier to improve the quality of the component.

Questions (40 marks; 45 minutes)

1 Explain what Figure 44.2 shows. (4)

2 From the case study, give two reasons for the quality problems experienced by PcNow. (2)

3 Assess two marketing implications for PcNow of the data in Figure 44.2. (8)

4 Assess the advantages PcNow may achieve from the discussion group formed to discuss the quality problems. (10)

5 Explain how Cara might convince the firm's management to change the layout of the production facilities. (4)

6 Once these changes have been made, the firm needs to ensure that quality is maintained and improved. Assess the implications for the firm of implementing a total quality management initiative. (12)

Extended writing

1 'Quality control is about building quality in, not inspecting it out.' Evaluate this statement. (20)

2 Evaluate whether quality management is solely a matter for the resource management function. (20)

3 Evaluate the extent to which quality is a major competitive issue in service businesses. (20)

45 Economic influences

> **Definition**
>
> Economic influences deal with changes in the economy as a whole (sometimes known as the 'macro' economy) and how they affect different businesses.

Linked to: Demand, Ch 5; Supply, Ch 6; Income elasticity of demand, Ch 9; Role of an entrepreneur, Ch 23.

45.1 What is 'the economy'?

Each of us goes about our business in our own way. A teacher receives a monthly salary paid directly into the bank, and draws out the cash needed to buy the shopping, buy petrol and give the children some pocket money. The children may spend this on chocolate, Coca-Cola and packets of crisps.

Although, as individuals, we 'do our own thing', the actions and decisions taken by millions of people and businesses make up 'the economy'. Collectively, chocolate purchases in Britain add up to £3,500 million per year. This, in turn, provides the income for chocolate producers and shopkeepers, who employ tens of thousands of staff.

If the value of all spending on all products bought in the UK is added together, it comes to an annual figure of over £1.5 trillion (a thousand billion). This spending provides the vast revenues that companies need in order to pay for Britain's 30 million workers, and enough profit left over to pay for business growth.

The key thing to remember is that the economy is intertwined. Cadbury is successful only if families have enough cash to be able to buy chocolate bars. So, if there was a big cutback in consumer spending, perhaps in the wake of government spending cutbacks, many firms would struggle, including Cadbury.

When times are bad, almost every business suffers; this, in turn, can lead to job losses. When the economy is recovering, things get better for almost all firms.

45.2 Current economic climate

Business thrives on confidence. Confident consumers are willing to dip into their savings for a holiday, or to borrow to buy a new carpet or car. Confident investors are willing to put more money into businesses in return for shares. And the companies themselves will spend to invest in their future: new factory buildings, new machinery and new computer systems. All this spending can create an upsurge in economic activity.

The reverse also applies: gloom can spread doom. Therefore, the **economic climate** is important. The sections that follow give an idea of the factors that help to create an economic climate, either of optimism or of pessimism. These factors include:

- the business cycle
- changes in inflation
- changes in interest rates
- changes in exchange rates
- changes in taxation and government spending.

45.3 The business cycle

The business cycle is the pattern of boom then slowdown that has been a feature of the UK economy for more than 150 years. When the economy is growing rapidly (around 3 per cent a year), consumers and companies have the confidence to spend and invest. This extra boost to output risks creating an unsustainable boom, which may lead to a bust, such as the one in 2009.

Figure 45.1 shows the tricky period for the UK economy between the start of **recession** in 2008 and the second quarter of 2014, when the economy finally returned to its pre-recession peak. The straight black line shows the **GDP** trend excluding the recession and the unprecedentedly slow recovery. The graph also shows the normal progress of the UK economy. For more than 200 years, it has grown at an average of just under 2.5 per cent per annum – that is, growth is normal. Therefore, the general expectation is that the underlying market conditions will be positive, with the size of markets expanding on a regular basis.

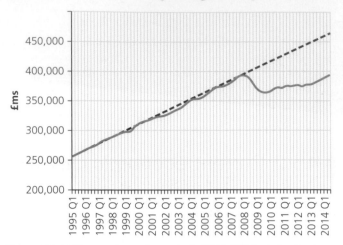

Figure 45.1 UK gross domestic product, 1995–2014; chained volume measures, quarterly figures, seasonally adjusted (source: ONS)

When market conditions are as tough, as in 2008/2009, there are likely to be failures as businesses run out of cash (Woolworths, La Senza and many others went under). There may also be huge pressures placed on company workforces, as people are forced to choose between redundancy and **real** wage cuts. In the recessions of 1980 and 1990, job losses pushed unemployment up above three million. The recent recession saw instead a huge squeeze on people's real incomes, meaning that the pain was shared more fairly across the population. Government statistics show that between July 2008 and March 2014 earnings rose 8.6 per cent while prices rose 16.9 per cent. This made people 7.1 per cent worse off (even worse if the tax to be paid on the extra earnings is included). In addition to this squeeze on incomes, Figure 45.2 shows why consumer confidence was hard hit in 2009, with people worried whether they would be next for a redundancy notice. No wonder that, at times, even products like chocolate and chewing gum saw falls in sales volume as market conditions tightened.

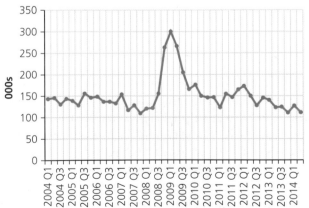

Figure 45.2 UK redundancies per quarter (source: ILO, quoted by UK Office of National Statistics)

'There's no evidence that the business cycle has been repealed.'

Alan Greenspan, former chairman of the US central bank

'Never has so much money been owed by so few to so many.'

Mervyn King, governor of the Bank of England, on the £1,000 billion bail-out from taxpayers to Britain's banks

45.4 Inflation

Inflation measures the percentage annual rise in the average price level. For consumers, inflation increases the cost of living. The rate of inflation is measured monthly, but presented as a year-on-year figure. So September 2014 inflation of 1.2 per cent meant that the prices of the average household's shopping basket were 1.2 per cent higher than in September 2013.

Does this matter? Traditionally, it mattered most to those with cash savings, such as pensioners. Steady inflation erodes the spending power of money and therefore makes each £1,000 of cash savings worth less. In the period between 2009 and 2015, it mattered because the weakness of the labour market meant that earnings were hardly rising at all, year on year. Therefore, every 1 per cent of inflation meant a 1 per cent reduction in the value of employees' earnings. In turn, that meant squeezed living standards.

The most widely quoted index for measuring inflation is the Consumer Prices Index (CPI). This data series is produced by the government's statistical office each month. It selects 700 items that we buy most often, then measures changes in the price charged for this shopping basket in thousands of different stores and locations. The data is then converted into an index to make it easier to understand and use by students, journalists and others.

An index means converting a series of data into figures that all relate to a base period where the data = 100. This allows users of the data to see at a glance the percentage changes and trends. In Table 45.1, column A shows the total price of buying the shopping basket. Column B converts that data into an index. This starts by saying 'let £402 = 100', then all the other figures in column A are related to that base figure of 100. For example, the figure for 2014 is £514.15/£402 × 100 = 127.9. Column C then calculates the percentage change each year based on the data in column A (or column B – it should give the same figure).

	A. Shopping basket price (£s)	B. Consumer Price Index 2005 = 100	C. Annual % change in inflation
2005	£402	100	–
2006	£411.25	102.3	2.3
2007	£420.9	104.7	2.3
2008	£436.2	108.5	3.6
2009	£445.4	110.8	2.2
2010	£460.3	114.5	3.3
2011	£480.8	119.6	4.5
2012	£494.45	123.0	2.8
2013	£506.9	126.1	2.6
2014	£514.15	127.9	1.4
2015 (est.)	£524.60	130.5	2.0

Table 45.1 Measuring inflation, 2005-2015

The advantage of index numbers is that you can see quickly that, for example, inflation amounted to 27.9 per cent between 2005 and 2014. So index numbers help you understand trends rather more easily. Their other huge benefit is that they enable direct comparisons to be made between different data series. In the case of inflation, the interesting recent comparison would be with earnings. This data is shown in Table 45.2 and Figure 45.3. It shows average earnings outstripping prices in 2006 and 2007, but then being dragged back until – from 2011 – they were well behind the rise in prices.

	Consumer Price Index 2005 = 100	Earnings Index 2005 = 100
2005	100	100
2006	102.3	105.7
2007	104.7	108.9
2008	108.5	111.6
2009	110.8	113.7
2010	114.5	115.1
2011	119.6	117.3
2012	123.0	118.6
2013	126.1	120.6
2014	127.9	121.8
2015 (est.)	130.5	123.6

Table 45.2 Consumer Price Index v. Earnings Index, 2005-2015

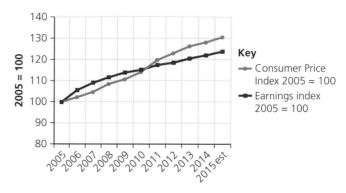

Figure 45.3 Consumer Price Index v. Earnings Index, 2005-2015 (source: Office of National Statistics, October 2014)

Effects of inflation on businesses

1 Firms with large loans benefit from inflation because inflation erodes the real value of the money owed. So when they have to repay the loan, it doesn't feel as painful because of the fall in the value of money. As an extreme example, a house in south London has just been sold for £1.2 million. When bought, 20 years ago, its price was £80,000. It was bought with a £50,000 mortgage. Repaying a £50,000 mortgage seems a lot easier now that the sale has provided £1.2 million of cash.

2 But inflation can damage profitability, especially for firms that have fixed-price contracts that take a long time to complete. For example, a local building company might agree a £5 million price for an extension to a local private school, which is expected to take three years to finish. If inflation is higher than expected, profit could be wiped out by the unexpectedly high cost increases created by the unexpectedly high rates of inflation.

3 If costs in Britain are rising faster than prices elsewhere, UK companies will find that they are losing their ability to compete effectively with foreign firms. Renault has launched a new small car for India priced at £2,200. That would hardly pay the labour costs if the car was produced in Britain.

45.5 Interest rates

The interest rate is the price charged by a bank per year for lending money or for providing credit. Individual banks decide for themselves about the rate they will charge on their credit cards or for the overdrafts they provide. But they are usually influenced by the interest rate that the central bank charges high street banks for borrowing money: the bank rate. In Britain, this is set each month by a committee of the Bank of England. As shown in Figure 45.4, the standard rate of interest in the UK has generally been around 4–5 per cent. In March 2009, though, the rate was cut to its lowest point in the Bank of England's history – 0.5 per cent. And it remained there as a way of helping to revive an economy hit very hard by the 2009 recession.

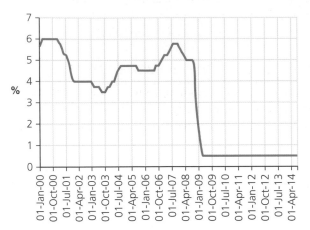

Figure 45.4 UK bank interest rates, 2000–2014 (source: www. bankofengland.co.uk)

The Bank of England committee is asked to set interest rates at a level that should ensure UK prices rise by around 2 per cent per year. If the committee members decide that the economy is growing so strongly that prices may rise faster than 2 per cent, it will increase interest rates. Then people will feel worried about borrowing more (because of the higher repayment cost) and may cut their spending. This should help to discourage firms from increasing their prices.

For firms, the level of interest rates is very important because:

- it affects **consumer demand**, especially for goods bought on credit, such as houses and cars; the higher the rate of interest, the lower the sales that can be expected
- the interest charges affect the total operating costs (that is, the higher the interest rate, the higher the costs of running an overdraft, and therefore the lower the profit)
- the higher the rate of interest, the less attractive it is for a firm to invest money into the future of the business (because of the opportunity cost – the high interest rates available for keeping money safely in the bank); therefore, there is a risk of falling demand for items such as lorries, computers and factory machinery.

If interest rates fall, the opposite effects occur, to the benefit of both companies and the economy as a whole.

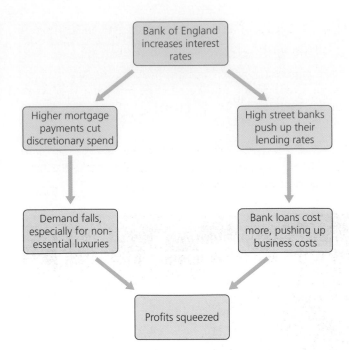

Figure 45.5 Logic chain: effect on costs and revenues of rising interest rates

45.6 Exchange rates

The exchange rate measures the quantity of foreign currency that can be bought with one unit of domestic currency. Movements in the exchange rate can dramatically affect profitability because the exchange rate affects prices of imported and exported goods. In exams, the value of the pound (£) is usually considered only in relation to the US dollar ($) or the euro (€).

Appreciation of the pound occurs when the value of the pound rises. This means each pound can buy more dollars or euros. Depreciation means a fall in the value of the pound. It can buy fewer dollars or euros. Table 45.3 gives a numerical example of appreciation and depreciation.

	Example	Impact on exports	Impact on imports
£ appreciates	£1 was $1.60, but now buys $1.80	UK exports get pricier, so sales volumes slip.	Imports to UK get cheaper, making it harder for UK firms to compete.
£ depreciates	£1 was at €1.30 but now slips to €1.15	UK exports get cheaper, so sales volumes rise.	Imports to UK get more expensive, so UK firms can compete more effectively.

Table 45.3 Summary of effects of exchange rate changes

The impact of a high exchange rate

On firms with large export markets

UK firms that sell a high proportion of their output overseas will prefer a low exchange rate (that is, a weak pound). Why is this so? The best way of explaining is via a numerical example.

America is an important export market for Morgan Cars. Morgan charges its UK customers £25,000 for a basic two-seater Roadster.

Figure 45.6 Morgan Roadster

To achieve the same profit margin in America, Morgan has to charge a price in US dollars that will convert into £25,000. If the exchange rate against the US dollar is £1 = $1.60, Morgan has to charge its American customers:

£25,000 × $1.60 = $40,000

If the pound appreciates to be worth $2, to generate the same £25,000 of export revenue per car, Morgan must charge its American customers:

£25,000 × $2 = $50,000

In other words, Morgan would have to increase the US price of its cars by $10,000 to maintain the current profit made on each car sold. The price increase would be off-putting to car buyers, so sales would fall.

On firms that import most of their raw materials or stock

Retailers such as Sports Direct, which import much of their stock, like a strong pound. A high exchange rate reduces the cost of buying goods from abroad. For example, Nike trainers are imported from the American producer. If the US price of a pair of trainers is $40, the price paid by Sports Direct is as follows.

If the exchange rate is £1 = $1.60, the trainers will cost Sports Direct:

$40/$1.60 = £25

However, if the exchange rate goes up to £1 = $2, the same trainers cost £20 ($40/$2 = £20). A high exchange rate benefits Sports Direct because it buys imports more cheaply, allowing it to make more profit per pair of imported trainers sold to UK customers.

The impacts of a low exchange rate

The impacts of a weak exchange rate are the reverse of the impacts of a strong exchange rate. Exporters, especially manufacturers, can be damaged by a strong pound. Exporters love to see the pound depreciate in value.

On the other hand, companies such as Sports Direct are damaged by a low exchange rate because their imported stock costs them more. If Sports Direct reacts to the falling exchange rate by raising its prices, the company could lose customers. If the company does nothing, it will make less profit on each sale of an imported item.

45.7 Taxation and government spending

In addition to economic change, businesses can be affected by economic policy decisions taken by government. If worried about inflation, a government could decide to increase income tax. This would take spending power out of the pockets of consumers, softening the upward pressure on prices, but cutting demand for the products and services produced by businesses. What might be right for the economy as a whole could be damaging for individual businesses.

Why would any government take actions that could damage businesses and therefore threaten jobs? The answer is simple: because ministers may believe that short-term pain may be necessary for long-term gain. This might be correct, but it will be no consolation to any business squeezed out of business by an unexpected tax rise.

The other main weapon government can use to achieve its policy goals is to change the level of government (known as 'public') spending. At present, just over 40 per cent of the British economy is generated by public spending. The rest is mainly generated by private consumers (you and me). The government spends huge sums on the health service, defence, roads and much else. If the government was concerned about rising prices, it could consider cutting back on its own spending. This would reduce the income of businesses involved in education, road-building, and so on. They, in turn, may have to make redundancies, thereby dampening down consumer spending, which should help to keep prices from rising so sharply.

> 'The last thing you want to do is raise taxes in the middle of the recession.'

Barack Obama, US President

It follows, therefore, that sensible businesspeople keep an eye on government activity. Years ago, the government announced its tax and spending plans in the Spring Budget, which was always kept secret until the government announced it. Today, an 'Autumn Statement' announces, six months in advance, the government's public spending plans. This ensures that firms can anticipate the tax decisions that will be announced in the spring.

Table 45.4 shows how a government could use its power over taxation and spending to tackle different economic problems.

45.8 The effect of economic uncertainty on the business environment

In late 2013, investment bankers Goldman Sachs made their forecast for oil prices for the coming year. They expected a price rise to $105, with $115 a distinct possibility. In fact, by December 2014, the world oil price was below $60 a barrel. Some very highly paid bankers got it all wrong. This, in turn, would mean that airlines would have paid too much for their fuel, and that suppliers of sustainable energy such as wind power would now be under severe economic pressure.

This gives an idea of what economic uncertainty looks like. If it is extremely difficult to forecast the level of supply and demand in the oil business (and therefore the price), how much harder is it to forecast the level of demand throughout an economy? It verges on the impossible. Therefore, every business has to make its plans for the coming year with little certainty about the overall state of the economy, and even less certainty

	Government spending up	Government spending down	Government puts taxes up	Government puts taxes down
To help reduce the level of unemployment	Extra spending on road-building, health and other services with big workforce			Reduce income tax to enable families to keep and spend more of the money they earn
To cut the growth rate when it is rising too fast		Cut the spending on health, education and defence, to take a bit of spending from the economy	Increase income tax to force people to think harder and more carefully about what they buy	
To improve the competitiveness of British firms	Extra spending on education			Cut company taxation (corporation tax)
To cut the rate of imports, especially of consumer goods		Cut benefits (e.g. state pension) to cut people's ability to buy imports	Increase VAT on all goods other than food and drink	

Table 45.4 The impact of a change in taxation and government spending

about certain economic variables that are especially prone to big ups and downs. These include:

- the value of the pound; in the ten years from 2005 to 2014, the value of the pound against the euro fluctuated between £1 = €1.02 and £1 = €1.52; that variation of 50 per cent adds huge uncertainty to the plans of UK exporters
- the rate of economic growth; in that same ten-year period, UK annual growth varied between +3.2 per cent and −5.0 per cent
- the value of oil; between 2005 and 2014, the world oil price varied between $41 and $133 once again, making planning extremely difficult.

The lesson businesses need to take from the uncertain economic environment is to always be prepared for changing times around the corner. In good times, make sure your cash balances are being built up sufficiently to cope with a sudden worsening of your position. And in bad times, keep alert to the opportunities that may soon be about to open up.

Five whys and a how

45.9 Economic influences – evaluation

When companies publish their annual results, commentators groan if the boss blames disappointing results on external factors such as the weather or the weakness of the economy. Business journalists admire chief executives who achieve their targets no matter what. Yet that may not be realistic. If you are running Coca-Cola, you have huge control over your pricing and therefore can probably find a way to boost profits to meet analysts' expectations. Not long ago, people assumed that Tesco was in a similar position. The squeeze on household spending, the rise of Aldi and Lidl and a series of strategy mistakes by Tesco make it look very different now.

In truth, it is always the case that firms are vulnerable to external factors. Even monopolies (when a single firm dominates a market) are subject to changing consumer habits, as Microsoft and even Apple have found in recent years. If things seem to be going wonderfully well – and every commentator thinks your business is bulletproof – it is probably time to worry. The one-time boss of monopolist microchip supplier Intel, Andy Grove, once said that 'only the paranoid survive'. That remains grimly true.

Questions	Answers
Why might Aldi and Lidl struggle when the UK economy starts to generate higher real incomes?	Because their sales boom in the 2010–2014 period may have been due to 'downtrading', as people switched to lower suppliers – therefore, the reverse may happen as the economy recovers.
Why may certain types of consumer find that 'their' inflation is higher than the CPI?	The CPI is based on the *average* shopping basket so it may not represent the price increases faced by pensioners, who spend differently (far more on energy bills than in other age groups).
Why might a rise in interest rates hit profits at a business such as Tesco?	Higher interest rates hit consumers' **discretionary income**, so spending falls (and so does Tesco revenue); also higher rates force Tesco to pay more on its bank borrowings/overdrafts.
Why might a UK manufacturer worry about a depreciation in the pound?	Although a falling pound helps competitiveness, it does mean higher costs for imported materials. This might be a worry, especially if UK rivals buy or make in this country instead of importing.
Why might a government want to increase the tax on air travel?	To raise tax revenue while appearing to be a 'green government' by taxing air travel.
How are real incomes measured?	By deducting price rises from the changes in people's incomes, e.g. 3 per cent more income but prices up 5 per cent – you are 2 per cent worse off in real purchasing power.

Key terms

Consumer demand: the levels of spending by consumers in general (not just the demand from one consumer).

Discretionary income: a person's income after deducting taxes and fixed payments such as rent and utility bills.

Economic climate: the atmosphere surrounding the economy (for example, gloom and doom or optimism and boom).

GDP: gross domestic product is the value of all the goods and services produced in a country in a year.

Real: changes in money (for example, wages) excluding the distorting effect of changes in prices. So a fall in real wages might be that wages are unchanged, but prices have risen.

Recession: two or more quarters of negative economic growth.

45.10 Workbook

Revision questions

(35 marks; 35 minutes)

1 Explain why a fall in spending in London could have a knock-on effect on the economy in Bradford, Plymouth, Norwich or anywhere else in the country. (3)

2 Explain whether the Bank of England should raise or cut interest rates in the following circumstances:

  a) A sharp recession has hit the UK economy. (3)

  b) House prices have risen by 16 per cent in each of the last two years. (3)

  c) Household incomes and spending have been rising rapidly. (3)

3 Outline how an economic downturn could affect the level of unemployment. (5)

4 a) Outline a change in government spending or taxation that could boost sales at Mothercare. (3)

  b) Explain the possible impact on a supermarket chain of an increase in inflation. (4)

5 What is meant by 'an appreciation' in an exchange rate? (1)

6 A British detective agency has been hired by a French woman to tail a man. The fee is €500 per week. After four weeks, the sum of €2,000 is due to be paid, but the rate for the pound against the euro has fallen from 1.30 to 1.15.

  a) What sum will the detective agency receive in pounds for this four weeks' work? (3)

  b) What may stop the agency from simply putting the euro price up? (3)

7 Outline two possible reasons why a UK manufacturer of chemicals might be concerned if the value of the pound depreciated. (4)

Data response

External pressures on the grocery market

The booming discount supermarket chain Aldi is on the verge of overtaking upmarket Waitrose to become the UK's sixth biggest supermarket as the German-owned grocer continues to open new stores and steal customers from its bigger rivals. Industry data show that, while Tesco and Morrisons continue to decline, Aldi's share of grocery till receipts rose to 4.8 per cent in the 12 weeks to 20 July 2014. A year previously, the discounter's market share was 3.7 per cent, according to figures from retail analysts Kantar Worldpanel.

Over the same period, Waitrose's market share edged up to 4.9 per cent from 4.8 per cent last year, while Tesco dropped to 28.9 per cent from 30.3 per cent. The data confirm the trend of shoppers abandoning mid-market players in favour of more upmarket rivals and the discounters, with increasing numbers of shoppers cherry-picking from both ends of the market. 'Waitrose has continued to resist pressure from the competition, testament to its policy of maximum differentiation, and has grown sales by 3.4 per cent. This figure is well above the market average and thereby has lifted its market share.'

Despite this positivity, *The Grocer* magazine has questioned whether Waitrose is now starting to suffer.

Its profit margins at 5.4 per cent are well above industry averages, and perhaps shoppers are starting to query its value for money. Partly because of its high prices, Waitrose offers free delivery to online grocery shoppers. With online sales booming, it may be that Waitrose profits start to get squeezed by the free delivery, given that picking and delivery is far from free from the shop's point of view.

The numbers come against a backdrop of a challenging market. Kantar says grocery price inflation has fallen for the tenth successive period and now stands at just 0.4 per cent – its lowest level since prices were first measured in 2006. As a result, market growth has fallen to 0.9 per cent.

Tim Vallance, head of retail at property group JLL, said:

'The figures highlight the impact that the big four's response to the rise of the discount retailers is having on the grocery sector, with vicious price cutting leading to shrinking market growth. As shoppers continue to demand a more convenient offer in an increasingly digital world, supermarkets need to think about how and where their customers shop and need to focus on choice, provenance, quality, service and convenience to differentiate from the discounter offering.'

Sources: adapted from www.4traders.com, 30 July 2014, and *The Grocer*, 9 August 2014

Questions (40 marks; 45 minutes)

1 Assess the possible implications for Waitrose of a fall in 'grocery price inflation' to 0.4 per cent a year. (10)

2 At this time in mid-2014, the rate of interest had been 0.5 per cent for five years. Assess how the position of Waitrose might have been affected by an increase in interest rates. (10)

3 Evaluate whether Waitrose would have been wise, at this time, to have differentiated itself further by switching entirely to Fairtrade supplies. (20)

Extended writing

1 Jaguar Land Rover exports 80 per cent of all the 500,000+ cars it produces in Britain. Evaluate the most probable response from the company if the pound appreciated sharply against other currencies. (20)

2 In the last recession, Tata Steel closed one of its Scunthorpe steelworks, making hundreds redundant. Evaluate the strategies Tata could have adopted to prepare for recession. (20)

46 Legislation

Definition

Legislation is defined as laws initiated by government but passed by parliament that relate to business operations and therefore employees, the general public and the environment.

Linked to: Introduction to managing people, Ch 16; Business objectives, Ch 25; Economic influences, Ch 45.

46.1 Introduction to legislation

UK businesses are subject to laws (legislation) passed by both the UK parliament and the European parliament. Since both UK and EU law are passed by parliaments, laws are affected by party politics. Conservative governments suggest they interfere as little as possible with the workings of business. In other words, they claim to take a **laissez-faire** approach. This means trusting businesses to do their best for their customers and employees – in other words, let the market regulate business activities.

'The most enlightened judicial policy is to let people manage their own business in their own way.'

Oliver Wendell Holmes, nineteenth-century author

Labour governments are more suspicious that businesses may act in their shareholders' interests, not those of their customers. Therefore, there is a greater temptation to bring in laws to regulate business activity. Before the Labour government established the National Minimum Wage in 1999, employers could, and did, pay as little as £3 an hour. The 2014 rate of £6.50 per hour is not riches, but provides some protection for the lower paid.

There are five main areas in which the law affects businesses:

1 consumer protection

2 employee protection

3 environmental protection

4 competition policy

5 health and safety.

46.2 Consumer protection

Consumer protection law is designed to ensure that consumers are treated fairly by the companies from which they buy. This covers issues such as whether a product does what it claims to do, whether products are correctly labelled and measured out and the rights of the consumers to refunds or exchanges of faulty goods. Consumer protection legislation should ensure that no firm can gain an unfair competitive advantage by taking short-cuts in how their products are made. If all products and services must meet a minimum legal standard, companies cannot use unsafe/cheaper materials to gain a competitive edge.

Two Acts of Parliament are especially important:

1 The Sale of Goods Act. First passed in 1893 and updated in 1979, this is the law that says 'goods must be fit for the purpose for which they are sold'. Before this law, nineteenth-century crooks sold 'cures' for 'bad blood' or cancer – and customers had no right to demand their money back. Today, if you buy shoes and holes appear in the soles within weeks, the Sale of Goods Act makes sure you can get your money back.

2 The Trade Descriptions Act. This was introduced in 1968 and updated in 2008. It forces companies to ensure that every claim and statement about a product is true. Before it, a beer producer could proclaim in advertising that 'Guinness is good for you'. In recent years, Danone has repeatedly been forced to back down on over-claims about the health virtues of products such as Activia.

The effect of consumer protection law on business has been to create more of a 'level playing field' in which competition has to be more on the basis of real product benefits, not simply on imagination and willingness to deceive. At every stage, companies have argued against new laws, suggesting that they will undermine competition. There is little evidence for this.

46.3 Employee protection

Employment law sets out, and aims to protect, the rights of employees at work. These rights include the right to fair pay, sick leave, maternity and paternity leave, employment contracts being honoured, relationships with trade unions, the ability of employers to shed staff and the responsibilities of employers who make staff redundant. Of these, the easiest to remember (and to see the implications of) is the National Minimum Wage legislation that was introduced in 1999. Table 46.1 sets out the implications of employment legislation for businesses.

Key area of employment law	Possible implications for firms
Minimum wage	Increased labour costs, which may lead to increased automation in the longer term and increased unemployment; on the plus side, employees may be more motivated by a fair wage satisfying basic needs
Right to a contract of employment	Meets employees' security needs but can reduce employers' flexibility in how they use their staff
Increased right to sick, maternity and paternity leave	Increased cost of paying for cover for these staff; however, staff may feel more valued as they feel well treated by employers, reducing staff turnover levels, which saves the costs of recruiting new staff
Redundancy	Reducing capacity becomes expensive due to statutory payments to staff made redundant; this can mean that closing a factory or office has a negative impact on cash flow in the short term
Trade union rights	Employers can be forced to deal with a trade union if enough staff are members; this does bring benefits as well as drawbacks

Table 46.1 Implications of employment legislation

As a general rule, businesses like to have minimal legal constraints on their activities. A business craves flexibility in the way it deals with its staff; legislation tends to impose certain restrictions on how staff are dealt with. UK business leaders argue that more employment legislation makes them uncompetitive relative to their international rivals. Yet UK employment legislation is not as tight as that in major rivals such as France and Germany. In its 2014–2015 report on global competitiveness, the World Economic Forum ranked the UK fifth in the world for 'labour market efficiency'. Yet there are still politicians who try to claim that Britain's labour market is over-regulated.

> 'Morality cannot be legislated, but behaviour can be regulated. Judicial decrees may not change the heart, but they can restrain the heartless.'
>
> Martin Luther King, civil rights leader

46.4 Environmental protection

Laws governing the impact of business on the environment are a key area today, given the increased acceptance of the need to legislate to protect the environment. A wide range of laws governs issues as diverse as the materials that firms must use for certain products, the processes firms are allowed to use in manufacturing and the extent to which firms must ensure their products are recyclable at the end of their lives. Environmental protection laws, perhaps more than any others, seem to most firms to be a source of additional cost without much of an upside. Firms in the UK are also subject to EU laws; this is an area in which several EU directives have led to increased expectations of businesses. Of course, all these firms feel a sense of injustice that they are competing against non-EU countries with less stringent environmental laws. The reality is, though, that companies such as Dyson have succeeded in Japan and America precisely because consumers in those countries want well-designed, environmentally friendly products.

Real business

Hoover panic

Towards the end of August 2014, UK newspapers reported on panic buying of vacuum cleaners. New EU rules were to start on 1 September making it unlawful to sell vacuum cleaners with an engine with more than 1,600 watts of power. Although James Dyson made it clear that the power of the engine was barely related to its efficiency, media scare stories created a sales surge amounting to a 400 per cent increase. The EU's concern was to halt a 6 per cent annual rise in electricity usage on household electric goods – as part of Europe's promise to cut carbon emissions by 20 per cent by 2020. UK newspapers treated the story as another opportunity to bash the European Union; in fact, vacuums sold today are every bit as efficient as before – with better design compensating for smaller engines.

Among the various pieces of environmental legislation, especially important ones include the following:

1 Landfill tax, which was introduced in the UK in 1996 following a European Union 'directive'. It forces businesses to pay £80 per tonne to deposit 'active waste' in landfill sites (council rubbish dumps). This adds to business costs and therefore can be said to damage international competitiveness. The other way to look at it is that it encourages businesses to minimise and then recycle waste instead of dumping it.

2 The Environmental Protection Act 1990 (updated in 2008), which sets out the structure of waste management and emissions control for the UK. Perhaps its most notorious feature is the requirement for 'risk assessments' – that is, full analyses by companies of the possible environmental risks from different aspects of their business. This is time-consuming and bureaucratic, but has probably helped in the significant reduction of river pollution in the UK. In 1990, a swim in the Thames was a suicide mission. Today fish, at least, have returned to the river.

46.5 Competition policy

Even the strongest believers in laissez-faire see the value in government intervention to boost competition. The need becomes most obvious when one company tries to buy up a rival. If Cadbury (with about 33 per cent of the UK chocolate market) bought Mars UK (which has about 20 per cent), the resulting giant would surely find it easy to push prices up and consumer choice down.

In 2014, the new Competition and Markets Authority (CMA) took on the functions of the now-closed Competition Commission and Office of Fair Trading. The government-funded CMA is responsible for:

- investigating takeovers and mergers
- investigating possible anti-competitive practices

- bringing criminal proceedings against individuals who commit **cartel** offences.

If the CMA is completely successful, UK consumers will benefit from real competition between companies doing their best to win market share. Sadly price-fixing remains surprisingly common, as evidenced by the number of companies 'busted' for this illegal activity.

'If there were no bad people there would be no good lawyers.'

Charles Dickens, novelist

Real business

In October 2013, the UK's cement industry was forced to change its practices by the competition authorities. The industry (dominated by three multinational companies) would no longer be allowed to share sales and production data, and the largest producer was forced to sell off one of its biggest cement factories. The competition authorities suggested that over-charging had cost the struggling construction sector £180 million over the period 2009–2013.

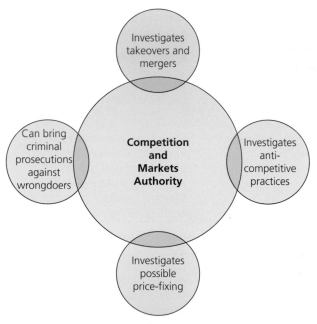

Figure 46.1 Logic circle: functions of the CMA

46.6 Health and safety

Health and safety legislation is designed to ensure the safety of employees and customers within the workplace. The Health & Safety at Work Act 1974 places the major burden on employers. They have to provide a safe working environment for their staff. The main areas covered by the legislation include the physical conditions in which staff are required to work, precautions that firms are required to take when planning their work and the way in which hazardous substances must be treated in the workplace.

The job of the Health and Safety Executive is to identify and prosecute any serious lapses by companies. In its 2014 annual report, the Executive prosecuted a scaffolding company that was found guilty and fined £300,000 (plus £124,000 in costs) after an employee was killed by an overturned skip lorry.

Despite the tight laws in Britain, there are still a worrying number of deaths at work. The annual toll is set out in Table 46.2. Even more striking is that there are as many as 230,000 workplace injuries a year. Health and safety cannot be taken for granted.

Industry sector	Number of workers killed
Agriculture, forestry and fishing	27
Manufacturing	14
Construction	42
Service industries	41
Extractive and utility supply	9
Overall	133

Table 46.2 Deaths at work, 2013–2014 (source: Health and Safety Commission)

Five whys and a how

46.7 Legislation – evaluation

Legislation seeks to ensure that all firms compete on a 'level playing field'.

This is a noble goal because one country's legislation can only create a level playing field in the home market. Super-tough laws, perhaps on the environment, add to costs and therefore may make it hard for UK firms to win contracts overseas. Although that could be a price worth paying, it may be better still for all developed trading countries to agree common standards. This is what happens within the European Union.

For those who argue that laws are unnecessary because market forces will drive unscrupulous firms out of business, there is a disappointing lack of evidence to suggest that this argument is valid. Though plenty of businesses are convicted of breaking the law, it is a real challenge to find just one example of a firm that has been forced to close as a result of doing so. Is the incentive to avoid prosecution strong enough?

Key terms

Cartel: an agreement between producers to control supply and thereby control prices. This is illegal, but not unusual.

Laissez-faire: literally means 'let it be', implying leaving businesses free to choose their own policies and practices: trusting in the free market.

Questions	Answers
Why are any laws needed to regulate business behaviour?	Because evidence shows that businesses are willing to compete on the basis of the lowest standards as well as on the highest.
Why do businesspeople often rage against the amount of 'red tape' they face?	Because red tape implies something time-consuming but pointless; perhaps they do not realise that laws such as the Sale of Goods Act help every business to become better.
Why are cartels illegal?	Because they operate as a conspiracy against the customer.
Why do some commentators accuse companies of 'greenwash'?	Greenwash means dressing up a business or product as friendlier to the environment than it really is; laws force firms to meet standards.
Why might health and safety rules threaten the survival of a business?	If poor safety standards have been keeping it competitive, being forced to comply with the rules might finish off a poorly run business.
How much of a problem is the minimum wage for the competitiveness of UK firms?	Not much; wage costs are a small fraction of total costs for most companies; so although the minimum wage means a lot to low-paid workers, it is not a big issue for most UK firms.

46.8 Workbook

Revision questions

(30 marks; 30 minutes)

1 a) Explain, in your own words, the meaning of
   the term 'laissez-faire'. (3)

   b) Explain what a follower of laissez-faire
   might think about governments setting a
   National Minimum Wage. (4)

2 From the chapter, explain one advantage and
   one disadvantage to UK businesses of being
   based in the European Union. (6)

3 Briefly describe the main aims of the
   following legislation:

   a) employment laws

   b) consumer protection law

   c) health and safety law. (6)

4 Explain two possible consequences
   of a tightening of environmental
   protection laws for one of the following:

   a) a supermarket

   b) a chemical manufacturer

   c) a bank. (6)

5 Briefly explain why many UK firms would welcome
   a relaxation of environmental protection legislation. (5)

Data response

Forbes Bricks

Maintaining a legal factory is a lot harder than you might expect – just ask Dave Maisey, managing director of Forbes Bricks Ltd. Forbes is one of a handful of bespoke brick makers left in the UK. It can tailor-make any shape, size, colour or material of brick; this feature explains its lasting popularity among those looking for bricks to restore or maintain older properties. A medium-sized firm, Forbes owns a single factory in Kent, with a loyal workforce of skilled and semi-skilled staff. Dave, however, has the look of a tired man. Charged with managing most aspects of the business, he is also ultimately responsible for the firm's compliance with the legislation affecting the business. His biggest headache, he says, is health and safety: 'They just don't seem to understand that making bricks is a dusty business. You can't make bricks without dust, and the inspector we had round the other week was measuring dust levels all round the shop floor, tutting as she went.'

The inspector from the HSE (Health and Safety Executive) was at the plant to measure the level of dust particles in the air and to assess the measures taken by the firm to ensure that staff suffered no long-term respiratory damage from the dusty working conditions.

Dave continued: 'I'd only just finished a full risk assessment on the new kiln we've bought, so luckily I managed to impress her with that. The inspector went over the accident record book, and our whole Health and Safety manual. I spent the whole day with her, time I could have spent out on the road finding new business, or working with the boys to find a better solution to some of the stockholding issues we've had recently.'

Two weeks after the inspector's visit, Dave called a meeting of the firm's directors to discuss the recommendation from the HSE: to spend an extra £105,000 on extractor units to reduce the dust levels in the air to standards acceptable under UK and EU law. Dave was also about to find out what purchasing director Andy Hemmings discovered when he visited a similar factory in China recently. Dave feared that Andy had found a factory with poor working conditions, paying well below Forbes' rates to staff and offering similar bricks at half the price.

Questions (30 marks; 35 minutes)

1 Outline two reasons why Dave seems unhappy
   about the legislation affecting Forbes Bricks Ltd. (6)

2 Explain Dave's general responsibilities to his
   staff according to UK health and safety law. (4)

3 Evaluate whether the case study proves that different
   legal standards make it impossible to have fair
   competition between firms from different countries. (20)

Extended writing

1 A laissez-faire 'think-tank' has recommended that the
   government should allow small firms to be exempt
   from all employment legislation. Evaluate the value
   of that recommendation to UK businesses. (20)

2 An important objective of business-related
   legislation is a 'level playing field'. Evaluate
   the extent to which this is possible in a
   globalised world. (20)

47 The competitive environment

> **Definition**
>
> A competitive environment involves measuring the directness and toughness of the competition within a market or sector within a market.

Linked to: Demand, Ch 5; Price elasticity of demand, Ch 8; Pricing strategies, Ch 12.

47.1 What is a competitive market?

Markets used to be physical places where buyers and sellers met in person to exchange goods or to haggle over price. Street markets are still like that. In online or digital markets, there is no face-to-face negotiation, but the potentially huge number of buyers and sellers makes transactions highly competitive.

A competitive market features intense rivalry between producers of a similar good or service. The number of firms operating within a market influences the intensity of competition; the more firms there are, the greater the level of competition. However, the respective size of the firms operating in the market should also be taken into account. A market consisting of 50 firms may not be particularly competitive, if one of the firms holds a 60 per cent market share and the 40 per cent is shared between the other 49. Similarly, a market composed of just four firms could be quite competitive if they are of a similar size.

Consumers benefit from competitive markets. Not so the firms themselves. In competitive markets, prices and profit margins tend to be squeezed. As a result, firms operating in competitive markets try hard to minimise competition, perhaps by creating a unique selling point (USP) or using **predatory pricing**.

It could be argued that marketing is vital no matter what the level of competition. Firms that fail to produce goods and services that satisfy the needs of their target consumers will find it hard to succeed in the long term. Ultimately, consumers will not waste their hard-earned cash on products that disappoint.

47.2 The degree of competition within a market

One dominant business

Some markets are dominated by one large business. Economists use the word 'monopoly' to describe a market where there is a single supplier, and therefore no competition. In practice, pure textbook monopolies rarely exist; even Microsoft does not have a 100 per cent share of the office software market (though it does have a 90 per cent share). The UK government's definition of a monopoly is somewhat looser. According to the Competition and Markets Authority, a monopoly is a firm that has a market share of 25 per cent and above.

Monopolies are bad for consumers. They restrict choice, and tend to drive prices upwards. For that reason, most governments regulate against monopolies and near monopolies that exploit consumers by abusing their dominant market position.

Deciding whether a firm has, or does not have, a monopoly is far from being a straightforward task. First of all, the market itself has to be accurately defined. For example, Camelot has been granted a monopoly to run the National Lottery. However, it could be argued that Camelot does not have a dominant market position because there are other forms of gambling, such as horse racing and football 'in-play' betting, available to consumers in the UK. Second, national market share figures should not be used in isolation because some firms enjoy local monopolies. A good example of a dominant local market position was the airport operator BAA. The company used to own three of London's four airports. Acting on complaints made by airlines, the government forced BAA to sell off Gatwick airport in December 2009 and Stansted in 2013. Increased competition should lead to improved customer service and lower landing fees (and therefore air fares).

Companies work hard to try to create monopoly positions for themselves. This might be achieved by technical innovations that make it harder for new entrants to break into the market. Apple spends millions of dollars on research and development in order to produce cutting-edge products. Apple's 14-year-old iPod is still the market leader in MP3s with a 70 per cent share of the massive US market. In 2014, Apple sold $14 billion of iPods. To ensure that Apple maintains its dominant market position, new product launches involve innovations that make it hard for competitors to keep up.

Figure 47.1 iPad

Competition among a few giants

The UK supermarket industry is a good example of a market that is dominated by a handful of very large companies. Economists call markets like this **oligopolies**. The rivalry that exists within such markets can be very intense. Firms know that any gains in market share will be at the expense of their rivals. The actions taken by one firm affect the profits made by the other firms that compete within the same market.

In markets made up of a few giants, firms tend to focus on **non-price competition** when designing the marketing mix. Firms in these markets are reluctant to compete by cutting price. They fear that the other firms in the industry will respond by cutting their prices too, creating a costly price war in which no firm wins.

The fiercely competitive market

Fiercely competitive markets tend to be fragmented; made up of hundreds of relatively small firms who each compete actively against other. In some of these markets, competition is amplified by the fact that firms sell near-identical products called commodities; these are products such as flour, sugar or blank DVDs, which are hard to differentiate. Rivalry in commodity markets tends to be intense. In such markets, firms have to manage their production costs very carefully because the retail price is the most important factor in determining whether the firm's product sells or not. If a firm cannot cut its costs, it will not be able to cut its prices without cutting into profit margins. Without price cuts, market share is likely to be lost.

In fiercely competitive markets, firms will try, where possible, to create product differentiation. For example, the restaurant market in Croydon, Surrey, is extremely competitive. There are over 70 outlets within a two-mile radius of the town centre. To survive without having to compete solely on price, firms in markets like this must find new innovations regularly because points of differentiation are quickly copied.

47.3 Competition and market size

Big markets

In 2014, British consumers spent £2,700 million on 'bagged snacks'. Walkers regular crisps was the market leader, with sales of £475 million. More money was spent on Walkers crisps in the UK than the entire worldwide revenues of Manchester United football club. But even though brand owner PepsiCo had 14 of the 25 top sellers in the market for bagged snacks (think Doritos, Quavers, Sensations and many more), it still faced serious competition. Although the market number two (Pringles) had sales of 'just' £180 million, Pringles gives Walkers serious competition, forcing the market leader to have to keep innovating in order to stay at number one. Walkers also faces competition from niche brands such as Kettle Chips. Started in 1988, it took the brand until 2004 to reach £35 million of annual sales. In 2014, its sales had nearly trebled to £98 million. A market share of 3.6 per cent may seem trivial, but Kettle's adult niche allows it to be one of the most profitable brands in bagged snacks.

Small markets

The market for dishwasher powder is less than a tenth of that for bagged snacks. At £250 million a year, there is only room for two brands: Finish, which once dominated this sector and still has a 52 per cent market share, and Fairy, with 25 per cent of the market. The remainder consists of other brands and supermarket own labels. In such a market, it would be hugely difficult for any other brand to break in. Both Finish and Fairy are backed by generous advertising budgets, which act as a barrier to others entering the market.

Changes in the competitive environment

The number of firms operating within a market can change over time. If new competitors enter, a market will become more competitive. New entrants are usually attracted into a new market by the high profits or the rapid growth achieved by the existing firms. After the Europe-wide success of airlines such as easy Jet and Ryanair, a huge number of imitators came into the airline business, including Air Berlin and Wizz Air. Although most of these have struggled to be profitable, their lower prices have unquestionably benefited the traveller.

In markets that are suffering from low or negative profitability, firms tend to exit, leaving the market less competitive than it was. In 2014, many UK 'payday' lenders withdrew from the market after the Financial Conduct Authority placed restrictions on the level of interest rates they were allowed to charge.

Key quotations

'People of the same trade seldom meet together, even for merriment and diversion, but the conversation ends in a conspiracy against the public, or in some contrivance to raise prices.'

Adam Smith, *The Wealth of Nations*, 1776

'Competition is not only the basis of protection to the consumer, but is the incentive to progress.'

Herbert Hoover, US President, 1929–1933

'Like many businessmen of genius he learned that free competition was wasteful, monopoly efficient. And so he simply set about achieving that efficient monopoly.'

Mario Puzo, *The Godfather*, 1969

47.4 Responses of businesses to a changing competitive environment

In a market that has become more competitive, firms may be forced into the following actions in order to defend market share.

Price cutting

Many firms attempt to fight off a competitor by cutting price. If the competition can be under-cut, consumers will hopefully remain loyal to the company that has cut its prices. Firms that use price-cutting as a way of fighting off the competition will normally try to cut their costs in line with the price cut in an attempt to preserve profit margins. If profit margins are already tight and costs have already been cut as much as possible, it probably will not be possible to respond to a new competitor by cutting prices.

Increase product differentiation

Product differentiation is the degree to which consumers perceive a brand to be different from, and in some way superior to, other brands of the same type of product. Some firms may be apprehensive about responding to a competitive threat by cutting price because the long-term result could be a deteriorating brand image that could hinder, rather than help, sales. Many consumers still associate price with product quality. If product differentiation can be increased, consumers will be less likely to switch to products supplied by the competition. To a degree, differentiation helps a firm to insulate itself from competitive pressure. Firms that want to increase differentiation can do so in the following ways.

Design

An eye-catching design that is aesthetically pleasing can help a firm to survive in a competitive market. By using design as a unique selling point, British manufacturers can compete on quality rather than on price, making them less vulnerable to competition from China and India. Good-looking design can add value to a product. For example, the BMW Mini relies upon its retro 1960s styling to command its price premium within the small car market.

Unique product features

In markets that are highly competitive, some firms react by redesigning their products to ensure that they possess the latest must-have feature. For example, in the car market, Toyota's hybrid drive technology has appealed to consumers who are interested in buying an environmentally friendly car with very low emissions.

Collusion

If faced with a real threat to the survival of the business, some managements take the apparently easy way out and try to do deals with their supposed competitors. In other words, they get in touch to fix prices, cut promotional expenditures or find any other way to boost profitability. If two or more companies feel equally threatened by the level of competition, there is every reason to agree to this in the short term. With much tougher legislation these days, it has become more difficult to make this work in the longer term, because there are strong incentives for one cheating firm to whistleblow ('rat') on the others. The first one to whistleblow gets 100 per cent immunity and therefore no fines or any other form of punishment.

Five whys and a how

47.5 The competitive environment – evaluation

The best way a business can ensure its survival in a competitive world is to find something it is good at, and stick with it. Cadbury is great when it concentrates on making chocolate; Heinz is brilliant at making and marketing baked beans or ketchup. Even if the massive Hershey Corporation brings its chocolate from America, Cadbury need not fear.

The hard thing is to get to the stage at which customers are subconsciously looking for your brand on the shelf, and buying it without thinking too much about price and quality. They want Nike on their feet and Apple in their hand. In 2014, in the UK, Pepsi added £33 million of sales while Coca-Cola suffered a £25 million sales decline – despite the huge and expensive launch of Coke Life. That is a reminder that 'do nothing' can sometimes be the right course of action. Instead of panicking about the possible impact of Coke Life upon Pepsi Max, Pepsi stayed confident in its product range. Clever stuff.

Questions	Answers
Why may it be hard to break into a small market if there are already strong, established brands present?	Because there isn't enough market size to justify the huge costs of trying to break through existing customers' purchasing habits.
Why might there be a change in the competitive environment a company faces?	A new company may enter the market or one might leave, as £100 million brand Huggies did in 2013 – withdrawing from the UK market for disposable nappies.
Why are so many top brands (Heinz, Coke, Pepsi, Pampers) US-owned?	Quite hard to say, but it may be that the Americans learnt more quickly than the British about the power of advertising and branding.
Why do company bosses often say 'we welcome competition'?	Because they think that is the right story to tell consumers; but it is simply not true; companies love to be in a powerful market position where they have a strong degree of control over price.
Why might Mars be able to make more profit from its Dolmio sauce brand than from its Mars bar?	Perhaps because Dolmio has a stronger market position in sauces (indeed, number one with £138 million of sales in 2014) than the Mars bar has in the chocolate market (in sixth position, with sales less than a fifth of Cadbury Dairy Milk).
How might the toughness of a competitive environment be measured?	By a measure such as how much market share is taken by the top three companies. In the UK, for chocolate, it is 70 per cent; in table sauces, it is nearly 100 per cent; but for sugar confectionery, it is below 40 per cent.

Key terms

Collusion: when managers from different firms get together to discuss ways to work together to restrict supply and/or raise prices.

Non-price competition: all competitive strategies other than price, such as branding, product design and technological innovation.

Oligopolies: markets dominated by a few large companies.

Predatory pricing: pricing low with the deliberate intention of driving a competitor out of business.

47.6 Workbook

Revision questions

(35 marks; 35 minutes)

1 What is a monopoly? (2)

2 Explain two reasons why monopolies exist. (4)

3 How may an increase in competition within the UK banking market affect shareholders of banks such as Lloyds and HSBC? (3)

4 Analyse two factors which could decrease the level of competition within the car market. (6)

5 Outline two reasons why a supermarket such as Waitrose may be concerned if Mars and Cadbury merged into one business. (6)

6 Explain how product differentiation may help a firm to adjust to a more competitive market. (4)

7 Explain why many large firms prefer to buy out smaller rivals, rather than competing against them head-to-head. (4)

8 Discuss whether it is right for some firms to use tactics such as predatory pricing to influence market structure. (6)

Data response 1

BA bosses accused of price-fixing by Virgin 'whistleblowers'

In 1993, British Airways found itself in court accused of using anti-competitive tactics in an attempt to force a much smaller new airline, called Virgin Atlantic, out of business. The so-called 'dirty tricks' used by BA included spreading malicious rumours about Virgin's solvency, in order to deprive the company of credit. After a bitter legal battle in the High Court, BA apologised and agreed to pay Virgin over £600,000 in compensation.

How times change. Nearly 20 years later, the same two companies stood accused of collusion. In April 2010, BA managers were summoned to appear in court to answer allegations that they had met with their rivals at Virgin to agree on a common fuel duty surcharge to impose on both BA and Virgin consumers. Over a period of a year and a half, both airlines increased the fuel surcharges paid by passengers on long-haul routes from £5 to £60.

In the UK, the Competition Commission was then responsible for investigating alleged cases of anti-competitive behaviour. Unfortunately, anti-competitive behaviour such as price-fixing is still very common in the UK, despite the fact that it is illegal. One of the main problems faced by the new Competition and Markets Authority is the difficulty faced in acquiring the necessary evidence needed to prove that anti-competitive behaviour has taken place. The Authority now offers so-called 'whistleblowers' immunity from prosecution in exchange for information that enables a prosecution to take place. In this case, the evidence used to convict BA came from their co-conspirators. Virgin's chief executive stood as the main witness for the prosecution!

Questions (30 marks; 35 minutes)

1 What is meant by the following terms:
   a) anti-competitive tactics
   b) 'whistleblowers'
   c) 'collusion'? (6)

2 Explain why anti-competitive behaviour such as price-fixing is illegal. (4)

3 Assess two possible reasons why anti-competitive behaviour persists despite the fact that it is illegal. (8)

4 Assess whether the Competition and Markets Authority was right to offer Virgin immunity from prosecution. (12)

Data response 2

The prices of consumer electronics, such as toasters, satellite TV set-top boxes and MP3 players, have tumbled in recent years. Supermarket chains like Tesco now sell DVD players that previously cost hundreds of pounds for less than £10. So, why have the prices of these goods fallen? In part, the price falls reflect the falling price of the components that go into consumer electronics. Low prices also reflect the fact that there is now more competition in the market. In the past, consumers typically bought items such as TVs and computers from specialist retailers – for example, Currys and Comet. Today, the situation is somewhat different; in addition to these specialist retailers, consumers can now buy electrical goods over the internet and from supermarkets. Some industry analysts also believe that some of the supermarket chains are using set-top boxes and DVD players as loss leaders.

In today's ultra-competitive environment, manufacturers of consumer electronics face intense pressure from retailers to cut costs so that retail prices can be cut without any loss of profit margin. To cut prices without compromising product quality, manufacturers such as the Dutch giant Phillips have transferred production from the Netherlands to low-cost locations like China.

Questions (35 marks; 40 minutes)

1 Describe two characteristics of a highly competitive market. (4)

2 Explain why the market for consumer electronics has become more competitive. (4)

3 Examine three factors that would affect the competitiveness of a manufacturer of DVD players. (9)

4 a) Use a dictionary or A-Z to find out the meaning of the term 'loss leader'. (3)

   b) Why do supermarkets use this tactic? (3)

5 Assess whether, in today's competitive market for consumer electronics, firms must constantly cut costs and prices if they are to survive. (12)

Extended writing

1 Evaluate the benefits to mobile phone buyers of the fierce competition between Samsung and Apple. (20)

2 With the demise of Rangers F.C., Celtic has a monopoly in Scottish club football. Evaluate whether this proves that monopoly is something no business should wish for. (20)

48 Quantitative skills for Business

Linked to every chapter in the book.

48.1 Introduction

Unlike the other chapters of the book, this purely provides questions (the answers can be found at the back of the book). It is to help you test your knowledge and understanding of an important aspect of the subject. Page 37 of the Edexcel

Specification sets out the exact skill requirement for AS level exams. The questions in this chapter match page 37 precisely, making it perfect for revision.

48.2 Calculate, use and understand ratios, averages and fractions

Look at Table 48.1 then answer the questions that follow.

Sales rank	Brand	Company	Sales 2013 £ millions	£ms change since 2012	% change since 2012
	Total category 2013 sales		£271.6m	£8.2m	3.1%
	Total own label 2013 sales		£1.8m	£0.5m	41.4%
1	Extra Gum	Wrigley	186.4	14.2	8.3
2	Airwaves	Wrigley	35.0	0.9	2.8
3	Orbit	Wrigley	12.8	−1.5	−10.8
4	Mentos Gum	Van Melle	8.1	−0.4	−5.2
5	Five Gum	Wrigley	5.3	−0.6	−10.1
6	Hubba Bubba	Wrigley	4.8	0.2	5.3
7	Trident Gum	Mondelēz	4.7	−1.3	−22.2
8	Juicy Fruit	Wrigley	2.4	−1.0	−30.6
9	Jawbreaker Gum	Zed Candy	1.6	−0.4	−21.5
10	Trebor Extra Strong gum	Mondelēz	1.5	−1.6	−50.4

Table 48.1 Chewing gum sales, top ten, 2013 (source: *The Grocer*, 21 December 2013)

1 a) Calculate the average 2013 sales figure among the top five in the UK market for chewing gum. (3)

  b) Why may that figure be less valuable than many averages? (4)

2 What fraction of the total market was represented by the sales of Wrigley's Extra Gum (be willing to round the numbers to provide a simple fraction)? (4)

3 a) In 2013, Maynards Fruit Gums outsold Orbit Chewing Gum 5:1. Use that ratio and the data provided to give the 2013 sales figure for Maynards Fruit Gums. (4)

  b) In the UK market for chocolate, brands outsell supermarket own labels in a ratio of 12:1. In the case of sugar confectionery, the ratio is 4.5:1. Explain two possible reasons for this. (8)

48.3 Calculate, use and understand percentages and percentage changes

Table 48.2 shows unit sales of Apple's three main products.

	iPod	iPhone	iPad
Q2 2013	4,569	31,241	14,617
Q3 2013	3,498	33,797	14,079
Q4 2013	6,049	51,025	26,035
Q1 2014	2,761	43,719	16,350
Q2 2014	2,926	35,203	13,276

Table 48.2 Unit sales of Apple's three main products (figures in 000s)

4 a) Calculate the percentage change in iPod sales between quarter 2 of 2013 and the same quarter of 2014. (3)

  b) Calculate the percentage change in iPhone sales between quarter 2 of 2013 and the same quarter of 2014. (3)

  c) If iPhone enjoys a 12 per cent sales increase between quarter 2 of 2014 and quarter 2 of 2015, what will its new sales level be? (3)

  d) In quarter 2 of 2014, what percentage of the sales of all Apple's three products came from the iPad? (3)

48.4 Construct and interpret a range of standard graphical forms

A line graph is a great way to show trends over time in comparative data. Figure 48.1 shows UK exports to four developing countries over the period 1998–2013. Look at the graph and then answer the questions below.

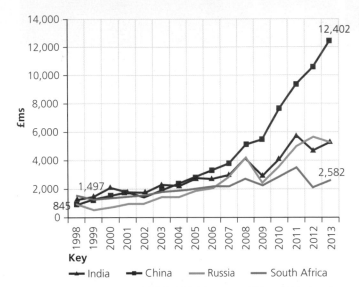

Figure 48.1 UK exports, 1998–2013 (source: Office of National Statistics)

5 a) Explain two important features of the data shown on the graph. (6)

  b) Estimate the £ms increase in UK exports to China between 2007 and 2012. (2)

  c) Calculate the percentage change in UK exports to China between 1998 and 2013. Then do the same for the percentage change in exports to South Africa. (5)

  d) Explain two possible reasons why the figure for China is so much greater. (8)

Another type of data that needs illustrating is proportions. This is often done by pie charts, though Figure 48.2 does the equivalent, using a stacked bar chart. This makes it easy to show changing proportions, in this case of the different consumer electronic products sold by Apple Inc.

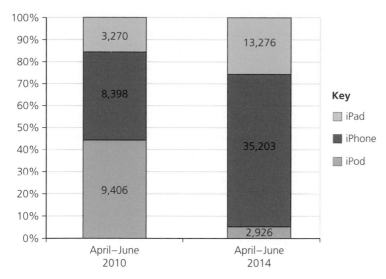

Figure 48.2 Global sales of Apple products (000 units) (source: Apple quarterly accounts)

Figure 48.3 Trends in UK manufacturing September 2014 (source: Office of National Statistics)

6 a) Explain two important features of the data shown in Figure 48.2. **(8)**

b) Calculate the percentage increase in total unit sales of Apple's products between 2010 and 2014. **(3)**

c) Assess what use Apple might have been able to make out of the data shown in Figure 48.2. **(8)**

48.5 Interpret index numbers

In business, data series are often converted into index numbers. It makes the data easier to interpret and far easier to compare with data that might be correlated.

Look at the graph showing trends in UK manufacturing (Figure 48.3) and then answer question 7.

7 a) i) Explain what is meant by 'Index 2010 – 100'. **(4)**

ii) Outline two possible reasons why this data has been presented in Index form. **(4)**

b) Assess the trend in car manufacturing with production of aircraft and spacecraft. **(8)**

c) The black line shows the trend in total UK manufacturing between 1997 and 2014. Assess the main features of this data over the period. **(8)**

48.6 Calculate cost, revenue, profit and break-even

A small bakery specialises in French bread. Each loaf is priced at £1.20 and has a variable cost of 40p. Weekly fixed costs are £600 and 1,200 loaves are sold per week.

8 a) Calculate the total costs of producing 1,200 loaves in a week. **(3)**

b) Calculate the total revenue per week. **(3)**

c) Calculate the weekly profit. **(2)**

d) Calculate the break-even point and the margin of safety for the bakery. **(6)**

e) Calculate the weekly profit if a price rise to £1.40 cuts demand to 1,100 loaves. **(5)**

(Quantitative skill 6 only applies to second-year A level and will be dealt with in *Edexcel Business A level Year 2* by Marcousé, Hammond and Watson, 2016.)

48.7 Interpret values of price and income elasticity of demand

In the year to June 2014, Wrigley put the price of its 'Hubba Bubba' brand up by 10 per cent. The result was a 9 per cent fall in sales volume. Therefore, its price elasticity of demand was −0.9.

9 a) What would have been the effect on Hubba Bubba sales revenue of this 10 per cent price rise? (3)

b) What would the effect be on the brand's profit level (in the short term)? (3)

c) Why might the long-term effect of this price rise be more worrying than the short-term effect? (5)

In January–June 2014, the UK economy grew at 3 per cent. Across the whole UK car market, income elasticity is estimated at +3.5.

10 a) Calculate the percentage increase in UK car sales that could be expected in January–June 2014. (3)

b) With an income elasticity of +3.5, what term could be used to describe cars as a product category? (1)

c) Based on the above information, explain what might happen to UK car sales if there is ever a repeat of the 2009 recession, with its 6 per cent fall in GDP. (4)

48.8 Use and interpret quantitative and non-quantitative information in order to make decisions

In 2014, a total of 912 new confectionery products hit the market. Within that total, the highest category for launches was 'seasonal chocolate', with 178 new products. These launches were attracted by the strength of this category, with sales rising 15.1 per cent to £580 million, even though the market as a whole was static. Quite apart from selling £58 million of its market leading Creme Eggs, Cadbury saw sales double in 2014 for its 'Dairy Milk Egg and Spoon'. Ferrero and Mars are among the companies trying hard to win a bigger share of this high profit-margin sector (source: *The Grocer*, 4 October 2014).

11 a) Explain two reasons why seasonal chocolate saw such a high number of new product launches in 2014. (8)

b) i) Calculate Creme Egg's share of this market sector. (3)

ii) What is the implication of a brand being the market leader with that level of market share? Explain your thinking. (4)

c) A key Mars brand is Maltesers – which has annual sales of £120 million but quite a small share of the seasonal chocolate sector. Assess how the Malteser brand might be used to boost Mars sales within this sector. (8)

48.9 Interpret, apply and analyse information in written, graphical and numerical forms

The final set of questions on quantitative skills relates to Table 48.3 and Figure 48.4. The data is based on the best estimates available in November 2014 of the sales performance of the Sony PS4 console compared with its rival Microsoft Xbox One.

Data in millions of units sold	PS4	Xbox One	PS3*
Oct–Dec 2013 (launch in Nov)	4.5	3.0	1.9
Jan–Mar 2014	3.0	2.0	2.0
Apr–Jun 2014	2.7	0.8	0.7
Jul–Sep 2014	3.3	1.7	1.4
Oct–Dec 2014			5.0
*Launch: same months, but 2006/2007			

Table 48.3 Launch sales estimates for PS4 and others

12 a) From the data in Table 48.3, what conclusions can Sony draw so far? (4)

b) On the basis of Table 48.3, what sales forecast might Sony make for Oct–Dec 2014? Give an estimate and explain your reasoning. (6)

c) Figure 48.4 shows the cumulative sales figures for each console. Assess whether this information is more or less useful than the ordinary quarterly sales figures shown in Table 48.3. (6)

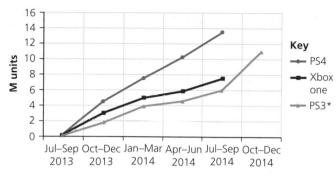

Figure 48.4 Cumulative launch sales: PS4 v. Xbox One v. PS3 (sources: various, including company press releases)

d) Assess how Microsoft might react to the sales data provided. (8)

All the answers to these questions are on pages 316–317, at the end of the book.

49 How to revise for Business exams

Good revision can add as much as two grades to your A level result. The aim of this unit is to help you to appreciate what makes up a quality revision programme.

49.1 Aims and objectives

A good revision programme should be aimed at achieving specific targets that will maximise your chances of success in the exam. How should these targets be set?

The basis for setting revision targets can be found in three places:

1 the specification (syllabus)

2 past papers (unfortunately, these are in short supply at the start of the life of a specification)

3 examiners' reports.

The specification

The specification tells you the knowledge and skills the examiner is looking for. Knowing the skills the examiner is looking for will help you to produce better-quality answers in an exam. However, like all skills these can be developed only through practice, so it is important to start your revision early. In fact, you should try to review your work every few weeks to make sure there are no gaps in your notes and that your files are well organised. This way it becomes easier to revise at the end of the course because everything is in place.

Definitions of higher academic skills

Higher academic skills include: analysis, synthesis and evaluation.

Analysis (breaking down)

This is:

- identification of cause, effect and interrelationships
- the appropriate use of theory or business cases/practice to investigate the question set
- breaking the material down to show underlying causes or problems
- use of appropriate techniques to analyse data.

Analysis involves a chain of argument linking ideas and concepts, and showing the relationship between them. You may analyse why something happened or the consequence of something occurring.

Look back at previous answers you have written and try to find examples of how you could extend your responses. Were there any occasions when you could have used business theory such as elasticity, motivation or break-even to strengthen your arguments and provide a higher level of analysis?

Synthesis (bringing together)

This is:

- building the points/themes within the answer into a connected whole
- logical sequencing of argument
- clarity through summarising an argument.

This skill is particularly important when you have a piece of extended writing such as a report or an essay. In a good essay, for example, each paragraph will have a clear purpose. The arguments will be well organised and lead to a logical conclusion that builds on the earlier analysis. In some exams, the synthesis marks may be awarded separately; in others, they will be part of an overall mark for an answer.

Evaluation (judgement)

This is:

- judgement shown in weighing up the relative importance of different points or sides of an argument, in order to reach a conclusion
- informed comment on the reliability of evidence
- distinguishing between fact and opinion
- judgement of the wider issues and implications
- conclusions drawn from the evidence presented
- selectivity: identifying the material that is most relevant to the question.

Past papers

Previous exam papers are very important in helping you to prepare for your exam. They will show you exactly what sort of questions you will face and the number of marks available. They will also give you a feel for the type of words used in the question. It goes without saying that exam questions must be read carefully. However, there will be key words used in the questions that tell you how to answer them. There is, for example, a great difference in the answers expected for the following two questions.

1 Assess the key elements of ABC plc's marketing strategy.

2 Evaluate the key elements of ABC plc's marketing strategy.

Unless you know what is expected from these two questions, you are unlikely to know how much detail is required or how your answer ought to be structured.

Examiners' reports

These are available for each examination and can be found on www.edexcel.com. They are written by the principal examiner of each exam and provide an insight into what candidates did well or struggled with. By looking at these reports, you will learn candidates' weak areas of subject knowledge and common problems in interpreting questions.

▌ 49.2 Resources

The following list contains items that will be of value in preparing for an exam. They should all be familiar to you before you begin revising, and should have played a constant part in your studies throughout the course.

1 Class notes
2 A copy of the specification
3 Past exam papers, mark schemes and examiners' reports
4 A revision plan
5 Newspapers/cuttings files of relevant stories
6 This textbook
7 Access to your teacher
8 Other students

Class notes

Since these are the product of your work and a record of your activities, they will form a vital part of your understanding of the subject. They should contain past work you have done on exam-style questions and model answers that will help to prepare you for the exam. As you make notes, try to make sure these will be legible and useful later on in your revision. Make sure you keep them in the right order as you go; having to sort them out later is much more of a challenge.

A copy of the specification

The specification tells you several important things:

- what knowledge you could be tested on
- what skills the examiner will be looking for
- how the marks will be allocated
- what you will be expected to do in each exam paper you sit.

Past exam papers, mark schemes and examiners' reports

By working from past papers, you will develop a feel for the type of question you will be asked and the sorts of responses you will be expected to give. Examiners' reports will give you an insight into what they thought worked well and what surprised them in terms of the responses. This in turn will give you some idea of how and what they want to assess in the future.

A revision plan

As described in the previous section, this will help to keep you on target to achieve everything that you need to cover before the exam.

Newspapers/cuttings files

Since Business is a real-life subject, the ability to bring in relevant examples will boost your answers and grades. By studying what is happening in the business world, you will be able to apply your answers much more effectively; this is because you will develop a better understanding of the key issues in different markets and industries. It will also help you to draw comparisons between different types of business, which can lead to good evaluation. Keeping some form of 'business diary', where you track at least one story a week, is a good way of keeping up to date with what is happening. When making notes about your story, try to highlight the underlying business issues and relate it to theory rather than just describe it. This will help you to analyse cases and business situations.

This textbook

In this textbook, focus especially on the 'Five whys and a how' and 'Evaluation' sections at the end of each chapter.

Access to your teacher

Asking your teacher for help is vital. She or he is able to give you useful advice and insights, to quell sudden panics and suggest ways to improve your performance. Don't hold back – ask! Whenever you get a piece of work back where the mark is disappointing, make sure you know what you need to do differently next time. Read any comments on your work and try to improve in the specific areas mentioned in the next piece of work.

Other students

Talk to other students to help discuss points and clarify ideas. Learning from each other is a very powerful way of revising. Studies often show that you remember something much more when you have to explain it to someone else. Why not agree as a group to revise some topics? Study them individually and then get together to test each other's understanding. This works very well. Remember you can all get A★s if you are good enough, so there is no problem helping others to improve their performance (as long as it is all their own work in the exam) and you will almost certainly benefit yourself from working with others.

▌49.3 Learning the language of the subject

Clear definitions of business terms are essential for exam success. *The Complete A–Z Business Studies Handbook* (see Further reading), is very helpful for this. They count for much more than the odd two-mark question here or there. By showing the examiner that you understand what a term means, you are reassuring her that your knowledge is sound; this is likely to help your marks for other skills as well. If the examiner is not convinced that you understand what a concept actually means, then they are less likely to reward the other skills at a high level. Even on very high-mark questions, it is important to define your terms.

For revising business definitions, you could use:

● definition cards
● past papers
● business crosswords and brainteasers.

There are many possible sources of good definitions of business terms. In this book, key terms have been highlighted and given clear and concise definitions. Your definitions should be written without using the word in question. ('Market growth is the growth in the market' is not a very good definition, for example!)

It is important, then, that you can produce high-quality definitions in an exam. This can be done only through learning and practice. Possible ways to achieve this are as follows.

Definition cards

Take a pack of index cards or postcards, or similar-sized pieces of thick paper. On each one, write a particular term or phrase that you can find in the specification document. Remember to include things like motivation theories where a clear definition or description can give an excellent overview. It is extremely unlikely that you will be asked to know a precise definition for any term that is not specifically in the specification.

On the back of each card write an appropriate definition. This could come from your class notes, a textbook or a dictionary such as *The Complete A–Z Business Studies Handbook*. Make sure that the definition you write:

● is concise
● is clear
● does not use the word being defined in the definition.

Learn them by continual repetition. Put a tick or cross on each card to show whether or not you came up with an acceptable effort. Over time, you should see the number of ticks growing.

Shuffle the cards occasionally so that you are not being given clues to some definitions because of the words or phrases preceding them.

Try doing the exercise 'back to front', by looking at the definitions and then applying the correct word or phrase.

Past papers

By using as many past papers as possible, you can find out exactly what type of definition questions are asked. More importantly, you can see how many marks are available for them, which will tell you exactly how much detail you need to go into in your answer.

If possible, get hold of examiners' mark schemes. These will again give you a clear idea of what is being looked for from your answer.

Business crosswords and brainteasers

You will be able to find many examples of word games in magazines such as *Business Review*. By completing these, you are developing your business vocabulary and linking words with their meanings.

49.4 Numbers

All business courses contain aspects of number work, which can be specifically tested in exams. It must be remembered, however, that there are two clear aspects to numbers:

1 calculation

2 interpretation.

The calculation aspects of business courses are one area where practice is by far the best approach. Each numerical element has its own techniques that you will be expected to be able to demonstrate. The techniques can be learnt, and by working through many examples they can become second nature. Even if mathematics is not your strong point, the calculations ought not to cause problems to an A level student. Something that at first sight appears complex, such as break-even, requires only simple techniques, such as multiplying, adding and subtracting. Going through the 'Workbook' sections of this book will provide invaluable practice. Ask your teacher for a photocopy of the answers available in the *Teacher's Guide*.

Once calculated, all business numbers need to be used. It is all very well to calculate the accounting ratios, for example, but if the numbers are then unused the exercise has been wasted. You must attempt to follow each calculation by stating what the numbers are saying and their implications for the business.

49.5 General tips for revision

1 Start early.

2 Know the purpose of your revision.

3 Work more on weaker areas.

4 Use past papers as far as is possible.

5 Keep a clear perspective.

Finally, do no more revision on the night before the exam; it won't help and can only cause you anxiety. Eat well and get a good night's sleep. That way you will be in good physical shape to perform to the best of your abilities in the exam.

Further reading

Business Review (available from Hodder Education, see www.hoddereducation.co.uk/magazines).

Lines, D., Marcousé, I. and Martin, B. (2009) *The Complete A–Z Business Studies Handbook* (6th edn), Hodder Education.

Answers to the questions in Chapter 48

1 a) Add £186.4 + £35.0 + …. Then divide by 5 = £49.52m.

b) Because the top seller is so much more than the others (the fifth − *Five Gum* − only has £5m of sales, so bears little relation to the average)

2 £186.4m/£271.6m = 0.686, rounded to 7/10.

3 a) £12.8 × 5 = £64, so Maynards had sales of £64m.

b) 1 Adults are more likely than children to eat chocolate, and know/care more about brand/ quality and can afford to pay more.

2 There is more differentiation with chocolate, with more powerful, historic brand names like Cadbury and Galaxy.

4 a) % change = change/original × 100

So it is 2,926 − 4,569 = −1,643 / 4,569 × 100 = −36%

b) 35,203 − 31,241 = 3,962 / 31,241 × 100 = +12.68%

c) 35,203 × 112 / 100 = 39,427.36

d) 13,276 / (13,276 + 35,203 + 2,926) × 100

= 13,276 / 51,405 × 100 = 25.8%

5 a) 1 It shows change in value of UK exports to four selected countries, misses out many others; what was the basis for the selection?

2 It shows that exports to China have increased disproportionately to the others on the graph.

b) £10,500 − £3,900 = £6,600ms

c) China: £12,402 − £845 = £11,557

£11,557 / £845 × 100 = +1,367.7%

South Africa: 2,582 − 1,497 = 1,085

1,085 / 1,497 × 100 = + 72.5%

d) 1 China has grown exceptionally rapidly in recent years.

2 Perhaps Britain has grown its market share in China.

6 a) 1 By 2014, iPhone had become the most important product by far for Apple.

2 Total Apple sales have increased hugely since 2010, despite the collapse of iPod sales.

b) 2010 total: 3,270 + 8,398 + 9,406 = 21,074 (000s)

2014 total: 13,276 + 35,203 + 2,926 = 51,405 (000s)

% increase = (51,405 − 21,074) / 21,074 × 100 = +143.9%

c) They may have to plan for when to discontinue the iPod. They may need a completely new product to reduce their dependence on the iPhone. (Will the Apple Watch do that? Surely not.)

7 a) i) All the other years' data is in proportion to 2010 − the base year.

ii) 1 The different data sets will all have their own scales, perhaps in units with millions of cars per year, but only 20 or so airplanes. Indexing the data brings it onto a common scale, making comparisons possible.

2 It shows trends at a glance.

b) Aircraft has grown more or less steadily with minor dips in 2002 and 2009, whereas car manufacturing has been erratic, with a major fall in 2009, and steady recovery since.

c) Manufacturing output remained very flat between 1997 and 2007, but then plunged in the 2009 recession. It still hadn't recovered its previous peak by the second quarter of 2014.

8 a) £480 variable + £600 fixed = £1,080

b) 1,200 × £1.20 = £1440

c) £1,440 − £1,080 = £360

d) Break-even = Fixed costs / Selling price − variable costs p.u.

£600 / £1.20 − 40p = 750 loaves

Margin of safety = 1,200 − 750 = 450 loaves

e) New profit = (£1.40 × 1,100) minus (£600 + 1,100 × 40p)

= £1,540 − £1,040 = £500

9 a) It would have risen slightly (approx. 1 per cent) as the percentage price increase is higher than the percentage sales decline.

b) It would rise (as the fall in sales would cut total costs; so revenue up, costs down).

c) In the longer term, the loss of sales volume might provide space for new entrants to the market, and might lead to reductions in distribution levels, as retailers are always short of space.

10 a) Economy + 3% × Income elasticity + 3.5 = 10.5% sales increase

b) Luxury

c) A fall of 6% × 3.5 = 21%

11 a) 1 The upward trend in this category that has seen a 15.1 per cent increase to £580m.

2 The mention at the end about it being a 'high profit–margin sector'.

b) i) 10 per cent

ii) With just 10 per cent, it would seem quite an open market, so other brands may try to break into the market.

c) They could either go for Malteser versions of existing seasonal products, such as Malteser Father Christmases, or else try to work at newer 'seasons', such as Halloween or Mothers' Day.

12 a) 1 Post-launch sales for Jan–Sep 2014 for PS4 were 200 per cent of launch compared to 215 per cent for PS3 and 150 per cent for XBox One.

2 More importantly, it looks as if PS4's sales are set to outdo PS3's, perhaps by a significant margin.

b) They could expect nearly 12m of unit sales in Oct–Dec 2014 if one year from launch matches increase in PS3. Workings: 5.0 / 1.6 = +263%

PS4 4.5m × 263% = 11.835 million

c) The cumulative figures give a sense of the progress of ongoing sales, perhaps giving rise to concern for Microsoft's One, which seems to be flagging in mid-2014.

d) 1 They might feel they have to attack PS4 aggressively, using price and promotions (free games, perhaps) to claw their way back.

2 Or they may already be thinking of bringing forward the development and launch of Xbox Two.

Index